Amy Levy

Her Life and Letters

Amy Levy

(photograph by Montabone
taken in Florence in January 1889;
first published along with Oscar Wilde's
tribute to Amy Levy in
Woman's World 3 [1890]: 51)

Amy Levy

HER LIFE AND LETTERS

Linda Hunt Beckman

Ohio University Press

Athens

Ohio University Press, Athens, Ohio 45701
© 2000 by Linda Hunt Beckman
Printed in the United States of America

Ohio University Press books are printed on acid-free paper ⊗ ™

09 08 07 06 05 04 03 02 01 00   5 4 3 2 1

The photograph of Amy Levy on the cover was taken in July 1879 at Brighton.
This and the other photographs in this volume are from her own album, now in the
possession of Levy's grandniece, and are reprinted with her permission.

Library of Congress Cataloging-in-Publication Data

Beckman, Linda Hunt.
  Amy Levy : her life and letters / Linda Hunt Beckman.
  p.cm.
  Includes bibliographical references and index.
  ISBN 0-8214-1329-5 (cloth : alk. paper) — ISBN 0-8214-1330-9 (pbk. : alk. paper)
    1. Levy, Amy, 1861–1889. 2. Women and literature—England—History—19th
century. 3. Authors, English—19th century—Biography. 4. Jewish women—Great Britain—
Biography. 5. Lesbians—Great Britain—Biography. 6. Jews in literature. I. Title
PR4886.L25 Z53 2000
828'.809—dc21
  [B]   99-086688

My life was jarring discord from the first.

"A Minor Poet" by Amy Levy

Contents

Illustrations

Preface and Acknowledgments

In the obituary that Oscar Wilde wrote for Amy Levy that appeared early in 1890, he gave her writing—both her prose and poetry—high praise. About *Reuben Sachs,* Levy's novel about Jewish life, he observed, "To write thus at six-and-twenty is given to very few," and expressed his regret that "the world must forego the full fruition of her power."[1] Despite the respect that Levy earned in her own time and in the period immediately following it, the work of this late-Victorian Anglo-Jewish woman of letters was largely unknown until recently although her name remained in scholarly memory.

In the 1990s Levy began to attract the attention of scholars, in part because of a surge of interest in the poetry written by Victorian women; the history of and the literature produced by England's Jews; and the experience of women who, like her, were female pioneers at England's ancient universities, especially when they went on to live in an independent and unconventional manner. This biography, together with her letters (annotated and published here for the first time), will help place Levy in literary and cultural history and give scholars, students, and casual readers a context for developing their own understanding of Levy's significance. In 1993 much of what Amy Levy published became easily accessible; coincidentally, her papers had recently become available to scholars after a century of being in private hands.[2]

I am indebted to Camellia Plc., which owns these manuscripts, documents, sketches, and other items, and whose owners gave me permission to quote from Levy's papers and to publish most of her letters; and to Barbara Hait, the eldest surviving grandchild of Levy's eldest sibling, who allowed me to cite passages from manuscripts to which she holds the copyright and to publish Amy Levy's letters to Vernon Lee.

Looking back over the years that I spent on this book, I find other individuals and institutions who deserve acknowledgment for letting me do research in their manuscript collections: the William Andrews Clark Memorial Library, University of California, Los Angeles; the Harry Ransom Humanities Research Library at the University of Texas at Austin; the British Library; the Library of Congress; and the Department of Special Collections, Miller Library, at Colby College. I want to thank the Harry Ransom Humanities Research Library for allowing me to quote from letters in the Richard Garnett Collection and from Elizabeth Pennell's journal; the British Library for letting me cite passages from manuscripts in the Macmillan Collection and from the diary of Michael Field; and Special Collections at Colby College for giving me permission to quote from Vernon Lee's manuscript letters and from the papers of Irene Cooper Willis. Nancy Reinhardt, the curator of Special Collections at Colby College, went out of her way to assist me in my research many times, and Bruce Whiteman, the head librarian at the Clark Library at UCLA, was outstandingly kind in his efforts to help me resolve what turned out to be an intractable problem.

I am grateful to the Ohio University Research Committee, whose grant enabled me to go to London in the fall of 1992 to examine the Amy Levy Collection, and to the English Department, the College of Arts and Sciences, and Honors Tutorial College at Ohio University, all of which provided funding that enabled me to travel to collections in England and the United States and to hire research assistants. Special thanks go to

Sharona Levy (no relation to Amy), whose own research on Levy was inspiring; and to Ann MacEwen, Dollie Radford's granddaughter, who gave me permission to quote from Dollie's diary and from some letters in her possession.

Most of all, however, I want to thank certain people who facilitated my work in numerous practical ways but who also made the writing of this book an adventure and an opportunity to widen my circle of friends and loved ones: Anthony Joseph, a distant kinsman of Amy Levy, who gave me access to the reminiscences of Lucy Levy Marks, Amy's first cousin, and whose research on the genealogy of England's Jews was helpful; Katharine Solomon, Amy Levy's grandniece, whose unfailingly generous assistance—in the form of memorabilia, photographs, oral history of the family, research, and analysis—has made the biography more accurate, insightful, and interesting; and Richard Beckman, whose contributions to my book and my life are immeasurable.

Amy Levy

Her Life and Letters

1

Prologue

On November 10, 1861, Amy Levy was born into a comfortably middle-class family with deep roots in England, where her mother's ancestors had arrived in the early eighteenth century. From 1879 to 1881 she was a student at Newnham, the second women's college at Cambridge University, and in the course of the 1880s she published three volumes of poetry, three novels, translations, a number of essays, and a great many short stories. She avoided Jewish topics in her published fiction until 1888, when she produced *Reuben Sachs*, a novel about Jewish life. That novel was perceived as an attack on the Jewish community largely because of the materialism and ruthless ambition of some of its characters and the social world they inhabit. While many Victorian novels indict British society for the same failings, such a representation of Jewish life from the pen of a Jewish writer seemed to corroborate long-standing anti-Semitic assumptions. This may be one of the reasons that Levy's work—even though much of it is not explicitly Jewish in content—was neglected for so long. For the most part, however, her neglect was a result of the larger obliteration of Victorian women poets and of women writing in all genres in the last two decades of the nineteenth century.[1] Levy's career ended abruptly, for she committed suicide in September 1889 when she was not quite twenty-eight.

In 1993 Melvyn New published *The Complete Novels and Selected Writings of Amy Levy, 1861–1889,* a major event in what might be called the Amy Levy Renaissance, although renewed interest in her writings preceded New's edition.[2] The availability of so much of her work in his volume is a major reason for the attention she is now receiving in literary journals and doctoral dissertations, in books wholly or partly on the poetry written by Victorian women, at academic conferences, in classrooms, and in cyberspace.[3] Simultaneously, the editors of reference books are soliciting entries about her life and work or revising what they already have. Those seeking information about her life, however, will find a great many biographical errors, romanticizing, myths, and falsehoods.

Many of Levy's texts—the letters, of course, but also poems, stories, and essays—allow an understanding of the evolution of her consciousness. One sees her subjectivity taking shape in negotiation with her discordant experiences as a member of various groups, all of them marginal. I will begin by discussing the myths and misconceptions about Amy Levy because the distortions of her image are a key to the artistic innovations and strategies that make her writing so remarkable. Assessing these distortions also helps to illuminate the time and place in which she lived and wrote.

Unaware that Levy had been educated at one of the first two women's colleges at Cambridge, James Warwick Price, in an essay written in 1912, identifies her as "a Jewess" and "a Clapham factory girl." Claiming that she had had only "four terms of schooling at suburban Newham" [*sic*] but "read voraciously at her loom," he attributes her suicide to her reading, suggesting that it created a "promise" that could not be fulfilled. Price's portrait is full of specific, erroneous detail: "She had looked through her squinting, cob-webbed garret panes and seen nothing but a world which knew her not."[4] The remarks of the Irish poet Katharine

Tynan, in contrast, are factually incontrovertible, but the tone of her description of Levy and its fascination with her appearance reveal an exaggerated response to the fact of her Jewishness that could easily lead to a different kind of mythologizing. Having met Levy in May 1889 at the first dinner of a club for women writers, Tynan reminisces: "I remember . . . that tragic personality . . . sitting opposite to me, her charming little Eastern face dreamy in a cloud of tobacco smoke."[5] The editor and writer Harry Quilter, in an essay on Amy Levy, also romanticizes her looks although he had seen her only in a photograph: "a small dark girl, of unmistakably Jewish type, with eyes that seemed too large for the delicate features, and far too sad for their youthfulness . . . I had rarely seen a face which was at once so interesting, so intellectual, so beautiful, and, alas! so unhappy."[6] The novelist Grant Allen ignores Levy's Jewishness, focusing instead on her rejection of traditional Victorian notions about the path a woman's life should follow. In an 1890 essay decrying higher education for women as an obstacle to the goals of the eugenics movement, he invokes her name: "A few hundred pallid little Amy Levys sacrificed on the way are as nothing before the face of our fashionable Juggernaut. Newnham has slain its thousands and Girton its tens of thousands."[7] Painting a different picture, Clementina Black, Levy's best friend, wrote to the *Athenaeum* only a few weeks after the suicide, reporting that Amy Levy never "left her father's house otherwise than on visits to friends or holiday journeys" and that her "fits of extreme depression" were the result of "the exhaustion produced by strenuous brain work."[8]

More recently, Gail Kraidman, in a 1988 encyclopedia entry, suggests that Levy's writing may have been "suppressed" because she was "politically controversial," describing her as "active in radical and feminist organizations such as the Men and Women's Club."[9] Deborah Nord groups Levy with Beatrice Webb and Margaret Harkness as part of "an amorphous community" of unmarried women who "understood their own marginality . . . as a condition of their sex but also as a product of their socialist politics, of their aspirations to enter male-dominated areas of work, or of their religion or class."[10] Nord's language is somewhat

ambiguous, but readers are likely to infer that Levy was a socialist. Angela Leighton (in an anthology of Victorian women's poetry that she
edited with Margaret Reynolds), while not placing Levy so specifically on
the political spectrum, also represents her as a social reformer, asserting
that she "was active as secretary of the Beaumont Trust, an organization
run by her father to solicit funds for educational facilities for the East
End."[11]

Price's facts are so wrong that one is at first at a loss to conjecture
where he got his image of Amy Levy, but apparently the large emigration of poor, uneducated Jews from Eastern Europe to England in the
1880s had by 1912 led to the construction of a stereotype associating Jewish people with poverty and deprivation instead of linking them to diamonds and materialistic values, the image that upset Jewish readers of
Reuben Sachs. Extraordinarily, one still finds traces of Price's portrait of
Levy in recent discussions of her life. The Feminist Companion to Literature by Women reports that "she is supposed to have worked in a factory,
lived in a garret and taught in London" (the notion that she was a
teacher, usually of poor Jewish children in the East End, is found in several discussions of Levy in the period after her death). Even Leighton, in
her preface to Levy's poetry, refers to a "garret above the roofs of London" that never existed.[12]

The impressions of Tynan and Quilter, though kindly meant, suggest that Levy's contemporaries—those who were not her close
friends—were unable to see her clearly because her image was obscured
by their tendency to see a "Jewess" as mysterious, exotic, and foreign
(and, like Quilter, to project onto a Jewish face the intellectuality that
was part of the stereotype). Grant Allen's distorted portrait is another
matter entirely. Befriending Levy after she became famous as a writer,
Allen exploited her untimely death as grist for his views about the so-
called New Woman[13] of the fin de siècle in the essay cited. The New
Woman was the subject of Allen's 1895 novel The Woman Who Did, its
title reflecting Allen's conviction that emancipation for women should
take the form of rebellion against monogamy and sexual constraints, not
the pursuit of an education equivalent to that available to men.

And why did Clementina Black place her friend so squarely in the domestic sphere—a woman who rarely leaves her father's house—when, in fact, Levy led an independent, public life? It seems especially odd that Black would endorse a widely held myth about the dangers of intellectual endeavor for women when she herself was an indefatigable woman of ideas, trade union activist, suffragist, and novelist. Her portrait of Levy as a highly conventional Victorian woman can be understood only as damage control: an attempt to bolster Levy's reputation in the face of a "sordid" end for the sake of her literary reputation and to mitigate the suffering of the surviving family.

In the recent image of Levy as a radical, a socialist, or a social reformer, we find assumptions that probably relate to more modern notions about intellectual Jewish women. This portrait is to a great extent derived from the work of feminist scholars who are, like most academic feminists, to some degree left wing or, at least, liberal, and interested in activism on behalf of progressive social change. It is likely that these feminists, in many cases themselves Jewish, have had a desire to see her as a precursor, and this inclination has found fertile ground in what is known about the social milieu in which she moved and in the political atmosphere of her time. In 1883–84 Henry James wrote to a friend, "The air is full of events, of changes, of movement." Eileen Sypher explains that he was "referring to the rumblings of social unrest he heard all about him as he wandered through London." As a consequence of the severe economic depression of 1884–87, the large "impoverished restive 'underclass'" became visible, and there emerged "new powerful collectivist ideologies, such as socialism."[14] Some of Amy Levy's good friends were dedicated socialists or social reformers, and so were many of her acquaintances, but, as we will see, Levy's overwhelming commitment was not to politics but to her art and to her career as a woman of letters.

Amy Levy's papers were sold at auction by Sotheby's in 1990 and are now available to the public for the first time. Her letters, a calendar for 1889, unpublished manuscripts, and other items in this collection (some of which lead the scholar to other accurate sources of information) make it possible to see Levy with considerable clarity.[15] These new documents do not undermine her image as a woman whose feminism occupied a central place in her consciousness; indeed, an apprehension of the devaluation of women and the need to widen their opportunities were integral to Levy's sense of self and of society at a very early age, and the desire to right the wrongs experienced by her sex continued to be important throughout her life. Moreover, some of her fiction and poetry indicates that she had a critique of the social injustices of her era that went beyond the subjection of women. But Deborah Nord's discussion of Levy can easily leave the impression that she was close to Webb and Harkness and that she shared their political commitments, when this was not the case. Only *some* of Levy's friends were leftists; a few seem to have been quite conventional; others had connections to "the sect / They call 'aesthetic'" ("To Lallie," New's ed. 381). In her own writing she espouses neither socialism nor "art for art's sake," and a careful scrutiny of the evidence shows that Levy was not a member of the Men and Women's Club and was neither a socialist nor a social activist. The president of the Beaumont Trust, which raised money for the new immigrant poor, had the same name as Amy Levy's father, and its secretary was an "A. Levy," but neither Amy nor her father was involved with it.[16]

That there are many legends and mistaken ideas about Levy should not be surprising. The misconceptions about her are multifold and inconsistent partly because, as Bryan Cheyette says, "'the Jew'" in liberal society is "a perversely imprecise sign."[17] During the period in which Levy lived and wrote, for example, Jewish people achieved a considerable degree of assimilation even though they were regarded as an unassimilable racial other. And the inaccuracy of the way she is remembered has been heightened because in addition to being Jewish she belonged to other groups about which her society had stereotypes. For one thing, she was a depressive. Levy's letters and 1889 calendar show her struggling with what was almost certainly a biochemical vulnerability to major depression;[18] in one of her letters she self-mockingly refers to this disability as "the great-devil that lyeth ever in wait in the recesses of my heart."[19] In late Victorian society, episodes of depression were likely to be understood not as an illness but as affectations of melancholy prompted by "poetic temperament."

Levy's bouts of depression appear to have been exacerbated by identity conflicts stemming from her position as a New Woman (a woman who, instead of centering her attention on home and family, strived for an autonomous, achievement-oriented existence); in her time the domestic "angel" was still the ideal. Moreover, Levy was a woman whose desire was homoerotic. While Margaret Reynolds is right in saying that lesbianism at this particular "historical moment" was "neither invisible nor condemned in certain contexts,"[20] it was far from easy to structure one's life around romantic relationships between women, especially for a Jewish woman,[21] and such relationships were not granted public recognition.

One feels that Levy would not have been surprised to learn how difficult it has been to establish the truth about who she was. My discussion of her writings, especially her fiction, will show that she was highly aware of her marginalization, and it will explain how the contradictions in her identity prompted her to develop innovative literary strategies for the representation of people who, like her, were outside society's sense of itself. While Levy's diverse subject positions gave her access to contradictory perspectives that were healthy for her art, the many ways in which she was on the margins of her society placed considerable strain on her life. Levy's dilemma can be understood only in the light of her time and place while aspects of late Victorian British culture are themselves cast in a new light by the reflection of who Levy was, what she did, and what life did to her.

Judith Walkowitz provides a sketch of how the changes women were undergoing altered the London scene in the next-to-last decade of the nineteenth century:

> An ability to get around and self-confidence in public places became the hallmarks of the modern woman. Not only could she be seen in the shopping districts of the West End and in the poor neighborhoods of the East, but she also made an appearance in other public spaces, alone or with friends, at concerts, picture exhibitions, the galleries of Albert Hall and the pits of the playhouse. "Our social life has changed," proclaimed the *Women's*

Penny Paper at the end of the decade. "One could hardly walk a quarter of a mile in any street in London without seeing instances of it, particularly in [the] dress and manner of women, in the things they do, in the words they say."[22]

Levy was one of the women who inhabited the public spaces of London in the 1880s, and her experiences before and during that decade bring into sharp focus how the changes that gave rise to the so-called New Woman could mark the life of an actual person. A student at one of the new secondary schools established to provide girls with an education based on solid academic achievement,[23] she became a member of the pioneering generation of women at Cambridge; for the remainder of her life Levy defined herself as a woman with a university education even while she grew increasingly critical of the academic mind. A feminist, she expressed her sexual politics in her writing and observed closely the activism on behalf of women of many of her friends. An ambitious, professional writer who shrewdly gauged the literary market, Levy gave considerable thought to the needs of women in the professions. Prone to falling in love with members of her own sex, she had friends who entered into long-term romantic partnerships with other women. Even Levy's emotional instability is in part related to her rejection of conventional gender roles, for, as Elaine Showalter asserts, the "New Woman was also the nervous woman. Doctors linked what they saw as an epidemic of nervous disorders . . . with the changes in women's aspirations."[24] And Levy was an emancipated Jewish woman at a time when most Jewish women's lives were even more traditional than those of their gentile sisters.

Levy's life was marked by the opportunities and predicaments of Anglo-Jews at a pivotal moment in their history. England's Jews had received full political rights in 1858, two years before she was born. Although they were allowed to matriculate and take degrees at Oxford after the Oxford University Reform Act of 1854 was passed and at Cambridge after the Cambridge University Reform Act of 1856, they were unlikely to feel comfortable at these schools until the University Test Act of 1872 abolished all religious tests at both of the ancient universities (even those for fellowships, university prizes, and posts). After 1872 Jews were no longer scarce at Oxford and Cambridge.[25]

Todd Endelman gives the British a mixed evaluation on their treatment of the Jews. Emphasizing that conditions in England throughout the Victorian period were far more favorable for Jews than in any other European country, he says that "Jewishness . . . was not an insurmountable obstacle to social advancement"[26] and points out that by 1881 "the native Jewish community had achieved a high degree of acculturation to the dominant cultural patterns of middle- and upper-middle-class English life."[27] Endelman acknowledges, however, that England was "hostile to the notion of cultural diversity" and explains that " circles and institutions quite willing to tolerate Jews as intimate associates were not willing to endorse the perpetuation of a separate Jewish culture or to see any value in the customs or beliefs of the Jewish religion."[28] This seems to suggest that a Jew could win full acceptance by eschewing specifically Jewish beliefs, practices, and customs, but Endelman goes on to say that "unflattering stereotyped remarks in the press, on the stage, and in literature reflected—as well as reinforced—popular feeling that Jews were, at heart, really not like other Englishmen, no matter how thoroughly anglicized they might appear."[29]

The experience of Levy's family, assimilated to a considerable degree but still strongly affiliated with the Jewish community, animates what scholarly studies tell us of contradictions in the status of English Jewry. That the three brothers who outlived Amy Levy left England probably has something to do with those contradictions. In the 1890s William (Willy) and Edmund (Ned) Levy emigrated to El Salvador. No doubt they were seeking economic opportunity, yet their willingness to settle in a land not part of the British Empire and in no way English in either culture or language suggests that although their sister in her published work insisted that Jews were an integral a part of English society,[30] Ned and Willy felt that they would always be outsiders in the dominant culture of the land where they and a good proportion of their ancestors were born.[31] Donald, the youngest boy in the family, emigrated to Canada sometime between 1900 and his death in 1907.

Michael Ragussis emphasizes the relentless efforts made throughout the century to convert the Jews (not seen as being at odds with an ideology of toleration); despite these efforts, he and other scholars report that the new "science" of ethnology, which began to be influential in the 1840s, gained adherents as the century went on (reifying racial differences and ranking racial groups, e.g., the superiority of the Indo-European over the Semitic).[32] Although Jewish people attained positions of status in the Victorian period and became integrated into the fabric of British society, hostility to the Jews increased in the 1870s. Ira Nadell says, "The Jewish stereotype now had a scientific basis according to racial anti-Semitism."[33]

Andrea Freud Loewenstein insists that Benjamin Disraeli, the baptized Jew who became a prime minister, "embodied the contradictory dialectic centered on the Jews. He was . . . proof that a Jew could indeed become an English gentleman—and a personification of the stealthy Jew who, concealing his identity, inveigles his way into the Christian body, polluting the whole."[34] This increased suspicion of the Jews was reflected in and heightened by novels about "secret" Jews subverting and vulgarizing English society.[35]

In the 1880s a flood of Jewish refugees from the pogroms in Eastern Europe introduced "foreign" Jews into British life. These immigrants arrived at a moment when the definition of English identity (an increasingly vexed issue throughout the century) was reaching a crisis as a result of theories of racial difference, the growth of nationalism everywhere in Europe, and the expansion of the empire, which created a heightened awareness of the alterity of non-Western people.[36] Explaining that the figure of the Jew complicated efforts to define what it meant to be English precisely because the Jew was not understood as entirely foreign, Michael Galchinsky says, "As both progenitor and rejector of Christianity, the Jew was both inside and outside the English national faith at the same time."[37] Thus concern over English national identity engendered anxiety about Anglo-Jewry, a group within England's own gates.

Agreeing that public attention became focused "on Jews to a degree hitherto unknown in Britain," Endelman emphasizes the importance of "the arrival of tens of thousands of East European immigrants . . . along with the spread of racial thinking and the crisis of liberalism" and acknowledges that "anti-Semitism was more overt and focused in the last decades of the century than before."[38] This change in climate had an impact on the lives of those Jewish people who, like Levy, did not want to be confined to what one of the characters in *Reuben Sachs* calls "the tribal duckpond." And so cultural shifts and upheavals affecting Amy Levy's subject positions as a woman and as a Jew left their imprint on her brief life. Some of these changes created opportunities for her at the same time that they created conflicts; others generated limitations that, it seems, she felt painfully.

Stephen Greenblatt says, "A culture's narratives . . . are crucial indices of the prevailing codes governing human mobility and constraint."[39] Levy's writings are such narratives, addressing as so many of them do the question of whether and to what extent a person in the various groups to which she belonged is free to reconfigure fundamental aspects of identity, and often showing that society makes such a conversion impossible, or that it comes only at a very high price. Many of Levy's writings are important as literature, but nearly all are intriguing cultural documents, revealing an intelligent, witty, troubled, gifted, ironic, and singular young woman navigating the turbulent waters of her time.

2

Childhood and Family

Most of Amy Levy's forebears on both sides had come to England in the eighteenth century, establishing themselves in Falmouth, where (according to the handwritten account of Lucy Levy Marks, Amy's first cousin), their maternal great-grandfather "bought a small sailing ship and traded between Cornwall and Spain."[1] Levy's parents, Lewis and Isabelle (who were cousins), thus had deep roots in English soil, and, like many other Englishmen, Lewis's affluence was made possible by British colonialism. Lucy Marks's narrative tells us that her own father, Nathaniel Levy, and his brothers (one of whom was Lewis), went to Australia "at the height of the gold-digging fever," establishing a small store in Melbourne as well as "driving a wagon stocked with shirts, pants, socks," and other necessities, which they sold to the miners in more remote parts of that country. Marks says that "the miners, who had no 'cash,' paid with gold nuggets, thus laying the foundations of a fortune" for Nathaniel, Goodman, and Lewis Levy. Returning to London, the brothers invested in the stock market. This must have happened before Lewis's marriage. In the census of 1861 (the year of her birth) Levy's father is listed as an export merchant, but in 1881 he described himself to the census taker as a stock and share broker, an occupational shift that indicates that the family experienced upward mobility during her childhood.

Born in what was then the south Lambeth section of London, Amy Levy was second in a family of seven children. She was very close to her sister Katie, Levy's elder by twenty months, their intimacy evidenced by the letters in this volume (Katie is often addressed as "Saint" in these letters). The youngest girl in the family, Ella, was born in 1872, and Levy had four younger brothers: Alfred, born in 1863; Willie, born in 1865; Ned, born in 1870; and Donald, who was born in 1874.

In many ways the family exemplifies what historians report about Anglo-Jewry at the time. Native Jews, especially those who, like the Levys, were upper middle class, lived much like non-Jews, having "become overwhelmingly English in manners, speech, deportment, and habits of thought and taste."[2] At the same time, Endelman says, the social ties of most Jewish people were primarily with other Jews, but this social cohesion "was not matched by any corresponding loyalty to religious practice. Over the course of the nineteenth century, there was a continual decline in synagogue attendance, home observance, Hebrew literacy and other fundamental hallmarks of Jewish knowledge and practice. Already at mid-century regular synagogue attendance on the sabbath was uncommon within Anglo-Jewry in general." Only on the Day of Atonement was synagogue attendance the norm. Endelman also tells us that in the late Victorian period "the dietary laws were not strictly observed," and "much of the native-born middle class also neglected to give their offspring a religious education. Some parents, probably a minority, engaged a teacher to instruct their children one or two hours a week."[3]

The Levy family shows these tendencies in its desire to behave much like other English people, its strong identification with Anglo-Jewry, and its casual attitude toward religious observance. Amy's governess was a young gentile woman, Emily Pateman. As the two childhood letters included in this volume show, Pateman was allowed to take her charges to visit Christian churches (one of them St. Paul's), and Amy is comfortable about telling her parents of the beauty of these churches. In another letter (not included), the child Amy writes happily to her parents about the Christmas tree she enjoys at her aunt's house.[4] Although a few of the letters indicate that the Levys practiced their religion to some extent, the Jewish dietary laws cannot have been important, for in 1876 Amy and two of her brothers were sent to board at a "gentile" school.

Like many Victorian families, the Levys engaged in home theatricals. A printed playbill shows that they performed Act IV of *The Merchant of Venice* in 1880. Katie played Portia, Amy was Shylock, and the other actors were two more Levy children and three of their young friends. Endelman says affluent Jews fully participated in English culture while strongly identifying with Jews as a group; that the Levys chose this particular play to perform shows how much they fit the pattern he describes. On the one hand, nothing could be more characteristic of Victorian bourgeois life than home theatricals; on the other, the choice of play reveals a preoccupation with things Jewish and an interest in the way Jews were perceived by the dominant culture (Ragussis calls *The Merchant of Venice* "the ur-text of the representation of Jewish identity in England").[5]

Twice in 1880 and once in 1883 the Levys staged performances of *The Unhappy Princess*, a play for children that Levy wrote in 1880.[6] The characterization of Princess Morosa, a seemingly fortunate young woman who is prone to melancholia, shows that Levy could laugh even at this aspect of herself, and, though its plot is hardly original, the drama reveals its author's quirky, delightful sense of humor. (Morosa's mother, the queen, willing to do nearly anything to allay her daughter's despondency, says, "What would you like? A doll? A sweet? / A little slave to pet or beat?"). Levy names the governess "Girtonia" (after the other women's college at Cambridge) and has her be pedantic with her doleful royal pupil:

"It's sad to think that you might grow
Into a woman and not know
A preposition from a noun,
Or what is Corsica's chief town,
What times the sun should rise and set,
Or what the bound'ries of Tibet!"

The playbills tell us that in staging these plays the parts not performed by Amy Levy and her siblings are played by girls from three Jewish families, the Leons, the Isaacs, and the Mocattas.[7] These names appear in other artifacts from Levy's girlhood, including a book in which she recorded the birth dates of friends. During Levy's girlhood, Connie Leon and her sister, Annie and Emmie Isaac, and Grace and Ella Mocatta filled out pages in Levy's "Confessions Book" (this popular album, as its cover says, was a place "to Record Opinions, Thoughts, Feelings, Ideas, Peculiarities, Impressions, Characteristics of Friends, & C." (See Figure 1 for one of Amy's own entries.) In several of Levy's letters written from boarding school she refers to Connie Leon, and in one, written to her mother (not included in this book), her references to Connie's father and mother indicate that the two sets of parents were well-acquainted. Katie remained friends with Annie and Emmie Isaac over the years, for in letters written from Europe in the 1880s Amy sends love to "the sisters Isaac," and Emmie's name appears in Levy's account of Katie's wedding (letter 24); Amy herself kept up the connection because her 1889 calendar shows that she spent a day with them. Clearly the Levys had close ties with these and other Jewish families, connections that demonstrate, despite their willingness to go beyond Jewish social networks in regard to schooling, the social cohesion that was so characteristic of Jewish life in the Victorian era.

It would be useful to know more about the Levy family's involvement with Judaic practice, whether the children received any religious training, and what relationship they had with the organized Jewish community. Although the basis for conjecture is not as full as we might wish,

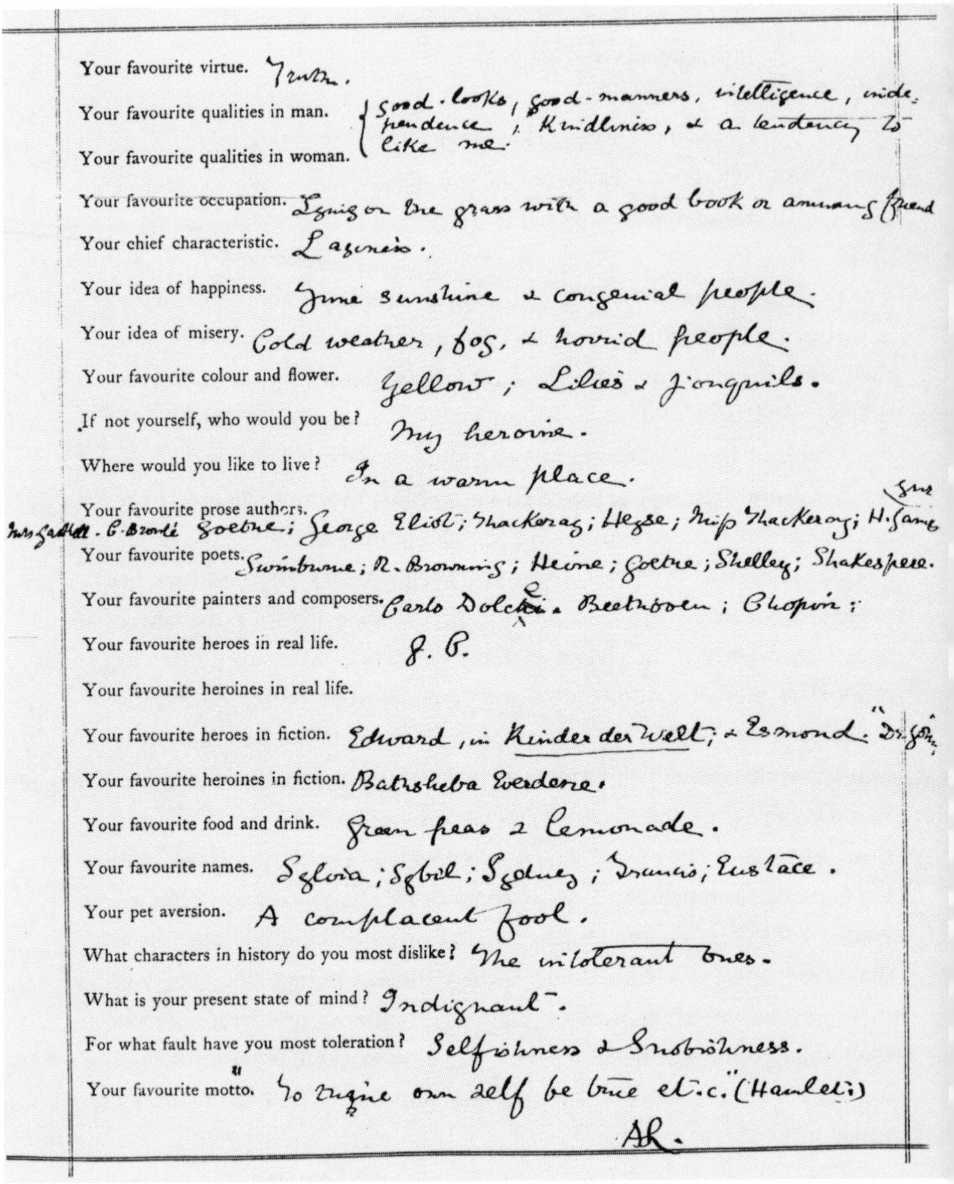

Your favourite virtue. *Truth.*

Your favourite qualities in man.
Your favourite qualities in woman. *{ Good-looks, good-manners, intelligence, inde- pendence, kindliness, & a tendency to like me.*

Your favourite occupation. *Lying on the grass with a good book or among friends*

Your chief characteristic. *Laziness.*

Your idea of happiness. *June sunshine & congenial people.*

Your idea of misery. *Cold weather, fog, & horrid people.*

Your favourite colour and flower. *Yellow; Lilies & Jonquils.*

If not yourself, who would you be? *My heroine.*

Where would you like to live? *In a warm place.*

Your favourite prose authors. *Mrs Gaskell. C. Brontë Goethe; George Eliot; Thackeray; Hesse; Miss Thackeray; H. James*

Your favourite poets. *Swinburne; R. Browning; Heine; Goethe; Shelley; Shakespere.*

Your favourite painters and composers. *Carlo Dolci. Beethoven; Chopin;*

Your favourite heroes in real life. *R. B.*

Your favourite heroines in real life.

Your favourite heroes in fiction. *Edward, in Kinder der Welt; & Esmond. Dr. ...*

Your favourite heroines in fiction. *Bathsheba Everdene.*

Your favourite food and drink. *Green peas & lemonade.*

Your favourite names. *Sgloria; Sybil; Sydney; Francis; Eustace.*

Your pet aversion. *A complacent fool.*

What characters in history do you most dislike? *The intolerant ones.*

What is your present state of mind? *Indignant.*

For what fault have you most toleration? *Selfishness & Snobbishness.*

Your favourite motto. *To thine own self be true etc. (Hamlet.)*

A.L.

Figure 1. Amy Levy's Confessions Book entry

there are some clues. At fourteen she published (in a children's magazine called *Kind Words*) a short piece analyzing the character of the biblical David. She concludes a rather prodigious psychological scrutiny of David by saying, "His pathetic child-like faith is decidedly the brightest spot in his character—to the darker ones we have already alluded, and . . . we can only add that, faulty as he was, in the life of David we have one of the grandest moral lessons of Scripture."[8] Although this analysis is hardly proof that Amy had any religious education, it does indicate that, as a young adolescent, she was familiar with and respected the Hebrew Bible.

Another piece, written when Levy was seventeen, was published in the *Jewish Chronicle,* a weekly newspaper that was (and is) an institution important to Anglo-Jewry. This lengthy letter titled "Jewish Women and 'Women's Rights'" is about the importance of paid professional work for women, and in it Levy brings together her Jewish and her feminist identities.[9] One other possible piece of evidence is that her cousin Lucy says in her memoir that she and her siblings had Hebrew lessons once a week.[10] The two Levy families were close, which suggests that Lewis and Isabelle Levy's children may have had private Hebrew lessons too. And Levy's letters provide a few hints that the family was at least somewhat observant. In fall of 1881 Levy says in a letter written from Dresden to her sister, "Being Friday, you can't go—sorry?" in response to something Katie has said about not going to a "ballette"(letter 9). Katie may not have been able to attend because she was required to be at home on Friday night, the start of the Jewish sabbath. In another letter written that same fall Levy seems to be referring to fasting and attending services on the Day of Atonement when she asks Katie, "How did everybody fast?" and (referring to herself), "Did you not miss your stalwart escort of last year?" (letter 16).[11] She goes on to say, "Please tell Mama that I went to Synagogue yesterday." In 1988 Sharona Levy, while writing a dissertation on Amy Levy, interviewed Beth Lask Abrahams, the woman who held Levy's books and papers for most of the twentieth century[12]. Abrahams, then in her nineties, told Sharona Levy that the family sometimes attended the Reform synagogue in Upper Berkeley Street (which is mentioned in *Reuben Sachs*). Like the Leunigers and Sachses in Levy's novel, and like most British Jews of their time, the Levy family may have attended religious services primarily on the Day of Atonement.

Whatever their degree of religious observance, the Levys appear to have had no qualms about allowing their children to read freely and to participate in secular literary activities even when these involved "advanced" ideas. Among Amy Levy's childhood drawings is one of a woman standing on a soap box dressed in a bloomer costume, her sign reading, "Women's Suffrage! Man is a Cruel Oppressor!" Her precocious attraction to women's rights is noteworthy, for she reviewed Elizabeth Barrett Browning's feminist epic "Aurora Leigh" for *Kind Words* when she was thirteen and at the same age published "The Ballad of Ida Grey" in the *Pelican*, a feminist journal.[13] Indeed, Lewis Levy, her father, must have been drawn to progressive ideas; in Levy's Confessions Book, he gave the answer "Mr. Darwin" to the question, "If not yourself, who would you be?"

Lewis Levy's desire to be Mr. Darwin is significant, as is his choosing, in his Confessions Book entry, Carlyle as one of his favorite prose authors and Milton, Shakespeare, Byron, and Schiller as his favorite poets. He appears to be a man to whom both science and literature were important, and his friendship with Asher Myers, the editor of the *Jewish Chronicle* and "a man of scholarly and historical inclination,"[14] supports the inference that Lewis was intellectual. He and Amy were not the only members of the family oriented toward learning and the arts. Levy's letters show that Katie too read and loved literature; she seems to have been preparing herself for higher education when marriage intervened. In 1881, when she was twenty-one, and so well past the age at which the typical Victorian girl completed her schooling, she was attending the London Academy.[15] Ella Levy, Levy's little sister, attended North London Collegiate, a secondary school founded by Frances Buss in the early 1850s (Buss was a major figure in the movement to provide high-quality education for girls). Although we have no information about which secondary schools the boys attended or why none of them went to a university, Willie at least seems to have had an interest in intellectual matters for he attended two meetings of a discussion club Levy belonged to in the first half of the 1880s.

The Philistinism of most of the Jews in *Reuben Sachs* (the exceptions being Leopold Leuniger, Esther Kohnthal, and to some extent Reuben), particularly that of the female characters, who are depicted as spending their time shopping and going to parties, may be drawn from life, but the portrait is not based on Levy's own family. This is important because from the first appearance of her novel there has been a tendency to assume Levy was writing autobiographically, and even Meri-Jane Rochelson, in her excellent discussion of *Reuben Sachs*, asserts that Levy "explores what seem to be areas of her own discontent," going on to draw parallels between Judith Quixano, the female protagonist, and its author.[16] Levy may well have felt that the Jewish community's rules and values were stultifying, but her own family, while part of that milieu, had broader interests (though the letters show that her mother was conventionally Victorian in regard to propriety in matters involving social relations between the sexes).

Endelman agrees that Jewish life was narrow: "The cultural and intellectual horizons of middle-class Jews were limited, and hence they rarely ventured into the larger world to find enlightenment or drink at the fountains of high culture. Indeed by comparison with other Western Jewish communities, Anglo-Jewry was remarkably ill-educated and Philistine, taking little interest in literary and artistic matters of a general nature."[17] The Levys, then, were an atypical Victorian Jewish family in two ways: they were literary and intellectual, and they believed in giving girls an excellent education. This notion of what they were like is borne out by what we know of the activities that Amy and Katie (and possibly the older boys) engaged in as children and young people.

Amy and her older sister Katie shared a love of literature, drawing pictures of characters from their favorite works, such as Louisa May Alcott's *Little Women*, Walter Scott's *Marmion*, and Mme. de Staël's *Corinne*. In childhood and in their teens, they put out literary magazines. The first of these was called the "Poplar Club Journal" (its motto "Excelsior!"). The surviving pages (in the Amy Levy collection) contain stories, plays, and verse, with illustrations, and, since the stories appear to be written in more than two handwritings, Alfred and Willie may have been contributors; or perhaps the two older girls contrived to make their writing look diverse. Most of the writings are unsigned; some are written by "Citizen Amy" and some signed "Amy Levy." Inevitably, one thinks of the Brontë children, though the remnants of the "Poplar Club Journal," while precocious, do not even begin to be as rich in imaginative energy as are the young Brontës' narratives about Gondal and Angria. Also, the writing of the Levy children is various, not set in invented kingdoms that recur, and not about characters who appear again and again. There is no reason to think that Katie and Amy, with or without their brothers, withdrew into a fantasy world during their childhood.

Nevertheless, there is no question that these journals are the work of young people who, as children and even as adolescents, lived to an unusual extent in their imaginations. To provide a sense of the "Poplar Club Journal" we will examine one issue from 1873, when Katie would have been about fourteen, Amy twelve, Alfred ten, and Willie eight (even this issue—the most complete of what survives—exists now only in fragments). In the final scene from a play called "Queen Eleanor & Fair Rosamund," the latter kills herself, and Eleanor says "exultingly," "Now lie there thou frail piece of clay; & be a witness that Eleanor of Aquitaine has now revenged her wrongs; & she alone now reigns the mistress of her husband's heart." The melodrama in that play is matched by that in another item in the same issue, "The Nun," which is doggerel about a "wretched nun" who says,

Why came I ever here
To this dreadful living grave.
The convent means a prison-house,
And nun means but a slave!

Whether the sentiment is antipapist and its attitude a reflection of how English these children were, or whether the view of the convent is the product of their Jewishness is hard to say (it may well be the latter, for there were and are, after all, Anglican nuns). "The Nun" may also have been inspired by their reading of Scott's Marmion, in which a nun is immured within convent walls as a punishment.

This "poem" (like many of the contributions to the journal) is followed by editorial comment, in this case, "Very well if it were not for the wrong meter of the last line of the first verse" (signed with the initials A. L.) and "Very good" (signed "Katie Levy"). Other editorial comments in this issue are made by fictitious personae: "Lord Spendthrift" and "Reverend B. Bubbles." There is also a letter informing its readers that those members who fail to produce their contributions will be fined, concluding, "I remain gentlemen, yours respectfully, Citizen Amy." That young Amy Levy was the driving force behind the "Poplar Club Journal" is indicated by this letter (where she speaks, albeit facetiously, in the voice of authority), the illustrations (which are clearly Amy's, the style recognizable from her many childhood sketches), and the fact that she is the only one of the contributors who attaches her name to her work.

The magazine and its successors, called "Harum Scarum" and the "Kettledrum," provided a workshop for her writing as it developed.[18] In writing for "Harum Scarum," produced during Amy Levy's adolescence even though she was often away at school (see the mention of this journal in letter 10), Levy signs her stories "The Follower of the Faithful," and the illustrations (again hers) are drawn by "New Boots" (this pseudonym, with a small drawing of a pair of boots, is at the bottom of each sketch). The writings are much better written than those in the "Poplar Club Journal" (though less amusing). Levy's extant scrapbooks contain numerous sketches of scenes from the stories that appeared in "Harum Scarum" (medleys that were themselves "published" in the next issue).

What seems odd is that there was an even later manuscript literary journal, this one called the "Kettledrum"; remnants of several issues and one complete magazine survive. A folder titled "The Kettledrum Goes to Japan" includes a pen-and-ink drawing of a Japanese scene, a sign that the aesthetic movement, which had a fascination with Japanese art, had made an impact on Levy. The only complete issue is dated March 1880 (when she was already a student at Newnham). Its stories are written in apparently different handwritings; the ones obviously penned by Levy are signed "The dog with the bad name."[19] The "Table of Contents" lists nine different pen names. The stories, with the exception of one called "Lallie: A Cambridge Sketch" (by "The dog with the bad name"), are fairly hackneyed (not necessarily an advance over those in "Harum Scarum"), and the drawings appear to be Levy's work. Again there are editorial comments, this time in a section called "Gentle Hints from Member to Member." These responses to stories in previous issues include two comments on a piece called "Euphemia," one of which says, "Euphemia is a brilliant specimen of character drawing—we cannot rank it with the other contributions—it is simply hors de concours" [sic], while the other asserts, "Euphemia is good, but not as good as the commencement promised." Both handwritings—the facetious overpraising of "Euphemia" and the qualified praise—are Levy's.

One begins to wonder who wrote these stories and editorial remarks. Levy may have involved friends from Newnham in this magazine, but it seems unlikely. The cursive script varies, but the "Gentle Hints" section raises suspicion because of the number of remarks that address the subject of handwriting, for example, "What a fortunate individual is the critic who knows the handwriting of all good writers—past and present!" Another remark from this section asserts:

The members need be under no apprehension as to "U.G.L.Y." and "The dog with the bad name" being one and the same person; all contribs this month having been written on the same sort of paper, it would be foolish to say that all are the productions of one prolific author. The paper which raised so much disquiet in the minds of some, is the regulation paper of the now defunct "Harum Scarum."

The disclaimer protests too much, encouraging one to wonder if Amy and Katie, now nineteen and twenty-one, wrote the entire issue while pretending to be a whole group of people, or whether Amy Levy put the "Kettledrum" together entirely on her own.

And what would it mean if this were so? Perhaps Levy's creative writing had become so bound up with the production of the literary journals she and Katie produced as children and teenagers that at this stage she could best prompt her imagination by re-creating yet another such magazine. Levy's translation from Goethe's "The Shepherd," which appeared in the June 9, 1880, issue of the *Cambridge Review*, is listed in the table of contents of the "Kettledrum" (authored by "The dog with the bad name"), and in the same year Levy published a story called "Euphemia" in *Victoria Magazine*. So, whether or not Levy was working with a group, her sister, or "pretending" on her own, the endeavor did result in at least two pieces of writing that found publication in the real world. And yet there is no denying that Levy's penchant for adopting personae, which in this issue of the "Kettledrum" takes the form of pen names and editorial comments that are tongue-in-cheek and in some sense fictitious, is striking.

We should not touch on the subject of personae without giving attention to two entries in Levy's Confessions Book.[20] There is a page signed by "Maryanne Salvation" and another signed by "Satan." Anyone familiar with Levy's handwriting would see quickly that these are hers, but the questions on these pages are answered from the perspective of Christian notions of good and evil personified. Her purpose was obviously to amuse her family and friends; thus Maryanne Salvation gives "Having anything better than anyone else" as her "idea of misery"; "The Flesh" as her "pet aversion"; and "The wicked shall perish like grass" as her "favourite motto." In contrast, "Satan" gives "Seeing people happy" as his "idea of misery"; "Pity" as his "pet aversion"; and "Take care of number one" as his "favourite motto," and (wonderfully) "Mrs. Aphra Benn" [*sic*] as his "favourite poet." In addition to Levy's inclination to adopt a mask, her sense of humor and her freedom to be irreverent are striking. Her parents must have been aware of their daughter's irreverence, for the album is obviously a family parlor game. While their Judaism would have made these satiric pages less shocking than they would have been to Christians (Satan, despite his appearance in the Book of Job, is not a figure in Judaism), that Levy was free to joke about moral questions in this manner indicates that she grew up in an unusually tolerant late-Victorian household.[21]

Early letters show exchanges between Levy and her parents marked by affection and fun. In one undated letter to her mother, surely written before she was twelve, Amy says with hyperbolic irony, "I was not of course at all surprised when . . . the house was dull without us; for am I not the glorious star, in fact the angelic treasure of our small community?" The same letter (1) contains a note to her father that concludes with a picture of how "fat" she has grown since he last saw her. Levy's remark in her essay "Jewish Children" that for Jews "Love of offspring might, indeed, be described as our master-passion" (New's ed. 529), would seem to come from her own experience as well as observation of other Jewish families. Another item in the Amy Levy collection, a musi-

Figure 2. Isabelle Levy

cal composition thirteen pages in length (an additional sign that the Levys, including their kin, had an interest in the arts), is called "The Amy Valse." Written by "S. Levy" (certainly a relative, perhaps even her paternal grandfather, Solomon Levy), it suggests that an adoring extended family was part of young Amy's life (see Figures 2, 3, 4, and 5 for photographs of Lewis, Isabelle, Katie, and young Amy).

In turn, Levy's letters and papers from her adolescence and afterward show her involvement with and fondness for her younger siblings.

Figure 3. Lewis Levy

Figure 4. Katie Levy

While at boarding school she spent some of her free time with Alfred and looked in on Willie, who had sprained his foot, reporting on his condition to her parents. In the letters written to Katie in her twenties, she frequently mentions her brothers with concern, often commenting on and criticizing decisions her parents have made in regard to them; in 1887 Levy also reports that she has sent a book to her "brother in America" (this would have been Willie, who was twenty-two at the time and may have gone to the United States to consider emigrating). Levy's relationship with Ella, nine years younger, seems also to have been affectionate. One of Levy's scrapbooks has a drawing of a little girl with her legs crossed and her dress pulled up to her knees. Under this sketch are these lines:

Figure 5. Amy Levy as a child of about seven

Here little Ella Levy sits
She shows more leg than quite befits
Her age, position, rank and sex;
No cold conventions Ella vex.
She thinks she has a perfect right
Her trotters[22] to expose tonight.

Levy's sisters were faithful to her memory. Ella Levy put her sister's papers in the hands of Beth Lask (later Abrahams), whom she met in the 1920s while doing philanthropic work among the immigrant Jews in the East End.[23] Lask was interested in literary Jewish women, and Ella must have felt she had found the best person to entrust with the job of keeping Amy Levy's work from being forgotten (these papers now constitute the Camellia Collection: Amy Levy Archive).[24] Katie too tried to perpetuate Amy's literary reputation. It is moving to find a letter from Levy's older sister to the Macmillan Company, dated May 24, 1932 (forty-three years after Amy died):

In 1888 you published my sister's novel *Reuben Sachs*. I possess several short stories by her which came out in different magazines, e,g, *Temple Bar, London Society,* Oscar Wilde's paper, *The Woman's World,* & others. There are also some unpublished stories. Not many in all. Would you care to consider the publication of these in book form? . . . Some of her poems have appeared in recent anthologies. Her memory is still alive.[25]

3

Brighton High School for Girls

Despite their Anglo-Jewish ties, Lewis and Isabelle Levy gave their children a good secular education and allowed them to mix freely with Christians. At fifteen Levy was fortunate enough to attend Brighton High School for Girls, run by the Girls' Public Day School Company (founded in 1871 by feminists Maria and Emily Shirreff to provide secondary schooling with higher standards for girls).[1] Brighton had a headmistress fresh out of Newnham College, Edith Creak (see Figure 6). She was one of the "original five" students at Newnham, which had been established in 1871 as the second women's college at Cambridge. That Levy's parents allowed her to study at Brighton (and eventually at Newnham) shows that they were unafraid of assimilation. Both Amy and her younger brothers Alfred and Willy attended Brighton (although it was a girls' secondary school, it also offered primary education to young boys).[2] By and large the Levy children appear to have been welcomed into Christian circles, and at Brighton Levy became friends with several non-Jewish girls, the most noteworthy being Constance Black, who later became Constance Garnett, the first translator of Russian literature into English (see Figure 7); this friendship eventually led to an even closer bond with Clementina, Constance's older sister, who was Levy's elder by six years.[3]

The lively letters Levy wrote to Katie during this period give a glimpse of life at one of the reformed secondary schools that were established in the late Victorian period to give young women a good education. Levy's school offered her, along with geography, history, French, German, and higher mathematics, the chance to study Latin, significant because a classical education had traditionally been at the center of the schooling only boys received. As a result, knowledge of the classics became one of the salient marks of their higher status. We can be sure that Levy prized the opportunity Brighton offered, for at thirteen (a year or so before she started high school), in her review of "Aurora Leigh," she

Figure 6. Miss Creak

Figure 7. Constance Black [later Garnett] (photograph probably taken during her years at Newnham College)

had pardoned Barrett Browning for including too many "learned allusions" on the grounds that "it is only natural that she should wish to display what public opinion denies her sex—a classical education."[4]

Levy's letters show she had fun at this school in the seaside resort of Brighton, studying hard but in her free time engaging in activities such as a jaunt with her brother Alfred to Preston Street, where they "refreshed" themselves (presumably with a cold beverage), ice skating, going to the beach, and paying visits to the Royal Pavilion (a pleasure palace built in an Oriental style by the prince regent in 1818).[5] At the pavilion she and her friends spent their time "sentimentalizing, lounging in the drawing rooms, and inspecting the pictures" (letters 4, 6, 9, and 5). Despite these distractions, we can believe that Levy studied hard because in her last year at high school she sat for the Cambridge Senior Local and got second-class honors.[6]

Martha Vicinus tells of the homoerotic "raves" that girls in these schools often had for one another or for teachers, and Levy's letters show that she laughed at herself but was unashamed of her "grand passion" for Brighton High School's young headmistress. Levy does not disguise her feelings for her teacher in her letters to Katie although, characteristically, her tone is satiric; Miss Creak, she says slangily, "has flung out minute crumbs of sweetness lately to her wormy adorer, who bagged a divine, passion-inspiring—whenever-I-think-of-it—embrace today at the sanctum door. Frankly I'm more in love with her than ever—isn't it grim?" (letter 8).[7] Such sentiments obviously raise the question of sexual orientation, although in dealing with the nineteenth century one must always take into account the wide latitude society permitted women in their feelings for one another. The Brighton letters in this edition are full of references to romantic feelings between girls and for teachers. Vicinus tells us that most of these girls and women "spiritualized" their passionate attachments, "loving through self-discipline" and finding "satisfaction through the suppression of desire."[8] It may have been harder for Levy to spiritualize her homoerotic feelings than it was for the gentile girls because Judaism does not have the spirit/body split so important in Christianity.

In addition to these letters, Levy, while in her teens, wrote a poem called (mysteriously) "Alderleifest" that is of interest only because it expresses love for a woman (three revised versions, all with words crossed out and replaced, indicate she was never satisfied with it). She also produced three pieces of prose that, in different ways, reveal her pre-occupation with intensity of feeling between women. Her Newnham geology notebook has a fragment called "Euphemia" (not the published story). It begins with its protagonist lying on the floor and sobbing, al-most unable to believe that her close and satisfying relationship with a girl named Kitty has come to an end. Looking out the window, Eu-phemia then sees Kitty, for whom she has powerful feelings, walking and talking in an intimate way with another girl and responds by inwardly berating her former friend as if rejected by a lover.

The other two writings are related to Levy's own obsession with Miss Creak (who was only twenty-one when Levy started at Brighton).[9] The first is Levy's unpublished story, probably written while she was at Brighton High School, "Miss C's Secretary," which may have been in-tended for the entertainment of her schoolmates.[10] Its young male pro-tagonist, Edgar, is in delicate health. He develops an unrequited passion for a formidable, highly competent headmistress, "Miss. C.," who hires him to correct Latin exercises and do other tedious clerical tasks. Al-though Edgar has been "brought up to sneer at 'blue' women" (female intellectuals), "he soon could not help regarding with no little respect, this busy, offhand young woman, who did not 'nag' or 'whine' like his mother;—nor invariably use superlative expressions, like his sister. Somehow Edgar began to think that women were not *all* hysterical & il-literate!" In short, the male protagonist meets a New Woman and ad-mires her.

He soon realizes that he is in love with his employer and "cannot keep himself from telling her of his feelings." She responds coolly: "'I am very sorry at what you have just told me, Edgar, & more so, that you shall have so far lost control over yourself. . . . I do not wish to speak of it again.'" Soon after this conversation, Miss C. discovers that Edgar has succumbed to consumption. The final sentence of the story announces, "The grim calf-love comedy was over. Miss C's secretary was dead at his post."

The story is a naked expression of what must have been the wishes and fantasies of its young author (and probably of many of the budding feminists at this reformed secondary school). In addition to transposing everyday power relations, Levy had revised through reversal one of the most conventional romance plots of the nineteenth century. The story of a woman who is unable to live after her hopes for love are dashed was more often told in the poetry of the nineteenth century than in the fiction: Tennyson's "Lady of Shallot" and poems by Felicia Hemans, Letitia Landon, Christina Rossetti, and other less-known female poets. Such a role reversal must have been a heady experience for the adolescent Amy, and it must have been equally satisfying to be able, by a stroke of the pen, to convince Edgar that women can be strong and self-sufficient rather than annoying and pathetic.

Writing "Miss C's Secretary" probably played an important part in Levy's attempt to reinvent herself as a woman who was altogether different from the domestic creature held up as the ideal in the Victorian period. The new woman exemplified by Miss C. has dignity and authority. Instead of living for love, she has important labor to do, work so demanding that she gives to a male hireling the menial tasks that it generates. When he is foolish enough to lose control of his emotions, she speaks to him sternly but with "all scorn swallowed up in a great fear and compassion": compassion seems to have been the one traditionally feminine quality that the young author wanted to preserve.

Another item in the London collection is a letter addressed to "My dear friend":

I do not know how to reply to your letter of yesterday—I was both grieved & surprised to receive it. I had had no intention that the pleasant intercourse of the last weeks should end in any thing important; I had merely hoped to preserve their pleasant memory. Yr letter, with its declaration, has rendered this impossible; what I shd. merely have remembered as the tokens of warm but Platonic friendship must now gather a new and less delightful meaning from your petition—I had hoped to have found what is for a woman both as rare as precious,—a man friend; but the ordinary type of—lover! How impossible it is for me to accede to your demand, you will perhaps understand when I say that I am already betrothed to the worthy Professor —— of —— College, Camb., who is to become my husband when his great work on "The Sages of Greece" (wh. has already occupied 10 yrs. of his life) is completed & *sold*. Hoping that you will consider this decision final,

    I am yrs, very sincerely. E. E. M. Creak

My first response to this astonishing document was to wonder how Levy had managed to steal such a personal letter from her beloved headmistress's private correspondence. After a few moments, of course, I recognized that the handwriting is her own, as are the characteristic abbreviations,[11] and realized that the letter is a forgery—another example of the adolescent Amy using her imaginative abilities to engage in a fantasy about being a New Woman. Once again we see her using her pen to empower a woman and to put a man in his place. This unusual fictional text, moreover, provides insights into Levy's psyche that are not apparent in "Miss C's Secretary." It is important that in the letter the rejecting woman has her worth romantically affirmed by a man who is, significantly, a scholar. It is noteworthy that Levy's imagination, well-developed though it was in her teens, did not permit her to make Miss Creak a great scholar. Even more important, young Amy Levy gave the fictional Miss Creak something that the real one did not have: a fiancé. This invention suggests that its author was unable to envision a satisfactory life without romantic fulfillment, even for an educated female professional. This desire for love is inscribed in the poetry Levy wrote as a young woman, as we shall see.

    Both "Miss C's Secretary" and the letter "from" Miss Creak probably have a parodic dimension. Levy's letters from high school are so full of humor, irony, and reports of hilarity that it is easy to imagine her reading both pieces aloud to the other girls at Brighton to amuse them. Yet what is most striking is Levy's great admiration for her headmistress.

There is no question, of course, that in some sense Levy was "in love," but putting aside for the moment the question of Levy's sexual orientation or even her sentimental life as a girl, what is striking about the Miss Creak material is Levy's propensity for taking on a persona (already evident in the editorial comments of "Lord Spendthrift" and the Rev. B. Bubbles) and the degree to which she wanted to *be* Miss Creak. Levy's mother had borne seven children; a similar destiny appears not to have appealed to the adolescent daughter, for in an early letter to "Mama" from high school, young Amy congratulates her on the acquisition of a new nephew and then says: "Poor Aunt Bessie with 10 children" (letter 4).

In the letter to Katie about her crush on Miss Creak, Levy predicts divergent futures for her sister and herself: "You married, maternal, prudent . . . with a tendency to laugh at the plain High School Mistress sister who grinds, and lodges with chums and adores 'without return'" (letter 8). Although she did not get all the details right, she prophesied correctly about the general direction of their lives. She followed in the footsteps of her alter ego and mentor Edith Creak, in 1879 becoming the second Jewish female student to enter Cambridge. The tone of Levy's youthful vision of things to come, expressed in the above passage from her letter, is playful and amused, eager and confident in its expectation of an adult life as a New Woman. The poignancy is almost unbearable when these remarks are juxtaposed with her words in a letter to Clementina, written in 1888: "O Clemmy, Clemmy, is everybody's life like this? I ought to have made something out of mine, but it's too late" (letter 36).

Levy's surviving letters to Katie from high school are uniformly exuberant, resounding with amused mockery, both about others and herself. In one letter, however, she mentions being "away half the term" (letter 7). This prolonged absence may have been the result of a bout of depression (in letter 3, the first one from Brighton, she apologizes to her parents for mentioning that she has "the blues"). Only once in the letters does a dark side to life at school appear: Levy expresses discomfort about the attitudes the other girls have or might have toward her Jewishness. She writes about being told by "Conny" that another classmate "did not like to visit Jews" and that this girl has made unpleasant allusions to Levy's "race and religion" ("Conny" is very likely Constance Black since the other Conny at school was Constance Leon, also Jewish). In response to such an attitude toward Jews, Amy's remark to Katie is "Filthy?" She then says, about her friend Conny, "but what if she shared them? The thought has quite haunted me." But if another girl, Ann, is found to harbor "anti Hebrew notions," Levy's attitude is feisty: should her suspicions that this girl is anti-Semitic be confirmed, she will punish Ann by means of the power of the pen, refusing to delete some parts of the story that she is working on that Ann would find "objectionable" (letter 9).

Some of Levy's surviving cartoons and drawings reveal that, while still an adolescent, she took an interest in the way Jews might differ in appearance from gentiles. Because the sketch titled "Scene from 'Wild Roses'" was signed by "New Boots," we know it served as an illustration for the journal "Harum Scarum." Two others, part of a series Levy titled "Katie's Courtship" (showing Katie with several different suitors) cannot be dated definitively, but their style suggests that they too were done during her high school years. In these sketches some figures have noses that could certainly be described as Semitic while others do not. Only one of the two "Jewish" faces in "Scene from 'Wild Roses'" could be considered ugly, and in a cartoon captioned "Katie's Courtship: a little triumph!" while the viewer is a bit startled by the beaked nose on one of the men, he is not less attractive than the four figures with conventional features. These drawings do not necessarily reveal negative attitudes toward Jews or being Jewish although Levy's interest in the way noses differ indicates sensitivity to the racial discourse of the period.

One item in the "Katie's Courtship" series is a cartoon of a man with a large hooked nose who is behind a woman with conventional features. He is starting to put his arms around the woman's waist, and the text tells us that he wants to kiss her. The caption reads,

> *Katie:* Now d'out zer Isaac. I've got to fry the fish.
> *Isaac Harris:* Oh one more for the sake of Shabbos and Pesach!

Levy is teasing her older sister in a good-natured way, but there can be no question, especially if one knows that fried fish was what Israel Zangwill was to call "the national dish" of the Jews in England,[12] that Jewish looks, culture, and religion are perceived here as comic and vulgar. Some of the humor seems to lie in the satiric removal of Katie from her position in the refined upper middle class. Tagging her sister as foreign (Katie speaks what is supposed to be a mixture of Yiddish and English), Levy conflates foreignness with demotion within the class hierarchy. Anglicized Jews like the Levys were condescending toward Jews who were less assimilated and were highly class-conscious because of a fear of not being accepted as English.

In July 1879 Levy published "Run to Death" in the feminist *Victoria Magazine*.[13] Written in 1876, when she was fifteen, "Run to Death" is about the pursuit and murder of a gypsy woman and her baby by prerevolutionary French nobles while they are out hunting. This powerful story situates Levy within the female tradition, for many nineteenth-century English women poets wrote poems that protested against the persecution of the weak by the strong. The victims were usually female, but their vulnerability was magnified by other aspects of their identity, and Levy's drawings of figures whose features set them off from the dominant culture indicate her awareness that as a Jewish woman she was doubly marginalized. "Xantippe," the dramatic monologue that is still Levy's best-known poem, was completed at around the same time that "Run to Death" was published or soon after.[14] On October 9, 1879, Clementina Black wrote to Richard Garnett, asking him to join "Miss Levy's thanks to my own for the time and consideration you have given to her poem. . . . She certainly does write verse with a most surprising facility and frequency, and with an ease of rhyme which I fancy is quite unusual. Her prose is at present certainly inferior to her verse. For the next few months, I am afraid, both will have to be put aside; she goes at the end of this week to begin her first [term?] at Newnham Hall."[15]

Newnham College

The publication of "Run to Death" and the attention that the respected man of letters Richard Garnett gave to "Xantippe" must have heightened Levy's confidence in her powers, and the surviving letters she wrote from Newnham, all from her first year, are full of elation. The accounts of other students, some included in a book called *A Newnham Anthology*[1] and other reminiscences cited by historians, report that the experience of being at one of the early women's colleges at Cambridge or Oxford was exhilarating. Historians such as Martha Vicinus, Carol Dyhouse, and Philippa Levine tell us that the young women at both universities "shared a common purpose and determination."[2] Levy's sense of adventure and freedom is palpable in her letters even though women students were carefully chaperoned inside the classroom or tutorial, whether or not male students were present. Chaperonage was felt to be necessary even when the teaching situation was single-sex because the lecturers were invariably men (at least at first). When male students were present, more often than not, they were hostile.[3]

In her letters Levy never mentions the unwelcoming attitude of so many of the men she must have encountered at Cambridge, but her unpublished verse play, called simply "Reading," shows that she was aware of it. One is struck by Levy's ability to create lines of verse in this short comic play—often with varying lengths and a variety of rhyme schemes, sometimes couplets in iambic pentameter—that have enough flexibility to simulate conversation at the same time that the rhymes wittily defy expectations, often by rhyming a word with one that follows in the dialogue of the next speaker. Levy could make fun of sexist men and of the women who wish to invade their sanctuary. Seeing the humor in both sides of an issue, Levy writes satire that almost, but not quite, lacks a stable viewpoint. Professor Ego's name conveys the narcissism and arrogance that she associates with men, qualities she mocks in this piece as well as in other writings (including letters) throughout her life; she also laughs at the extraordinary failure of the imagination that makes what the encroaching women want so incomprehensible to Professor Ego's pupil Bob Bumptious.

But Cornelia Conix and Janet Gerund, students at Newnham Hall, are satirized too, as their names suggest. Both are absurdly zealous in their determination to become erudite, so that as soon as the two arrive at the hotel by boat during the Long Vacation, the former cries, "Let's waste not time; you read your 'Mill,' and I / will fetch my 'Huxley.'"[4] Janet replies,

> It's in the boat; a-lying on the seat
> Are some poor efforts in iambic feet,
> And faulty Attic; over which my brain
> Has been a-boiling since the morn; Refrain
> I beg from reading; fling them in the mere!

Cornelia responds,

> You silly goose! I'll do it, never fear.

Both the men and the women are ridiculed, and yet what Cornelia says to Bob, near the end, rings powerfully, certainly an expression of the author's deeply felt sentiments, attitudes that underlie her defense of the weak in the poem "Run to Death":

> *Ah sir, I detest*
> *The shallow sentiment of men like you,*
> *Who kill us, use us with as much remorse*
> *As they would kill a stag; or ride a horse,*
> *But like to keep us sound, and free from vice,*
> *Fattened with meekness, for the sacrifice.*

The Newnham records show that Levy first lived in Norwich house, which, from 1877 to 1880, housed students for whom there was no room in the first building, Newnham Hall. The college took its name from the parish in which it was built in 1875, just outside the town of Cambridge (it had begun in temporary quarters four years earlier). Unlike the other women's college at Cambridge at that time (Girton, founded in 1867, was more imitative of the men's colleges), Newnham attempted to create a family-style life and a feminine atmosphere. Martha Vicinus says that its "white-trimmed brick buildings" were designed to be pleasantly inviting, but "internally the colleges were rather spartan, as befitted a generation determined to use its new opportunities to serve others."[5]

There is only one indication that Levy sometimes found the work at Newnham daunting. In an unpublished poem, "To Myself" (in her geology notebook and probably never intended for eyes other than her own), we see how hard on herself she could be if she failed to live up to her own academic expectations and how the idea of suicide was never very far from her mind, even in her youth. In this poem, one hopes, she is exaggerating the savagery of her self-reproach for poetic emphasis. Possibly responding to negative reception of her work or perhaps only expressing her own sense of incompetence, she wrote,

That is the end of your geology,
[the second line is illegible]
Damn you, poor thing! That's only one small part
Of things you've failed in; more for want of heart
Than want of brain; I will make bold to state:
Yet (second thoughts) the brain is not first rate.
You do great things? You strut as poet? Pshaw![6]
Poor funny thing, hardly worth a straw!
You dare, dark worm, to raise a bleary eye
To yon fair lily blooming pure & high![7]
Here, I'll advise you; brace your little soul,
Hie to a chemist, pay a copper dole
Of jingling coin, first taking care to ask
For "Yon brown fluid in the little flask,
With that great label on it: P, o, i,—."

Although in her letters Levy acknowledges no similar trepidations about her ability to accomplish what was expected academically, it is clear that the work was hard. She tells her mother, "I rather wish I had not so many subjects" (letter 12), and tells Katie about the time she spends studying: "I do an average 6 hours a day—sometimes 7, sometimes only 5. I get so grimly fagged that I can't do more." In a fragment of a letter written shortly after she arrived at Newnham, in which she describes how she and the other students decorate their rooms and act as hostess for one another, she mentions turning down two invitations in order to "grind" (letter 10). Yet she praises the quality of the education, expressing confidence that she will overcome shyness and be a more active participant: "The teaching here (excepting the French) is really crack—I feel myself getting on with my classes. . . . Tonight we have a debate—subject Browning & Tennyson; I was to have led the opposition (in favour of R. B.) but backed out of it, yet think of speaking" (letter 11).

Edith Creak, still part of Levy's life, remained so involved with her alma mater that Levy frequently mentions her presence (the Newnham records show Creak was in residence there during two summer sessions that Levy also attended); in the letter cited above, Levy reports that she has "had an awful lot of sweetness" from her former headmistress. But other young women also evoke enthusiastic description. Helen Gladstone (the prime minister's daughter) receives particular notice: "I had the bliss of being helped by her the other day in the gym when I was practising—she has a sort of queenly graciousness for all young or new girls, & is a sort of 'cock' at Newnham." Vicinus writes that homoerotic crushes and relationships were as important an aspect of life at the new women's colleges as they were at the reformed secondary schools,[8] and one cannot help speculating about Levy's interest in Helen Gladstone, especially since Levy is so taken with this new acquaintance that she includes in her letter a sketch of Gladstone's face in profile.[9] The irreverence that is so characteristic of Levy's voice in the letters from high school is a prominent feature in all of these letters. In an early one (letter 10) she describes a visit to the "Local Museum . . . with a rather good collection of pictures—there is one specially famous one where John the Baptist is represented in specs!" In another letter she reports: "I have howled a good deal since I have been here. I must look up some Greek for the benefit of the worthy Mr. Jenkinson, at whose class we invariably roar, so adieu" (letter 11). In the early fragment, however, some of Levy's comments hint that she felt awed by being at one of England's two beautiful, ancient universities. Katie is told of "the great stained glass windows" in one of the buildings and its "old deep carved stalls such as one reads about, and the candles in the middle only make the unlit part look more mysterious" (letter 10). A school notebook has a scribbled, unfinished sonnet that expresses the gratitude Levy felt as well as her reverence for "the pearls, the golden gems of ancient lore" that the university has to offer.

In her three published poems about Cambridge and in "Lallie: A Cambridge Sketch," Levy allows herself to voice deep feeling for the city that she calls "O fairest of all fair places, / Sweetest of all sweet towns!"[10]

"Lallie" has several moving descriptions of the university and its environs, especially one about the end of a day spent on the river Cam. It shows how deeply the loveliness of Cambridge had touched its author:

> They . . . were rowing slowly among the grey old bridges, with their quaint devices; on one side of them green meadows stretched, and tall trees hid the glory of the setting sun; on the other rose the stately college buildings, dull red and grey; lichen-grown and ivy-dressed; the stern outlines softened and mellowed by that incorrigible aesthete, Lady Nature.

The word *aesthete* is another sign that Levy was attuned to the burgeoning aesthetic movement. More important, "Lallie" is a fable in which Levy expresses the difficulty and the danger of the transformative process women students were supposed to undergo as a result of their residence in the new women's colleges. Two female characters are of central importance in the story, young Lallie (the protagonist), not a student (she is the daughter of a professor), and Rhoda Chodmonley, a "Newton" girl whom Lallie admires but also calls "a horrid clever thing." The narrator tells us about Rhoda: "It was the calm cheerfulness, which characterized her, that should rather have been called an 'affectation.' She was . . . a modern production—the offspring of a period of social and intellectual transition;—and, as such, was it to be wondered at if she bore the marks of acute psychical pain?" That this passage is crossed out in the surviving manuscript is certainly evidence of Levy's ambivalence about acknowledging that being a woman at Cambridge was hard on the pioneers. But she did not delete Rhoda's response to what appears to her to be the younger girl's assumption that "happiness depends on one's knowledge of the classics": "Lallie has never felt the old 'Faust-feeling' evidently." One poem and another story written at Newnham reveal that Levy shared Rhoda's fear that as a woman with scholarly and literary ambitions she was an overreacher.

Neither Lallie nor Rhoda finds fulfillment at the end of this story.

The two are opposites, it would seem: a rather traditional Victorian maiden and a New Woman. Even without the passage Levy rejected, the narrative allows the reader to understand that her New Woman character is under a strain. But it is traditional Lallie who dies—she simply fades away—after Frank Duchesne, the man she loves, marries Rhoda. Lallie thinks of herself as another Undine, a creature without a soul. These allusions to the fabled water spirit who can receive a human soul only by intermarrying with a mortal provide, on the level of myth, a reason for Lallie's death. [11] On a psychological level her identification with Undine, expressed *before* Lallie learns that Frank will wed Rhoda, seems to come primarily from a sense of undeveloped subjectivity that results from not being able to reconstruct herself as a woman who wants to be more than an adored and desired wife. The reader feels that Lallie dies because, to use her own words, she is "a useless little drone." But in "Lallie" Rhoda is not altogether triumphant. In this story as in Levy's letter "from" Miss Creak, even the woman who has reinvented herself must be loved. And so Rhoda marries—but as a married woman she can no longer be a Cambridge student. In the end, then, Rhoda and Lallie are doubles, not opposites, because measured by the gauge of whether a woman can successfully undergo the conversion that Levy herself was attempting, both women fail.

"Lallie" reveals the fear Levy must have come to feel once she was at Cambridge—the apprehension that she was cutting herself off from a normal woman's life. This sense of the magnitude of what she had entered into so lightly—eager to adore "without return"—does not seem misplaced. Showalter says that Beatrice Webb recorded in her diary a conversation that she had with "Alfred Marshall, a Cambridge professor who was 'the single most effective enemy of degrees for women.'" He told Webb with a laugh that if women "'ceased to be subordinate, there would be no object for a man to marry. . . . If you compete with us we shan't marry you.'"[12] Recent scholarship tells us what happened to the 720 women who went through Newnham in the years between its establishment in 1871 and 1893: "374 were employed as teachers in 1893. Ten or so were married."[13]

Even if Levy's sexual orientation was homoerotic, female sexuality is, many theorists think, to a considerable extent malleable: if Levy had not gone to Cambridge University, she might well have married, and marriage would have given her a place in the Jewish community that she could not find as a single, university-educated intellectual woman.[14] This is not to say that Levy wished that she had married. The picture of Jewish marriage she provides in *Reuben Sachs* is certainly bleak. Nor is there reason to suggest that the women who went to Oxford and Cambridge in those early days did not prize the freedom and opportunities that their lives offered or that Levy herself regretted her decision to go to Cambridge. Some of the pioneering women at the universities found satisfaction in romantic friendships and lesbian relationships while others may have had little difficulty accepting celibacy. Levy's youthful poetry tells us that, for her, love and sexual fulfillment were not easily dispensable.

The Amy Levy archive contains quite a few unpublished poems. The one beginning "O! deem not" was in the possession of Levy's friend Euphemia Malder Stevens (called Effie), whom she first met at Brighton High School; the copy Effie sent to Lewis Levy after Amy's death is dated "1878 or 1879," so it was composed before Levy became a Cambridge student. Several lyrics were written in her geology notebook, which has "1880" on several pages, and two other manuscript poems carry that date. The poems that are important to this part of Levy's story are "A Prayer," "Félise to Her Lover," "*Poeta Esuriens,*" "The Sleepy Poet to His Frame," and the sonnet beginning "Most wonderful and strange."[15]

"Félise to Her Lover," as its subtitle "See Swinburne's *Poems and Ballads*" indicates, is a response to Algernon Swinburne's "Félise" and has such a close intertextual relationship with it that the speaker in Levy's poem several times quotes directly the cynical words about love spoken by Swinburne's narrator.[16] Levy's Félise responds to rejection by the man who had adored her the previous year when she was "calm and cold" by endeavoring to avoid reproaching him. Instead, she tries to play his game, speaking about love as scornfully and cynically as he has spoken, insisting that her love will not endure; at the same time, she describes his body sensuously ("Long lines of limb that sway like a reed") and remembers his kisses. Toward the end, however, she reverses herself. In Swinburne's "Félise" the male narrator is disdainful of "lifelong loves" and says, "Can I forget? yea that can I, / And that can all men." But Levy's Félise realizes that "A sorry gift of constancy / The gods on women here below / Too oft bestow." Once the man kisses her, Levy's Félise is far from aloof; indeed, in the final two stanzas she is transported by passion:

> My lips are fire from your lips' touch
> they cling & clutch,
>
> They suck the foam which is honey & gall,
> They sting & scorch, they cleave & kiss!
> I am all love—no scorn at all!—
> Gods, if all moments were as this
> then life were bliss.

These are hot words from a poet about whom it has been said, "Whatever else may be thought of Amy Levy's love poems, there can be no question that hers was a very chaste muse."[17]

Instead of representing a woman who can enjoy the passion of the moment, however, Levy ends up depicting a woman whose body is, as Angela Leighton says about the speakers in the poetry of Letitia Landon, "a trapped object of desire and pain."[18] Recent studies by Leighton, Isobel Armstrong, and other scholars say that Letitia Landon (L. E. L.) and Felicia Hemans, writing in the 1820s and 1830s, were the poets that many Victorian women poets looked to as precursors. Some of these poets, particularly Landon, approach "art as an overflow of the female body."[19] Elaborating on this aesthetic, Leighton argues that some of this poetry by nineteenth-century women objectified "woman's body as a convulsively impassioned art form, as a self-improvising poetry as well as a sexual spectacle."[20] Rejected by her lover while she still feels passion for him, Levy's Félise ceases to be a person capable of agency: "I am all love."

While we do not have a date for "Félise to Her Lover," it would seem to have been written during Levy's Cambridge years (or before) when she wrote other poems (none of them as accomplished) about sexuality. The poem beginning "O! deem not" is startlingly sexual too. Like Levy's Félise, this speaker is in the grip of feelings that are beyond her control and that threaten to grow even more intense. Her words seem to pour out of her and rise to a climax, and her feelings are expressed in images of overflow and hunger (her love "bleeds so deep" and, later on in the poem, "no broken wayside / blossom feeds / My great heart-hunger").

The "favourite poets" that Levy lists in her Confessions Book entry are all male: Swinburne, Robert Browning, Heine, Goethe, Shelley, and Shakespeare. It has not been possible to establish definitively what female poets Levy read, other than Christina Rossetti,[21] Elizabeth Barrett Browning, and Felicia Hemans, though it is unlikely that Levy could have been unfamiliar with the work of L. E. L., whose poems were standard fare for literary girls throughout the century; some of Levy's early unpublished poetry calls to mind Landon's work. "Xantippe" shows that she was reading both Brownings, but also, I would guess, Augusta Webster, whose impressive feminist dramatic monologues appeared in the 1870s. Webster's work shows a strong commitment to exposing various forms of social injustice and is probably among the influences on "Run to Death."

Much of the poetry written by Victorian "poetesses" is intensely emotional, melancholy, and preoccupied with betrayal by men. While Levy's "Félise to Her Lover" reveals how attentively Levy read Swinburne, it also has, as do her other unpublished poems from this period, the mark of the poetic lineage that goes back to and includes Hemans and Landon. Isobel Armstrong says, "Even when there seems no direct link between these earlier and later writers it does seem as if they worked within a recognizable tradition understood by them to belong to women."[22]

One can see why, even without influence, Victorian women poets would have been drawn to themes that emphasized women's vulnerability to betrayal and objectification and to the idea that poetry is an outpouring of emotion and sensation. Throughout the century a woman's life was full of constraints, sacrifices, and enforced passivity, and the feminine was understood "as a nature which occupies a distinct sphere of feeling, sensitivity, and emotion quite apart from the sphere of thought and action occupied by men."[23] By 1879, when Levy entered Cambridge, the best Victorian women poets either no longer worked within these conventions or, as Isobel Armstrong explains, had "assimilated an aesthetic of the feminine" so as to "revolutionize it from within." She means that poets in the latter group ostensibly adopt "an affective mode, often simple, pious, often conventional," but that "those conventions are subjected to investigation, questioned, or used for unexpected purposes."[24]

Levy's *"Poeta Esuriens,"* written in 1880, both conforms to the woeful and highly emotional mode associated with female poets and breaks with that tradition by adopting a male persona. The speaker in another early poem, "The Sleepy Poet to His Frame," is male too. Levy may have been trying to make these poems seem less autobiographical,[25] but in these two poems Levy would have had an additional motive. She is writing about emotional need and erotic feeling that is not linked to a particular beloved person, and it would be understandable if she felt that was a highly transgressive act for a woman speaker. *"Poeta Esuriens"* and "A Prayer" (New's ed. 365) were, the manuscripts show, intended to be part of a book called by the title of the former poem (in English, "The Hungry Poet"). Like "Félise To Her Lover" and "O! deem not," *"Poeta Esuriens,"* "The Sleepy Poet," and "A Prayer" tell that Levy as a young woman experienced powerful longings for love and was acquainted with sexual desire. This poetry is in the female poetic tradition in its expression of unmet needs, unhappiness, and (in all but "Félise to Her Lover") self-pity, but in other ways (that go beyond the use of a male speaker in two of them) they are singular. The speakers in *"Poeta Esuriens"* and "A Prayer" see themselves as unlovable, unable to be the object of another's passion, and therefore barred from normal human experience (and from satisfactions that they crave) for reasons that are unspecified but suggest a deep feeling of inferiority. The sense of self these poems express is similar to that of Lucy Snowe in Charlotte Brontë's *Villette,* also a woman of deep passions, whose need for love made Harriet Martineau so uncomfortable.[26]

In "The Sleepy Poet to His Frame" (comic in its attitude to problems taken seriously elsewhere, it was probably never intended for eyes other than Levy's own), the speaker knows where to place the blame for lack of love and erotic satisfaction:

> Little Body, all misshapen,
>   Now to slumber were a sin,
>   You have brought enough of sorrow
>   On the soul which groans within.

Levy's reasons for dwelling on lack of physical attractiveness will be taken up later. What is most important here is that these poems, especially "A Prayer" and "Poeta Esuriens," articulate either a resigned or desperate sense of lacking what it takes to attract the love of another human being. This feeling leads to the expression of what the speaker in "Poeta Esuriens" calls an "endless Hunger which is never stilled." In Augusta Webster's "By the Looking Glass" and Eliza Cook's "Song of the Ugly Maiden" the speakers articulate a similar sense of the painful consequences of being plain (such sentiments are part of the female poetic tradition).[27] But Webster's and Cook's poems are dramatic monologues; the reader need not assume that the sentiments expressed are those of the poet.

Levy's reiteration of this consciousness of being physically unattractive and of emotional and physical starvation, and her intention to write a book of poems on this theme, encourage the reading of these poems as personal utterances. A passage in a letter Levy wrote to her mother in 1881 (assuring her that she would not be compromising her virtue if she were to teach English to some German boys) provides additional support:

But seriously, you needn't have any fears on my account. I regret to say that I am as safe as Grandmama could be; there wouldn't be any impropriety (excepting from an outside point of view) in my teaching any number of young men. I have never excited in anyone a desire to 'forget themselves' in any way, which has its advantages, especially in my present circumstances. (letter 15)

The manuscript of the final poem from this group, "Sonnet," is in her geology notebook (no wonder Levy had trouble with geology), and it is the only poem in that notebook that Levy ever published. The notebook contains two versions. The first, dated October 1880, reads as follows:

> Most wonderful and strange it seems, that I
> Who but a little time ago was tost
> High on the waves of passion and of pain,
> With aching heart and wildly throbbing brain,
> Who peered into the darkness, deeming vain
> All things there found if but One thing were lost,
> Thus calm and still and silent here should lie,
> Watching and waiting,—waiting passively.
>
> The dark has faded, and before mine eyes
> Have long, grey flats expanded, dim and bare;
> And through the changing guises all things wear
> Inevitable Law I recognize:
> Yet in my heart a hint of feeling lies
> Which half a hope and half is a despair.[28]

The notebook reveals that lived experience lies behind the poem. Levy added another stanza (so that it is no longer a sonnet), dating it November 1880, in which she berates herself:

> Thou foul, thou fool, who in the little space
> In which the passion-tempest ceased its roar
> Among the caverns of thy soul, didst dream
> That it had past away, parted to return no more.

It would seem that during 1880, while at Cambridge, she was caught up in some personal drama that evoked intense feeling, emotional turbulence, and painful disappointment. And news of that drama reached the family because Levy's cousin Lucy Levy Marks reports that Amy had an unhappy love affair at Cambridge.[29] Of course, it is possible that the romance was largely one-sided.

But these youthful poems are not simply the expression of Levy's individual sense of homeliness, of being someone doomed to live without love, or of her personal experience of disappointment in an affair of the heart. A comparison (that Levy invites) between *"Poeta Esuriens"* and Shelley's "The Exhortation" prompts us to go beyond what has already been said about resemblances between the poetry Levy wrote in her youth and the work of other nineteenth-century women poets. Her early work makes a significant contribution to questions posed by Elaine Showalter when she was defining the major task that feminist literary theorists and critics should undertake: "How can we constitute women as a distinct literary group? What is the *difference* of women's writing?"[30] *"Poeta Esuriens"* begins with an epigraph from "The Exhortation": "Poet's food is love and fame." Shelley goes on to deconstruct this binary, arguing that for poets fame is "love disguised." But critics examining the poetry produced by nineteenth-century women argue that for them love and fame could not be deconstructed, that they remained polarized, and this is what we find in *"Poeta Esuriens"* and other writings by Levy from her Newnham years. Caroline Lindsay's "Love or Fame," written in the 1890s, expresses the same sentiments as Hemans's "Woman and Fame," published in the 1820s. Lindsay's speaker, given a choice by the Delphic oracle, chooses recognition for her poetic gift only to return years later to pray, "O give me Love! Take back the bay-crown'd lyre!"

The scholarship of Angela Leighton, Margaret Reynolds, Dorothy Mermin, Isobel Armstrong, and others emphasizes the importance of Sappho and of Mme. de Staël's Corinne (from her 1807 novel by that name) to nineteenth-century women poets.[31] The Sappho these writers are preoccupied with is legendary rather than historical: the homoeroticism of the Greek poetess is not part of the story.[32] For Levy's female predecessors and contemporaries, Sappho was a poetess who leaped from a cliff out of unrequited love for a young man, and her tragic betrayal was understood as the consequence of her achievement as an artist; Corinne, who is crowned with a laurel wreath as she spontaneously declaims her poetry from the Capitol in Rome, is another Sappho, for the man she loves ultimately rejects her for a conventional, domestic woman.

Levy's interest in the Sappho-Phaon legend is evidenced by her translation of two passages from Franz Grillparzer's play *Sappho* (1817), which appeared in the *Cambridge Review* in 1882. In the passage from Act I the poet from Lesbos tells Phaon, her legendary male lover, why she has chosen him. Life (equated here with love), she says, is more important than any fame that can come from artistic success ("Life's highest aim is, after all, to live"[33]). But Sappho also believes that "poor Art is ever driv'n / To beg of life's abundance." In short, she needs to love Phaon, but that is in part so that she can use him as a muse. In the second passage that Levy chose, from Act IV, Sappho berates Phaon because he has left her for another woman. Distorting the past, she remembers her solitude as a kind of paradise when she "made gold-stringed melody" and was protected from "Earth's sorrows."

By juxtaposing these two passages, Levy brings out the ironic relationship between them, creating a fragment of verse-drama (like her "Medea" although much shorter) that has form and meaning. She provides a view of the Lesbian poet that is quite different from the one offered by the many earlier versions of the story by women because "her" Sappho, while represented sympathetically, is not simply an innocent victim. Claiming that "one rough man" tore her away from a happy existence, Sappho forgets that she initiated the relationship and that she always planned to use Phaon for her own artistic aims.

But first (two years earlier) Levy had written *"Poeta Esuriens."* The speaker is a male poet "who craves love and fame, / Hungers for ever, hungers and yet lives: / A starving soul within a weary form." In making the speaker in this poem male, even if the affection he longs for is not romantic love, Levy creates a problem. The poem is in the Sappho-Corinne tradition in that love and poetic success are at odds, but for a man emotional fulfillment and literary achievement were not in conflict. The speaker asks, "O friends, your praise is sweet which greets my song—/ Can you not give me Love, sweeter than Praise?" And goes on,

> I was glad
> When men cried out, "he has the gift of song,
> His notes are notes of music; he can see
> Beyond the common bounds of human gaze."
> Thus then, they called me "Poet." I was glad
> For that which now I weep at; for I
> Thought to draw men's hearts to love me. . . .

The speaker's plea for love and his repeated complaints about his "endless Hunger" are bathetic rather than moving largely because the relationship between his lovelessness and his artistry is neither obvious nor explained. Even without this problem, the reader would still be likely to feel embarrassed and put upon by so much raw self-pity. Levy's speaker is too hungry to express himself as openly and directly as he does. "Poeta Esuriens" would require more formal devices to create the necessary distance, or it would need to be recast as a narrative or dramatic poem. Levy must have realized this because she finally used some of the lines in "Poeta Esuriens" effectively by putting them in the mouth of the protagonist in her version of "Medea."

Despite its male persona and its humorous tone, "The Sleepy Poet to His Frame" is also in the Sappho-Corinne tradition because of the way it polarizes love and fame. In this poem, however, Levy suggests that greatness as a poet can be compensation for the love the speaker cannot win. Although most of "Sleepy Poet" lacks poetic power, its last five lines show Levy's promise. The speaker tells his body how it has let him down in not remaining awake, for now he "must leave unwritten" the great work

Which was to have roused mankind,
Till all men cried out in rapture,
"Lo, a prophet! What's his name?"
And the women showed the children
How the Thames was all aflame!

The relationship between love and achievement had been a theme in Levy's work even when she was at Brighton High School for Girls. "Miss C's Secretary" defies literary tradition in that achievement by a woman evokes love (however unwelcome), and the fictitious Miss Creak who writes a letter to a young man turning down his proposal and telling him of her betrothal to a Cambridge professor is allowed to have both. But the stories and poems written during Levy's time at Newnham suggest that while at Brighton she had been able to give her letter writer a happy combination of love and work because she did not yet know the real world. As we have seen, "Lallie: A Cambridge Sketch" presents a no-win situation for women since Lallie, who lives for love alone, suffers disappointment and death, and Rhoda, for whom romantic fulfillment and the scholarly life *seem* to be harmonious, ends with only the former. In Levy's poem "A Prayer" the only way the speaker can satisfy her creative imagination *and* her libido is to ask her fancy to compensate for lack of erotic satisfaction by allowing her to "image love / The bliss, without the woe."

There can be little doubt that Levy, while at Cambridge, was preoccupied with a painful recognition: by choosing to attend a university and by choosing as a goal worldly success in the arts, Levy had not seen (to cite lines from *"Poeta Esuriens"*) "the band of shadowy figures shutting off / The poet from the happy herd of men." For "poet" here, we can read "educated woman of letters" and for "men" read "men and women" because these poems show that Levy was concerned not just about love and marriage but about becoming distinctly different from most people—whom she saw as living satisfactory lives of conformity, a life she did not want but was afraid to give up. It is conceivable that when Levy wrote *"Poeta Esuriens"* she had in mind Landon's "Stanzas on the Death of Mrs. Hemans," where the speaker says,

The meteor-wreath the poet wears
Must make a lonely lot;
It dazzles, only to divide
From those who wear it not.

In 1881, after her second year, Levy left Newnham. It is impossible to know precisely why she left before her final year and without taking her Tripos (final exams). The letters from this period—with one exception—reveal confidence, strenuous effort, and high spirits while the literature produced indicates emotional tumult and provides insight into the psychological burden of being a woman at Cambridge in her era. The anomalous letter, of which only a small fragment survives, was written (probably to her mother) from Italy, where she was traveling with Clementina. Levy says, "I expect to be quite well long before 3 months & to be in full work for the summer term." Is this letter from her first or second year? Either is possible—the records show that she was in residence at Newnham during the "Long Vacations" of both 1880 and 1881. The important question the fragment raises, of course, is what was wrong with her? The likelihood is that she had a breakdown, an episode of clinical depression. Did it result from an accumulation of stresses and the inner conflicts we have been examining? Did some crisis set it off? There is no telling. She completed her second year at Cambridge but left for reasons not related to her health.

One cause of her decision to leave may have been the publication of her first book, *Xantippe and Other Verse*. Its title poem had already earned Levy attention, and now it was reprinted in a volume containing other work. Richard Garnett was to give Levy's first dramatic monologue the following appraisal: "'Xantippe' is in many respects her most powerful production, exhibiting a passionate rhetoric and a keen, piercing dialectic, exceedingly remarkable in so young a writer. It is a defense of Socrates' maligned wife, from the woman's point of view, full of tragic pathos, and only short of complete success from its frequent reproduction of the manner of both Brownings."[34] Xantippe explains bitterly that as a maiden she had possessed a "soul which yearned for knowledge," but that after her marriage she allowed herself to dwindle into a "household vessel" when she realized that the great philosopher "Deigned not to stoop to touch so slight a thing / As the fine fabric of a woman's brain / So subtle as a passionate woman's soul" (New's ed. 358 and 360).

Levy's pamphlet-sized volume includes "A Prayer." Two of its other poems, "Ralph to Mary" and "Translation from Geibel," both weak artistically, use images of hunger to represent the yearning for emotional experience. *Xantippe and Other Verse* also contains the sonnet beginning "Most wonderful and strange" (without the anguished stanza that was added to the manuscript), "Felo de Se" (both a parody of and a tribute to Swinburne),[35] and "Run to Death." The poorest poems in Levy's first book are the three that deal with the intensity of the soul's hunger (she had not yet learned how to write effectively on this theme, which, for her, was loaded with emotion). The other four are fine, especially "Xantippe." Like Augusta Webster, whose dramatic monologues include one spoken by Circe, the goddess who turned Odysseus's men into swine, Levy exonerates a legendary woman whose story had previously been filtered through the misogyny of the culture.

To publish a book of poetry with such a remarkable title poem at the age of nineteen must have assured Levy that she was unusually gifted, especially considering the notice that *Xantippe and Other Verse* received. An article in the *Literary World* uses Levy's volume as ammunition in the war of ideas over the question of higher education for women. Its male author challenges pieties about women's place, asserting that the university experience is salutary because "this temporary isolation from the countless calls and duties of homelife is essential to a woman in the earlier stages of her intellectual development." When he finally gets around to commenting on Levy's poetry, he credits "Xantippe" with the power to persuade the unconvinced that "women have souls," and goes on to say about the book as a whole: "From the first page to the last the workmanship is firm and sound. Slovenliness in literary finish has always been a fault attributed to women, and with more or less of truth; but Miss Levy has so far benefited by her training and opportunities, that there is hardly a line which will not pass muster in the most rigorously critical examination."[36] Levy's achievement thus becomes a sign of how the university experience can alter women for the better. With *Xantippe* hailed in such a manner, one can understand why she would have concluded that it was time to leave the academic world to concentrate on forging a literary career.

Her newspaper article "Newnham College," dated March 4, 1881, suggests an additional reason for leaving: Cambridge women had just won permission to take the Tripos. Reporting this as a triumph, Levy nonetheless observes that the privilege for the first time imposed on women students a "fixed course of study," explaining that "mathematical classes [are being] organized for unhappy people whose souls are yearning for Plato or Mill."[37] Given her very specific aspirations, she may well have felt that further study of mathematics was unnecessary.

Levy's article also refers to the influence of the aesthetic movement on the décor of students' rooms, to which it devotes considerable attention. Reminiscences of other students at Newnham in these early years place a similar emphasis on the zeal that these young women put into decorating; Carol Dyhouse explains that these dormitories were a place to "read and study unfettered by the obligations of domestic life."[38] What is most interesting about Levy's article is that it reveals the extent to which university women were viewed as a new species in need of "anthropological" explanation. She seems determined to show that Newnham women are not all that different from other young women whereas, in fact, most of them probably were far from ordinary. Indeed, many of those writing from a perspective friendly to the aims of the new women's colleges spoke openly about their hopes that the university experience would produce a new kind of woman.[39]

5

Levy's Fictive Selves
The Hungry Poet, "Miss Creak," and "Leopold Leuniger"

During her two years at Cambridge, in addition to "Lallie," Levy wrote three better and more important stories; each of them shows her struggle to resolve personal issues having to do with identity. "Euphemia" (the story, not the fragment) is about a woman whose fierce desire for emotional and erotic fulfillment is at odds with her artistic gifts and ambitions. It appeared in *Victoria Magazine* just before the start of her second year and is, from a literary point of view, the least successful of these narratives; ironically, it is the only one that she published. The other two stories exist in manuscript in the Amy Levy Archive in London.[1] "The Doctor," written during her second year,[2] contrasts Mrs. Fairfield, a domestic woman, with Agatha Arundel, a female physician. Unlike Lallie and Rhoda in Levy's earlier story, these two women truly polarize conventional womanliness and New Womanhood, and writing this narrative may have helped Levy to reject the part of her psyche that had been socialized to conform to Victorian notions about female nature and role.

She appears to have wanted to publish "The Doctor" because the manuscript is a "fair copy," the series of crossed-out addresses on the back of the last page evidence that she carried it with her all her life. It is one of Levy's best stories (though it has features that mark it as an early work), but she may never have been able to place it because the attack on "the angel in the house" was too radical for its time. The third of these narratives, "Leopold Leuniger: A Study," is evidence that while at Cambridge Levy was in conflict about her Jewishness. Scribbled in Levy's geology notebook, this story does not appear to have ever been recopied, so she probably did not consider publishing it. Her protagonist is a young Jewish man who is so infatuated with the landed classes that his longing to be accepted by them leads to a desire to efface his origins. Each of these three very different stories is about transformation of identity—attempted and then abandoned, successful, or failed. One might say, to borrow a phrase from Ragussis, that Levy was preoccupied with "the trope of conversion."

Euphemia, Agatha Arundel, and Leopold Leuniger are strikingly different from each other, and yet the subjectivity of these characters would seem to be Levy's own at certain times and that of other speakers and important characters in her later writings. Postmodern theorists say that "self" is not an inherent, coherent core of identity but a process of construction and performance in which many social and cultural forces collaborate, and this is true for Levy (although a few of the writings, at least the ones produced before and during 1886, disclose that she also believed that temperament and certain qualities of character were inborn, and for her, as for most people in her era, these aspects of identity were linked to race and nationality).

Clifford Geertz emphasizes the importance of narrative in the process of constructing identity, asserting "that we assemble the selves we live in out of materials lying about in the society around us . . . that from birth on we are all active, impassioned 'meaning makers' in search of plausible stories."[3] In childhood and adolescence Levy lived to a considerable extent in a world of her own construction and enjoyed inventing various characters—personae—that she used as voices. This propensity continued into adulthood and went beyond writing editorial comments by "Lord Spendthrift" and filling out pages of her Confessions Book as "Maryanne Salvation" and "Satan." Her identity can be understood in terms of what might be called fictive selves, diverse figures whose various narratives gave form to her experiences and helped her to see meaning in them.

Levy's major personae and their narratives came out of the clash of her various subject positions. These fictive selves overlapped one another, so that, while at Cambridge, at the same time that the Hungry Poet was one image Levy had of herself, she continued to adopt a persona that can be called "Miss Creak," an emotionally self-sufficient and immensely capable New Woman. Rather than extolling the satisfactions of an independent, achievement-oriented life, however, Levy's early, unpublished poetry (aside from her light, satiric verse) exposes an artistic soul that hungers for passion and personal fulfillment and anguishes over their absence. The protagonist of "Euphemia" has the same obsessions. These themes (and hunger imagery) continue to appear in Levy's more accomplished and mature poetry and fiction although the meaning of this motif widens in scope and she learns how to bring out its philosophical implications. The hungry self in Levy's texts—surely a voice from within her psyche—wants to experience life with such intensity that in some of her early poems even painful emotions are valued. The speaker in "Translation from Geibel" (in *Xantippe and Other Verse*) chooses not to forget "yearnings, wild desire, and wrath and woe."

In constructing this persona, Levy would have been aided by Walter Pater, who, in his conclusion to *The Renaissance* (1873), wrote: "Not the fruit of experience, but experience itself is the end. . . . To burn always with [a] hard, gemlike flame, to maintain . . . ecstasy, is success in life." Because of "the awful brevity" of life, the best way to spend one's time is "in art and song. For our one chance lies in expanding that interval, in getting as many pulsations as possible into the given time. Great passions may give us this quickened sense of life, ecstasy and sorrow of love, the various forms of enthusiastic activity . . . which come naturally to many of us. Only be sure that it is passion—that it does yield you this fruit of a quickened, multiplied consciousness."[4] Pater's paradigm for the way one should live, of course, is highly romantic, certainly influenced by Byron and Shelley and their personae. The voice of the Hungry Poet in Levy's early poems is inflected by the voices of these poets and some-times, it seems, by the voice of Letitia Landon as well.

Hungry Poet themes and images appear in Levy's work throughout her life, and her letters and what was said about her by others reveal that she spoke about herself and her own life in these terms. In 1882 she wrote to Clementina from Europe that if she "weren't . . . always crying out 'More, More'" she "shd. be happy" (letter 18). After Levy's Newnham years both her writings and the reminiscences of friends and acquain-tances consistently make it clear that what she craved was not just *any* kind of intense emotional experience: to rephrase Pater, the Hungry Poet wants the "ecstasy," not the "sorrow of love" and yearns for other kinds of joy. In 1891 Edith Cooper and Katherine Bradley (Michael Field) reported in their shared diary what the Radfords had told them about Levy: "She demanded happiness of life—it refused her demand, and she refused life."[5]

The novelist and aesthetician Vernon Lee (who became a major fig-ure in Levy's life) offers the clearest picture of Levy as the Hungry Poet: "I used at one time to have frequent discussions on art and life with a cer-tain poor friend of mine. . . . 'You see,' said my friend, 'you see, there is a fundamental difference between us. You are satisfied with what you call *happiness;* but I want *rapture and excess.*' Alas, a few years later, the chance of happiness had gone."[6] By 1886, when these conversations with Vernon Lee took place, Levy had addressed the theme of depression in "James Thomson: A Minor Poet," "A Minor Poet," and "Sokratics in the Strand," and these writings indicate that Levy only half believed the explanation she gave to her friends for her dissatisfaction with life. Re-gardless of what she told others (and even sometimes herself), she un-derstood that the fervor of her craving for joy came from being robbed of ordinary happiness by what Richard Garnett called her "habitual melancholy."[7]

The Hungry Poet gives voice to some of Levy's deepest longings, yet many of her writings can be thought of as having been written in the guise of "Miss Creak." These, of course, show her commitment to female autonomy and new roles for women—"Miss C's Secretary"; "The Doctor"; "Reading" (her verse-drama about women at Cambridge); "Fragment" (subtitled "By a Very Sentimental Fellow"), an unpublished, witty poem that satirizes the uncomprehending sexism of men; the novel *Romance of a Shop*; a poem called "Rondel (Dedicated to Mrs. Fenwick-Miller)"; and essays such as "Middle-Class Jewish Women of To-Day." Levy's life as a single woman dedicated to a career in letters testifies to the presence of "Miss Creak" as a major component of her identity.

Levy created one more major persona, a figure that represents a dimension of her subjectivity that found expression in her life and in her fiction. "Leopold Leuniger," the name of the young Jew in Levy's early story, can serve as the name for this alter ego. Leuniger appears again in *Reuben Sachs* and in "Cohen of Trinity." In "Leopold Leuniger: A Study" he is entirely sympathetic, and the reader identifies with his desire to win acceptance by the upper-class gentile world. Eight years later, in *Reuben Sachs*, although he is no longer the main character, his denunciations of Jews and Jewishness have as much weight as Reuben's love for his people in a dialogue between the two on what it means to be a Jew and the moral nature of Jewish life (Leo's is one of the important voices in the novel's polyphony on these themes). In "Cohen of Trinity," however, Leuniger is never allowed to speak, and his desire to gain acceptance by the aristocratic crowd at Cambridge is made to look contemptible. His reappearances reveal how deeply he was lodged in Levy's imagination, and the changes he undergoes, as well as the shifts in Levy's attitude toward him, show how her feelings about being Jewish evolved over time.

That when she gave fictional embodiment to one of the most important voices within her psyche Levy created a male character—and that many of the protagonists in her fiction and speakers in her poems are men—is probably related to her homoeroticism. Certainly scholars working on lesbian writers often interpret the construction of male characters as a means of encoding discomfort with femininity and even with female gender identity. Catherine Stimpson says that for Gertrude Stein "the language of self was male and masculine" and that in her early autobiographical novels the characters who represent herself in her fiction were male because she chose to identify herself with the power and potential that men had in society.[8]

But Leopold Leuniger, far from being powerful, is a fault-finding, self-hating Jew, and when Levy later gives two other short stories ("Sokratics in the Strand" and "Cohen of Trinity") a male protagonist, he is deeply troubled and suicidal, as is the primary speaker in her dramatic monologue "A Minor Poet." And most of Levy's fiction has female protagonists; even in *Reuben Sachs* Judith Quixano takes over the last third of the novel. All but one of Levy's dramatic poems give women the only or the central voice, and, though some critics have thought otherwise,[9] there is no reason to think that in her lyrics the speakers are not female.[10]

My speculation is that Levy uses male personae (even for such an important alter ego as Leopold Leuniger) because when she was probing the experience of a character or speaker who belonged to a group misunderstood by society—a Jew and a person suffering from depressive illness—she preferred not to complicate the question by giving that character the additional burden of being a woman. By handling the problem in this manner Levy does seem to have accepted the male as the generic human being; nevertheless, her strategy shows that she understood, as Elizabeth Spelman says, "how one form of oppression is experienced is influenced by and influences how another form is experienced." She goes on to explain that "sexism and racism must be seen as interlocking, and not as piled upon each other."[11] By the time Levy wrote *Reuben Sachs* she was ready to take on the particular predicament of the Jew *and* the "Jewess."

That Levy was able to use a male protagonist effectively in her early story about a Jew at Cambridge implies that at a young age she found it easy to imagine the world through the eyes of the other sex. One would not expect this from reading "Félise to Her Lover," where Levy's speaker is in the grip of essentialist thinking about how the sexes differ, but the poetry and especially the fiction that she wrote during her two Cambridge years suggest that a variety of disparate notions about women and men were flickering through Levy's mind and sometimes bursting into flame. Even when the ideas that underlie the writing seem traditional, she is clearly brooding about gender, and this, evidently, gave her the imaginative freedom that she needed to create Leopold Leuniger as a stand-in for herself. Levy's sexual orientation may have made it easy for her to imagine herself as a man. Knowing her desire was different from that of most women would have contributed to her ability to reject the binary of gender as an absolute, though her attempts to undergo the metamorphosis from Victorian girl to New Woman must have helped too.

In the Confessions Book entry to which she signed her own name, Levy answered the questions about "favourite qualities in man" and "favourite qualities in women" by bracketing the two and listing the same qualities for both.[12] It does not appear to have occurred to any of the other people who filled out the pages of her book that men and women might have the same virtues, not even to Edith Creak and Clementina Black, both of whom were strongly committed to women's rights. Hardly anyone, perhaps feminists least of all, challenged masculinity and femininity as meaningful categories in Levy's time though women's rights reformers were eager to redefine women's roles and female identity.

The impulse to minimize differences between the sexes that her bracketing of favorite qualities reveals may be part of the reason why in "Poeta Esuriens" she failed to take into account the inescapable importance of being born male or female in late nineteenth-century society. But Levy does not make that mistake in any of her other writings. If anything, in what was probably the first of her three identity narratives, "Euphemia," Levy leans in the other direction, betraying her concern about the price that society exacts from the woman artist by creating a protagonist with the soul of an artist and then having her abandon her art because she is a woman.

Without question, Euphemia is a Hungry Poet. Trying to explain her dissatisfaction with life after being lectured about "the principles of

. . . harmony . . . underlying all things," she cries out, "Harmony? when everything is discordant and incomplete. Don't we all come into the world with fine healthy appetites for happiness, and aren't we all sent out of it unsatisfied, like hungry children going supperless to bed?" The word *hungry* and the extension of hunger as a metaphor are among the many connections between this story and the early poetry that Levy did not publish in her lifetime. Euphemia has the ardor that is characteristic of the speakers in those poems, and, like them, she finds it hard to satisfy her appetite for life. The theological and philosophical implications of Euphemia's sense of disharmony and dissatisfaction are heightened by what she says about her inability to believe in God and her reference to "Caliban upon Setebos" as a poem that "expresses my meaning."[13] Advised to fill her life with study, Euphemia vows to "try to fill up my fifty or sixty years of life with work." But then she drops her books, declaring, "What are they? wise, *dead* books . . . I want to *live*."

Several years pass, and Euphemia goes on the stage. She is both author and performer, telling the enthralled audience of "her hopes, her aims, her inspirations—of the wrongs of her sex, which she shall set right, of the disjointed times, which she shall make whole." The young woman seems to have found her answer to the riddle of life by using her talents as an actress to work for women's rights, but the story ends with a surprising twist. Euphemia tells the narrator, an avuncular physician, that she is leaving "her brilliant career" to get married: "I see you don't understand us women. What is fame to us? Does it satisfy the hunger of our hearts for love, the wild craving in our souls for protection and guidance, for something in our turn to protect and guide? Fame and a brilliant career don't fill up our lives—we want something else."

And so Euphemia's quandary is resolved by choosing one pole from the love and fame polarity. But Levy wants to reconcile her heroine's decision to give up achievement for love with her earlier hunger for a meaningful universe and for transcendent experience. Attempting to show that Euphemia has not chosen mere domesticity, Levy sends the young couple off to Iowa, where the new husband will be a doctor in "a young, wild colony" doing "rough work" that "few would undertake."

The word *wild* is important because Levy wants to give her heroine a life that would satisfy "the great hopes, great beliefs, great aims" whose thwarting Euphemia had complained of as a discontented adolescent. In this story Levy cannot imagine a woman with an artistic nature being fulfilled except through a romantic union, but she is unable to imagine a union that would not require a woman to abandon her artistic aspirations. Unable to push her imagination beyond existing literary and social conventions, she makes Euphemia a wife whose wild desires will be met only vicariously through the achievements of a husband who does heroic work. Caught in a double bind, Levy cannot resolve her heroine's dilemma satisfactorily.

Probably written at most a year later, "The Doctor" takes a different attitude toward love and career as alternatives. Nevertheless, the stories, especially taken together, are further evidence that Levy, while at Cambridge, was torn by the conviction that emotional and professional fulfillment were mutually exclusive for a woman. "The Doctor" was written later than "Euphemia," so one could conclude that before she left Cambridge Levy had cast her lot with the Miss Creaks of her society, and in doing so had made a decision about the kind of woman she was to be. As letter 8 shows, she had opted for that identity before she left Brighton High School, but if Levy was now allying herself with the New Women of her time, she was doing it with less of a sense of choice and more awareness of the costs. This may account for the savagery of her assault on the "womanly woman" who tells the story. But there is no reason to assume that in writing "The Doctor" Levy had resolved her conflict with any finality.

Far more sophisticated and successful as a work of fiction than "Euphemia," "The Doctor" is the first story in which Levy uses her predicament as a person marginalized in multiple ways to develop innovative narrative strategies that allow her to represent characters who, like herself, are outsiders. The contradictory subject positions that contributed to Levy's emotional instability apparently heightened her awareness that both writers and readers have difficulty getting beyond the belief systems their societies make available and that "truth" about people from groups outside the mainstream is difficult to establish.

Levy represents an outsider (the New Woman physician) from the viewpoint of someone whom readers from dominant cultural groups would identity with or approve of, and in doing so she exposes the inadequacy of such a witness. Her mainstream narrator's comments about the character she views as the other are thrown into question. And when it becomes apparent that this narrator cannot satisfactorily represent a woman who, because of her difference, she finds repellent and incomprehensible—that she can see such a person only in terms of stereotypes—the reader is prompted to recognize and question his or her own assumptions about single, professional women. "The Doctor" is Levy's first piece of fiction in which she contests received ideas about a group susceptible to misinterpretation by deploying the very preconceptions that make up the stereotype.

The reader never sees the female physician (a figure that functioned as an emblem for women breaking out of conventional roles in Levy's era) in an unmediated way. The woman doctor is seen through the eyes of the first person narrator, Mrs. Fairfield, a young widow who journeys with her infant and a maid to start a new life in a town she has never seen. Almost upon arrival the child becomes ill; the mother calls in a male physician, Dr. Wright. As Mrs. Fairfield tells her story, we learn that she has highly traditional ideas about men, motherhood, and woman's place. She appears to be that familiar Victorian heroine, the domestic woman. Literary tradition demands that she be selfless and sweet.

Slowly, however, the narrator reveals herself to be unreliable and to have an almost paranoid sense of herself as a helpless victim of more independent women. Her words gradually bring into focus "Agatha Arundel, M.D.," Dr. Wright's professional partner—for whom the narrator feels hatred. Young Mrs. Fairfield dislikes "Miss Arundel" before the two even meet: "Where would be the beautiful chivalry, the tender protecting respect paid by man to woman if she jostle and fight him in the public crowd? I know a great many clever people would have plenty to say against this sentiment of mine and, I daresay, could completely crush me with their arguments; but there are some things in which feeling counts more than logic. So I prepare myself, rather ruefully, to receive a visit (for the first time in my life) from a 'strongminded female.'" Mrs. Fairfield's adjective *strongminded* (a Victorian code word for women who questioned the cult of domesticity) and other loaded words make up what Mikhail Bakhtin would call her social dialect. Mocking the discourse of mainstream Victorian gender ideology, Levy shapes a narrator from whom the reader increasingly recoils.

Agatha Arundel, the doctor, is allowed to speak in the story, and her words and manner are restrained, forthright, yet caring. When cholera breaks out in the town, the young mother insists on waiting for the overworked Dr. Wright, refusing to let the female physician minister to "Baby." The woman doctor tries to reason with Mrs. Fairfield, speaking "in subdued tones, but quite calmly": "'I must entreat you for your child's, for Dr. Wright's sake, for once to waive your prejudices. It is important that Dr. Wright should have as much rest as possible;—he will not be home till late this evening. Surely, you will not send for him, worn out as he will be?'"

Agatha Arundel's words and manner reflect her broader, less self-absorbed consciousness, a worldview stemming from her educational opportunities and her involvement in concerns beyond the personal. Proponents of university education for women, describing life at Newnham and Girton, emphasized how the opportunity would transform the young women who attended. An 1889 *Woman's World* article sums up these expectations when it speaks of students learning to understand "that it is desirable that women's lives should cease to 'lie stagnant in the round of personal loves,' that women should not abandon, but—look beyond and so see in a clearer light the 'daily round' which is all in all to a large majority."[14] Mrs. Fairfield and Agatha Arundel speak in styles that are carefully juxtaposed: their dialogue is an example of how, in Bakhtin's phrasing, "each word tastes of the context and contexts in which it has lived its socially charged life."[15] The social dialects of the two women emphasize their divergent ideological perspectives.

Mrs. Fairfield's stereotypical preconceptions about Agatha Arundel's appearance turn out to be wrong, alerting the reader to the young mother's prejudice. The plot reaches its climax when Mrs. Fairfield turns "Miss" Arundel away from her door though the child has become seriously ill. The widow's remarks at this moment of crisis reveal her sentimentality about motherhood, her precepts about what is womanly, and also her implacable hostility: "Which of us do you think more likely to understand the child, you, a stranger, or I, its mother? . . . O I daresay I haven't sat with men and listened to lectures which would make any modest woman blush . . . I daresay I haven't discussed everything under the sun, decent or indecent, with a man; but I am a mother." Even when it becomes clear that the child is dying, the mother continues to see herself as a victim, lamenting, "They are all conspiring against me—it is hard, hard."

Mrs. Fairfield goes to get the male doctor, but is too late to save the baby. Astonishingly, almost immediately after the child's death the mother accepts a proposal of marriage from Dr. Wright. This may seem like a ridiculous contrivance, but Levy's skillful construction of her unreliable narrator's voice—obsessive, frightened, aggressive, and self-absorbed—is so compelling that Mrs. Fairfield's final demonstration of monstrous selfishness is not implausible. Because of her repeated admissions that she feels helpless without a man, the reader accepts the ruthlessness of this woman.

In approaching the last of these three stories, "Leopold Leuniger: A Study" and in thinking about the problems that Levy might have had as a Jew at Cambridge, one must remember that in the last part of the nineteenth century British society was both tolerant toward Jews who comported themselves much like English Christians and increasingly anti-Semitic. Endelman, who, without denying its existence, tends to downplay the impact of anti-Semitism in Victorian England, writes that the persistence of anti-Semitic stereotypes could "occasionally" generate "mild feelings of self-contempt" in those Jews who craved full acceptance by the larger society.[16]

"Leopold Leuniger: A Study" indicates that while at Cambridge

Levy experienced feelings of self-contempt about her Jewishness that were far from mild. It tells of the friendship between Leopold and Gerald, the son of an earl. Their intimacy, the narrator observes, spans "the widest of social gaps," Leopold being the grandson of "a rich Jew in the City," whose grandfather "had bought old gold and silver, and given the best price for artificial teeth." For the narrator of this story, and probably for Levy herself, the immense gulf between the two young men is created by a compound of class and "race." Leopold and Gerald are both privileged young men, but Leopold's moneyed background is tainted by the crass way his grandfather's fortune was made.

Of course, the condescension that the landed classes felt toward those in commerce throughout the Victorian period is pertinent here, but the coarseness of buying artificial teeth is inseparable from Leopold's grandfather's Jewishness, the result making for an even wider class gap between Leopold and Gerald than if the former were not Jewish. Admitting that Jewish society "jars me utterly," Leopold complains that his father does not want him to stay on at Cambridge as an tutor after graduation: "I pointed out to him that coaching was a highly genteel employment, that scions of nobility and gentry have been known to engage in it." For this young Jewish man, the world of learning that opened up for him at the university is the birthright of the British upper classes, and members of that elite group are his models for how to live.

Upon visiting Gerald's country estate, he is at first uncomfortable with his friend's sister Lilian, whose grace and refinement he attributes to "generations of culture." Three weeks pass, with "Leopold, Sydenham, and his sister spending their time together riding, walking, reading, and making music." It is Lilian who articulates what Cambridge means for the young Jew: "I think the best thing in the world must be to be an undergraduate. He comes up and sees the grand old historic buildings, and he thinks, 'I am part of all this intellectual life which has been growing and growing through the centuries—.'"

When Gerald's brother arrives with some aristocratic friends, Leopold overhears him speak disparagingly of Jews in general and of his cousin Reuben Saxe[17] in particular: "I think it is a disgrace to society that such people should be received. The whole race is a low-born, underbred [illegible] of moneyed intruigers" [sic]. The young Jewish man hurries to his room. Deeply stung, he thinks that he, "Leopold Leuniger . . . had no right to be staying in this place—the people whom he met would have acknowledged him on no other standing than as Sydenham's friend . . . he had been trying to deceive himself all these weeks . . . the moonbeams fell . . . onto a table near where lay . . . a well-worn copy of Heine; Heine the Jew-poet; Heine his best-beloved of singers." By placing the anti-Semitic phrase "Heine the Jew-poet"[18] in Leo's mind and juxtaposing it to a phrase that reveals how important this Jewish writer is to him, Levy evokes powerfully the youth's sudden spasm of self-hatred as well as his sudden loss of faith that he can ever be accepted by the kind of people he has come to feel are the only ones worth knowing.

Michael Ragussis and Bryan Cheyette explain that starting in the 1870s the cultural construction of Jews in England was deeply inconsistent. It was believed that they could be transformed by a superior civilization, but they were also seen as having racial characteristics that were unassimilable and even a threat to the social order. *Culture and Anarchy* (1869) is the paradigmatic expression of this contradiction because of its clash of universalist and racial ideas. For Matthew Arnold "hellenized Jews" could become the representatives of the universalist culture he was espousing, yet, he asserts: "Science has now made visible to everybody the great and pregnant elements of difference which lie in race, and in how signal a manner they make the genius and history of an Indo-European people vary from those of a Semitic people."[19]

Levy depicts what happens to Leopold Leuniger as a consequence of his attempt to live his life in accord with the Arnoldian idea that outsiders to English society can be civilized by accepting its superior culture. Hoping that his love for Western learning and music and his abilities as a poet, violinist, and scholar qualify him for a warm reception by the old England that Sydenham's country house represents, he overcomes his initial anxiety and begins to believe he can gain entry. The overheard conversation destroys his hopes. Believing that people like the Sydenhams set the standard, he concludes that no matter how English a Jew is, he can never be truly assimilated.

The point is driven home by the way that Leopold, in his moment of disillusionment, implicates even Heinrich Heine as a Jew in the racial sense—Heine, who remains a "Jew-poet" regardless of the stature he has achieved as a poet throughout Europe and despite his conversion to Christianity.[20] Leopold is stunned into despair by the conviction that one cannot stop being a Jew: that self-transformation or self-reinvention is impossible. The contradiction in Victorian Britain's attitude toward Jewishness is exposed by the contrast between Leopold's belief that he is worthy of acceptance at the story's midpoint and his perception of his own (and Heine's) inferiority at the end.

It is difficult to determine what attitude to take toward Leopold's internalized self-hatred because the narrator stays so close to his consciousness. A key may be found in a passage that treats Lady Lilian's attitude toward higher education for women. When Lilian speaks so eloquently about the charms of Cambridge, Leopold reminds her that there is now a "college for Ladies in Cambridge." She replies, "Oh but that wouldn't be at all the same thing . . . I should feel that I was a blot on the landscape; destroying the picturesqueness and doing dishonour to the tradition of the place." Leuniger responds, "'I think you are right' . . . he had been very eloquent over the wrongs of women time after time at the 'Union,' but looking at the graceful delicate woman before him it seemed right to him that she did not wish to become one of those ladies the sight of whom was so familiar to him, who paraded the Cambridge streets in 'Peacock' gowns, long fur-lined cloaks, and big furry hats, and always managed to get the front seats at the university lectures."

The reader will be tempted to insist that Lady Lilian's creator, Amy Levy, cannot be endorsing Lilian's retrograde viewpoint on higher education for women. Levy and her friends at Newnham are the very young women in "Peacock" gowns (loose, comfortable dresses, worn without corsets) who were causing such a fuss in Cambridge lecture halls. One feels that Levy must be using Leopold's conversion away from progressive attitudes on women's rights and Lady Lilian's traditionalist views to undermine our confidence in the effect of upper-class country house life on him. The passage about women at Cambridge can be used in this way to unlock the meaning of the emotional crisis that prompts Leopold to conclude that as a Jew he has no right to be at Gerald's estate. From Levy's life and attitudes at the moment that she wrote this story (and the feminist views she espoused) we can conclude that Leopold's response to the overheard conversation, rather than being epiphanic, is a delusionary, self-hating moment in which he aligns himself with the dominant social order, mistakenly accepting its definition of the Jew. But this reading of "Leopold Leuniger" depends on extratextual evidence—knowledge about its author. Levy may have provided no internal clues because at the time she wrote the story she was ambivalent in her attitude toward her people—too close to Leopold's idealization of the Gerald Syden-hams and Lady Lillians she had met at Cambridge and too troubled about what it meant to be Jewish.

By the 1870s uncertainty about who was English and what English-ness meant led to a concern about secret Jews—what Ragussis calls "masked Jewish identity" and "Jewish invaders"—that would have af-fected Levy's feelings about assimilation. Anthony Trollope's novels be-came obsessed with the threat of "a world in which Jews reinvent their own identities in order to hide their Jewish origins"; his secret Jews can be converts to Christianity and even become Christian clergymen.[21] The second half of the 1870s were, of course, the years in which Levy moved from childhood to young womanhood, and, because she enrolled at Brighton High School, the period in which she began to mix mostly with gentiles.

She was probably well aware of the notion of vulgar Jews who qui-etly attempt to infiltrate and subvert English society. That the idea of "Jewish invaders" caused her considerable anxiety is evident in "Leopold Leopold: A Study." Trollope's absence from the list of Levy's favorite novelists in her Confessions Book entry, therefore, becomes notewor-thy.[22] Whether or not Levy had read his fiction by 1880, the presence of these novels in the consciousness of educated, novel-reading people must have had a negative impact on her sense of whether she could allow herself to be absorbed into the dominant culture.[23] Endelman says that at the turn of the century, when large numbers of young Jewish men and women began to go to public school and then to Oxford and

Cambridge, "they encountered values and outlooks that undermined their faith and forged personal relationships that eroded their communal allegiances."[24] If, during and after her Newnham days, Levy gave serious thought to subordinating and neutralizing her Jewish identity, she would have been responding to her pioneering experience at one of England's ancient universities in a manner similar to that of other young Jews two decades later. But "Leopold Leuniger: A Study" reveals the negative reception that Levy, while at Cambridge, believed awaited Jews who tried to go too far in the direction of assimilation.

Reading this story, it is impossible not to feel that one of the interwoven strands involved in Levy's early departure from Cambridge was a sense of social inferiority as a Jew or at least the conviction that as a Jew she would never gain acceptance there. Her two years at Newnham seem to have awakened anxieties about Jewishness that had not existed previously: the rather feisty response to anti-Semitism expressed in the letter written from Brighton High School (letter 9) gave way to a much more troubled attitude. Vicinus says that at the new women's colleges "there were always 'in' and 'out' groups, determined by sports, intellect, money, or some current fashion. Patronizing condescension was common."[25] It is certainly possible that Levy's Jewishness lowered her position in Newnham's social hierarchy. Whatever did happen, it does seem that at Cambridge Levy's "Leopold Leuniger" fictive self was born, a side of her consciousness that continued to be preoccupied by Jewishness as a problem and a puzzle. Ultimately this preoccupation led to her most deeply felt works of fiction, *Reuben Sachs* and "Cohen of Trinity," but it also appears to have caused her considerable pain.

6

Europe and London
1881–1885

In autumn of 1881 Amy Levy, turning twenty in November, was in Dresden, Germany, with her friend Madge.[1] Levy was to spend the four years after Cambridge traveling on the Continent frequently, alone or with friends. The letters from Dresden show that she continued her education, "going in for a course of German reading," participating in a Shakespeare club, and "studying Greek with a Cambridge man." Her mother seems to have expressed concern about the propriety of those private lessons in Greek, for Levy responds dryly, "He has a wife and baby, both of them very nice of their kind" (letters 14–16). She writes of succeeding finally in getting pupils to whom she can teach English, only to find that her mother forbids it on the grounds that it is improper for a young woman to tutor male students. Although she accepts her mother's decree, it is clear that there were tensions (albeit commonplace ones) in that relationship.

These letters from Europe suggest that the family fortunes were unstable. In the fall of 1881 she is pleased that "Papa . . . has at last struck oil," while in July of 1882 she asks Katie, "Are we going to be in a very bad way financially all this winter? I mean to get regular work of some sort if I possibly can" (letters 14 and 19). Levy's distaste for "consuming the paternal substance" (letter 17) and her determination to earn money probably stemmed both from the recognition that the family coffers could use replenishment and from the impulse toward self-sufficiency and professionalism that would satisfy her determination to approach life as "Miss Creak."[2]

The letters from this period are full of anecdotes about adventures, some enjoyable and others unpleasant, such as boating at night on Lake Lucerne in July 1882 (letter 19) and, in the summer of 1884, being frightened about staying alone in an inn in the Black Forest, where a priest made an unwelcome nighttime visit to her room. Although she makes the latter into an amusing story, it is clear that she was keenly aware of her vulnerability to sexual assault: "I bolted my room & put chairs against an inner door . . . he was a hale man in the 30's & I was quite at his mercy: I had a grim night" (letter 23).

In two other letters written from Baden (in the Black Forest) in 1884—one to Katie and one to her friend Dollie Radford—Levy provides an amusing account of running into Karl Pearson and his friend Harry Bond. A socialist, evolutionary biologist, and mathematician, Pearson was a member of the discussion club Levy joined in 1882 and was part of her London network of London friends and acquaintants. She told Dollie: "Carl Pearson has been staying at a village a little way off; we . . . were introduced to his peasants. He is a sort of little god among them—wh. he rather enjoys I fancy in spite of much philosophy and mathematics" (letter 22). Levy's sarcasm about the self-importance of Karl Pearson (and the friend he is traveling with) is an example of her usual derisive attitude toward male egoism and arrogance. Her remarks about Pearson in these letters are consistent with the portrait Judith Walkowitz paints in her discussion of the Men and Women's Club, which describes him as a man of "immense, humorless, and self-important rectitude."[3]

Levy, of course, encountered many new people in her travels. In her descriptions of silly people as well as interesting ones in the letters writ-

ten from 1881 through 1884, Levy's mode is mockery, and she spares neither the acquaintances she finds ridiculous or vulgar nor the ones that
will become friends. In Switzerland, at the Hotel Sonnenberg in
Lucerne, she became acquainted with "Miss Cross," the sister of John
Cross, George Eliot's widower,[4] and either met Lady Katie Magnus or
got to know her better. Although one would not suspect it from the way
that Levy jokes about her (letter 19), Magnus was an accomplished
woman who, the year before she and Levy encountered each other in
Switzerland, had published a book about the history of the Jews.[5] Lady
Katie seems to have become a friend of the Levy family, serving as
"referee" (sponsor) when Ella applied for admission to North London
Collegiate in 1885. The friendship may have been important for Levy,
helping her to feel more positive about her Jewish background, for Lady
Katie moved in the larger, gentile world of letters and yet remained
strongly affiliated with the Jewish community. In 1888 Levy was to contribute translations of poetry by Jehudah Halevi and Heinrich Heine to
Magnus's *Jewish Portraits*.[6] Levy's letters and 1889 calendar tell that she
stayed in contact with John Cross's sister in the years ahead, so her stay
at the Hotel Sonnenberg had the effect of enlarging her social circle.

Travel did not get in the way of Levy's writing. Many of the poems
in her second published book were written in Dresden, and a letter written in 1884 (letter 23) mentions that she is working on a novel (which she
apparently abandoned). Levy's own copy of her 1884 volume *A Minor
Poet and Other Verse* contains notes about where and when many of the
poems were written[7] and makes it possible to chart her sojourns abroad
and her homecomings (many letters are dated, but most often the year
is missing). From Dresden she went to Lucerne, where in 1882 she completed her blank verse "fragment" of Medea.

Returning home in 1882, she spent most of 1883 in London, where
she wrote "Christopher Found." The juxtaposition of its three voices,
each character having a different relationship to the tale that emerges,
make this innovative poem not so much a dramatic monologue as a kind
of short story in verse. Adelaide, the main speaker, is a woman whose
love for Christopher is so unswerving despite many years of futile

searching that she cannot even imagine that her lover might be less faithful than herself. Citing Shelley's argument against monogamy in "Episychidion" (that "love divided is larger love"), which she rejects, she concludes her section of the poem with an affirmation of uncompromising belief in the relationship: "Till the world be dead, you shall love but me, / Till the stars have ceased, I shall love but you."

Levy then gives us an exchange between a lodger who inhabits the room in which Adelaide died and the "chatelaine" of the rooming house, whom he calls a "worthy, worthy soul." The landlady's voice, replete with colloquialisms and the rhythms of gossip, conveys her ordinariness, and her words reveal her empty piety, but the woman is not a person without worth. She tells the lodger that she tried to care for Adelaide during her illness and shows a bit of sympathy and respect: the dead roomer was "A lonesome woman" and "Paid her rent / Most regular, like a lady."

Yet the landlady's sensibility throws Adelaide's idealism into relief, exposing how maladapted she was for life in this world:

> They say (at least Ann Brown says), ten years back
> The lady had a lover. Even then
> She must have been no chicken.
> > Three months since
> She died. Well, well, the Lord is kind and just.
> I did my best to tend her, yet indeed
> Its bad for trade to have a lodger die.

While this speaker's pragmatism makes Adelaide's high-mindedness seem silly, Adelaide's idealism casts the landlady's acceptance of things as they are in a questionable light. In "Christopher Found" Levy's success in evoking contradictory sensibilities, each having legitimacy, foreshadows her ability to take advantage of the dialogic potential of fiction on which Bakhtin expounds.

Returning to Dresden, Levy finished "A Minor Poet" in 1883. For most of 1884 she was at home in London (as Dollie Radford's diary records), but by August she was in Germany, first in Alsace,[8] then in Baden, returning to England either late in 1884 or in the first half of 1885. From 1881 through 1885 (and throughout the remainder of Levy's life), she lived an independent existence when in London but resided in her parents' home—first at 11 Sussex Place, Regents Park (where the Levys had lived since 1872), then from December 1884 until sometime in 1885 at 26 Ulster Place, Regents Park.

These two houses were part of a belt of terraces built by the architect John Nash in the second decade of the nineteenth century. This belt is not in the park but forms a built-up area around it, separated from the park by a carriage road called the Outer Circle. Sussex Place is on the Outer Circle, a most desirable location, while Ulster Place is on the Marylebone Road, a site that is not so imposing and would have cost somewhat less to rent (certainly the reason for the move). Nash's Regents Park terraces are discussed in a book on Georgian architecture in London, which describes them as "dream palaces, full of grandiose, romantic ideas. . . . Carved pediments, rich in allegory, top the trees," and assesses their architectural value: "rows and rows of identical houses" characterized by "thin pretentiousness" and "poverty of design."[9]

The Levys stayed at their second Regents Park address only briefly, taking a more ordinary house in Bloomsbury (mid-Victorian in style, with huge porticos) by August 1885, a move that put the British Museum only a walk away. Becoming a member of the library at the museum in autumn of 1882, Levy often wrote or studied in its Reading Room, eating at its lunchroom for women.[10] It was most likely at the British Museum, which "became a stomping ground of the 'bohemian set,'[11] that Levy became acquainted with Eleanor Marx (Karl Marx's daughter), Olive Schreiner, Margaret Harkness, Beatrice Potter (later Webb),[12] and Dollie Maitland (see Figure 8), who married the poet Ernest Radford in October 1883.[13] These women were all socialists or social reformers; Harkness, Potter, and Marx did social investigation and political organizing among the poor in the slums of the East End, and all but Beatrice Potter were or became involved with imaginative literature as writers or translators.

Schreiner's *Story of an African Farm* came out in 1883; Dollie Maitland Radford published poetry in magazines in the 1880s (her first book appeared in the 1890s), and Margaret Harkness wrote four novels about the working class, starting with *The City Girl* (1887). Clementina Black, already a close friend of Levy's, was part of that crowd; she too combined social reform with fiction writing.[14] Clementina, who had used the museum Reading Room since she moved to London with her sisters Emma and Grace in 1879, was good friends with Richard Garnett (who was its superintendent until 1884)[15] and his family. (Constance Black, Levy's

Figure 8. Dollie Maitland Radford

schoolmate, was to marry his son Edward in 1889.) Levy's ties to the Black family would have fostered her relationship with Garnett, whose responsibilities as an official of the British Museum must have made him a constant presence.

In "Readers at the British Museum," an essay Levy published in *Atalanta* in 1889, she describes the Reading Room, with its "motley crowd of readers, in various stages of industry and idleness, absorbed in their books, bustling, hither and thither with important faces, gossiping, lounging, or even, in some rare instances, fast asleep." Praising the Reading Room for its "comfort and convenience," Levy mentions that "the lighting is by electric light; and so carefully is the temperature regulated by means of an elaborate ventilating apparatus, that an enthusiastic American lady once compared the atmosphere of the place in summer to that of a cool and shady dell."

In 1884 about 20 percent of the five hundred people who used it daily were women.[16] These female readers were not always welcome. In "The Recent Telepathic Occurrence in the British Museum" (1888) Levy has a prematurely myopic and enervated professor who, while "poring over manuscripts" in the Reading Room pauses to grumble, "What a tramping and whispering on all sides! It's the women—they've no business to have women here at all." He assumes that women come to the library for frivolous reasons: to find "the answer to an acrostic, the pattern of some bygone fashion for a ball." Levy no doubt knew that some of the male scholars held such attitudes because in the mid-1880s journals often printed complaints about the presence of women. The *St. James Gazette* quotes a reader who said that "the ladies were an absolute nuisance there, that they chattered, held *levées,* read novels, painted pictures, and rustled their silks to the serious disturbance of men who went there to work."[17] Levy and her friends were not using the Reading Room to do acrostics.

For these women the library met many needs in addition to allowing them to pursue their scholarly interests. It allowed Eleanor Marx to scrape together an income by doing research for wealthier writers and, in some cases, by writing their books for them.[18] Deborah Nord writes about a "loosely organized community or network" of unmarried women "in revolt against the constraints of bourgeois family life," using Harkness, Potter, and Levy as examples.[19] Nord says that these relationships helped to alleviate the strain of living in a nontraditional manner, allowing emancipated women to see in one another "their own ambitions reflected and affirmed."[20] The library provided one of the important spaces where such women could meet, get to know one another, and see each other frequently.

Some of the relationships that began or were sustained through regular encounters at the British Museum remained casual while others grew into genuine friendships. Eleanor Marx told the German socialist Max Beer that she and Levy knew each other from the library:

> Amy . . . was a good friend of mine, and only a few years my junior. I am the only one of my family who felt drawn to Jewish people. . . . We used to meet there [at the British Museum]; I was working on Ibsen translations and she on the German poets, Lenau, Heine and others. She had a particular liking for Lenau, the poet of melancholy and human liberation, but her affinity was with Heine, the sublimated essence of Jewish genius. There are a good many English writers who have tried their hand at translating Heine's Lieder. Amy was the best of them.[21]

While organizing Jewish workers in the East End, Eleanor Marx became interested in the fact that she was descended from Jews and finally came to consider herself Jewish (although not in the religious sense). Max Beer and more recent commentators on Marx's life suggest that this is one of the reasons why she was attracted to Levy,[22] and their conversations may have addressed the question of what it meant to be Jewish, an emotionally charged subject for both of them.

The two also had in common a tendency toward severe depression. In 1881, after her mother's death, Eleanor had a breakdown,[23] and in 1882, after terminating her engagement with her fiancé (Hyppolite Lissagaray, a French Communard), Eleanor fought despondency.[24] In 1884, only a month after Eleanor's decision to live with Edward Aveling, friends observed that she was depressed, and in 1887 she attempted suicide; in 1898 she succeeded in killing herself.[25] Hence it is no surprise that Eleanor Marx wrote to a friend after Levy's suicide in 1889 that she felt sympathy for Amy's "hopeless melancholy."[26]

Eleanor Marx was a close friend of Dollie Maitland Radford's before and after Dollie's marriage. References to "Tussy," Marx's family nickname, are plentiful in Dollie's diary: "Met Tussy at the Museum; walked with her to Newman Street." Other entries in 1883 and 1884 refer to socialist lectures Dollie and Eleanor attended together and describe evenings with Marx and her friends from the Social Democratic Federation. Dollie describes William Morris's socialist lecture "How we live, and how we might live," as "a beautiful address."[27] After joining William Morris's Socialist League in January 1886, the Radfords moved to Hammersmith to be near him.

Levy's name appears frequently in Dollie's diary from 1883 through 1886 but is conspicuously lacking in entries that refer to left-wing activities or social gatherings that included socialist leaders. Clearly, despite Levy's friendship with Marx and the Radfords, she did not share their interest in left-wing politics.[28] In her book *Eleanor Marx* Yvonne Kapp says that the leaders of the Social Democratic Federation (SDF) were anti-Semitic and that the Fabians ignored Jewish socialists; only in the Socialist League did some Jews feel welcome, and these were working-class Jews attracted to its anarchist wing.[29] Socialist attitudes toward Jews would have made it hard for Levy to be involved in the movements that her friends found attractive, but even if these attitudes had not existed, her class anxieties would have kept her out.

It is important to bear in mind that while the Levys were undeniably bourgeois, they did not have "old money," and Amy's letters to Katie throughout the 1880s show that she worried about the family finances. The move from Sussex Place tells a story of economic decline. But Levy's concern about her class position was not merely the result of the rise and fall of the family income. The cartoon showing Katie and a suitor exchanging remarks in a language that is supposed to be Yiddish shows that even in Levy's adolescence she was sensitive to the linking of class, Jewishness, foreignness, and vulgarity in the consciousness of her time.[30] The social position of England's Jews was always tenuous, especially after immigrant Jews poured into England, most of them members of the laboring classes. Like other middle-class "native" Jews, Levy seems to have felt a need to keep a firm hold on her niche in the upper middle class, so it is not difficult to understand why social movements on behalf of those at the bottom of the class hierarchy would not have the same appeal for her that they had for the Radfords or for her other friends.

This does not mean that Levy had a distaste for social groups. Whether or not she first met Dollie at the British Museum (or through the three Black sisters, who had moved to London), her ties to Clementina and Dollie would have been tightened through her participation in the informal network of women who frequented the British Library. That some of her friends were part of large, forward-thinking families—the Blacks (five sisters and three brothers), the Radfords (Ernest Radford had two sisters and several female cousins), and the young Garnetts (three brothers and three sisters)—created an avenue that allowed Levy to meet and mix with like-minded women and even with men.

The picture that emerges helps to complicate and qualify what Nord tells us about women who adopted an unconventional style of life in the 1880s. She quotes Beatrice Potter Webb, who wrote that Margaret Harkness "is typical of the emancipated woman who has broken ties and struggled against the prejudice and oppression of bigoted and conventional relations to gain her freedom."[31] Although Harkness's situation was probably not uncommon, some emancipated women were able to use their families to make contact with other unconventional young people, and these clans were a resource for women like Levy whose own families did not give them access to women and men with heterodox ideas.

Dollie's diary shows that she and Levy saw each other frequently in the first half of the 1880s. Most of the activities Dollie recorded are commonplace—Amy and Dollie go shopping, they play tennis, in the spring of 1883 they (along with Clara, Dollie's sister) spend a few days in the country at Hastings.[32] But these young women were intellectual and independent, and, unlike the female characters in most of Levy's fiction, their lives did not revolve around the rituals of courtship. While at Hastings they met and spent time with Dykes Campbell (Samuel Taylor Coleridge's biographer) and his wife, and about a month later they went up to Cambridge for the weekend with Ada Radford, Louie Jeeves (an artist), and Constance Black.[33] The diary entries show that the Radfords and Levy were all pursuing careers as professional writers (as do Levy's letters 20 and 22). In February 1884 Dollie records, "Fairy tale back from 'Home Chimes,'" "sent songs to 'Ladies Pictorial,'" and "Amy Levy . . . called."[34] In December of that year (after her marriage) Dollie wrote, "Amy Levy came in after dinner and talked to us of her work—and of many other things. It appears that my verses . . . were published in London Society [sic] this summer. Amy saw them."[35]

By February 1881 Ernest Radford had introduced Clementina Black to a club whose meetings he had begun attending in March 1880.[36] Drawing its members and guests from London's artistic and political circles, this club provided an organized way for intellectuals of both sexes in their twenties and thirties to see each other regularly.[37] The names of Ernest Radford's and Clementina Black's friends and relatives soon began to appear in its Attendance Book.. Dollie's name first shows up in May 1881 and Levy's in May 1882. Levy's ties to the Black, Radford, and Garnett clans, her friendship with Ernest Radford (which seems to have been as important as her friendship with Dollie), and her involvement with this club are evidence that, despite what Nord writes, in the first half of the 1880s Levy was not wholly dependent on an "unstructured . . . urban female community" of unmarried emancipated women.[38]

The club to which Levy belonged (which seems to have had no name) was not unusual. Walkowitz reports that "mixed discussion clubs held in drawing-room settings . . . proliferated in 1880s London," naming, in addition to the Men and Women's Club (which began in the middle of

the decade), "the Proudhon Club, the Browning society, the Zetetical Society, and for more radical souls, the Fellowship of the New Life [and the]
Fabian Society."[39] Dollie mentions "the Club" regularly in her diary: it
met twice a month and devoted alternate evenings to music and conversation and to meetings in which one member would give a paper, followed by discussion. The record that remains of those meetings tells
who attended but is thin about what was on the agenda: in a short note
to Dollie, dated "February 84," Levy wrote that she has "captured" a
"Miss Solomon" with "a lovely voice" who will sing Mozart's "O per
pieta" for the group; Dollie's diary shows that in May 1883 she read a
paper titled "To The Progressive Soul All Friendships Are Momentary";
in July 1883 Robert Parker[40] gave a "paper on Suicide"; and at a meeting
on December 2, 1884, at the Levys' home at Ulster Place, the topic was
the comparative reliability of biography and autobiography. The club's
Attendance Book shows that in June 1884 it held a picnic.[41]

The Attendance Book discloses that some of those involved with
this group were already prominent. On May 19, 1885, Levy brought to a
meeting George Bernard Shaw; Augustine Birrell, who had made his
name with a volume of essays, *Obiter Dicta*, in 1884; and Sydney Lee, at
that time assistant editor of the *Dictionary of National Biography*.[42] Other
guests sponsored by Levy were May Garnett (Richard's daughter) and
Lewis Levy, her father, both of whom attended a meeting held at her
home at Sussex Place. The club met at Levy's home five times before it
disbanded in 1885, and Dollie wrote in her diary that the guests "dined
with the Levys" before the meeting on December 2, 1884. The hospital-
ity of Amy's parents (and the participation of her father) demonstrates
that they accepted her life outside the Jewish community and that Levy
had not "broken ties . . . to gain her freedom."[43] But even though Willie
Levy attended two meetings (not the ones at his home), neither he,
Katie, Alfred, nor Ned Levy joined the club. Their lives remained en-
twined with those of friends and with activities from the world of Anglo-
Jewry.

It is harder to know about Levy's state of mind while she was in London than during her periods abroad, for her travels produced confidential

letters to Katie. While at Newnham she had been a cheerful correspondent, despite the troubles suggested by the fiction and poetry from that
period, but the letters written between 1881 and 1885 show that Levy was
gradually modulating the relentlessly high-spirited voice of her adolescence. Without losing that voice entirely, these letters often refer to or
resonate with personal unhappiness. In a letter to Katie written from her
pension in Dresden, Levy expresses her sadness in the self-dramatizing,
heavily ironic manner reminiscent of her earlier correspondence with
her sister: "My youth is dead, my ♥ is Broken—sour & Sara-like old age
come upon me ere my time. Madge and I sit like two aged crones & talk
about the past—by mutual consent avoiding any reference to the future"
(letter 17). Such passages, full of posture, might be only the result of the
ordinary, episodic misery of the young, but her allusion to her broken
heart, however playfully couched, reveals that she has been disappointed
in love.

Three of the poems in A Minor Poet, together with "A Ballad of Last
Seeing,"[44] form a group. They tell the story of a failed romance with a
woman, and they again bring up the subject of Levy's sexual orientation.
Nord reads Levy's love poems (eleven of which are to or about a
woman) as instances in which she uses a male persona, and for the most
part Melvyn New agrees. I will offer further biographical evidence that
Levy's sexuality was homoerotic, but textual evidence alone shows that
passion for men is all but absent from her love poems.[45] In the poems not
explicitly addressed to or about beloved women, the lover's gender is unspecified, so these too are probably about romantic and sexual feeling between women.[46] "To Sylvia," written in Dresden in 1882, was published
that year in the Cambridge Review.[47] Among Levy's papers in the London
collection is a torn-out page, with "Mrs. Stanford, Cambridge, July 1881,"
in Levy's handwriting under the poem. I have been unable to establish
who this woman was, but the presence of this name, place, and date are
evidence that Levy was writing about an actual emotional episode. The
recurrent musical imagery supports my grouping of these four poems.
When "To Sylvia" was reprinted in A Minor Poet, the graphic under its
title was a bar of music; the lyric itself speaks of the beloved woman

singing and playing the piano, and the final stanza ends with the line "Sylvia and song, divinely mixt, / Made Paradise."

"Sinfonia Eroica" (a much better poem, in fact one of Levy's finest), also composed in Dresden in 1882, is subtitled "To Sylvia" so that the two poems are linked explicitly (the name "Sylvia" is of course traditional in English love lyrics). It tells of a concert "in a great hall" on a June day; again the beloved woman fuses with the music. Describing the outline of the beloved's throat, the speaker says, " . . . I knew / Not which was sound, and which, O Love, was you." Like "O! deem not," composed when Levy was only seventeen or eighteen, "Sinfonia Eroica" is orgasmic:

> My spirit's murky lead grew molten fire;
> Despair itself was rapture.
> > Ever higher,
> Stronger and clearer rose the mighty strain;
> Then sudden fell, then all was still again.

The speaker in "A Ballad of Last Seeing" is also at a concert, where she is overcome by feeling:

> It is so very long ago,
> > A little thing, I am aware;
> I heard the music's ebb and flow,
> > I raised my head and saw you there.
> Cold was your face, as cold as fair,
> > You did not stay to smile or greet;
> Sunshine and music filled the air
> > The last time that I saw you, sweet.

> Beneath the arching portico
> > Carved round about with carvings rare
> You paused a space, then turned to go,
> > I watched you down the sculptured stair.

I did not hear the organ's blare
　　Sole heard I your departing feet;
I cared so much, you did not care,
The last time that I saw you, sweet.

This poem is the only one of the four that is reproachful: "I cared so much, you did not care."

The poem has an "Envoy" in which the speaker seems to have overcome her resentment, insisting that she treasures her last glimpse of the woman she had loved:

　　Friend, if indeed it must be so,
　　　　And we no more on earth may meet,
　　One time was dear to me I know—
　　The last time that I saw you, sweet.[48]

This envoy is troubling, for the refrain, repeated for the third time, strikes a false note. The other woman's coldness at this final encounter is in no way endearing—so why should it be "dear" to the speaker? The reader may wonder if the repetition of the word *sweet* has an edge to it. Perhaps Levy omitted "Ballad of Last Seeing" from her second book of poems because it has a bitterness that is out of tune with the other poems in the group.

"In a Minor Key," written in Dresden in 1881 (thus probably the earliest in the sequence), is longer than the others, and, being a narrative, it reveals more about Levy's actual relationship with Mrs. Stanford. This is not to say that its account of the love affair is factual; "In a Minor Key," because it tells a story, helps us to know more about the emotional meaning of Levy's attachment to this woman. The poem's title provides the central metaphor, the figure suggesting not that the relationship lacked importance but that, like a minor key or mode in music, it had a melancholy, plaintive beauty.

Moreover, just as music in which the intervals are higher by a half tone than the corresponding major intervals is somewhat less familiar to the Western ear, this love affair was different, that is, of a kind that is less common. The speaker (unidentified by gender, but there is no reason to think that Levy is adopting a male persona here) tells of her feelings for a person who wore "blue gowns." What is different about this relationship, then, is possibly its homoeroticism. At the same time, the poem suggests that there may be an additional (though perhaps related) aspect to its difference. "In a Minor Key" draws a distinction between the not easily categorized affection that the speaker has "to-day" for the woman who wore blue gowns and the more ordinary romantic love she felt for this person during the first phase of her attachment.

The second part of the poem (the asterisks signify the passing of time) begins with a question: "Is it love that I have to-day?" The speaker is much sadder now, and she insists that her present behavior is entirely unlike the earlier manifestations of her affection for this woman and devoid of the conventions of love: she writes neither songs nor sonnets, no longer paces by this woman's home, brings no flowers, and does not cry over the relationship. But then the speaker's feelings erupt, her words flooded with emotion:

> And yet—and yet—ah, who understands?
> We men and women are complex things!
> A hundred tunes Fate's inexorable hands
> May play on sensitive soul-strings.

These musical metaphors evoke deep, unrestrained feeling, and they link this speaker's supposedly more mature, more subdued affection to the blissful passion of "To Sylvia" and "Sinfonia Eroica"—and to the figurative use of stringed instruments to express sensation and feeling that is common in nineteenth-century poetry by women.[49]

The last three stanzas of "In a Minor Key" emphasize fierce loyalty rather than erotic emotion, and the speaker says, "I do not think I love you—quite." In the next to last stanza the speaker admits that she does not understand her own feelings: "And yet—and yet—I scarce can tell why / (As I said we are riddles and hard to read)." In this last section the speaker contradicts what she has said about no longer pacing by the home of this woman, admitting, "I paced, in the damp grey mist, last night / In the streets (an hour) to see you pass." And so by the close of the poem the reader is far from sure that the speaker's emotions have changed much from "early" to "late." While the poem ostensibly makes a distinction between romantic, passionate love (major) and the deep, tenacious affection one feels for a very dear friend (minor), that distinction actually collapses.

The only stable meaning in "In a Minor Key" is that human beings in the grip of intense feelings can be riddles even to themselves. This is probably all Levy could be sure about as she looked back on her relationship with the woman who, in the last word of the poem, she calls her "friend." Feminist scholars today often puzzle over the actual nature of the romantic friendships between women in Levy's era. This poem suggests that the homoerotic woman of that time may herself sometimes have been puzzled about such affairs of the heart, perhaps believing that, to quote Levy's speaker, "What's felt so finely 'twere coarse to class." "In a Minor Key" can be read as a record of Levy's attempt to transmute passionate love into friendship as she started a new life in Dresden in the fall of 1881. "Sinfonia Eroica" and "Ballad of Last Seeing" were composed later, and they indicate that as time passed Levy decided that she had indeed been in love.

An unhappy, abortive, or even an unclassifiable love affair is, of course, an ordinary, though sometimes excruciating, source of misery. But the letters Levy wrote throughout this period often startle the reader by moving from chatter to sudden pessimism even in the midst of apparent good news. The following letter, written on her birthday, is an example: "My pupil has lately taken up with her love troubles & joys—her fiancé (an awful creature) has been staying here; it is a secret engagement etc. I don't like being twenty at all. I think my arrival in the world was rather an unfortunate occurrence for everyone concerned. A new poetry club at Newnham was inaugurated the other day with the reading of 'Xantippe'" (letter 13).

Some of this unhappiness is related to physical ills unusual for someone in her twenties: abscesses, eye infections, neuralgia, and increasing deafness, certainly sufficient reason for sadness, especially the hearing loss.[50] She is obviously uncomfortable in the following passages (from letter 17), yet the rapidity with which she moves from self-satirizing complaints about her health to thoughts of suicide is startling: "I write to you out of the very depths of affliction brought on by a diseased body. God must love me awfully for he chasteneth me without cease. . . . Really if this confounded neuralgia don't stop I shall have to hie to a chemist—no, not a chemist—the river; for the German chemist is alas! not permitted to retail the death-fraught drug to the chance customer."

Throughout the decade Levy frequently mentions her increasing deafness. From Germany in 1884 she writes to Katie: "Fr. my point of view you are such a lucky beggar! Fixed income, good ears" (letter 23). Indeed, her loss of hearing must have cut her off from the music that was so important to her and affected her social life. Friends referred to it after her death. In 1891, after meeting the Radfords, Katherine Bradley wrote in the journal she shared with Edith Cooper, "The husband and wife knew Amy Levy and a delightful silent smoking companion she could be—she was deaf and often quiet."[51]

Levy's translations and poems appeared in the *Cambridge Review* every year from 1880 through 1883, and most were reprinted in her second volume of poetry. Between 1883 and 1885 Levy also published two literary essays[52] and "Between Two Stools," a funny and poignant epistolary narrative about a Newnham alumna who attempts to readjust to life among the "Philistines." Its protagonist, Nora, returns home to find herself appalled by the position of women in conventional society: "A woman is held to have no absolute value; it is relative, and depends on the extent of the demand for her among members of the opposite sex. The way the women themselves acquiesce in this view is quite horrible" (New's ed. 413–14). In this story Levy puts to good use her proclivity to hold in mind mutually exclusive, yet legitimate, modes of apprehending life. But in "Between Two Stools" her focus is not so much on juxtaposing people with irreconcilable ways of perceiving the world than with examining the fluidity of personality that an individual may experience as she moves from one environment and set of values to another.

The reader who knows about Levy's life will be surprised to find that in this story she questions the high-minded ideals that Cambridge offered women far more than she targets bourgeois manners and mores. Nora gradually comes to see Reginald Talbot, the professor with whom she had thought she was in love during her Newnham days, as "colourless" and "cramped," and she muses over whether "his atmosphere is too rarified for me." "Between Two Stools" offers a critique of the academic male personality, a theme Levy was to take up in later stories. From a biographical perspective, what is most intriguing is the suggestion that even though Levy was living her life as "Miss Creak" she was not yet entirely at peace with the transformation of female subjectivity that she associated with the university experience.

Of course, Levy could have decided to satirize Nora rather than life among the Philistines in order to cater to her conventional audience, readers of *Temple Bar*, a popular magazine; on the level of ideas, however, the story is anything but conventional. Although it would be anachronistic to assume that Levy would have agreed with Judith Butler that "words, acts and gestures, articulated and enacted desires, create the illusion of an interior and organizing gender core,"[53] there is no doubt that "Between Two Stools" examines gender as a social construct that is enacted as performance. Nora changes costume (she is immediately taken to a dressmaker because her family is shocked by the "absence of stays and crinolette" when she arrives home), setting, and activities (she spends her evenings in ballrooms instead of reading "Swinburne on the roof"). Losing interest in "fine scholarship," she gets a thrill from withdrawing, together with a male partner, from the crowd at a party to do what was called "sitting on the stairs" ("You go and sit down in a little corner . . . and talk about everything under the sun . . . your soul if you like . . . conscious that it is not quite real").

After participating in the social rituals of mainstream society for a while, her sense of the erotic alters, so that she writes to her friend

Agnes, still at Newnham: "A woman likes to be deferred to, to have her ideas treated respectfully; but on the other hand she likes to be taken possession of, regulated, magnificently and tenderly scorned, even, at times. We have been slaves so long that we rather enjoy, metaphorically speaking, the application of a little brute force on the part of our lords and master" (New's ed. 421). By having Nora change dramatically, Levy demonstrates that gender identity can be deconstructed and reconstructed as a person moves from one social group to another—but that these conversions are far from painless.

Nora's Newnham experience makes her aware of the inadequacies of bourgeois life, and she is shaken by the reappearance of emotional and sexual responses that she thought she had rejected, admitting in her last letter that she has lost "faith in myself, my feelings, and even my 'soul.'" The title of this story externalizes this young woman's identity crisis in a humorous proverbial expression. Despite the facetiousness of the title, at the end she is "disgusted, sorry, and just a little sick of everything" (423)—unable to find a place for herself in the life that her background provides yet disillusioned by the alternative universe that she had for a while found so limitless and desirable. The theme of being caught between worlds, both of them unsatisfactory or inaccessible, had resonance for Levy, and she was to return to it six years later in "Cohen of Trinity."

Levy has the protagonist of "Between Two Stools" become more conventionally feminine in regard to the kind of man she finds attractive, but she also has her challenge prevailing pieties about the tenacity of women's love. Nora quotes lines spoken by the male narrator of Swinburne's poem "Félise": "This year knows nothing of last year." Levy makes sure that the reader takes note of the appropriation of this "masculine" sentiment, for Nora asserts, "Is it not a terrible poem? and yet I think it is the story of many women's lives" (422).

When Levy wrote her response to Swinburne's "Félise," her Félise found falling out of love impossible because "the gods" have given women "a sorry gift of constancy." The protagonist of Levy's "Medea," composed in 1882 (at most a year earlier than "Two Stools") agrees, saying, "woman's chiefest curse" is that "her constant heart clings to its love." Levy may never have been as convinced of the truth of this tenet of nineteenth-century gender ideology as are her speakers; that she returned to the theme of woman's constancy repeatedly in the years that she was at Cambridge and just afterward does, however, indicate that she was obsessed by the question. She seems to have reached a turning point in 1883, for in "Christopher Found" Levy suggests that, at least from a pragmatic point of view, a commitment that persists when hope is gone is excessively idealistic.

"To E.," a lyric, suggests that personal experience taught Levy that a woman could experience the death of one love and the birth of another. Because this poem appears last in *A London Plane-Tree* and concludes with ominous words ("on me / The Cloud descends"), readers have assumed that Levy is speaking of her final depression.[54] But the poem was first published in *London Society* in 1886, and it refers to "three years gone by": "To E." is probably about Levy's time in Switzerland or Germany in 1882 or 1883. The description of the landscape ("mountains in fantastic lines / Sweep, blue white, to the sky, which shines") supports this dating. The poem's satiric attitude toward platonic friendship suggests that Levy, looking back, felt regret that she and "E." had not given physical expression to their feelings.[55]

"Sokratics in the Strand," the other important work of fiction from these years, is about depression and suicide. Levy tackles the representation of a despairing poet, distancing herself from her character through a shift in gender as well as by depicting him as poor and unable to publish his work, and she uses (and modifies) narrative strategies developed for "The Doctor." This time, instead of choosing a narrator who is an important character in the fiction, she tells the story from the point of view of an unintrusive, omniscient narrator; nevertheless, it allows readers to understand a person society misunderstands; they see him through the eyes of characters with whom they can more easily identify. Horace's friend Vincent, a successful barrister, full of energy and optimism, argues with and laughs at the depressed poet. The barrister finds his friend amusing and his condition only a passing phase; he assumes, as would most people in Levy's era (and some in ours), that Horace's problem is that he is prone to self-dramatization.

"Sokratics in the Strand" is similar to Levy's story about a female physician in that it challenges received and unexamined assumptions about a group that her society was prone to stereotype. But the 1884 story has much more of an interlocutory or dialogic spirit, for in "The Doctor" the reader becomes quite certain early on that the narrator's depiction of the female physician is distorted by bigotry. In "Sokratics," truth, though not indeterminate, is debated by Horace and Vincent, each of whom provides convincing arguments. Horace insists that there is no way that he can find existence tolerable, and the question at issue is whether such a person has a right to take his own life.

The mood is kept relatively light, at least superficially, as the two joust verbally about self-murder. The reader feels that Horace's insistence that it is wrong to meddle with the "natural healthy impulse of insane persons to destroy themselves" is valid yet is likely to agree with Vincent "that the instinct against suicide, stronger than any logical conclusion, will always lie at the root of [man's] nature" (New's ed. 428). Similarly, Horace is persuasive when he says about himself, "Body and soul, there is a flaw in the machine," and Vincent makes sense when he replies, "Don't talk as if you were a steam-engine."

As the debate continues, however, it becomes evident that speaking about human nature in terms of universals is problematic because each individual must cope with his specific set of circumstances and his own nature. Vincent assumes that all aspects of experience are developmental stages that everyone goes through. His idea is undermined by the narrator's description of the barrister puffing "with some complacence at [a] big cigar" as he says, "You poets . . . expect too much from life" (429). Vincent's prejudices are so palpable that readers are prompted to question whether they too lack empathy for those suffering from serious depression.

A paragraph following the powerful close of the main section of the story, just after Vincent leaves Horace by himself, starts with the voice and point of view of the omniscient narrator. The language used here stands out from the dialogue of the two young men (which is consistently jocular and ironic) in its freedom from mannerism: "For a moment, a mighty anguish, an unutterable yearning for the life which was so near and yet so far, rose up within him and almost overpowered him. He flung himself down . . . and taking up a volume of *Die Welt als Wille und Vorstellung*[56] which lay near, hurled it from the room" (430). At this point, just before the epilogue, the angle of vision becomes restricted to that of Horace, and the language becomes permeated by his moody consciousness: "There were times when he liked to nurse and dandle his sorrow; to feed it with philosophy; to mature it with metaphysics; but tonight his own despair made him afraid." The diction and alliteration in this passage provide access to the depressive's inner life by evoking his literary habits of mind. The words are double-voiced: their indisputably sincere tone conveys the terror that is missing from Horace's spoken dialogue, and yet the passage, cast as it is in third person, gives authorial acknowledgment to Horace's desperation, removing doubts about its authenticity.

The epilogue gives us a change of narrators. The new speaker, a character in the story who tells us that the depressed poet has died, is unconvincing when he declares his "own belief" (although "opinions differ") that Horace did not kill himself. That this narrator, like Vincent, is a self-satisfied lawyer who thoroughly enjoys his worldly success as a member of an elite clique is evident from his cozy references to "legal circles" and "professional secrets." His animal spirits are in sharp contrast to Horace's fragility. The man's inadvertent self-portrait subverts confidence in his assertion that "Poets . . . rarely commit suicide" (430). For people like Vincent and this final narrator, the depressive's agony is imperceptible because inconceivable: such people cannot grasp the anguish of those afflicted by what Horace calls his "unfitness for life."

One of the ironies of "Sokratics in the Strand" is that at the time that Levy wrote it, she may well have been struggling to hold onto the positions articulated by its two life-affirming voices even as she subverted them. The variety of perspectives in this story gives us an idea of the warring voices in her own head. Writing to Katie from Germany in

August 1884, six months after the story appeared in the *Cambridge Review,* Levy is obviously struggling to maintain emotional stability. This is the letter in which she gives a name to her episodes of depressive illness, saying that she tries "to ignore the great devil who lyeth ever in wait" but that "the devils are awful bad in the intervals of basking" (letter 21).

An undated, never published poem found in manuscript among Levy's papers bears a title written in Greek letters that translated reads "Aristarchus."[57] The poem takes the form of a dialogue between polarized internal voices representing the speaker's soul and heart. The soul-voice, highly Victorian in values and language, preaches optimism and effort. Life is "a precious gift" and one should "Work, think & hope, rejoice and strive, believe." The heart, using evolutionary diction, nevertheless takes the attitude that so much effort is not worth the trouble. Why try "To be the highest of the creeping things, / And stretcheth to full extent the pygmy brain? Of what avails?" To that second voice life is "a void."

Levy's writings, while giving expression to her doubts and despondency, reveal that, however arduous it may have been to find the emotional energy, she forced herself to continue to strive. In the same year that she wrote "Sokratics," a serious piece of fiction about a disturbed state of mind so close to her own, she began to address a popular market. In 1884 *London Society,* a magazine that provided light reading for a wide audience, began publishing her series of fictionalized travelogues. Signed "Melissa," all but one of these narratives take the form of letters that describe places Levy actually visited.[58] Drawing on both invention and experience, she keeps the pieces jocular and anecdotal. Melissa and her friends are students from "Princess Ida's College," the school's name inspired by Tennyson's 1847 poem *The Princess* and Gilbert and Sullivan's 1884 comic opera *Princess Ida.*

London Society also published "Mariana in the Ballroom" in 1884. In this lighthearted poem, Levy mocks the melancholy and melodrama of Tennyson's "Mariana" (which Leighton calls "that most seductive of poems to women poets"[59] because many of them wrote poems about women who were reclusive and dying). Levy's Mariana is a young lady who, instead of wishing she were dead, flirts with another man while waiting for her lover and thinks about how she will punish him. And despite having said regretfully in an 1882 letter (letter 19) that "being educated has taken away all chance of my producing 'potboilers,'" Levy, between 1883 and 1885, published in *London Society* three romantic stories to which the term "potboiler" applies.[60]

But these publications are signs of Levy's professionalism, not of insufficient creativity. Recording in her notebooks how much money she made from each transaction, she was determined to live by her pen as much as she could[61] and understood that this would sometimes require a calculated manipulation of silly conventions. An 1884 letter to Dollie Radford shows her joking about her potboilers:

> Heroes don't want many "lines"; give them . . . a rare grave smile, a white hand, & "celebrated sneer." I am at present taking a young man through scene after scene of most thrilling interest solely by means of a loud, genial laugh & an electric eye. The cultured but passionate heroine makes a speech, then "their eyes met" or she hears that laugh neighing out sympathetically from some hidden & remote corner. It is very subtle. (letter 20)

The letter is evidence that Levy was highly conscious that she was writing formulaic stories for what we would today call the mass market.[62]

A Minor Poet and Other Verse, the most important product of this period, came out in 1884 when Levy was twenty-three, and it included most of the poems she had written since Cambridge. They are nearly all sad, and many are about death and suicide. Once again the mood and preoccupations of Levy's poetry link it to the conventional melancholy of the female tradition in nineteenth-century poetry. But if almost all of Levy's work is mothered by British "poetesses," her second book makes clear that its fathers (along with Browning and Swinburne) are poets writing in German who were part of the pessimistic tradition in philosophy and literature. *A Minor Poet* includes translations of two lyrics by Nikolaus Lenau, "To Death" and "The Sick Man and the Nightingale," and two

poems inspired by Heinrich Heine, "A Farewell" and "A Dirge."[63] The latter takes its epigraph from a poem of Heine's that Levy had translated
faithfully and published in the *Cambridge Review* in 1882.

Several reviewers of *A Minor Poet* in 1884 note that Levy is indebted
to Heine, but, curiously, they do not connect the sadness of her mood to
his *Weltschmerz*. To do so would be to acknowledge that Levy's woeful-
ness had intellectual roots, and for some male reviewers, apparently, poetry by women was about feelings that had no relationship to ideas. In
addition, for many reviewers and readers the female poetic tradition remained so distinct that they could not conceive of significant influence
across the gender barrier. The reviewer for *Oxford Magazine* says reduc-
tively, "A Minor Poet [*sic*—he means the title poem] is the soliloquy in
blank verse of the type of Mrs. Browning, delivered by a moody man before he takes cold poison" (why only *Mrs.* Browning?).[64] This same writer
praises Levy's translations and adaptations from Heine, then complains,
"If she would only keep from subjects of morbid attraction." In fact,
Heine's poems are at least as morbid.

Levy was drawing on two morbid and melancholy poetic traditions,
but reviewers of *A Minor Poet and Other Verse* seem unaware of this. That
they deplore the relentless sadness of her work may reflect the changes
that were occurring in the conventions of women's poetry. In any case,
the grimness and despair that pervade some of the poems in *Minor Poet*
(unlike the sadness usually found in the work of Victorian poetesses and
in Levy's first book) are not merely an expression of the disappointments
of personal life and go beyond what can be blamed on the unfairness of
woman's lot.

That several of the reviews call attention to the illustration on the
title page explains what provoked discomfort. A. W. Dole (who praised
Xantippe and Other Verse) describes and comments on the frontispiece:

There is a well . . . beside which, upon the ground, sits a woman
. . . . The bucket rests upon the well-side, and the empty pitcher
lies near. Upon the top of the well is the mournful motto, "Non
in est veritas" ["Truth isn't in it"]. And we suppose we are to un-

derstand that in the teaching of the church which we see upon the hill in the distance, there is the same lack of truth.[65]

The reviewer for the *Court Circular,* who sees so much promise in the volume that he predicts that Levy will someday be more than a minor poet, hopes that she will find it possible "to discern the Divine harmony" and observes that the lack of such "wisdom" is what "spoilt poor Xantippe's life."[66]

Most of the monologues in Levy's second volume of poetry—for example, "Xantippe," "Christopher Found," "A Greek Girl," "A Minor Poet," and "Magdalen"—are spoken by personae who are in anguish (as is Medea). Although nineteenth-century women poets had long been writing poems about rejection and disappointment, Levy's poems transcend the personal by calling attention to the presence of her speakers in a world that has denied them the bare essentials that the human spirit requires to survive. Angela Leighton, referring to "Magdalen" as one among many poems about the "fallen woman" written by Victorian female poets, recognizes that, unlike the others, it is not "a work of social protest." Quoting Levy's Magdalen, who says, "And good is evil, evil good: Nothing is known or understood / Save only pain," Leighton observes, "Pain, which is the only residue from moral anarchy, is one of the keynotes of Levy's work, expressing her vision of a world which is unredeemed by faith, love, or social change."[67]

Isobel Armstrong compares "Magdalen" to Augusta Webster's "A Castaway" (about a prostitute). She pinpoints how it differs from "A Castaway" (and, though she does not say so, from most other poems by Victorian female poets about women who have transgressed sexually); the difference is that Levy's emphasis is on "the psychological damage of seduction and betrayal" rather than on social injustice.[68] Armstrong's observation calls attention to an important shift in Levy's poetry. After writing "Run to Death" and "Xantippe" (both completed before she entered Cambridge), she never again wrote a poem that so openly protested the social order. The aesthetic movement may have influenced her to question this mode, causing her to reject polemical poetry even before she entered Newnham. This shift in her attitude toward the purpose of art may be behind a comment Levy made at that time: "Mr. Garnett just expresses my own doubt about Xantippe's not being poetry."[69]

"Xantippe" and "Magdalen" exemplify what Dorothy Mermin says about the difference between dramatic monologues by Victorian women poets and those by men. Levy sympathizes with her female speakers rather than framing them with irony or otherwise creating authorial distance. The result, as Mermin says, is that instead of having "two sharply differentiated figures . . . the poet and the dramatized speaker—in women's poems the two blur together."[70] In "Xantippe" Levy's poetic voice embodies the sincerity the Victorians thought was natural to women's poetry. But what "Xantippe" loses by the lack of distance between poet and speaking subject is compensated for by the tension between the point of view of Socrates' wife, which it offers, and the vantage point of the traditional misogynistic legend that is its shadow.[71]

"Magdalen" has a different kind of tension. Levy's voice may blend with that of her dramatized speaker, but Magdalen speaks of deprivation so fundamental that it raises questions about whether there is any order or any meaning that can justify such suffering. These questions challenge attitudes that were at the heart of the Victorian worldview. Angela Leighton observes that Levy's "pessimism . . . is a . . . philosophical attitude in the face of a morally senseless world."[72] The philosophical dimension of Levy's poetry that Leighton notes is crucial. Levy's *A Minor Poet and Other Verse* is groundbreaking—different from the work of nearly all other Victorian women poets[73]—in that many of its poems (and not only those that are dramatic monologues or soliloquies) show people grappling with life in a world that lacks justice and meaning.

In many of Levy's poems, those who suffer are anomalous, but "Epitaph" assumes that for most people life is a cheat. It is subtitled "On a commonplace person who died in bed," and its speaker says matter-of-factly:

He will never stretch out in hands in vain
Groping and groping—never again.

Never ask for bread, get a stone instead,
Never pretend that the stone is bread.

The pessimism here is so sweeping that Levy makes a general statement about life, but for the most part, as Cynthia Scheinberg says, Amy Levy challenges the idea "that the true poet has some sort of prophetic access to universal feeling and truth."[74]

In keeping with her rejection of universals, Levy gives us poems that show the particularity of experience and the inequities in the human lot. As the speaker in "A Minor Poet" says, "I am myself, as each man is himself— / Feels his own pain, joys his own joy," and later, "One man gets meat for two, / The while another hungers." Further on this poet tells us that he feels himself to be "A creature maimed and marr'd / From very birth. A blot, a blur, a note / All out of tune in this world's instrument." (These lines provide a glimpse of what would seem to be Levy's understanding of her own susceptibility to cycles of recurrent depression. Her view is not far from that of modern psychiatry, which holds that susceptibility to depression is largely congenital.) "A Minor Poet," like "Sokratics in the Strand" and "James Thomson: A Minor Poet," explores the estrangement from the mainstream of humanity of those whose mental pain cannot be assuaged.[75]

Not surprisingly, both the nineteenth-century reviewers and even some readers today do not find the depressed speaker in "A Minor Poet" deserving of respect, worthy of sympathy, or comprehensible, thus proving Levy's point. The *Cambridge Review* notice disdainfully refers to the main speaker in "A Minor Poet" as "one of those men, the very largeness of whose ideal has helped to paralyze their *slight* powers of striving towards it" (emphasis added). The review in the *Jewish World* derides Levy herself, referring to her "mournful wailing," and indignantly asserts that "'A Minor Poet' is almost an apology for suicide."[76] "The word *almost* indicates that this writer cannot conceive of such a thing, but, actually, the poem (up until the epilogue) is exactly that—an apologia: a defense or vindication of self-murder. George Bernard Shaw, writing anonymously in *To-Day*, says that "Miss Levy's minor poet . . . has failed to persuade anyone to believe in him [and feels] out of sorts because he is not all that he ignorantly wishes to be."[77] Levy wrote to Dollie Radford, "I saw Mr. Shaw's article in To-Day. Perhaps he thinks it is criticism—I don't" (letter 22).

In our own time Melvyn New, while avoiding derision, calls the monologue "certainly not one of Levy's better efforts." His analysis of "Sokratics in the Strand," which, as he says, "revisits the same scene," may explain his dislike of "A Minor Poet" (which he does not explain). New likes the story but misreads it, trusting the final narrator's denial that the despondent man has killed himself. For New, "Horace . . . is, after all, a bit of a poseur," and Levy is "exorcizing what she perhaps feared were affectations of pain and anguish."[78] New's assumptions about both "Sokratics in the Strand" and Levy's attitude toward her own affliction suggest that he too finds it hard to feel fellowship with those whose suffering is so unendurable that suicide makes sense.

Levy conveys her understanding that people like her despondent poet are far outside the usual currents of human experience by playing on several meanings of the word minor although commentators on "A Minor Poet" have failed to notice this. Bernard Shaw's facetious notice is reductive and mean-spirited: "A Minor Poet is . . . one whose verse falls short, not only of Shakespere's and Shelley's, but of average excellence, just as a short man is not one who fails to attain gigantic stature, but one who is beneath the average height."[79] Other reviewers, less frivolous, take the word minor in its conventional sense, assuming that the title merely signifies that the depressed poet is second-rate. In our own time Angela Leighton—certain that in "A Minor Poet" Levy explained why she was going to kill herself five years in the future—hypothesizes that one cause of that suicide was "dissatisfaction with her art."[80]

To understand Levy's use of the word minor one needs to be aware of what the Oxford English Dictionary calls a "rare" meaning: the word can signify "in a minority."[81] When Levy calls her poet "minor" she is acknowledging that he has doubts about the value of his work, but, much more important, she is saying that his apprehension of life is different from that of most—that she is creating a speaker who articulates the lonely experience of those souls for whom acute emotional pain is commonplace.

In "James Thomson: A Minor Poet," Levy also plays with the meanings of *minor*. Admitting that she cannot "claim for Thomson the genius of a Homer or a Milton," she calls him "a minor poet," using the word conventionally. But then its meaning quickly shades into the less common usage—a poet who is in a minority (different)—when she acknowledges that Thomson "dwells on a view of things . . . which does not exist for the perfectly healthy human being" (New's ed. 502). Defending the value of this "passionately subjective" vision, she speaks of his "intense eyes fixed on one side of the solid polygon of truth . . . realizing that one side with a fervour and intensity" (501). Near the end Levy expresses her conviction that "James Thomson will take a recognized place among our poets, when the mass of our minor bards shall have been consigned by a ruthless posterity to oblivion" (509). The word *minor* has shifted back to the meaning it generally has when it is used to modify *poet*—unimportant or of secondary importance—as Levy, by a verbal sleight of hand, implies that in contrast to poets who now receive recognition, Thomson's reputation will endure, that he is not minor in the usual sense after all.

The primary speaker of "A Minor Poet" is recognizably the Hungry Poet, that voice in Levy's psyche that desperately longed for joy, love, and whatever else we mean today by the term *personal fulfillment*. In earlier poems such as "The Sleepy Poet" and "A Prayer" the speaker accepted intense feeling of *any* kind as coin that could be exchanged for artistic expression; conversely, in "Euphemia" the protagonist is willing to barter her career as an artist for happiness. But in the poems that make up *A Minor Poet and Other Verse* Levy's hungering speakers—unwilling to strike a deal—are in a rage about the unfairness of their lot or refuse to live if they cannot get what they require. These attitudes are evident in the lyrics as well as in the monologues. In "A June-Tide Echo" the month of June is berated for not sending delight; in "To Death" the speaker asks for death if "the flame of poesy" and "the flame of Love" grow old.

What makes the perspective of Levy's minor poet so disturbing is that he has given up and is ready to die. But far from being resigned, he combines fury with a refusal to go on with life, and when he begins his monologue he has already given up. His words have the fervor that is the keynote of the Hungry Poet in Levy's early poems even if now he is not willing to settle for just *any* emotional experience regardless of its quality. In a long passage from the middle of "A Minor Poet" the suicidal speaker articulates his sense of outraged entitlement. It begins with his refusal

> *To take my starveling's portion and pretend*
> *I'm grateful for it. I want all, all, all;*
> *I've appetite for all. I want the best:*
> *Love, beauty, sunlight, nameless joy of life.*

The poet compares life to "a feast" to which mankind has been invited: "The board is spread, and groans with cates and drinks; / In troop the guests; each man with appetite / Keen-whetted with expectance." Extending the metaphor, he provides a vivid image of how disappointing and unfair life is for a person like himself: "What's this? what's this? There are not seats for all!" The passage ends bitterly: "O, I have hungered, hungered, through the years."

The poems in Levy's second book challenge Victorian optimism so thoroughly that it is no wonder that her contemporaries in 1884 were unwilling to confront the bleakness of her vision. Despite Thomson's *City of Dreadful Night,* Swinburne's work, and some of the poems of John Addington Symonds, it was not until the 1890s that pessimism became familiar fare in English literature. In the mid-Victorian period, of course, some poets, most notably Arthur Hugh Clough and Matthew Arnold, wrote about being tormented by religious doubt. But Arnold holds out the hope that comfort may be found if people will only turn to those they love and "be true to one another!"

In her second book of poetry Levy sometimes does find meaning in human relationships. But the dramatic monologues are grim—and so are most of the short lyrics (the love poems, though hardly cheery, are the least negative). In "A June-Tide Echo" the speaker asks "the gods" for compensation for "the sick, slow grief of the weary years." Her demand is minimal—at first, one June day of gladness would satisfy and then, cutting back, merely "one fleeting hour"—but her modest request is refused. In "A Cross-Road Epitaph" the speaker tells how she turned to "Death" in desperation after crying out in vain to both God and "Love" (one assumes she means human affection of all kinds). Those reviewers who, like A. W. Dole, catch a glimpse of Levy's inability to find any consolation for human suffering in a silent and empty universe refuse to confront fully what he calls "its mournful key."

The reviewers may have been particularly prone to miss or minimize Levy's unflinching vision of meaninglessness and unfortunate happenstance because they did not expect or want philosophical despair from a woman. The reviewer for the *Jewish Chronicle* recognizes that the "acrid taste of the poems" is "in keeping with the canons of the modern poetic spirit which is nothing if not pessimist." While he finds this spirit disagreeable, it is clear that part of the problem for him is the sex of the poet: "The bitterness and disappointment which nearly every one of the poems breathes, and the tragic tendency indicated by the choice of the darkest episode in the story of Medea . . . suggest the masculine mind." That he is troubled by what he senses is a growing rebellion against what has been traditionally coded as feminine is implied when he says, "We do not know if the author will take as a compliment the remark that" the "notable gloom" of the poems "gives a masculine stamp to the poems."[82] An 1891 review of the second edition of Elizabeth Sharp's anthology of women's poetry shows similar discomfort. The writer complains about "its scientific terms and subjects," listing "Pessimism" as one of them, and concludes with a rejection of poems by women that "versify Mr. Spencer and Schopenhauer."[83]

Frank Harris writes that in the 1880s he was unable to recognize that good poetry could express despair; for him the gender of the poet was not the obstacle. Remembering a conversation about suicide that must have taken place sometime between 1885 and 1887, he quotes Philip Marston, a blind poet, who said, "I have no belief, none, cannot conceive how anyone can cherish any faith in the future, however faint." Harris says that he agreed, adding, "It was dear Amy Levy . . . who gave perfect expression to my thought," and cites the last five lines of "To Clementina Black." At the time, Harris says, he was interested only in the "sheer pathos" of Marston's and Levy's outlook but reports that "later that I came to see that their poetic achievement . . . had extraordinary importance."[84]

Commenting on *A Minor Poet* in 1891 (Fisher Unwin had just come out with a new edition), Arthur Quiller-Couch expresses hatred for Levy's pessimism. He says that the book is "symptomatic . . . [of] a great epidemic of hopelessness which has infected whole tracts of literature."[85] A few months later E. K. Chambers, in a generous, humanistic essay, starts off with the assertion that "the analysis . . . of modern pessimism can scarcely be dissociated from the study of that gifted writer whose work it permeates and informs, Amy Levy."[86] Dispassionately probing the meaning of the pessimistic impulse as philosophy, as cultural history, and as individual psychology, he describes Levy's poetry as "the record of a soul." These two pieces, so different in attitude, reflect the growing controversy over despair in the last decade of the nineteenth century. Although Amy Levy died in 1889, her work was part of the cultural conversation of the *fin de siècle*.

Levy's philosophical pessimism was, of course, connected to her personal unhappiness. In May 1883, during Levy's visit to Hastings with the Maitland sisters, Dollie wrote to Ernest that Amy "is rather sad, I wish I could persuade her how much happiness there is in the world: she is morbid and unhappy, & seems to have no springtime in her heart, & no elasticity of spirit."[87] While the chronic, pervasive sadness that Dollie remarks on must have had a biochemical component, we have seen that Levy had a variety of troubles during these years: disappointment in love, the deterioration of her hearing, a lingering ambivalence about her conversion to New Womanhood, the belief that she was physically unattractive, and the loneliness that came from feeling that she was different from most people in a variety of ways. Some of her unhappiness seems to stem from being Jewish.

The Amy Levy collection has the manuscript of an unpublished story called "St. Anthony's Vicarage."[88] Judging by the style and length, it is an early work (Levy's stories got shorter over the years, and this is a long one); the first address on the back of the manuscript—Sussex Place, Regents Park—establishes that it was written no later than 1884, when the Levys left that house.[89] Although the story is unsuccessful artistically, it is enormously interesting for its critique of British society and for what it reveals about Levy's attitudes toward her fellow Jews at the time she wrote it.

In "St. Anthony's Vicarage" Levy shows that duty, honor, laboring for one's fellow man, and marrying for love rather than social ambition (the values to which Victorian society gave lip service) are not rewarded. Toward the end, a man named Reuben Sachs and an aristocrat with an allegorical name, Lord Barrenhill, speak in favor of the exaggerated competitiveness that society actually endorses. The Jew functions as a signifier of Social Darwinism, and Barrenhill, who seems to represent what his class has become in the Victorian age, also speaks in favor of the aggressive pursuit of self-interest.

A family named Slagg, engaged in manufacturing and commerce (their name too is allegorical), are decent, if uninspiring. The third-person narrator of the story (who has conventional attitudes) endorses their values (the work ethic), but the moral center of the story is Sydney Aylmer, the vicar of St. Anthony's, a man whose university education means much to him. This saintly man labors tirelessly for his flock and his family. Honorable, self-sacrificing, hardworking, and scholarly, he dies unrecognized and poor. "St. Anthony's Vicarage" shows that Levy came to understand not long after leaving the university (and perhaps while she was there) that the ideals articulated at Cambridge were ignored or mocked in actual life. While Old Barrenhill, the father of "the youthful hereditary legislator," is not much better than the son, the story has one character from the landed classes—Sir George Travers—who appreciates what Aylmer stands for. There is no admirable Jew to counteract the impression made by Reuben Sachs (who has only a bit part). He appears only once, in conversation with Lord Barrenhill and Sir George Travers: "'I will make a very cynical remark,' said Reuben Sachs, the Jew, who chanced to be of the party; 'I don't believe in unsuccessful men. I never had the slightest faith in your mute, inglorious millions. The fit survive—they must—it's a law of nature.'"

A letter to Katie from Dresden written a few months after Levy left Cambridge leaves no doubt that she internalized the anti-Semitism encountered at the university: the stereotyping of the Jew in "St. Anthony's Vicarage" suggests far less visceral distaste than the revulsion she describes herself as feeling on a visit to a German synagogue:

> [A] beastly place it was. Zion unventilated& unrefreshed, sent forth an odour which made me feel [illegible] for the rest of the day. The place was crammed with evil-looking Hebrews. . . . This afternoon we call on . . . some wealthy Hebrews of our 'acquaintance' who, for Js [Jews], don't seem half bad. I say "for Js" because the German Hebrew makes me feel, as a rule, that the Anti-Semitic movement is a most just and virtuous one. (letter 16)

Levy's response to the Orthodox German Jews she saw in the Dresden synagogue is a classic instance of the condition that Sander Gilman analyzes and calls Jewish self-hatred. Gilman theorizes that members of a despised group (the Jews are his model) deal with their predicament by identifying with the group in power; they "select some fragment of that category in which they have been included and see in that the essence of Otherness, an essence that is separate from their own definition of themselves," projecting onto that fragment the qualities and behavior regarded as contaminating.[90]

It stands to reason that Levy was particularly put off by foreign Jews. Jewish immigration from Eastern Europe to England had became a tide by the 1880s, and, as Todd Endelman writes, the "poverty and overcrowding of [the] immigrant 'ghettos,' their alien sounds and smells, their un-English appearance, focused unprecedented public attention, mostly unsympathetic, on Jews in general."[91] The new arrivals made "native" Jews increasingly anxious about their place in society. In a letter to Katie from Switzerland in July 1882, Levy's word choice suggests, probably unconsciously, that she thinks of her fellow Jews (and herself) as not entirely English. After naming some of the Jews at the hotel, she goes on to say, "Among the *English people* . . ." (emphasis added).

In the same letter she writes with irony, "My dear, the sight of yr. co-religionists wd. delight you utterly; I simply sit & watch, sad but infinitely amused" (letter 19). It is evident that she and Katie found it embarrassing to encounter other Jews in public places because they had a painful sense that all Jewish people would be judged by the behavior of any representatives of the group and that they too participated in the judging. A letter from Titisee in the Black Forest two years later says: "There are some Jews here, of course. . . . They regard me with a knowing eye, but I think I puzzle them" (letter 21). Levy seems to have needed to feel that as a Jew she (and probably other Jews with whom she identified) were exceptional, another manifestation of her impulse to project "those qualities perceived as negative onto a subgroup within the general category of the Other"[92] even if in her view the "subgroup" was the majority of Jews.

Among Levy's drawings of people who are definitely meant to be Jewish is one that is particularly disturbing. This sketch, which I will call "Jewesses," represents Jews as they were seen and sometimes represented graphically by Victorians who hated Jews on racial grounds. It is different from Levy's earlier sketches, products of her high school years. Those "Jewish" faces, except for that crucial signifier, the "hooked" nose, are indistinguishable from countenances that conform to the conventions that governed how "English" faces were represented in popular illustrations of the era.

"Jewesses" was probably sketched during Levy's Cambridge years or in the period just afterward when she found the Jews she encountered in her travels so disturbing. It has two women seated at the theater, one of whom has hooded eyes and what seems to be a beaked nose. She is overly ornamented, with dangling earrings and a large necklace. A standing figure with features similar to those of the seated woman with the Semitic look may be the same person. She wears what appears to be a turban and dangling earrings, is dressed for the street, and holds a muff. She is distinctly unattractive if one judges her by "Anglo-Saxon" standards. Of the faces in profile, the two that have features associated with notions of Jewish physiognomy are outstandingly ugly, and the proportions of the hooked nose on one of these women are grotesquely exaggerated.

The faces in profile—apart from being female—are strikingly reminiscent of the caricatured Jewish faces in Robert Knox's *The Races of Men*.[93] Whether or not Levy knew Knox's book, which espoused the racial doctrines of ethnology (or others that are part of the same discourse), her drawing carefully imitates or caricatures features coded as Semitic, exploring the idea that Jews are so racially distinct from non-Jews that they can almost be considered another species. The dress and jewelry of the two clothed women with exaggerated Semitic features draw on stereotypes about ostentatious Jews.

These drawings reveal a new, much more troubled preoccupation with "racial" difference.[94] The draftsman would seem to be "Leopold Leuniger," Levy's self-hating Jewish persona. But Levy's gender is significant here because the ugly Jews in this sketch are all female, and the importance of good looks for a Victorian woman can hardly be exaggerated. Valerie Steele cites an anonymous writer for the *Quarterly Review*, "'We should doubt . . . whether the woman who is indifferent to her appearance be a woman at all.'" Steele notes that even John Stuart Mill held, in a letter to Harriet Taylor, that "'the great occupation of women' was 'to diffuse beauty, elegance, & grace everywhere.'"[95] Another sketch in Levy's scrapbook, of a blond woman wearing what seems to be a medieval pointed hat and a veil, suggests that Levy was far from indifferent to her culture's demand but understood why she could not comply. Under her drawing of the blond figure in the hat, Levy wrote, "The Fair One with Golden Locks (A Child's Ideal)." Levy's "Medea" provides more evidence that she came to understand that blond hair and fair skin were her ideal as a child because they were her society's ideal of womanly beauty. Referring to Jason's foreign wife, a Corinthian says that he dislikes "swart skins," "purple hair," and "black, fierce eyes," and adds, "Give me gold hair . . . and spare the strangeness." Levy's 1881 letter to Mama from Germany (letter 15), in which she says that no one has ever found her physically alluring, suggests that from her perspective Europeans (perhaps including Jews, who to a degree would have internalized the same aesthetic) were no more attracted to her than the Corinthian was to Medea.

That Levy incorporated fifteen lines originally written for her abandoned poem (and book) "Poeta Esuriens" into Medea's opening speech shows that she felt an identification with this "swart" heroine who lacked the looks prized by the people she lived among. The grafted passage in "Medea" expresses the desperate need for love that is the hallmark of the Hungry Poet and is preceded by these lines:

> *Alas, alas, this people loves me not!*
> *This strong, fair people, marble-cold and smooth*
> *As modelled marble. I, an alien here,*
> *That well can speak the language of their lips,*
> *The language of their souls may never learn.*

As Nord says, "Levy, the anomalous Jewish woman, surely stands behind the alien and enraged Medea, the stranger in a strange land who is marked as much in physical type as in temperament."[96]

Reading Medea's speech, cited here, is like hearing the voice of one of the ugly, caricatured Jews in Levy's sketch. Medea's words do not challenge Knox's anti-Semitic pronouncement, cited by Ragussis, that "Nature alters not"; that is, they do not challenge the idea that race is an aspect of identity that cannot be erased. In Levy's version, Medea is as much the object of racial hatred as of the cruelty of Jason, and she gives expression to Levy's own sense of the alterity of the strangers among whom she lives and articulates her wrath about being dismissed as alien. Isobel Armstrong says that Levy's "Medea" explores "the destructive impulse of the rejected," and one can imagine how therapeutic it would have been for Levy to give voice "to the fury and anguish of the woman who is dispossessed and denied."[97] "Medea" may have been revised several times in the two years between its composition and its publication in *A Minor Poet and Other Verse* in 1884. Each time Levy reworked (or reread) the poem, she would have experienced a catharsis that came from speaking behind the mask of a female character, a stranger in a foreign land, whose rage has become archetypal in the literary tradition of the West.

Levy stayed home in 1885. That she was in London for the first half of the year is established by her attendance at meetings of her club every month from January through May[98] and then by two letters at the end of August to her sister, who was honeymooning with her husband. The first of these provides a glimpse of Amy obviously still feeling the glow of Katie's exuberant, indecorous Jewish wedding, which took place the previous day. The second, written three days later, shows Levy having come down to earth, concerned about family matters, and making a characteristically ironic remark about her own "vitality and Lebenslust" that implies she is no longer in such a good mood (letters 24 and 25). These letters, written from Endsleigh Gardens, are the first indication that the Levys had moved to Bloomsbury.

Levy's account of Katie's wedding includes the names of "Paul" (Pauline), Charlotte, Dora, and Jenny, women that her 1889 daily calendar reveals she spent time with in that last year of her life. Jenny, to whom Levy asks to be remembered in the letters she wrote to Katie in the first half of the 1880s, is Jennette Rachel De Pass, born in 1859 (and so two years older than Amy), Pauline's surname is likely to be Meyerstein since the Amy Levy collection has a copy of *A Minor Poet* that is inscribed to "Pauline Meyerstein, with Amy Levy's love, June 1884." Charlotte and Dora are almost certainly Jewish too. The presence of these names in the letter Levy wrote to her sister just after her marriage and the fond inscription to Pauline are useful as reminders that even though Levy's correspondence and drawings from the first half of the 1880s betray feelings of alienation, shame, and self-loathing about her Jewishness, she must have been in regular contact with the Jews who came to the family home to see Katie and her brothers, and she appears to have maintained a degree of friendship with some young women from the Jewish community.[99] In Levy's "A Game of Lawn-Tennis," first published in 1886, the speaker brings to fond and vivid recollection a tennis match from her past and uses specific names: *"Paulina cries, "Play!""* and *"Those volleys of Jenny's.—return them."*

In January 1886 Levy published her last travelogue in *London Society*, about a visit to Cornwall. Called "Out of the World," it is superior to the others, an impressive essay. Melissa writes to her friend Psyche about how she spent August in London because of the "engagement and marriage of my sister Josephine." She reports that when the wedding preparations was [*sic*] over . . . when the boys had gone back to school . . . a great blankness fell upon my soul." Levy was giving her readers a thinly fictionalized account of what followed Katie's wedding in the autumn of 1885: an episode of depression and a therapeutic retreat to an inn in Cornwall.[100] Levy's vulnerability to depression was a constant, so it is hardly surprising that Katie's marriage to a Jewish barrister precipitated an episode. The "prudent" destiny that Levy had long ago predicted for her sister must have brought to the surface troubling questions about her own alternative paths.

7

Florence, London, and Florence
1886–1888

1886

Clementina Black and Amy Levy spent the winter and early spring of 1886 together in Florence. They had been in Italy together once before—sometime in 1879 or 1881—when Levy was recuperating, probably from a depressive episode. This time both needed rest and reinvigoration. Clementina, thirty-two years old, had left London to recover from the strain of "tenacious studies, town life, and the task of nursing several relations through their illnesses."[1] Much better after spending the autumn in Switzerland, she went on to Italy, where she and Amy, now twenty-four, stayed at the Casa Guidi, just south of the Ponte Vecchio, where the Brownings had lived from 1847 to 1861.[2] That Elizabeth Barrett Browning had spent so many years in this house (one of her volumes is called *Casa Guidi Windows*) must have been inspiring for both Black and Levy. In late March, just before Levy left for home, Black wrote a letter to Richard Garnett saying, "I have not written much since I came here . . . and Miss

116

Levy may without injustice be said to have done nothing—except indeed that she has done the great work of getting well. Her health seems entirely rested; she looks a different creature to what she was when she met me at Milan."[3]

Levy's love and respect for her closest friend is inscribed in "To Clementina Black," the dedication poem in *A London Plane-Tree*. In that lyric Clementina's honesty and "human goodness" are all that ameliorates an existence that otherwise is marked by dashed hopes and "creeds [that] are rent in twain." Levy's testimonial to Black's exemplary character is substantiated by the descriptions of others who knew her. Mary Cameron's assessment, written in 1892, is typical: "Only those who have worked with her . . . can fully appreciate her untiring industry, her tact and patience, and above all, her unvarying good temper under the most aggravating conditions."[4]

Clementina's personality also had a joyous component, and the frolicsome, girlish side of her relationship with Amy is commemorated in a humorous piece of verse scrawled in one of the latter's notebooks. Titled "Dedication" (Levy must already have been planning to dedicate her next volume of poems to her friend), it begins with a stanza that is teasing in tone:

> Dear Clementina, take my story,
> Altho' your name, I've often said,
> Not till indeed you'd gone to glory
> Upon my fly-leaf should be read.

Its final stanza refers to an incident that must have taken place during the last part of their 1886 Italian holiday:

> We've many memories to-gether,
> Of town and country, sun and rain;
> Not least that night of spring time weather,
> At Prato, when we missed the train.

Levy's sojourn in Florence was important for several reasons. Her visit to the old Jewish ghetto of the city is described in "The Ghetto in Florence," which appeared in the *Jewish Chronicle* in March. It was the first of five unsigned articles on Jewish topics that Levy was to publish in the *Chronicle* in 1886, her first narrative on a Jewish theme that she exposed to the public eye.[5] Beth Lask Abrahams says that Lewis Levy arranged for his daughter's venture into the world of Jewish journalism.[6] The *Chronicle* published two other articles on the Jews of Italy that year; these do not have Levy's stylistic stamp, but their existence suggests that the piece on Florence had already been assigned to her as part of that series before she left for Italy. Nevertheless, her first article reads as though it were prompted by her visit to the history-laden Florence ghetto.

Melvyn New describes "The Ghetto in Florence" as an "awakening to [Levy's] Jewish heritage."[7] The structure of the article intimates that the awakening was an effort: she is clearly straining to be affirmative. At first she seems able to give the ghetto glamour only by dwelling on its associations with Christian and Islamic culture: "From window, and archway and passage you obtain glimpses of the matchless architectural mass composed by the Duomo and Campanile" (New's ed. 518). Writing about the part that the ghetto played during Carnival week, she tells of how it was decorated to be the "Città di Baghdad" and that there are still "real camels" and "real studio-models posing as Orientals in all the glory of turban and fez."

Observing the present scene, she elicits the ghetto's Jewish past by taking note of its absence: "There is nothing that need remind one of the cramped life that once thronged and huddled and swarmed here, that need call up unpleasant memories of the sordid, struggling, choked existence that went on wearily from generation to generation." Once Levy has established that there is no necessity to feel the presence of the ghetto's former inhabitants, she chooses to imagine "the faces of ghosts, that peer so wistfully through the grated lower windows" and fancies the place to be haunted by "footsteps" (519). Distinguishing herself from the "many Jews here tonight [tourists], evidently quite undisturbed by 'inherited memory,'" she fashions a personal bond between herself and the oppressed Jews who used to live in Florence's ghetto and uses this connection to criticize her own relationship to Jewish religion and culture: "We ourselves, it is to be feared, are not very good Jews; is it by way of 'judgment' that the throng of tribal ghosts haunts us so persistently tonight?"

In the article's last paragraph Levy's moody prose seeks out romantic images: "When a pair of shrewd, melancholy eyes meet with your own, you are puzzled at the equal suggestion of Jew and Florentine in their glance. Who knows but that . . . those old and mystic races, the Etrurians and Semites, were kinfolk pasturing their flocks together in Asia Minor?" (520). Although this is a far cry from the "artificial teeth" that served as a metonym for Jewish vulgarity in "Leopold Leuniger: A Study," the romance is possible only because she is making an effort to associate Jews with a people that she already finds exotically attractive. When Levy describes a British Jew in "The Ghetto in Florence," her "Leopold Leuniger" persona, still unbending, holds the pen: "A sprightly, if unhandsome son of Shem urges us, in correct cockney, to take shares in a lottery." To take note of these things is not to minimize the importance of this article about Florence as a step toward improving her attitude toward her Jewish background.

If Florence was a watershed for Levy's sense of Jewish identity, it was also a turning point in her personal life because there she met and became friends with Vernon Lee (see Figure 9). In 1887 Levy wrote to Lee, "You are something of an electric battery to me . . . & I am getting faint fr. want of contact!" (letter 28). Violet Paget, who was thirty when she and Levy met, began calling herself Vernon Lee in her teens because she believed "that no-one would take her seriously as a woman."[8] Born in France, she was Welsh on her mother's side and considered herself British. Residing with her mother, Matilda Paget, who had a villa in Florence, she spent a portion of each year in London, where she was part of the literary scene. When she and Levy became acquainted in Florence, Lee had already published *Studies of the Eighteenth Century in Italy* (1880), the historical novel *Ottilie* (1883), and *Miss Brown* (1884), a novel that satirizes the aesthetic movement in England.[9] Her book on eighteenth-century Italy had brought her friendships with Robert Browning, Walter Pater, Henry James, Oscar Wilde, William Morris, William Rossetti, and many others though *Miss Brown* alienated Wilde, the Rossettis, and the Morrises.[10] A description of her by Irene Cooper Willis (who at one time had been a devotee) allows us to imagine the effect Vernon must have had on Levy, who, as we know from her response to Edith Creak, was attracted to strong personalities:

> As a talker she was always interesting and often arresting . . . those intensely inquisitive (although not penetrating) eyes, almond-shaped and set slightly aslant in the small but long Hapspurg kind of face, her slow, foreign articulation of words and the peculiar articulation of the syllables of words and the peculiar range of her voice compelled attention. . . . It was worth a journey to hear her pronounce:—"From my friends' matrimonial adventures I avert my eyes" and say: "There goes something primeval!"[11]

Willis gives another example of the kind of remark Lee might make in a social situation: "'Tell me, dear Eugènie, is adultery much practiced in England?'"[12]

At the time that Levy became acquainted with her, Lee had been in a romantic relationship with the poet and novelist Agnes Mary Robinson (called Mary) since at least the autumn of 1880.[13] When Vernon Lee was in London she stayed with the Robinsons, and when Mary was in Florence she stayed at the Pagets' villa, sharing a room with Lee.[14] But the letters that Levy wrote to Vernon Lee after she left Florence—which sometimes mention Mary—reveal that Levy was not aware of the special nature of their attachment: for example, "Miss Robinson . . . is very charming, but hasn't the same personal attraction for me that Miss Blomfield has,"[15] and "I am now expecting Miss Robinson to tea here; knowing her habits & customs I shall not be surprised if she fails to turn up." Both Levy's letters and poems indicate that Levy fell in love with Vernon Lee (and her feelings must have received a charge when Lee vis-

ited London only three months after they parted).[16] Most telling are two
of the five poems that she enclosed with a letter written during the following autumn ("To Vernon Lee" and *Neue Liebe, Neues Leben*"). Since
sending such poems to Vernon Lee at this juncture was tantamount to
announcing her love, these lyrics call for a biographical reading.

In "To Vernon Lee" Levy addresses her friend, recalling how in early
spring they wandered around the fields of Bellosguardo, "seeking for the

Figure 9. Vernon Lee (sketch by John Sargent)

daffodil / And dark anemone" while they talked "of Art and Life." The sonnet is subtly erotic; Levy's feelings are evoked most powerfully in the sestet in which she reminds Vernon that when they exchanged flowers, she encouraged Amy's awakening passion by breaking off and giving to her "a branch of snowy blackthorn" that Amy had thought "beyond my reach." In the last two lines Levy mentions that their conversation included the recognition that "the gods" have given her and Vernon antithetical "gifts"—"Hope unto you, and unto me Despair." From this one would assume that Levy understood the futility of her burgeoning love, but since the poem seems to have been sent to Vernon Lee as a billet-doux, the statement of how their temperaments diverge can be read as a challenge. Lee is asked to show the young poet—by returning her love—that she is wrong to despair.

"*Neue Liebe, Neues Leben,*"[17] the original title of the poem that was eventually translated as "New Love, New Life" for publication, poses that challenge even more clearly. In the first two stanzas of both versions love is imaged as a dead bird that awakens and sings of "joy and pain / Of sorrow and delight." Levy admits that past love has been a disappointment, that she has paid a dreadful price for allowing herself to feel passion, and that "this time is the last." The manuscript sent to Vernon Lee has two intervening stanzas (omitted when the poem appeared in Levy's *A London Plane-Tree and Other Verse*) which further stress Levy's misgivings about allowing herself to love again (the deleted stanzas are in this volume, following letter 26). As a courtship strategy Levy's expression of self-doubt was unfortunate, but the poems themselves reveal her growth as a poet.

"Out of the World," which appeared before Levy's encounter with Lee, demonstrates that Levy was ready to make important changes. She has Melissa humorously recall "the dear old days at Princess Ida's. Ah! those fierce old fights around the fire! . . . Malthusia has five children now . . . Agnostica has gone over to Rome; Democratica has married a capitalist and cuts all her old friends."[18] With these witticisms Levy/Melissa shows that she knows that her identity as a former student from a women's college is becoming outdated, and so, in this essay, Melissa re-positions herself, choosing a persona that at first seems merely a playful choice.

Insisting that she is a "Genuine Cockney," she assures her correspondent that while she is enjoying her removal from London, she is "not playing at Wordsworth, not trying to 'get at one with nature,' as one used to in the old days, before one had come to recognize one's limits" (54–55). The speaker in "Out of the World" is choosing to accept limits so she can invent an identity that she needs in order to speak and reflect on her experience. London-born and bred, she proclaims that she "prefers chimney-tops to tree-tops" and declares, "I do enjoy my diurnal Pall Mall" and "am not in the least indifferent to my weekly *Academy*" (55). As the cultural studies theorist Stuart Hall says: "There is no enunciation without positionality. You have to position yourself somewhere in order to say anything at all."[19]

Levy develops this idea with a negative example when the woman who shows Melissa around the grounds of a Carmelite convent is asked whether she planned to take the veil: "Alas! she had not the 'vocation'!" (55). Levy's point is that one needs to know who one is *not* in order to lay claim to who one is. Toward the conclusion of "Out of the World" she gives Melissa a statement that stakes out her position as a cockney by recognizing the play of difference and similarity that is involved in defining one's identity: "Much as I admire the superior peace, simplicity, and beauty of a country life, I know that my own place is among the struggling crowd of dwellers in the cities" (56).

By 1886, when Levy wrote this essay, she seems to have decided that she could exert control over the narratives assigned to her by society by finding her own place in them. This is not to say that she did not realize society's power to determine the boundaries of the self, and Levy makes this point in "Out of the World" when Melissa cites lines from Browning's "Caliban upon Setebos" about a fish from an icy stream that tries to live in the lukewarm ocean but can only sicken in that milieu. She does not quote the rest of Browning's passage—about how this poor fish is never again happy in the stream to which it must return[20]—for Levy's emphasis in this piece is not on the constraints that follow from the acceptance of a social position.

Instead, her emphasis is on the usable self that can emerge from an understanding of one's own past. For Stuart Hall "identities are things we make up, but not just out of any old thing,"[21] and Levy shows that she understands this, for the urban identity that Melissa lays claim to in "Out of the World" emanates from her creator's sense of a strong historical connection between Jews and city life, even though the essay does not mention Jews. Melissa's emergence as a cockney in this essay, which came out at the start of 1886, can be considered a rehearsal for Levy's appearance as a Jewish journalist.

At intervals throughout the remainder of the year Levy published "The Jew in Fiction,"[22] "Jewish Humour," "Middle-Class Jewish Women of To-Day," and, finally, "Jewish Children." Given Levy's discomfort about her Jewish background and her previous unwillingness to publish on Jewish topics, the articles that follow her piece about Florence's ghetto are startling in the ease with which she situates herself as a writer from within the Jewish community who has thought seriously about concerns and issues related to being Jewish. In "Jewish Humour," which appeared in August, Levy elaborates on her belief that the Jew is quintessentially an urban creature. Discussing what she calls the "Jewish Family Joke," she insists that its "distinctly urban quality is one of the chief features" (New's ed. 523).

Levy says in this essay that her sense of membership in the Jewish community comes from her similarity to other Jews in what she finds funny: humor is the cultural element that will keep "alive the family feeling of the Jewish race" as old traditions die and assimilation occurs (524). Stressing the particular Jewish propensity to combine laughter and pain, she outlines what she finds distinctive about Jewish humor: "The close and humorous observation of manners . . . ; the irresistible, swift transition to the absurd, in the midst of everything that is most solemn; the absolute refusal to take life quite seriously." Forging a connection between the two aspects of Jewish culture with which she most identifies, Levy asks, "Do we not recognize these qualities as common, more or less, to all bred and born in great cities?" This idea is developed further: "If they are more marked in the Jew, let us remember how long it is since he gave up pasturing his flocks and 'took (perforce) to trade'; he hardly has left . . . a drop of bucolic blood in his veins" (523).

These words have implications for Levy's artistic identity because in England the creation of poetry was conventionally associated with celebrating the natural world.[23] When Levy's "The Village Garden" was published in a prominent journal in 1889, it was accompanied by an unsigned article expressing the belief that urban living is superior, particularly for the intellectual and, by implication, the artist: "Merely by its existence around you, [London] quickens the brain, fosters thought that in the country would never come, and in some way by its own weight develops and facilitates mental industry."[24] That these ideas are iconoclastic is apparent from how delighted the writer is to have found a poem that affirms his or her sentiments.

We have seen that in making a place for herself as a poet, Levy had emphasized the lonely particularities of experience, risking the alienation of readers by writing about suffering that most could not identify with. Reading "Jewish Humour," one begins to perceive that Levy's poetics, not overtly Jewish, derives from her Jewish identity and that she is challenging notions about poets and poetry that are fundamental to the British literary tradition. With hindsight it is apparent that in positioning herself as both an urbanite and a Jew and by articulating the connection between those subject positions, Levy is using this essay to fashion an identity that would permit her to write poems that depart from the poetic mainstream. The sense of self that emerges foreshadows the direction she would take in her most serious fiction, the representation of Jews and Jewish life. In the years that followed Levy's *Jewish Chronicle* series she was to write a series of poems that celebrated the city and to include them (along with lyrics on other themes) in *A London Plane-Tree*, a book that invokes "an urban Muse."[25]

"Jewish Humour" allows us to see that all along Levy's poetry is in an important sense "Jewish" because of its focus on suffering and its rejection of universals. Levy uses Heine's body as an emblem both for human anguish and for the tribulations of the Jewish people: "The Poet stretched on his couch of pain; the nation whose shoulders are sore with the yoke of oppression" (522). Moreover, as Cynthia Scheinberg explains in her discussion of Levy's essay, Levy's rejection of universals is in itself Jewish. Unlike Christianity, Judaism has never aspired to be a world religion (in this sense it is "tribal"). Scheinberg asserts that "for Levy, Heine's identity as a Jew is very particular and cannot be made universal,"[26] but I believe that in "Jewish Humour" Levy makes Heine's physical self a metaphor for the peculiar suffering of *any* despised or devalued person or group.

And yet Levy wants to reclaim her membership in her own "family" and to affirm the significance of what is distinct and local, and so she even claims that "only a Jew perceives to the full the humour of another . . . we believe it impossible to impart its perception to anyone not born a Jew. The most hardened Agnostic deserter from the synagogue enjoys its pungency, where the zealous alien convert to Judaism tastes nothing but a little bitterness" (523–24). By referring wryly to the "Agnostic deserter," she reintegrates herself into the Judaic fold, and, riding the current of her boldness, she ends by choosing Jewish jokes over classical text: "Not for all Aristophanes can we yield up our national free-masonry of wit; our family joke, our Jewish Humour" (524).

"Middle-Class Jewish Women of To-Day," which appeared in September 1886, reveals that Levy's alienation from Anglo-Jewry was not only the result of the self-hatred engendered by the anti-Semitism of the larger culture. In this essay she writes that for the Jewish woman of her time, even more than for the gentile, marriage is made "the one aim and end of her existence."[27] Thus if a Jewish woman fails to marry, "her lot is a desperately unenviable one" (New's ed. 525), and if she has interests that go beyond marriage and family, "she must seek them . . . beyond the tribal limits" (526). Levy writes, "The assertion even of comparative freedom on the part of a Jewess often means the severance of the closest ties, both of family and race."[28] When she refers with pride to "distinguished women of today who are of Semitic origin" (527), her phrasing indicates that the women she names are among those who have paid the price of broken ties. These women are Helen Zimmern, a Schopenhauer scholar, who had been a member of the now defunct discussion club; Hertha Ayrton,[29] a mathematician and scientist, who was active, as was Levy, in the University Women's Club;[30] and Mathilde Blind, a poet, with whom Levy almost certainly had a nodding acquaintance through London literary circles. That she knew these women shows how much the essay is written out of personal and possibly bitter experience.

Did Levy's own parents put pressure on her to marry? She may have felt the weight of such expectations, either from them or from extended family and others in the Jewish community, which could have made it harder for to live life as "Miss Creak." In September 1886 Levy was not yet twenty-five and so not disqualified for marriage by age (Katie had been twenty-six when she wed), but, sexual orientation aside, her New Woman ambitions and habits of living made spinsterhood likely. "Middle-Class Jewish Women of To-Day" shows Levy using her gifts as a writer to fight for the right of Jewish women like herself to have options other than either "beating . . . in vain against the solid masonry of our ancient fortifications, long grown obsolete" or "scaling the wall and departing, never to return to the world beyond"(527).

The final article in the series, "Jewish Children," published in November, addresses "mental and nervous diseases among Jews." Levy seems to have been exploring the question of whether her tendencies toward depression and anxiety stemmed at least in part from her upbringing as a Jewish child and from being born with a temperament that she associated with her Jewishness. Careful to stress that "a love of children is one of the most deeply-rooted instincts of our nature," Levy warns that "the Jewish child . . . runs great danger . . . of being killed with kindness." Her description of the Jewish child, surely a retrospective self-portrait, is particularly interesting:

Such vivacity, such sense of fun, such sensibility and intelligence at so early an age, could only be the product of a very delicate and elaborate organism; a bit of mechanism that will not bear to be tampered with rashly. . . . Mental precocity . . . may nearly always be accepted as the sign of a highly developed nervous organization. And the Jewish child, descendant of many city-bred ancestors . . . is apt to be a very complicated little bundle of nerves indeed. (New's ed. 530)

Levy is asking the Jewish community difficult questions, but the article is not an attack. Signed "By a Maiden Aunt," this article is like the others that followed "The Ghetto in Florence" in that the first person plural pronouns appear to be used with confidence. These writings demonstrate what seems to be a successful rapprochement between Levy and her people.

The letter Levy wrote to Vernon Lee in the fall of 1886 (letter 26) shows that after returning home for the most part she took up the life she had left: residing with her family, moving in the world of London social activists and intellectuals, and working hard on her writing. She tells of "a very remarkable party" at which she is surprised that Fisher Unwin shows an interest in seeing her recent work ("he blushingly murmured that he thought we cd. manage a quadrille") and writes about "wrestling with a story & reading solid literature at the Museum!"[31]

Levy is frank about longing to return to Florence and admits how much the friendship with Lee means to her: "What a difference it has made to me to have known you." When she says cheerily, "As for me, I am rather good," the statement is convincing, especially taken together with the "Jewish" series, which is impressive as a record of personal growth. One of the most striking things about these articles is that Levy, seeking to make peace with her Jewish background, does so on her own terms: not religious, she insists that agnostics are bona fide Jews; troubled by the position of women in the Anglo-Jewish community, she states her objections; concerned about the way Jewish children are brought up, she speaks her mind.

1887

Levy's second letter (27) to Vernon Lee concludes, "With every good wish for 1887," and her four, possibly five, letters to Lee written that year are almost the only record we have of what was going on in Levy's life and mind in 1887. Because Beth Zion Lask knew of no publications for that year, she described it as "barren,"[32] and it is true that Levy published no essays or fiction (not even potboilers). But she had a poem, "Alma Mater," in the *Cambridge Review* in June (a slightly different version from the one published in *Plane-Tree*), another, "London in July," in the *Academy* in July, and two of her sonnets appeared in print in Elizabeth Sharp's anthology of women's poetry.[33] As Melvyn New observes, "While [Levy's] appearance in print may have been minimal, her productivity was monumental" considering the amount of work she published in the remaining twenty-two months of her life.[34] In a letter (29) she acknowledges this surge of creative energy: "I am so good that you wd. hardly know me, am in the 19th chapter of my novel, & am thinking seriously of a new volume of verse."

Levy's prose in her correspondence with Vernon Lee, eight letters in all, is formal, the tone restrained even when she is speaking with astonishing openness of Lee's importance to her. The letters are often elegant in style and sometimes witty, the kind of letter that a literary person would write someone she hoped to impress in hopes of forging a closer relationship. The correspondence suggests that Levy's life changed after meeting Lee becoming involved with a new circle of people who were Vernon's friends. Some of these were women Levy had known previously as members of the club (Mary Robinson, Bertha Thomas, and Helen Zimmern[35]), but now that she was Vernon Lee's friend, she seems to have begun to see them socially and on more intimate terms. Levy has Robinson to tea, takes an overnight trip with Thomas, and knows Zimmern well enough to say about her, "It is dreadful, the way in wh. she is broken up" (letter 29).

Levy writes about Dorothy Blomfield, a poet,[36] as if they have just become acquainted, and she feels that an important new friendship is blossoming: "Miss Blomfield attracts me immensely; there is something so generous about her; generous in an extended sense; & her sort of mind is so refreshing, after the academic mind wh., till within a comparatively short time, represented culture to me as distinguished fr. Philistinism" (letter 27). Levy's disillusionment with university life reaches a new level in this letter. Getting to know Lee and her friends apparently convinced Levy that to be a person of ideas did not have to mean taking "no pleasure in anything" or cultivating "intellectual exclusiveness" (letter 26). Though she says nothing overt about gender, she probably had in mind university types like Karl Pearson, who, as we know, Levy found offensive. She is not referring specifically to Pearson in letter 26 (he was a professor at the University of London, not Cambridge), but what she says, particularly about intellectual exclusiveness, calls to mind Judith Walkowitz's portrayal of the behavior and attitudes of Pearson, Thicknesse, and the other male members of the Men and Women's Club (some of whom had been in Levy's discussion club). These men disbanded the Men and Women's Club because they found the female members, who were not university-educated, "incapable of the level of scientific work" that the men felt themselves able to engage in.[37]

Levy was already friends with other intellectuals who were not part of the academic world—Clementina Black, the Radfords, Eleanor Marx, possibly Olive Schreiner (it is not clear when they met)—these cannot be the people Levy had in mind when she wrote disparagingly of those who "represented culture" to her before meeting Lee and her friends. The letters to Vernon Lee show that Levy remained close to Clementina and was proud that her friend was elected secretary to a women's trade union. Because Black's union, the Woman's Provident and Protective League,[38] was at the Industrial Hall in Bloomsbury, near Endsleigh Gardens, Clementina and Amy found it easy to see each other regularly, and the two remained intimate.[39] But Levy's letters to Lee in 1886 and 1887 demonstrate that she was no closer than she had been in previous years to sharing Clementina's dedication to alleviating the lot of the working classes; the Radfords, Schreiner, and, of course, Eleanor Marx felt that commitment keenly. This difference between Levy and her old friends, even though they shared her interest in literature, would have put her at a certain distance from them intellectually; the "sort of mind" she found in Dorothy Blomfield and, by implication, in Vernon Lee, may have been refreshing in that it offered ideas and interests more compatible with her own.

Clementina and Grace Black[40] had taken a flat on Fitzroy Street, where they were doing their own housework and, as Levy told Lee in the fall of 1886, "attending Socialist and Anarchist meetings." About the Blacks' new home, Levy comments, "I confess that my own Philistine, middle-class notions of comfort would not be met by their *ménage*" (letter 26).[41] Seven months later Vernon Lee visited that flat just before going to a socialist meeting with Clementina and Grace and found it amusing that they were willing to dispense with what were considered the amenities: "I went to Miss Black's anti servitoress lodging. It is extremely picturesque."[42] Levy's inability to be amused by the Bohemianism of the Black sisters, together with her lack of interest in the problems of the poor, makes her stand out even in comparison with Dorothy Blomfield, who took Levy to a club for working-class girls, and Vernon Lee, whose interest in the social activism of the period was merely voyeuristic.

The fascination that socialism and social activism had for many intellectuals of the period, whether or not they cared about social inequality, is apparent in the letters Vernon Lee wrote to her mother during the summer of 1887. On her visit to London she attended meetings of the Fabian Society, the Social Democratic Federation, and the Fellowship of the New Life as if they were tourist attractions, and she had intense conversations with Henry Mayers Hyndeman of the SDF. In one letter she reported satirically on the meeting she attended with the Black sisters: "We went in the bus to St. James Hall, where a socialist conference 'for the Rich classes' was going on in a small room. The audience was all well dressed, mainly women, with a sprinkling of aesthetic looking men. Stepniak, the Nihilist and author of *Underground Russia* was in the chair, an alarming person with a face like the paw of a bear."[43]

Earlier that afternoon, Lee had visited Levy, who probably declined the opportunity to attend the event at St. James Hall.[44] Her letter to Lee, written that same summer, about the working-class girls she met when

Blomfield took her to visit their club, is candid on the subject of class: "Somehow those girls fr. the streets, with short & merry lives, don't excite my compassion half as much as small bourgeoisie shut up in stucco villas at Brodesbury or Islington. Their enforced 'respectability' seems to me really tragic" (letter 31). There is a reason why Levy found it most easy to empathize with those who had a tenuous hold on middle-class status.

Reuben Sachs shows that Levy understood that Jews experienced a particular insecurity about their place in society. In a conversation with his cousin Leo about Jews and materialism, Reuben responds to Leo's idealization of Cophetua, the mythical king, for marrying without worldly motives by saying, "King Cophetua had an assured position. It isn't everyone that can afford to marry begger maids" (New's ed. 237). Levy's lack of an assured position in the social hierarchy is one reason why she would have been happy with her new friends. As intellectuals Vernon Lee and her crowd were more interested in art and philosophy than in socialist theory, and as feminists they wrote biographies of women and New Woman novels instead of organizing working women.[45]

There is another reason why Levy would have been glad that Vernon Lee had given her access to a new social circle. By 1887 some of her old friends had paired off and started families. Effie Malder Scott, her close friend since Brighton High School, had married Tom Stevens, a solicitor, and had one son; Eleanor Marx had added Aveling to her name, viewing her common law liaison with Edward Aveling as a marriage; the Radfords now had two children.[46] In contrast, Vernon Lee, Dorothy Blomfield, Bertha Thomas, Helen Zimmern, and other women Levy saw often after 1886 tended to be homosocial.

Not surprisingly, given Lee's own relationships, some of her friends seem to have been homosexual as well. Thomas's letters to Richard Garnett show that she and Zimmern shared a house in Canterbury, and the two traveled together to Florence and other places; it is difficult to be sure, but they may have been romantic partners.[47] Three of Dorothy Blomfield's writings—a poem, a story, and a letter—suggest that she too looked to women for emotional and erotic satisfaction. In the first, "A Roman Love-Song," a speaker expresses love for a woman (which in itself shows nothing since Blomfield could be using a male persona), but the second, "The Reputation of Mademoiselle Claude," is considerably more revealing.

The title character in the story is an unconventional American woman, Claude, who lives in France with her companion, Anne Harland, a twenty-three-year-old girl. We are told that Anne Harland's devotion to her friend "was beyond all bounds of ordinary friendship . . . it amounted to a religion, and a religion intensified by an imaginative and strongly passionate nature."[48] When an aristocratic bounder begins to spread tales that suggest he has had an affair with the older woman, the girl proposes that her twin brother defend Mademoiselle Claude's honor in a duel. The unsavory Comte kills the slim Mr. Harland, whose "likeness to his sister" is "extraordinary," and upon closer inspection the dead boy turns out to be—Anne Harland.

What did people reading such a tale in a popular magazine make of it at the time? Elements in the story such as the older woman's masculine first name, the girl's desire to be gallant in defense of the woman she loves, cross-dressing, and male impersonation seem likely to have been common signifiers of a lesbian relationship in the closeted homerotic writing of the period.[49] The narrator's reference to Claude's "motherly interest" in Anne's well-being seems an obvious cover for an erotic relationship, but most of those who read the story in *Temple Bar* in 1885 must have taken Anne Harland's passion at face value. Leighton, writing about the "poetic tradition of physical love between women," explains that the representation of such love was accepted because of what she calls the "sisterly gesture," which "permitted the expression of all sorts of desire, maternal, religious, political as well as sexual."[50] Notions about sisterly love would have concealed what was behind the intensity of emotion that connects Blomfield's characters, who never touch.

Dorothy Blomfield's letter written in 1885 to Vernon Lee provides a revelation about the history of her relationship with Lee:

I will do my best to follow the programme you laid down & you must forgive my having forgotten it so entirely last Friday. Isn't it almost too Utopian to expect a friendship to develop perfect equality of growth in every side of it? . . . However I think your programme a wise one, & as I have an egotistical & great desire to be a pleasure in your life in return for the pleasure & pain you are to mine, I will let things go quietly & refrain as much as in me lies from forcing anything upon you. I should like above anything I can think of at this moment to possess this real friendship . . . friendship that greater people than we have lived out in their lives—but good things ripen slowly & my great snare in life is hurry![51]

My reading of this letter is that Dorothy, having confessed love for Vernon, was told that, without burying her feelings altogether, she should keep them under constraint and aspire toward a "Platonic" friendship, one that was idealized but not romantic. Blomfield apologizes for departing from that "programme": on some occasion she must have displayed her devotion too intensely.

In 1885, Lee was in a committed relationship with Mary Robinson; it appears that Lee, while discouraging expectations of romance on Blomfield's part, wanted to keep her as a devotee. Evelyn Wimbush, whom Levy mentions in several letters, also had an unrequited passion for Lee.[52] One can see how Levy might have felt more open about her sexual orientation among the women in Vernon Lee's clique. How she felt when she found out (as she probably did, at least about Dorothy) that she, Wimbush, and Blomfield were all worshipers at the same shrine does not emerge in her correspondence with Lee.

Levy writes that she is especially happy to have met Blomfield, with whom she reads Italian, and who, Levy says, "is the only person I have ever met with whom it gives me any real satisfaction to talk about verse & verse-making" (letter 30). The letters also mention that she has "been abnormally productive, both of prose & verse" (letter 28); reveal that she keeps scheming to return to Florence and thinks of it often; and show that she is still so unaware of Mary Robinson's relationship with Vernon Lee that she can ask without self-consciousness, "Is it true that you are going to live en garcon [*sic*] instead of staying with the Robinsons?" (letter 29). Surely Levy is being flirtatious while obliquely testing for whether she has a chance to win Lee's affections when she says, "I really do mean to write a novel, & you are to be not the heroine, but the hero! At least he is to have elements of you in his composition; & to suffer fr. psychological spasms, wh. the poor heroine is to find rather misleading" (letter 30).

In what is probably Levy's last letter to Lee that year she is equally flirtatious, inviting Lee to imagine her in a "a black dress, open in front, & sticking out behind as much as even you cd. desire." Lee seems to have been trying to get Levy to give up the kind of outfit she had worn as a Newnham student—what was called "artistic dress"[53] (loose and comfortable)—in favor of the close-fitting dress with a bustle, requiring a corset, that was in vogue. In early June 1887 Vernon Lee was in London although Levy did not see her until June 11 at a gathering at Mary Robinson's.[54] Levy acknowledges that she is feeling a bit poorly at the moment, but the admission makes her hopefulness even more poignant: "I am seedy,[55] but apart fr. that, find life opening up, somehow" (letter 31).

Levy had begun an earlier letter to Vernon Lee (letter 30) with the words, "Here is bad news; fr. my own pt. of view, at least, very bad news indeed. I am not coming to Florence after all. I can't exactly give the reasons as they concern other people besides myself." Most likely Levy was protecting the privacy of her father because the family had undergone a financial crisis. According to Levy's cousin Lucy Levy Marks, her own father, Nathaniel, and her uncle Lewis "lost every penny they had" on the Stock Exchange when Lucy was "about fifteen" (she was born in 1872 so the catastrophe would have occurred around 1887).[56] Lucy Marks's account is undoubtedly exaggerated because the Levys continued to live at Endsleigh Gardens until some time after Amy's suicide; the glimpses of their style of life that Levy provides during the two years or so remaining to her life do not suggest that they were impoverished, but severe retrenchment (and debt) may have been necessary. The census of 1891 shows that the family was no longer living at their Bloomsbury address. In 1895 Lewis died in Johannesburg, where he had been residing and working as a stockbroker, so he does seem to have lost his niche in the London Stock Exchange.[57]

The worst event of 1887 for the Levys has to have been Alfred's death on May 27 at the age of twenty-four. Levy's "bad news" may refer to that event, and the tone of the letter, rather cheerful, may be more forced than it seems. Alfred's death certificate discloses that he died in a coastal village, Gorleston, had no occupation, and that the cause of death was "Paralysis, Exhaustion." This may mean he died of tertiary syphilis, also called General Paralysis of the Insane (GPI); he might have been away from home because his parents were angry with him. There are other possibilities. Like Amy, he may have suffered from depressive illness (which runs in families); perhaps he killed himself. Depression or the late stages of syphilis (or both) could have made it impossible for him to pursue any occupation toward the end of his life.

Alfred had been ill in the summer of 1885 (in letter 25 Levy wrote to Katie that "the heir apparent is considerably better"), and so it is possible that his health (mental or physical) had been failing for quite a while. None of Levy's 1887 letters to Vernon Lee mention a death in the family, but this may reflect the family's shame. Levy's sole allusion to Alfred's death appears in "Cohen of Trinity," which came out in May 1889, two years later. The full name of the story's suicidal protagonist is Alfred Lazarus Cohen, surely a reference to her dead brother who, by the power of the imagination, she can briefly resurrect. In linking Alfred to Cohen, a Jewish student at Cambridge who commits suicide because he cannot make himself comprehensible to the gentile world, Levy is not telling her brother's story in a literal way. Alfred, seventeen months younger than Amy, did not, as Cohen does, attend a university or write a book that made a big splash. By naming her protagonist Alfred Lazarus Cohen—and by attributing to him many of her own experiences, preoccupations, and interests—Levy recognizes that while their paths in life were divergent, she and her brother had much in common.[58]

In the autumn of 1887 Levy was active as a member of the University Women's Club, which, as she says in her essay "Women and Club Life," occupied "a small but daintily-furnished set of rooms on the upper floors of a house in New Bond Street" (New's ed. 534). The club's records show that Hertha Ayrton proposed a candidate for membership, with Amy Levy seconding the motion.[59] That the first and second Jewish women to attend Cambridge University worked together on club business strikes the imagination and prompts curiosity about their relationship. The University Women's Club had first opened its premises in January 1887, and Levy must have gone there frequently because many of her letters to Vernon Lee are on the club's stationery. In her essay on clubs she explains that they were necessary for women because they provided "a haven of refuge" where members could be "undisturbed by the importunities of a family circle, which can never bring itself to regard feminine leisure and feminine solitude as things to be accepted" (534).

1888

Despite Alfred's death the previous May, during most of 1888 Levy was apparently able to sustain the energetic activity, literary productivity, and, for her, unusually optimistic frame of mind that she had enjoyed since her visit to Florence in 1886. Maintaining old ties while making new friends, she seems to have made significant progress toward overcoming the "accursed shyness" mentioned in a letter to Katie in 1884 (letter 19). What remained of that shyness may have been charming. Since much has been said about Levy's melancholia, we should also note, to round out the picture, that Garnett describes her as "frequently gay and animated."[60]

The playful side of Levy's personality is evident in the poetry she published in the winter of 1888. "Rondel (dedicated to Mrs. Fenwick-Miller)," which appeared in the Pall Mall Gazette in February, is very light verse, yet we can make inferences from it about Levy's mood and attitudes. Mrs. Fenwick-Miller[61] kept her own surname when she married (merely changing her title to "Mrs." instead of "Miss"). Levy seems to have been inspired by this; perhaps she also knew that Fenwick-Miller's relationship with her husband was truly egalitarian.[62] The rondel

indicates a new faith on Levy's part that love and fame need not be antithetical, and this allowed her to write what can be considered an anti-
conversion poem. We have seen that at a young age Levy was challenged
by the possibilities of self-transformation. Could one be a New Woman
and still have the satisfactions of loving and being loved? Could a Jewess
become a secular Englishwoman? In this rondel, Levy, now twenty-six,
having successfully rejected domesticity for a life of achievement in the
public world, suggests that the goal need not be to change oneself into a
woman who does not want to be a wife; instead, wifehood can be rede-
fined. Levy may have taken this question seriously without wanting marriage for herself.

"Rondel" ends with the line "Married or single, I do not require / To
change my name." While the poem is obviously a feminist statement,
readers aware of Levy's preoccupations would not be going far afield if
they took the trope of refusing a name change in a second sense—as a refusal to anglicize a Jewish name and a Jewish identity. Starting in 1886
with her *Jewish Chronicle* series, Levy took on the identity of a persona
that could be called the Independent Jewess, a figure much like "Miss
Creak" in her autonomy and dedication to work, different only in that
she straddled the Jewish and gentile worlds. That Jews in the last decades
of the century were increasingly thought of as a racial group (and thus
immutable) makes Levy's strategy pragmatic but no less bold and hopeful than a more thoroughgoing transformation. Although Cynthia
Scheinberg did not know "Rondel" when she published "Canonizing the
Jew," the trope that she uses is noteworthy: "Levy herself never gave up
her Jewish name, and in choosing to publish as a Jewish woman, she took
up a particular challenge."[63]

At this time Levy began writing her urban poems (and experimenting with two fixed forms, the ballade and the rondel). In February and
March 1888 she published five lyrics about the city in a newspaper called
the *Star.* "Ballade of an Omnibus," one of these, celebrates the "city
pageant" that could be seen unfolding from the tops of the omnibuses
that were introduced into the London scene in the 1880s. Some of the
poem's humor comes from its juxtaposition of the archaic and the mod-

ern and from Levy's willingness to be self-referential: "The 'busman know me and my lyre / From Brompton to the Bull-and-Gate." Popular and high culture are also tossed together, with the speaker referring to herself as "A wandering minstrel, poor and free" (alluding to "The Mikado") and observing from her "summit" both "Croesus" and "Lucullus's phaeton." She envies neither of these classical figures because "an omnibus suffices me." Levy's lyre sings of the democracy of public transportation.

The poem reminds us that London in the 1880s offered women like Levy new opportunities for mobility and exposure. Her first novel, *Romance of a Shop* (which appeared later that year), conveys how transgressive it was for a woman to expose herself to the eye of the anonymous spectator. Gertrude's aunt is horrified by the sight of her niece "careening up the street on the summit of a tall, green omnibus, her hair blowing gaily in the breeze." In 1929 Katie Levy Solomon sent "Ballade of an Omnibus" to a London newspaper, along with the following letter: "The writer was among the first women in London to show herself on the tops of omnibuses. She excused herself to her shocked family circle by saying that she had committed the outrage in company with the daughter of a dean, who was also the grand-daughter of an Archbishop of Canterbury."[64] In this verbal snapshot we get a glimpse of Levy in a sassy and self-confident mood, delighted by the adventure she has shared with a pal who, given the account of her pedigree, has to have been Bertha Thomas.

"Ballade of a Special Edition,"[65] also a product of that winter, is about a figure that haunts Levy's writings—the hawker of tabloids who announces catastrophes. In "Sokratics in the Strand," such newsboys are part of the London crowd; in "Out of the World," Melissa imagines that she hears the hawker's cry; and in both *Romance of a Shop* and *Reuben Sachs* the announcement of a "Special Edition" is an important plot device. This image becomes an emblem of the power of calamity or death to interrupt any scene, no matter how tranquil. The figure of the newsboy conveys Levy's outraged understanding of how the media fed on the public's appetite for morbid news. Levy has her speaker fight back: she calls the hawker a "Fiend" and a "cheat" and insists that his news is apocryphal. The defiance in "Ballade of a Special Edition" is another sign of Levy's energy and optimism in the first part of 1888.

In "Women and Club Life," published in *Woman's World* later that year, Levy says that "the *flaneuse* of St. James's Street, latch-key in pocket and eye-glasses on nose, remains a creature of the imagination" (New's ed. 536). The *flaneur* is Baudelaire's word for the urban spectator, the man who strolled the streets of the metropolis looking at everything and everybody. Levy's observation about the *flaneuse* implies that while the city does not yet belong to women in the same way, she foresees a time when women will be as much at home in the modern cityscape as men. Aware that the sight of a woman alone in public still had the power to shock (and no doubt just as mindful that a female wayfarer was subject to the proprietary gaze), Levy made her way about London by omnibus and on foot, and some of the poems that finally appeared in *Plane-Tree* record those travels. The voice addressing a possible stranger in the last stanza of "Between the Showers" might even be that of a *flaneuse*: "Hither and thither, swift and gay / The people chased the changeful hours; / And you, you passed and smiled that day, / Between the showers."

There is no way of establishing when Levy wrote "A Ballad of Religion and Marriage," a poem so daring that she apparently felt that it could not be published.[66] Its vision of the future, wit, and overall tone suggest that it may have been a product of the first half of 1888, when she was in high spirits that were, for her, unusually sustained. Beginning with a reference to the defeat of an institution central to patriarchy—religion—the speaker affects a tone of dry amusement: "The Father, Son, and Holy Ghost, / Pale and defeated, rise and go." The humor of the second stanza is equally deadpan, with the words "Domestic round of boiled and roast" serving as a metonym for marriage. It is easy to imagine Levy smiling at her own understatement: married women are still at their "post," but they find "the whole proceeding slow." The refrain, which is phrased as a question at the end of the first stanza, is reworded in the second, becoming a declarative sentence that predicts the end of another institution at the heart of patriarchy: "Marriage must go the way of God." The boldness and optimism of Levy's revolutionary vision is contradicted by the measured tread of the rhythm, deepening the poem by problematizing its message.

In the final stanza the speaker prophesies that "in a million years at most, / Folks shall be neither pairs nor odd." The word *odd* may be evidence of how radical Levy allowed herself to be in this poem. Critics have usually assumed that Levy was using *odd* as George Gissing did in his novel *The Odd Women:* to refer to the so-called surplus women or redundant women of Victorian society, with the poem making a statement that in the absence of marriage coupledom will cease to be a meaningful category. This interpretation is not wrong, but *odd* probably carries a second meaning. Terry Castle tells us that *odd woman* and *odd girl* were among the slang terms for lesbian that "occur with . . . enticing regularity in . . . lesbian-themed writing."[67] "The Ballad of Religion and Marriage" may have been passed around in manuscript among Levy's friends, who would have enjoyed her encoded allusion to a future so liberated that the distinction between married and single *and* the distinction between heterosexual and homosexual would be meaningless.[68]

It must have seemed to Levy that her own good mood was matched by the nascent temper of the day—that release from constraints was in the air. The city was becoming more hospitable to women and easier for them to navigate; at least as bracing, the position of the woman writer was changing. Showalter says, "To the New Women of the 1880s and 1890s . . . feminine 'difference' was the basis of a developing Female Aesthetic." She cites Ella Hepworth-Dixon, who saw the writing of fiction as "'a political act of sexual solidarity'" and called for "'a kind of moral and social trades-unionism among women.'"[69] Oscar Wilde's *Woman's World,* new in 1888, played a part in creating a better atmosphere for women writers, for it provided an excellent place for women of ideas and talent to publish (often the articles take opposing views on women's issues).[70] It became the major outlet for Levy's writing at the end of her life, and the table of contents of the three volumes that were published from 1888 to 1890 reads like a roll call of her friends and acquaintances. The appearance of Elizabeth Sharp's anthology of women's poetry in the previous year had also been a major event in Englishwomen's literary history.

Levy's poetry had always contained signs of how much she was steeped in the work of her poetic foremothers, but her debt to them was not inscribed in the poems themselves through titles or subtitles as was her homage to the German male poets that she loved, and the list of favorite poets in her Confessions Book entry includes no women. Levy's "Dirge" (in *A Minor Poet*) is a good example of acknowledged and unacknowledged antecedents. Inspired by Heine's *"Mein Herz, mein Herz, ist traurig,"* it is also indebted to Christina Rossetti's "Dirge." In all three lyrics the anguish of the speakers is registered as unnatural (and therefore felt more keenly) because it is at odds with the apparent tranquillity and orderly well-being of things in the natural and the social world.[71] Levy's reticence about her female precursors is understandable because "poetesses" were not accorded much respect by the literary establishment, but now Sharp's collection—both by the quantity and quality of its poetry and by its feminist introduction—made a statement about how seriously the work of women should be treated.

Sharp declares that one hundred years earlier women poets found recognition more easily than in the present and that living writers in particular are "strangely, and one is inclined to say, ungenerously neglected." She adds, "Among the minor poets of this generation women have written more that is worthy to endure than men have done . . . the settlement of the question is within the power of every one who cares to go into the matter intelligently, sympathetically, and without prejudice."[72] A look at Victorian anthologies of poetry, even (or especially) those devoted to the work of women, reveals how much Sharp's book was needed.

Frederick Rowton's *Female Poets of Great Britain,* for example, published in 1850 (and reprinted many times), has an introduction in which he gabbles in the gender-lect of the mid-Victorian period that "Man's intellect is meant to make the world stronger and wiser, Woman's is intended to make it purer and better."[73] What is worse, he interjects his

commentary into the text itself, actually breaking up poems to inter-
sperse comments intended to guide the reader's response, often remark-
ing on whether the poetic text is appropriately feminine. Sharp's *Women's
Voices* is a sign that by the last part of the 1880s women poets were determined to wrest control from editors like Rowton and that they would
do so by working together. By allowing her poems to be included in
Sharp's book (and by attending the first meeting of the new Women
Writers' Club that was to meet for the first time in May 1889) Levy
openly aligned herself with other poets of her sex. The new esprit de
corps among literary women is probably what prompted her to write
"The Poetry of Christina Rossetti" for the first volume of *Woman's
World*.

Levy's papers reveal that at least by 1881 she was reading Christina
Rossetti, for she copied four lines from the second stanza of Rossetti's
"An 'Immurata' Sister" (in *A Pageant and Other Poems,* published that
year):

> *Men work & think, but women feel;*
> *And so (for I'm a woman, I)*
> *And so I should be glad to die*
> *And cease from impotence of zeal.*

Rossetti's stanza ends:

> *And cease from hope, and cease from dread,*
> *And cease from yearnings without gain,*
> *And cease from all this world of pain,*
> *And be at peace among the dead.*

William Rossetti, who edited his sister's poems (and knew that
Christina had written these lines in her notebook years before she used
them in her poem about a nun), said that the passage "was clearly a personal utterance."[74] Christina's sense of the limits on what was possible
for a woman must have given voice to Levy's own feelings of impotence

(and possibly despair) in 1881. Now, in 1888, the climate for women was changing in ways that would have allowed Levy to read Rossetti in a far more hopeful mood. Glancing at all of Christina Rossetti's published work, she lists "A Royal Princess," "Maude Clare," "The Hour and the Ghost," "The Ghost's Petition," and "Wife to Husband" as poems she can place "very high in our literature."[75] Levy is determined to consider her subject in relation to the entire canon of English poetry at the same time that she praises "Maude Clare" with the statement, "Only a woman could have written this poem" (180). Believing, it seems, in the "Female Aesthetic," she also needs to assure readers that she has enough literary sophistication to recognize Rossetti's limitations. Throughout, Levy alternates between apologizing for and praising Christina Rossetti, and she refrains from delivering a "verdict" or indulging "in prophecy as to its power of resisting the action of the waves of Time." Levy's insecurity, her ambivalence, is what is most valuable about this essay for our understanding of the woman writer in the fin de siècle. Even as female poets were gaining confidence in themselves and in one another, she found it necessary to take a defensive posture toward her subject. One wishes that Levy could read Angela Leighton's pronouncement: "Rossetti is undoubtedly one of the greatest poets of the nineteenth century. As a lyricist she is unsurpassed."[76]

The flood of work from Levy's pen that was published in 1888 includes the translations of Heine and Jehudah Halevi for Katie Magnus's *Jewish Portraits* and three short stories. Two of these stories show Levy moving in the direction that Showalter describes in her discussion of New Woman fiction: "Women novelists were seeking to create new kinds of narratives about female experience outside the conventional fictional destinies of marriage and death, availing themselves of a profusion of alternative fictional forms."[77] Among those alternative forms Showalter includes fantasies and allegories, and "The Recent Telepathic Occurrence at the British Museum" (published in *Woman's World*) shows Levy experimenting with fantasy. This story about male academics and female users of the British Library was described by Wilde as "a real literary gem . . . sent to me by a girl . . . who has a touch of genius in her work!"[78] "Griselda" (published in *Temple Bar*) is nothing new, one of Levy's potboilers though stylishly written. But the third of these fictions, "At Prato" (which appeared in *Time*), is another "literary gem," one that slipped from view to such an extent that Lask, Wagenknecht, and New, who do not mention it, must not have known of its existence.

Like "Griselda," "At Prato" is written to engage a wide audience—it is romantic and has an exotic setting. Its value as a commodity was no doubt enhanced by the presence of a woman who is a sad and beautiful sinner. But Levy defies conventions by refusing to punish the erring woman with death, and her story is not about Elinor but about Ivan Callendar, a Cambridge professor, who undergoes a profound transformation as a result of his encounter with her. Avoiding sentimentality, Levy combines graceful prose, a melodramatic plot that flirts with fantasy without quite shattering the conventions of realism, and the popular elements already mentioned. The story is written to entertain readers of light fiction, but it also has something to offer serious readers. "At Prato," like "The Late Telegraphic Occurrence," is about the arrogance and emotional ineptitude of intellectual Englishmen.

Callendar, "a tall, unmistakably English figure," assumes that he is superior to the Italians in Prato, especially "the strolling player and his wife" and the clown who entertain the crowd in the piazza on a moonlit night.[79] Chatting with the beautifully dressed Englishwoman, whom he has met accidentally, he displays racist assumptions that are placed in counterpoint to the attitudes of Elinor, the Englishwoman.[80] Ivan says about the crowd's enthusiasm for the clown, "'What a little it takes . . . to amuse these people'" (69) while Eleanor expresses curiosity about what it is that the clown does. Ivan assures her he does "'absolutely nothing . . . he can't do the simplest tricks of his trade.'" Eleanor replies, "'Perhaps he is clever and amusing. I wish I could understand Italian.'" In response, "Ivan permitted himself some assumption of masculine superiority"(70).

A funeral procession appears: "on the one hand, a masque of life, on the other, a masque of death, passing each other by without concern or recognition." The mysterious unknowability of life is emblemized by this polarity, yet Ivan assures Elinor that the dead person is at rest. With-out penetrating beyond the surface of life, this professor never doubts his ability to have answers, and so it does not occur to him that Elinor may not be the "English gentlewoman" that she seems. Noticing that her eyes are "inscrutable," he explains this to himself by quoting Francis Bacon. Wise as Bacon's words might be in some contexts, their function in the story is to reveal how Ivan allows his education to be a barrier to the truth.

Falling in love with Elinor—or, more accurately, with his idealized image of her—he bursts out, "'I love you . . . my whole life is yours—for you to take or refuse'" (72). When Ivan learns that Elinor left her hus-band for another man and, even worse, that she came to Prato that day with yet another lover, he is deeply shocked. Assuming that she needs to be "saved" and that this can be accomplished by contact with a pure woman, he exclaims, "'I have a sister, a good woman; let me take you to her.'" The revelation that Elinor planned their encounter affects him as if it were an even greater violation of morality than her adultery, but he still pleads "for the right to save her" (73) and is astonished when she van-ishes.

Near the end we are told, "Sometimes he wonders if it were indeed a living woman, or a beautiful sad vision that talked with him that night at Prato" (74). The story's conclusion leaves the reader with questions. On what level of reality did Ivan undergo the experience that triggered the "unaccountable indescribable . . . change affecting his whole person-ality?" And what did that transformation involve? Is the story in some sense an allegory for Ivan's spiritual and psychological crisis? Did the melodramatic and mysterious encounter literally take place? Did mis-taking appearance for reality in such a major way forever shake Ivan's sense of superiority?

Readers of this story should notice that when Ivan recommends the reading of *Romola*, Elinor, with the same hostility to George Eliot's solemnity that Elaine Showalter discusses,[81] retorts, "'I never could read 'Romola.' It's too much like an Italian *chiesa*, half museum, half church.'" And Levy's papers provide a postscript to "At Prato." The playful poem that Levy addressed to Clementina, which culminates in a reference to that night "at Prato when we missed the train" (cited at the start of chapter 7) has a middle stanza:

> Unto your Bradshaw, that misguiding
> Will o' the wisp, and hence to you.[82]
> Still in its mocking light confiding,
> Ivan and Elinor are due.

My guess is that "At Prato" began to germinate in Levy's imagination when she and Black visited Prato in 1886 and, observing a tall Englishman and a somewhat mysterious Englishwoman, gave them names and conjured up a tale about them.

Only one letter survives from Levy's correspondence with Vernon Lee in 1888 (32). Written in late June or early July, it is a response to a note from Lee that has brought the news that she will be going to Scotland but is "too smashed to see people."[83] Levy is disappointed but hardly crushed. Her life seems full. Dorothy Blomfield continues to delight her, and the two have just returned from a trip to her cottage in Geddington. Levy is correcting proofs for what must be *Romance of a Shop* while continuing to work on *Reuben Sachs*. She modestly acknowledges that the latter has "some stuff" but is dismissive about the former (writing to Katie—letter 33—Levy says that she cares about the reviews of her first novel only "for sale purposes; & it's as well to have the way paved for Reuben"). The distinction she makes between the two novels is worth thinking about, especially since Melvyn New argues that *Romance* is the better of the two; he notes that "it is almost twice as long as *Reuben*. . . . It seems possible that Levy's Jewishness has gotten in the way of a valid assessment of her achievements, most particularly as a feminist voice."[84] What New misses here is that Levy's "Jewish" novel is itself an important work of feminist fiction[85] and that *Reuben* is a far more ambitious and serious work. Levy makes this point in a manner that does not do justice to *Romance:* "I don't much care for the other one—wh. is slight & aims at the *young person*. You mustn't pitch into me about it—it fills its own aims, more or less, & I have purposely held in my hand." Also, Levy comments that Kit Anstruther-Thomson "is very unique & full of all sorts of beauties" though not a person she "cd. ever become intimate with . . . as with Dorothy." It is only in this letter (32) that Dorothy is not referred to as "Miss Blomfield."

Why was Vernon Lee "smashed" that summer, what had been going on in her life since meeting Amy Levy, and what was she like if we do not look at her through Levy's idealizing eyes? Lee's correspondence with her mother in 1887 and 1888 reveals that she was grappling with depression and ill health (not at all the "rock—morally & mentally speaking" that serves as Levy's metaphor for her in letter 32). She appears to have gone through a prolonged period of instability as a result of the termination of her relationship with Mary Robinson, who became engaged to a French Jew, James Darmesteter. In late August 1887 Robinson informed Vernon Lee of her decision to marry Darmesteter while Lee was visiting Kit Anstruther-Thomson at Charleton, an estate in Scotland that belonged to Kit's aristocratic and wealthy family.[86]

That month Lee had already begun a romantic relationship with Kit, probably understanding that Robinson was restless and making other plans; nevertheless, Lee's letters reveal that her health was shattered until at least 1889.[87] Kit, who had studied art in Paris, has been described as a "large, handsome woman whose interests until then were pretty evenly divided between horses and art."[88] It is hard to determine from Levy's comments whether at this point (early summer of 1888) she knew that Vernon and Kit were romantic partners. What she could not have known is that Vernon and Kit kept "a small pressed rose, preserved in an envelope, tucked among a sheaf of letters written by Vernon to Kit in 1887 and 1888"; on that envelope Vernon wrote, "Kit / Charleton, Aug. 24 / *Neue Liebe, Neues Leben*"[89]—the title of the love poem that Levy sent to Lee. That Vernon would use Levy's words to express feelings and hopes for a romantic liaison with someone else captures the pathos of their entire relationship. Lee cannot be blamed for not returning Levy's affection, but appropriating Levy's words of love shows an emotional insensitivity that was characteristic of her.

Writing about Vernon Lee, Irene Cooper Willis acknowledges that her friend's character was flawed: "There was, of course, a violently ego-tistical side to her. . . . She described herself perfectly once when she said to me: 'I *am* hard. I *am* cold. I like people as I like things, that is to say my likings are preferences for qualities that I can enjoy. Liking people does not for me mean devotion: it means only my answer, as it were, to qual-ities in them which please and charm me. . . . I have not got—I am per-fectly aware of it—a sympathy for people which goes out from me to them, independent of my own state of being bored or not.'"[90] Willis's perspective has to be measured against other evidence, of course, but Evelyn Wimbush's letters are themselves damning; they reveal that she was in love with Lee, who exploited her abject and obsessional passion.[91]

Was Levy still in love with Vernon Lee in 1888? Levy seems so happy in the letter she wrote that summer (letter 32), and her previous letter (31), in which she does not seem to mind that Blomfield too has received flowers from Lee, indicates that as time passed Levy revised her expec-tations of the relationship. Vernon Lee still had a special position in her emotional life, and Levy felt gratitude, aware that the past two and a half years had been a period of sustained well-being and extraordinary pro-ductivity at least in part because of their friendship: "Dorothy & I agreed that you made life interesting & vivid in quite a wonderful way; although I hardly ever see you, that time in Florence has made all the difference to me, & has made it more possible to carry on the—to me—burdensome business of living" (letter 32).

Levy's *Romance of a Shop* does not betray that its author finds the business of living burdensome. Most of the reviews that it drew refer to its "liveliness" and "vitality," and many of them, like the one in the *Spec-tator,* comment on the novel's "bright and sometimes witty" dialogue, its "epigrammatic sayings" and "sallies of mirth."[92] Fisher Unwin brought the novel out in October, and by the end of the month Levy left for Flo-rence. Just before her departure she wrote to the editor at Macmillan to say that she had completed the proofs for *Reuben Sachs.* Levy adds that if she has a "voice in the matter of binding," she "thinks the *Aspern Papers* with its double gold lines and dark cloth very nicely got up" but would choose "dark red cloth, not blue, for *Reuben Sachs.*"[93] If Levy's psyche had

had "Miss Creak" firmly at the helm—if achievement were enough—she would have felt buoyant about the almost simultaneous publication of her first two novels.

That she was not elated in the autumn of 1888 is probably an instance of what Richard Garnett had in mind when he said that Levy's "incapacity for pleasure . . . deprived her of the encouragement she might have received from the success" of her novels.[94] But the Hungry Poet in her did not allow achievement alone to be fulfilling. Levy continued to have an unsatisfied "appetite for all . . . Love, beauty, nameless joy of life" ("Minor Poet"). Trying to be philosophical about her disappointment, she was critical of this aspect of her personality, writing on the flyleaf of her own copy of her first volume of poems during her stay in Florence in 1888, "'The deepest root of moral disorder lies in an immoderate expectation of happiness.' John Morley, *Life of J. J. Rousseau.*"[95] As her moralizing would indicate, Levy was sad and lonely in Florence. Returning had been her goal since leaving the Italian city in March 1886, but even though she stayed again at the Casa Guidi, the city had lost its magic.

Vernon Lee had written to her mother from Kit's estate in October with a plan for how her friend might be put to use: "Miss Levy is ordered abroad for her health, and writes to me for addresses of pensions. . . . She is very forlorn, poor little body, for her deafness has not diminished. I suppose she might not do as Eugene's reader?"[96] There never was any chance that Levy would have cooperated with the scheme. In her first letter to Katie from Italy she mentions Eugene, Lee's half-brother, a bedridden poet who resided with his mother: "Lee-Hamilton has sent me his poems with a well-turned compliment scrawled on the fly-leaf. I called the other day, but thank God, he was out. . . . The poems are dreadful."

In the same letter Levy is frankly unhappy, consoled only by the presence of Bertha Thomas and the pleasures of reading *War and Peace* (in French): "the most enthralling book I have ever read . . . my guide, philosopher, & friend for the time being" (letter 33). Her second letter tells of meeting Vernon's friend Bella Duffy,[97] whom she describes as falling "upon me with apparent mash at once" (letter 34). She is joking, but Duffy became a friend, and, when Levy went home to London, Bella Duffy gave her as a gift the *Calendrier* for 1889 that is a major source of information about the last year of her life. Expecting *Reuben Sachs* to appear any day, Levy says facetiously to Katie, "any day you may wake to find yrself once more an aunt. (& Joe an uncle)," and observes that "Reviews of *The Shop* continue good, in a damn-with-faint-praise fashion." This letter, despite its jocular reports on activities, people, and books, shows how right Lee was when she described Levy as "forlorn."

Inserted between a report on her reading and the news that she has been invited to "five tea-parties" Levy admits, "I'm not well & horribly sad. I don't think so much time for thinking over one's sunken ships is exactly good for one." Toward the close she adds, "I hope to hear . . . that I've played my last card & lost" (letter 34). Katie Levy Solomon no doubt knew what Levy meant by the figures of speech she uses in this letter ("sunken ships" and "last card"), but over a hundred years later there is only conjecture. My surmise is that she was anticipating rejection by a lover or a person she wanted as a lover and knew that she should give up hope. In such a situation, she felt that receiving final word would give her some relief.

Levy's third letter to Katie reports that she is "rather better," perhaps because she and Duffy have begun to see each other "nearly every day. We have begun to read Dante together" (letter 35). Levy does not appear to be in the throes of her "devil." But the surviving fragment of a letter to Clementina, almost certainly written at this time, is the most fully articulated expression of what Levy experienced when depression washed over her (and the first sign that Levy feared insanity). That this note (letter 36) ends with a love poem about a woman supports my supposition that Levy once again was disappointed in love.

The lyric, never published before its inclusion in this volume, is, from a literary standpoint, quite fine. Titled "Imitation of Heine," it is Levy's own composition, but it manages, without being overly derivative, to capture Heine's sensibility perfectly. After two stanzas about a party where everyone is dancing with joyful abandon, the third stanza ends with the lines: "Then someone went by in the brightness—/ A woman with eyes like you." The poem concludes,

> The laughter, the leaping, the chatter,
> Went on as before without rest;—
> O I wished the walls wd. close round me
> And crush the life from my breast.

"The First Extra," which Levy had published that same autumn, has a speaker who tells of the "bliss" of *dancing* with a beloved person until a rose falls to the floor to be *"crushed"* to death (emphasis added). The similarity of the images in the two poems is striking, as is the way that in both joy turns into its opposite, and love is equated with death. The third stanza of "The First Extra" explains that "Love is like a rose" because it is "A tender flow'r that lives an hour / And is most sweet in death."

But who was Levy in love with? Vernon Lee's remarks about Levy in the letter to her mother give little reason to think that Levy could have had any reason for a resurgence of hopefulness about that relationship. Of course, Levy could have been enamored of someone she does not mention in her letters. But Dorothy Blomfield is a likely candidate.[98] Levy mentions her every time she writes to Lee, always with enormous affection and appreciation for her qualities of mind and character, acknowledging their intimacy most openly in the letter written in the summer of 1888, where she says "Dorothy and I" as if they were a couple; on holiday together, they behave like lovers: "We talked all the time, & drove about in the rain, in a high dog-cart with a frisky horse"(letter 32). Most telling, after being a presence in every letter written to Lee, Blomfield is all but absent from Levy's 1889 calendar, which she kept meticulously. Returning home on the January 17, Levy got together with other friends immediately; finally having tea with Dorothy on the last day of January, she never saw her again. Something happened to end that friendship (or love affair). A letter from Blomfield calling off the relationship may have been the "last card" that Levy was in a hurry to receive so that the matter would be resolved.

8

Two Novels
Romance of a Shop and *Reuben Sachs*

Like "At Prato," *Romance of a Shop* offers first-rate entertainment to a wide audience. Educated readers grounded in serious fiction as well as readers accustomed to reading trivial novels could (and can) read it with pleasure if they do not expect profound truths about life. Because the novel to some degree disrupts the traditional distinction between popular culture and high art, Levy's book anticipates the New Woman novel of the 1890s.[1] Deborah Nord is right in recognizing that a good deal of the charm of *Romance of a Shop* comes from its success at conveying "how difficult and yet how exhilarating it was to be a woman alone in London in the 1880s"; she cites Levy's protagonist, Gertrude, who has a "secret childish love for the gas-lit street, for the sight of hurrying people, the lamps, hansom cabs, flickering in and out of the yellow haze, like so many fireflies" (110).[2] Despite Levy's negative attitude toward the informal, servantless flat where Clementina Black lived with her sisters, she has the Lorimers live in much the same style (though she gives them considerably less freedom from social convention and does not have them attend political meetings).

Nord believes that "Levy's first novel . . . anticipates Gissing's novel *The Odd Women*" in that it is about orphaned sisters who are left "virtually penniless by a . . . reckless father" though she understands that Gertrude and Lucy Lorimer, Levy's heroines, "look forward to Gissing's Rhoda Nunn and Mary Barfoot" rather than to the orphaned Madden sisters.[3] The only really striking parallel between the two novels is the *donnée* of the two plots: what happens to middle-class girls reared to be dependent creatures who find themselves on their own? The two elder Madden sisters daydream about setting up a school while Gertrude and Lucy Lorimer use their small capital and their skills as photographers to set up a photography shop.

In mood, however, the two novels could not be more different, and this is a consequence of genre. While both can be classed as New Women novels, *The Odd Women* (1891) shows the influence of French Naturalism: as a result of both nurture and nature the Madden sisters lack the energy and discipline to take hold of their lives. In contrast, *Romance of a Shop* (as the title suggests) is a romantic comedy: Gertrude and Lucy Lorimer, vitalized by the need to fend for themselves and their sisters, are successful as artists, as entrepreneurs, and, to use a phrase from the novel, in "matters matrimonial." Moreover, Levy complicates the question of genre by having *Romance* adhere in a purposely exaggerated way to the conventions of Victorian realism.

Nord's complaint that the last third of the novel resembles a shoddy *Pride and Prejudice*—"all four sisters searching for the appropriate mate"—emanates from the misconception that Levy started out to write the kind of New Woman novel that Ann Ardis believes should be valued for its ideological experimentation.[4] The notices of *Romance of a Shop* reveal that by 1888 there was nothing daring about the representation of young, independent women attempting to earn their own living. One reviewer, summarizing the plot of Levy's novel, says it is about sisters who take "to photography as a means of gaining a living" and remarks, "This seems a sufficiently tame theme."[5] Another review discloses that this plot line had become conventional: "The notion of young ladies, who are suddenly turned out of affluence into poverty, supporting themselves by trade or something like it, is, of course, not new, but it is not yet exhausted. The last time we met it, it was dressmaking, now it is photography."[6] None of the commentators on Levy's novel were even slightly shocked by anything in it except the treatment of Phyllis, the youngest Lorimer, a beauty who falls from virtue not because she was in love but as a consequence of boredom. The reviewer for the *Spectator* hopes this turn of plot is "untrue to Nature."[7] Nearly all of the reviewers agree that Phyllis's fall is a fault even though Levy bows to convention by sentencing Phyllis to death by consumption, a turn of plot that allows its author to give the Victorian reading public what it loved—a heartrending deathbed scene.

To point out that readers of Levy's time would have found much that was familiar in *Romance of a Shop* is not to fail to appreciate her achievement. We must remember that she said that the book "aims at the *young person*," and "I have purposely held in my hand" (letter 32). Gertrude says about the man who nearly succeeded in seducing Phyllis, "Happiness . . . is not for such as he—for the egoist and the sensualist" (New's ed. 154), and in this novel she is right. While appearing to imitate reality, *Romance* gives the reader entree to a universe where bad people always fail to flourish and the good are rewarded. Although Phyllis is not evil, she is permitted to die young because one of the ways she stands out from her sisters is that her values are aesthetic, not moral. Examining the photographs that Gertrude has taken of the corpse of Lady Watergate, an adulteress, Phyllis says, "Poor thing . . . Mrs. Maryon told us she was wicked, didn't she? But I don't know that it matters about being good when you are as beautiful as all that" (93).

Romance of a Shop has an omniscient narrator with a singular and epigrammatic voice. That narrator is totally in control of the meaning of the text—that is, the novel is completely monologic. This is only one of the ways in which it conforms—a textbook example—to what are usually considered the conventions of nineteenth-century realism. The dialogue is realistically colloquial, often slangy, and Levy's protagonist gives the illusion that she is a real human being while never ceasing to be what in today's jargon is called a unitary self. Gertrude is "strong-minded" (independent and willing to challenge social convention albeit in mild ways), torn by contradictory impulses, and yet at bottom an "angel" who, despite her own longings, always puts the needs of others first. Phyllis too is characterized in such a way that she appears truer to life than she actually is. Called a "spoilt pet" by the reviewer for the *Spectator*,[8] she has a highly developed aesthetic sensibility and an underdeveloped moral sense. Her doom is predictable because her nature is fixed even though she is by no means a stock character. In this first novel Levy's approach to characterization is markedly different from that of other writers of New Woman fiction, who, as Ardis points out, usually invalidate the notion that "identity is single, seamless, and coherent."[9] Levy has characters (minor ones) who are familiar types: Fanny (the half-sister) is a comical old maid whom Levy, by authorial fiat, manages to marry off by contriving the return of a former suitor, and Sydney Darrell, Phyllis's villainous would-be seducer, is a familiar type. But stock characters in minor roles are standard in works of Victorian realism.

The novel also conforms to the conventions of realism in that it is full of the slang of the day and topical references—epigraphs from and allusions to actual popular songs, poetry, contemporary novels, and Gilbert and Sullivan operettas—and to political figures and tabloid journalism. Phenomena of the moment—like the advent of omnibuses—make an appearance, and references to England's expanding empire are plentiful. Levy's critique of the narrowness and materialism of mainstream middle-class life must have been somewhat thought-provoking at the time, and the novel's perspective is feminist, but not, as the reviews make clear, in a way that would jar any but the most conservative readers.

As a model of the realism of its age *The Romance of a Shop* even has a moral vision: first, that meaningful work, economic autonomy, and (if they have the inner resources that Phyllis lacks) the absence of chaperonage help women to become mature human beings; second, that "an ideal society" would be, as Gertrude says, "not of class, caste, or family —but of picked individuals" (120). Moreover, Levy's novel announces that it is an example of Victorian realism in that its plot is so firmly resolved: the narrator goes beyond the ending to tell us what happens to all the characters, even mentioning figures as unimportant as the Lorimers' landlords, the Maryons. It is here that Levy's exaggeration of the conventions of the classic Victorian novel—and its satire of the genre—is most obvious, for the reader is even told of the destiny of the studio and the flat at Twenty B Baker Street after the Lorimers have vacated it.

Steeped in the work of writers of genius like Thackeray and Charlotte Brontë, Levy at times in this novel makes her prose echo passages in *Jane Eyre* so audaciously that the effect is comic.[10] There can be no doubt that she learned her craft from the masters; it is equally clear that she learned from writing for the market that fiction was based on literary formulas. In *Romance* Levy works deftly with conventions that would be tired if she did not amuse the sophisticated reader with outrageous self-reflexivity. For example, when Frank Jermyn (now Lucy's fiancé) goes to Africa, where the British are having colonial troubles, he is believed to be dead after a newspaper hawker announces, "Terrible slaughter of British troops!" The narrator moralizes about death, "the great mystery," and Lucy struggles to bear her loss, but foolish Fanny remarks, "People always come back in books"(166). Six chapters later he is back.

An important theme in *Romance of a Shop* is the artist's need to accommodate her or himself to the tastes of those who consume art as a commercial product—without sacrificing all standards of quality. Frank Jermyn had originally planned to be a painter, and at the start of *Romance* Gertrude is writing a verse-drama about the French revolutionary figure Charlotte Corday. (The comparison with Levy's own *Xantippe* and *Medea* should be noted.) But Frank is happy to have a steady job doing photographs for *The Illustrated News*. He stops by the Lorimers' flat to show them an issue of another publication, "*The Woodcut,* damp from the press," because it has his wood engraving of a tennis court, together with Gertrude's poem about lawn tennis. She says ruefully, "It is rather a come down after *Charlotte Corday,* isn't it?" (126). Frank replies, "We all have to get off our high horse, Miss Lorimer, if we want to live. I had ten guineas this morning for that thing." He then observes that his work of high art—*The Death of Oedipus*—stands "with its face to the wall in the studio" (126).

Levy must have laughed while writing this novel, for her self-referentiality extends beyond its world. Gertrude's poem about tennis is actually Levy's "A Game of Lawn-Tennis," which had appeared in *Lawn-Tennis* two years earlier (and was reprinted in *Plane-Tree* almost a year later after her death). Another inside joke, one that at the time *Romance* came out could have amused only Levy's family and those who knew her well, is that Levy has wealthy Lord Watergate (whom Gertrude ends up marrying) live where the Levys had resided from 1872 to 1884. When Gertrude must go to Lord Watergate's home for the first time, Lucy says, "I know he lives in Regent's Park, and the address . . . is Sussex Place" (91). Arriving at his home, Gertrude observes "the white curve of houses with the columns, the cupolas, and the railed-in space of garden that fronted the Park" (92).

That Levy's first novel neither strives for profundity nor reaches for originality is not a demerit; she shows that she could do both in *Reuben Sachs*. But in *Romance* she is targeting a popular audience, and the novel is her answer to those who complained about the tyranny of "New Grub Street." Like her heroine Gertrude, Levy accepted the commodification of fiction, and she set out to show that commercial art need not be base. She achieves her goal by overconforming to the devices of what post-modern critics often call "Classic Realism."[11]

The truly great Victorian novels transcend realism's conventions (while often providing a vision of life that is anything but sentimental), and their meaning is sometimes as multiple as those in many works of fiction written in the twentieth century;[12] the omniscient narrator of the best works of Victorian realism may even lack what Penny Boumelha calls a "controlling 'truth-voice'";[13] the plot (to the extent that it is contrived) may be archetypal or covertly symbolic;[14] and the main characters not so consistent that they never surprise us by behaving out of character. The relationship of Levy's first novel to Victorian realism is parodic because *Romance* adheres so faithfully to formulas that its own artifice is exposed. In calling attention to its imitation of art rather than life, *Ro-*

mance of a Shop should be read as a product of late Victorian aestheti-
cism, which, as Regina Gagnier argues, was determined (paradoxically)
by "the emerging service and consumerist economy."[15]

Romance of a Shop is a clever book, but Levy's methods in *Reuben
Sachs* are more ambitious and complex and her purposes more serious.
Levy's article "The Jew in Fiction," the second in the series she wrote in
1886, had called for "a serious treatment . . . of the complex problem of
Jewish life and Jewish character," and she had finally responded to her
own call. When the novel opens, Reuben, a rising young lawyer, has just
returned from "the antipodes," where he had gone to recover from a nervous breakdown. His father, we are told, died years before, and the narrator establishes that his death was premature by reporting that
longevity runs in this family. As the various members of Reuben's family are introduced, we find that nearly all the men are defective—sick or
nervous. His cousin Esther's father is in a madhouse, and another cousin,
Ernest Leuniger ("of whom it would be unfair to say that he was an
idiot"), is "nervous, delicate," and has "a rooted aversion to society"
(204). He spends his time playing solitaire, a game that involves a board,
marbles, and a little glass ball. The meaninglessness of his obsessive
desire to win is apparent when, near the end of the novel, he is finally
successful: Judith, the female protagonist, is "vaguely kind" but unim-
pressed. This solitary game symbolizes the competitive individualism to
which Reuben and, to a lesser extent, nearly all the male Jews in this
novel dedicate their lives. Levy reminds us of the prevailing ethos by frequently employing the diction of Social Darwinism—old Solomon
Sachs, for instance, "was blest with that fitness for which survival is the
inevitable reward" (213).

Reuben betrays his cousin Judith because his ambition requires that
he marry a wealthy woman; the night after he rejects her "there was a
withered, yellow look about him," and his mother thinks, "He is not
well." By the novel's end he is dead. Judith is told that "his heart was
weak . . . cardiac disease was the cause of his death—cardiac disease."
The redundancy of the wording emphasizes that Reuben died as a result
of not attending to his own emotional needs. The Jewish women are

expected to be ambitious and competitive in a different way. Judith sees "herself as merely one of a crowd of girls awaiting their promotion by marriage" (209). Such marriages have little to do with love. While Judith's mother says, "No girl likes her intended—at first" (279), all of the married women are, as Rochelson says in her article on *Reuben Sachs*, "stunted or disappointed"[16] (about two-thirds of the way through the novel the focus shifts from Reuben to Judith Quixano, and the previously secondary feminist theme becomes prominent).

Although passionately in love with Reuben, once Judith has lost him she obediently makes a socially advantageous marriage to Bertie Lee-Harrison,[17] whose conversion to Judaism is treated satirically (he shops around, trying different religions, and has already "'flirted with the Holy Mother" and "joined a set of mystics . . . somewhere in Asia Minor" [205]).[18] At the novel's end Judith, married to Bertie (who remains an outsider), feels "a strange fit of homesickness, an inrushing sense of exile." Levy evokes her character's inner life by first having the narrator describe how Judith feels and then letting the narrative slip into free indirect discourse: "A sudden longing for old faces, the old ties and associations came over her as she stood there; a strange fit of homesickness, an inrushing sense of exile. . . . Her people—oh, her people!—to be back once more among them!" (289).

In "The Jew in Fiction" Levy had asked for novels that would represent "the Jew as we know him today, with his curious mingling of diametrically opposed qualities; his surprising virtues and no less surprising vices; leading his eager intricate life." Although it may not seem so from what has been said so far, Levy conforms to these objectives by offering a range of perspectives on Jews and Jewish life in *Reuben Sachs*. The attractive thing about the members of Reuben and Judith's extended family is that they love each other to an almost remarkable, though always credible, degree. When Reuben returns from his voyage at the start, he can hardly wait to see his cousins, the Leunigers, and the other kin that live with them or frequent their home. When he enters, his little cousins throw themselves at him adoringly, and he responds with affection. The Leunigers have taken Judith, a niece whose family has no money, into their home, and she "shared everything with her cousin Rose: the French and German governesses, the expensive music lessons, the useless, pretentious 'finishing lessons.'" When the young women went into society, "no difference had been made between them. The gowns and bonnets of Rose were neither more splendid nor more abundant than those of her poor relation" (208).[19] Reuben's mother, whom we might expect to dislike Judith out of fear that Reuben would make a materially disadvantageous marriage to her, "admires the girl immensely, and at the bottom of her heart was fond of her" (215). Recognizing that Leo "regards me at present as an incarnation of the seven deadly sins" (219), Reuben nonetheless feels tender toward his cousin. Of old Solomon, the family patriarch, we are told that "his love for his children had been the romance of an eminently unromantic career" (215). Levy is able to evoke all this familial affection without ever slipping into sentimentality, truly an achievement in a Victorian novel. In its representation of family ties the novel may be a conscious revision of the image of Jewish family disloyalty in English literature—for example, Trollope's *The Way We Live Now* (Ragussis traces the myth of family betrayal back to *The Merchant of Venice*).[20]

Reuben speaks movingly of Jewish "love of race, home, and kindred" and elaborates on the ties that hold Jews together:

> "If we are to die as a race, we shall die harder than you think. . . . That strange strong instinct which has held us together so long is not a thing easily eradicated. . . . Jew will gravitate to Jew, though each may call himself by another name. If prejudice died, if difference of opinion died, if all the world, metaphorically speaking, thought one thought and spoke one language, there would still remain unspeakable mysteries, affinity and—love." (240)

The word *affinity* is important here because it appears in the epigraph Levy uses at the start of "Leopold Leuniger: A Study." She quotes there from Clough: "Juxtaposition is great—but you tell me affinity is greater."[21] In that early story Leuniger is not drawn to his people, the Jews, but to Gerald Sydenham, an aristocrat, and to Gerald's sister, Lady Lilian. The affinity he feels with them turns out to be problematic because of the anti-Semitism of Gerald's cousin Lord Norwood and his friends. But the affinity for the Jews that Reuben speaks of in the novel is compromised by his own behavior. Much more likable than the minor character with the same name in another story that exists only in manuscript in the Amy Levy collection, "St. Anthony's Vicarage," Reuben is a man whose contradictory behavior far transcends the deviations from type allowed to most characters in realistic fiction. Despite his affirmation of love for his people, he eventually puts the achievement of power and social position ahead of his commitment to Judith. That she is his own kin reopens the question of family loyalty.

Reuben's cousin Leo (in the early story he had been Leopold) has not undergone a transformation in moving from one text to another. Still eager to be accepted by the aristocratic set at Cambridge, he believes that Jews and Jewish life are no different from what anti-Semites say they are. Eliciting Reuben's impassioned defense of his people by proclaiming that he looks forward to the "absorption" of the Jews, Leo asks, "'Where else do you see such eagerness to take advantage; such sickening, hideous greed; such cruel, remorseless striving for power and importance; such ever-active vanity, that must be fed at any cost? Steeped to the lips in sordidness . . . how is it possible that any one among us, by any effort of his own, can wipe off from his soul the hereditary stain?'"(239). His rhetoric comes so directly from age-old anti-Semitic diatribes—and his loathing of his own kind is so extreme—that the reader is likely to be uneasy about his judgment. That discomfort is warranted; Levy explores the theme of Jewish self-hatred in *Reuben Sachs* as she did in "Leopold Leuniger: A Study."[22]

That the novel and the story address this subject does not in itself mean that either rejects negative attitudes about Jews. In *Reuben Sachs* Leo's point of view has as much weight as Reuben's affirmative perspective. Both are presented for consideration and both are undermined.

Reuben *does* strive for power and importance, while Leo's antipathy for Jews is made suspect by the rhetoric he uses to attack them. Moreover, the identification he makes between the upper-class gentile world and the art and culture he learned to love at Cambridge is put in doubt when the narrator tells us that Lord Norwood, Leo's aristocratic friend, has an "exceedingly *borné* mind" [narrow, restricted] and lacks even "a drop of artist's blood in his veins" (246). Levy uses the narrative voice repeatedly in this way—to allow us to see Leo's aristocratic friends from another angle. The narrator describes Lady Geraldine (his friend's sister) for whom Leo has "a hopeless passion" as "a thin, pale person, with faint colouring, a rather receding chin, and slightly prominent teeth" (248).

Because the early story about young Leuniger is unpublished, readers have been unable to appreciate fully the way that Levy weakens Leo's point of view in her novel; nuances of meaning in Leo's relationship with the aristocrats that he idealizes emerge only intertextually.[23] In *Reuben Sachs* Gerald Sydenham, Leopold's friend in the story, is gone, and the aristocratic friend is the narrow-minded, haughty, and snobbish Lord Norwood. The object of Leo's affections is homely Lady Geraldine —not Lady Lilian as in "Leopold Leuniger," whose "tall slight figure" was described as "completely harmonious" and whose face was "fair." Not even Leo thinks Lady Geraldine is pretty, a suggestion, perhaps, that he is beginning to see his gentile friends more clearly.

We are told that "Reuben . . . understood perhaps more of Leopold's state of mind than anyone suspected, of the struggles within himself, the revolt against his surroundings which the lad was undergoing" (219). This glimpse of a different, younger Reuben who did not feel good about his Jewishness[24] is an indication that Levy believed young Jews were likely to undergo a developmental process in which self-hatred was a way station, not an endpoint. The narrative voice plunges the reader forward beyond the frame of the novel to reveal that Leo's attitudes will indeed change: "The time was yet to come when he should acknowledge to himself the depth of tribal feeling, of love for his race, which lay at the root of his nature" (229). That Levy could have her narrator make such a statement about this character—an alter ego for her—has considerable significance biographically.

But is the narrator in this novel trustworthy? The answer is sometimes yes and sometimes no. The reader is likely to accept what the narrator says about how Leo's feelings toward his people will change; the prediction is backed up by what has been implied about the stages of Reuben's own development (in that passage he says, understandingly, about Leo, "He is in a ticklish stage of his growth"). But when the narrator says, "If there is strong family feeling among the children of Israel, it takes often the form of acute family jealousy" (249), the remark strikes a false note, for there is so much evidence that the Sachses and the Leunigers are unusually fond of one another. The pronouncement is particularly suspect because the narrator makes this remark just as Rose and Judith are happily planning a party together, their camaraderie undimmed by the assertion that Judith "while she had her admirers, was by no means such a success as her cousin" (249).

We are likely to lose confidence in the narrative voice when it says about cousin Esther (who has refused to go to synagogue on the Day of Atonement), "She, poor soul, was of those who deny the existence of the Friend of whom she stood so sorely in need" (230). Given the irreverent attitude toward Judaism as a religion in *Reuben Sachs*, the reader may wonder who is this "Friend" the narrator is talking about? There has been no previous indication that the universe is watched over by a caring, or indeed, any other kind of God. If the narrator is referring to God, he cannot be a Jewish deity, so another thought comes to mind: is the narrator a gentile? If so, the many pronouncements of the narrative voice are put in doubt, particularly the ones that generalize about how physically unattractive, materialistic, and ruthlessly ambitious Jewish people are. Did Levy put these offensive remarks about Jews into the mouth of the narrator to expose that speaker's anti-Semitism?

The narrator's objectivity is again cast in a questionable light when she tells us that the aristocratic Norwoods "were not rich, not 'smart,' not politically important; but in their own fashion they were people of the best sort, true aristocrats, such as few remain to *us* in these degenerate days" (246, emphasis added). The narrator's sentiment suggests that she is a member of society's elite, and Levy's phrases—"people of the best sort" and "in these degenerate days"—mimic and mock the tone of a snob. The "us" in this passage excludes the Jewish characters—that is, nearly everybody in the novel. But a few pages later the narrator tells us that Reuben, the Jew, is much more open-minded and intelligent than Lord Norwood, disturbing the notion that we have identified the narrator as a snobbish gentile.

The relationship between the narrator and the narrative is slippery because Levy wants the reader to understand that it is impossible to establish the truth about the Jews. In "The Doctor" and "Sokratics in the Strand" Levy had employed narrative techniques that allowed her to represent people whose image was often obscured by received ideas. In those stories the stereotypes that distort society's view of people on the margins are undermined by indications that the speaker (narrator or mainstream character) is not reliable. The narrative strategies in *Reuben Sachs* have their seeds in those stories. But Levy herself was sure of where she stood in regard to women doctors and depressed people while she may never have been able to maintain a consistent attitude toward the Anglo-Jewish community.

Although narrated in the third person, *Reuben Sachs* lacks an omniscient point of view. The story is told either by one narrator whose perspective keeps shifting and who is a kind of ventriloquist (able to speak in several social dialects) or by divergent voices that are not explicitly differentiated from one another. The voice that tells us Reuben is superior to Lord Norwood has neither the same attitudes nor the same style of speech as the voice that asserts that the Norwoods are "people of the best sort." When the narrator tells us that the Leunigers had treated Judith exactly as they treated their own daughter, she appears to contradict what we have been told about strong family feeling among Jews often taking the form of jealousy. There is no denying that Levy's experimentation with narrative technique puts an enormous demand on the reader and leads to confusion.

Levy also makes extensive use of free indirect discourse. In her practice the shift from the narrator's perspective and language into the point of view and diction of the character and back again is usually abrupt, not the gradual modulation that is more common. Often when she employs this technique, she evokes inner life with exclamations and especially with questions. To illustrate:

> The thought of Judith took more and more possession of him [Reuben], till his pulses beat and his senses swam.
> Ah, why not, why not?
> Children on his hearth with Judith's eyes, and Judith there herself amongst them: Judith, calm, dignified, stately, yet a creature so gentle withal, so sweet, so teachable!
> He looked again and again at this picture of his fancy . . . alarmed at his own fascination. (241)

Levy's use of indirect discourse adds the style of thought and speech of her major characters to the cacophony created by the multiplicity of narrative voices in the novel.

In 1883 Levy had written a letter to the *Chronicle* about the half-Jewish novelist Paul Heyse, a German. Signed by Keran Numi, the pen name Levy used for all of her *Jewish Chronicle* writing (except the letter she wrote at seventeen), it indicates that at the age of twenty-three Levy believed that the various races and nations had particular qualities of mind and character and that she assumed those differences were a matter of "blood" (i.e., inherited). She said, "The Jewish nature, with its strange pride and strange humility; its surprising toughnesses and no less surprising sensibilities; its curious mixture of mart and temple; its quaint juxtaposition of the sublime and the ridiculous: this Jewish nature in full has not descended to Heyse, but his Jewish blood has perceptibly leavened his whole individuality."[25] One must bear in mind that, as Cheyette and Ragussis establish, nearly everyone in Levy's time had essentialist notions about "racial" character. This letter supports my reading of *Reuben Sachs* because it shows Levy's enduring interest in the "nature" of the Jew; it demonstrates, moreover, that even during the period when she seems to have been most troubled by her Jewishness, she maintained some connection with organized Anglo-Jewry and had a conception of Jewish character that was far from entirely negative.

But the letter shows certainty about "Jewish nature" while *Reuben Sachs* is interlocutory. To the extent that the novel responds to the question of what Jews and Jewish life are like, its responses conflict to such an extent that they may appear to cancel each other out. But they do not. Instead we get answers that are multiple—so that *Reuben Sachs* is truly polyphonic. The novel's variety of perspectives on Jews draws on layers of Levy's experience and feelings that evolved over time, but it would be too simple to say that when Reuben speaks in defense of the Jews he is the mouthpiece of the Amy Levy who wrote *Reuben Sachs* while Leo speaks for the Amy Levy who wrote the anti-Semitic letter about the "evil-looking Hebrews" in a German synagogue (letter 16). Even that letter, however disturbing, was not written without irony; at the very moment Levy was venting self-hatred and shame she was also scrutinizing and mocking her response to those foreign Jews.

In "Jewish Children," one of the *Chronicle* articles, Levy makes us see that George Eliot, even in a novel written in part to counter anti-Semitic ideas, was only partially able to extricate herself from the stock of notions and language found in the dominant discourse about Jews. Levy calls our attention to Eliot's descriptions of the progeny of Ezra Cohen, the Jewish shopkeeper in *Daniel Deronda*. She reminds the reader that the voice of Jacob Alexander Cohen, the pawnbroker's son, is described as "'hoarse in its glibness, as if it belonged to an aged commercial soul, fatigued with bargaining for many generations'"; that Cohen's daughter Adelaide Rebekah is described as having "'monumental features'"; and that the baby of the family "'carries on her teething intelligently'" and "'looks about her with such precocious interest'" (New's ed. 528).

Despite her recognition that even in her philo-Semitic *Daniel Deronda*, Eliot drew on unexamined assumptions about Jews to create some of the Jewish characters, Levy said in "The Jew in Fiction," published in the same year as "Jewish Children," "There is yet to be done for [the Jew] what M. Daudet has done for the inhabitants of Southern

France. No picture of English 19th century life and manners can be considered complete without an adequate representation of the modern sons of Shem." Alphonse Daudet was a French Naturalist, and in 1886 Levy called for what the Naturalists tried to provide: an ethnography, an objective picture of a society. But by 1887 or 1888, when Levy began to write *Reuben Sachs,* she had gained sophistication about the nature of fiction; she no longer believed that a novelist could represent "reality" objectively. My discussion of *Romance of a Shop* emphasized Levy's keen awareness that art was conventional in its very nature and that this understanding allowed her to work with fictional formulas in a knowing manner.

Reuben Sachs, like *Romance,* mimics literary conventions. Her narrator often appears to adopt the ethnographic stance of a Zola or a Daudet, both of whom describe the appearance and explain the ways of the lower classes, people living sordid lives that middle-class readers would not know about (Daudet's *Sapho,* published in 1884, is about a prostitute). That most members of the British reading public did not know about the social group represented in *Reuben Sachs* is apparent in the reviews: the writer for the *Academy* says the Jews "are a people of whom the outside world knows but little."[26] Evidence that literary people thought the Jews—or any fragment of society—could be represented without subjective bias is easy to come by, but the report on Levy's novel written by the reader for Macmillan is of particular interest. He says: "It is a most effective bit of narrow and close photography. . . . She apparently has no concealed moral or deliberate purpose—but simply describes for description's sake. The people are not made at all *excessively* [emphasis added] disagreeable; but are painted just (I should think) as they really are in the synagogue, shopping at Whiteley's, dining, and so on."[27]

In *Reuben Sachs* the narrator's many generalizations about the behavior and appearance of Jews *seem* to be descriptions of Jews "as they really are"—for example, strong family feeling among Jews takes the form of jealousy; "the Jewish people . . . so determined in laying claim to the successful among their number, have scant love for those unfortunates who have dropped behind in the race" (235); Reuben's sister Adelaide has "the gregarious instincts of her race" (222); "the race instincts of Rebecca of York are strong, and she is less apt to give her heart to Ivanhoe, the Saxon knight, than might be imagined" (242); "Leo was by no means free from the tribal foible of inquisitiveness" (243); Judith "was one of the few people of her race who look well at a distance" (251); "The charms of person which a Jew or Jewess may possess are not usually such as will bear the test of being regarded as a whole" (251); "Some quite commonplace English girls and men who were here tonight looked positively beautiful . . . among the ill-made sons and daughters of Shem" (251).

With statements of this kind Levy is imitating and parodying novels that contain negative remarks about Jews. By piling up *too many* generalizations about Jews, she caricatures fiction replete with anti-Semitic images and ideas. She also offers a critique of realism, and takes a particular jab at Naturalism, which took its thesis from the post-Darwinian biological tenet that human beings are merely higher-order animals and hence could be explained in novels that were scientific experiments. Possibly she is contesting the growing tendency in her time to believe that the method of empirical investigation and proof developed in the physical sciences—positivism—could be extended into all areas of speculation and inquiry.

Did Levy believe any of the remarks about Jews as a group that she included in *Reuben Sachs*? In the course of her life she had probably pondered the question of whether there was truth in all of them, and even in 1888 she must have found herself giving credence to some of these notions from time to time. We know from "St. Anthony's Vicarage" that Levy was deeply troubled by the rampant competition that marked life in late Victorian England; the character called "Reuben Sachs the Jew" articulates a heartless creed (although Levy is indicting Victorian society as a whole). That story was written no later that 1884; by 1888 Levy felt quite differently about Jews and Jewishness.

In *Romance of a Shop* Levy shows that the middle-class (non-Jewish) world that the Lorimers have left behind is unkind and materialistic. In

Reuben Sachs Levy again reminds the reader that English society in general is obsessed with competition, worships money, and treats its women as commodities: the many implicit and explicit allusions to *Daniel Deronda* set up parallels between Jewish life and the larger society in order to make those points.[28] That Levy charges the Jewish community with prizing worldly success and material things too highly is undeniable (what Reuben and others do and say supports that charge), but some of the generalizations made by the novel's narrator(s) imply that the Jews are *particularly* vulnerable to those criticisms.

Those who have read Victorian fiction should be able to run a random sample of the period's novels through their mind and recognize that the materialism of the Sachses and Leunigers and Reuben's decision to make a financially and socially advantageous marriage make Levy's novel, in these respects, generic rather than anomalous. One need not look only at *Daniel Deronda*. In *Vanity Fair* Becky Sharp approaches marriages entirely from the perspective of social advancement, and George Osborne's father forbids him to marry Amelia Sedley once her father has lost his money. In *Great Expectations* Wemmick, a likeable man, explains that what counts in London is "portable property," and even back in the rural marsh country where Pip grows up, Pumblechook and others fawn over Pip after he appears to have risen on the social ladder; Estella marries stupid and brutal Bentley Drummle because he is wealthy.

In Trollope's *Eustace Diamonds,* when Frank Greystock becomes engaged to penniless Lucy Morris, everyone, including his father (an Anglican dean), his mother, and the local bishop, believes he was mad to have made such a choice, and Frank can hardly bring himself to carry out his promise to Lucy. Indeed, the omniscient narrator speaks for the society when he says,

> A man born to great wealth may,—without injury to himself or friends,—do pretty nearly what he likes in regard to marriage, always presuming that the wife he selects may be of his own rank. . . . But . . . there is a middle class of men, who . . . literally cannot marry for love, because their earnings will do no more

than support themselves. As to [Frank Greystock], it must be confessed that his earnings should have done more than that; but not the less did he find himself in a position to which marriage with a penniless girl seemed to threaten him with ruin. All his friends told Frank Greystock that he would be ruined were he to marry Lucy Morris;—and his friends were supposed to be very good and wise.[29]

Readers who think Levy is unduly hard on her Jewish characters seem to forget that she was writing in such a literary tradition (and in such a world). Where she stood in relation to the idea that the Jews were even more enslaved to corrupt, worldly values than were gentiles—an assumption at the heart of what Christian society has always said was true about the Jews—is left open in *Reuben Sachs*. Without endorsing or rejecting the generalizing pronouncements about Jewish attitudes that are inscribed on its pages, Levy's novel asks the reader to think about Jewish ambition and materialism in a serious, critical way. Both Jews and gentiles have failed to see that *Reuben Sachs* examines rather than promulgates the tenet that the Jewish community is unusually devoted to the worship of Mammon.

But it is her narrator's remarks about the ugliness of Jews, more than anything else, that strike today's reader as anti-Semitic. Levy is especially likely to have had trouble freeing herself from the ideas about the physical appearance of Jewish people that are expressed by the narrative voice—we must not forget her drawings, particularly the sketch I dubbed "Jewesses." But as Levy began to see much that was positive in her Jewish heritage, how could she not have begun to question the accuracy of such descriptions even if cartoons, studies of racial difference, and novels all agreed that Jews were offensive physically? In "The Jew in Fiction" Levy refers to a "clever, vulgar, unpleasant novel *Mrs. Keith's Crime*" and says that "no outspoken picture of Jewish vice could be as offensive as the author's condescending acknowledgment of Jewish virtue. 'The Sardine', [*sic*] (as with characteristic refinement he is called throughout the book) is an impossibly, slangy Jew of wealth and position, who

spends his time doing good to ungrateful gentiles."[30] If Levy was of-
fended by a work of fiction in which a virtuous Jewish character gets his
nickname from the greasiness of his appearance (this is why the male
Jew in Clifford's novel is called the Sardine), does it seem probable that in
Reuben Sachs the narrator's remarks about the physical unattractiveness
of Jewish people should be taken at face value?

Similar and much more unpleasant descriptions of Jews were preva-
lent in the novels of Trollope. Because we can be pretty sure that Levy
read *The Eustace Diamonds* in 1882 (see letter 18), my examples will come
from that novel. Mr. Emilius (a Jewish convert who has become a Christian clergyman) is described as "a nasty, greasy, lying, squinting Jew
preacher" and as "a greasy, fawning, pawing, creeping, black-browed ras-
cal"; reference is made to his "hooky nose" and his "grease and nasti-
ness."[31] One observation about Reuben's appearance is very close to
Trollope's description of a Jewish character in *Nina Balatka* (1867). The
Jew in that novel is described as "a very Jew among Jews . . . the movement of the man's body was the movement of a Jew."[32] We are told
about Reuben that "his figure was bad, and his movements awkward; unmistakably the figure and movements of a Jew" (201).

Levy must have hoped that her readers would recognize that she
was very nearly using Trollope's phrasing and that her physical descriptions of Jews also echoed those of Julia Frankau, another Jewish novelist
accused of self-hatred. In *Dr. Phillips: A Maida Vale Idyll* (1887), Frankau
has her narrator observe that "Judaea, when it dances, is an ungainly
spectacle."[33] Levy would have borrowed anti-Semitic language from
other novels with Jewish characters for the same purpose that she borrowed stereotypical generalities: to ask the reader to recognize that a
writer, even a serious one, could not avoid producing a text that included
assumptions that were widely accepted and deeply felt in the culture and
that the words a writer uses, as Jonathan Culler says, carry "the meaning
speakers have given it in past acts of communication." Culler goes further: "And what is true of a word is true of language in general. . . . The
possibility of meaning something by an utterance is already inscribed in
the structure of the language."[34]

Levy's departure from realism in *Reuben Sachs* was fueled by such realizations; the novel shows an understanding that the ability of writers to imagine the world and produce meaning is limited and defined by the language and the belief system they receive from the systems of representation that their society makes available. Levy wants her reader to notice that her "Jewish novel," rather than photographing reality, draws on ideas and uses words that inescapably reproduce meanings that result from the way these ideas and words have been used by other users of the language in the past. Treating meaning as inevitably subjective and unstable, she calls attention to that subjectivity and instability. Epistemologically experimental, *Reuben Sachs* lacks a "controlling truth voice."[35]

Nevertheless, meaning in *Reuben Sachs* is not entirely indeterminate. While Levy may believe stereotypical thinking is inescapable (she had dabbled in it herself in her letter about Paul Heyse), she signals that it is foolish by having a fool, Bertie Lee-Harrison, engage in it. When he converts to Judaism, Bertie gives up "with considerable reluctance his plan of living in a tent" (248). While "secretly irritated" when Bertie says, "I am deeply interested in the Jewish character . . . the underlying resemblances, the elaborate differentiations from a fundamental type—!" Reuben says only, "You will find among us all sorts and conditions of men" (236–37).[36]

And after finishing the novel, readers have reason to feel that they have learned something about the Jews. On the one hand the novel is a jeremiad, a lamentation for a people that has sold its soul for money and power, that demands from its men a diseased and even suicidal style of life, and that mistreats its women. On the other, the communal life that Levy represents has warmth, vitality, kindness, and characters who truly love each other; isolated from the Jewish community, Judith is bereft. Eleanor Marx, who translated *Reuben Sachs* into German in 1889, seems to have found the representation of Jews and Jewish life in Levy's novel so attractive that it helped her to identify with the Jewish part of her background.[37]

Yet there is no denying that in Reuben's treachery toward the woman he loves—and toward himself—he becomes a figure for a deeply disturbing strain in Jewish life. The hypothesis that the affection these people have for one another has something redemptive about it, while not entirely erased, is seriously dimmed. At the novel's conclusion the narrative voice asks a question: "Is life indeed over for Judith, or at least all that makes life beautiful, worthy—a thing in anyway tolerable?" (292). That she is no longer part of the Jewish community, that she is in alien space, is evoked emblematically by the two references to the gold cross above the Albert Memorial outside her window.

Judith Quixano's predicament has implications for the survival of the Jews as a people, particularly if we know about the "Jewish tradition . . . that figures loss of place and of collective identity as feminine."[38] Levy leaves the outcome unresolved both for her protagonist (whose name means "Jewess") and, by implication, for the Jews. Nevertheless, one suspects that the novelist's own emotional investment in the future of her people is what prompted her to conclude with a conventional signifier of hope: Judith, unbeknownst to herself, is with child. The reader of *Reuben Sachs,* a novel in which meaning has been so indeterminate and the narrative voice so unreliable, is bound to be wary of putting too much trust in anything that the narrator says, but it would be a mistake, I think, simply to dismiss the novel's last sentence. We are told that Judith's child "shall bring with it, no doubt, pain and sorrow, and tears; but shall bring also hope and joy, and that quickening of purpose which is perhaps as much as any of us should expect or demand from Fate" (293).

9

London
1889

Levy left Italy on the eighth of January, a Tuesday, stopped in Paris for over a week,[1] and arrived home on the evening of January 18, a Thursday. On Friday Levy reported in her calendar that she "Saw Clemmy" and "dined at Katie's"; on Saturday she lunched with Jenny De Pass and spent the evening with Dora; and on Sunday she saw Pauline, and, after seeing Bertha Thomas, in the evening dined with Jenny De Pass and her family. That Levy would see her Jewish friends, Jenny, Pauline, and Dora, so soon after returning is unexpected. Perhaps Levy's friendships with these Jewish women (all mentioned in Levy's 1885 letter about Katie's wedding) deepened after she became more positive about her Jewish background in 1886, or it may be that she and they had been close all along. The 1889 calendar shows that she saw Pauline and Dora at intervals throughout the year while spending more time with Jenny than with anybody else except Clementina and, of course, Katie.

On January 13 (while she was in Paris) Levy had acknowledged the publication of her second novel—the one she took seriously—by writing in her calendar, "*Reuben* comes." Levy's calendar, Bella Duffy's parting gift, is an invaluable document, providing a record of who Levy saw and what she did every day in 1889 until her death in September. It paints a far more detailed picture of her London life than we have for any other year. The daily calendar brings into focus aspects of Levy's life that, in many instances, must have been present but invisible in preceding years because Dollie's diary and Levy's letters to Lee (our previous main sources when Levy was in London) contain only what mattered to Dollie or what Levy thought Lee would be interested in. (This not to say that Levy's last year of life may not have differed in important respects from preceding years.) The calendar shows that in 1889, in addition to seeing Clementina and the Jewish women just mentioned, she kept up with other old friends and spent quite a bit of time with Bertha Thomas, Olive Schreiner, a woman referred to in the calendar only as "M. Smart," and another woman, Margaret Bateson.[2]

Levy's life in 1889 seems a whirlwind of people, activities, and work. She records that she wrote *Miss Meredith*, her third novel, in six weeks, and on March 8, after reporting "finished *M. M.*," she adds, "Lunch with Clemmy and M. Smart. Dined at K.'s. To Effie's. The MS. tragedy!!" The day is typical in that it is so crowded (and the last item teases the imagination). Although there are entries in Levy's calendar such as "Wrote at the B.M." [British Museum], "wrote verse at home," and "wrote a sonnet (London Poets)," she does not record much writing. Yet 1889 was a highly prolific year. The calendar offers further support for Judith Walkowitz's assertion that by the end of the 1880s it was commonplace for women to appear in public places without a male escort and move freely about the city.[3] Levy goes "To the Philharmonic," the Lyceum, and "To a new gallery" with Bertha Thomas; attends "Ibsen's *Doll House* with M. Bateson" (shortly after its opening produced such a stir); lunches "with Clemmy and M. Smart at a vegetarian restaurant"; takes Effie Scott's son Henry to the Natural History Museum; sits "on the lees with Charlotte, Jenny, and Pauline" (a bank of the Thames sheltered from the wind); and, after lunch at "the Club," "Walked home with Bessy May."[4]

Her numerous companions include intimate friends whom she sees frequently, acquaintances who are active in various social movements, gentiles and Jews, and, a bit surprisingly, several men. She writes of "loafing with Clemmy" and notes that she went "To Olive Schreiner's in the evening." She has "M. Smart, Mr. Young and Mr. Cohen to tea"; goes "To Lady Magnus in the morning"; has "Margaret Bateson and Jenny to lunch"; goes "to an 'At Home' of the Fabian Society with her friend Effie's husband, Tom Stevens; and goes with Robert Garnett (one of Richard's sons) "To the theatre." Other entries include: "To Mrs. Eve's— met Mrs. Fawcett" (both women were leaders of the suffragist movement); "Called on Stepniak;[5] "Stepniak to tea," and "To tea at Bella Duffy's . . . we talked of the Soul."

Family is important. Levy sees Katie several times a week; takes her little sister Ella "to the Rossetti's (good singing)"; takes Katie's son Billy to play with Effie's little boy; visits "Grandmamma"; sees "Aunt Kate"; goes "to *Richard III* with Papa, Ella, and Donald"; and takes her nephews on a picnic. Despite her disillusionment with the university, Levy visits Cambridge several times; during one visit she hears a lecture on the "Immortality of the Soul," about which she writes dryly (I would guess), "Thinks it will be proved scientifically."

In April, on Easter Sunday, she walks "in Kensington Gardens with E. and I. Isaac" (Emma and Isabel, Jewish friends from her youth). In May she has "a party in my room (80)." (This is oddly phrased, but a friend remembered attending a gathering at the University Women's Club at Levy's invitation.)[6] When the summer comes, Levy takes a cottage at Dorking with Jenny, and they spend time with the novelist Grant Allen and his family at their cottage nearby (after dinner the Allens and their guests "Discussed the Woman Question . . . G.A. thinks marriage not permanent"). She goes rowing "to Gorling and back (9 miles)" with Bertha Thomas and buys "a wedding present for Conny Black." In July Levy calls "on Vernon Lee who was in town for a few days."

The celebrity that came with the publication of *Reuben Sachs* brought new literary acquaintances. The poet Rosamund Marriott Watson, who used the name "Graham Tomson," visits Levy, and they talk about her tumultuous marital history ("G. T. told me her history"). Levy goes to Graham Tomson's party, where she meets Hardy and Wilde; sees "George Fleming"[7] at "the Salon"; attends "the Robinsons' party" (Mary Robinson's parents regularly held parties for London literati); goes to a tea party "where I met Mr. Yeats"; "dines with the Macmillans"; attends "The Sharps' party" (Elizabeth Sharp had edited *Women's Voices*); and goes to "Mr. and Mrs. Moulton's *At Home*" (another gathering place for writers and artists).

Attending to the routines of life, Levy buys a hat; visits the dentist several times; and goes for fittings at the shop of a dressmaker, Mr. Nicholl, with whom she has "a row" (she calls him a "A cad and a wretch!"). She also does a good deal of reading of all kinds, including *Macbeth*, "a novel of Ouida's,"[8] "*Pierre et Jean* by Guy de Maupassant," *King Lear*, "D.G.R.'s *Vita Nuova*," *The Evolutionist at Large*, "Swinburne's new poems," and *Education* by Herbert Spencer. Every time she makes money by selling a story or poem she records the amount in her calendar. She keeps a list on the back of the diary of where she placed every story, poem, or essay; mentions that she "Read *M. M.* [*Miss Meredith*] to Clemmie"; writes that "Macmillan chucks poems"; reports (on the following day) that she "Took poems to Fisher Unwin"; goes over the "Proofs of 'A Slip of the Pen' for *Temple Bar*"; and records her attendance at the first meeting of the "Ladies Literary Dinner"; she adds to that entry, "Mona Caird in the chair. I received thanks for fiction."[9]

Elizabeth Pennell, an American with a satiric eye, described the Fabian "At Home" that Levy mentions in her calendar. This is the only affair sponsored by the Fabian Society that Levy attended in 1889 or, perhaps, ever; Pennell's journal entry helps us to imagine a social scene the margins of which Levy inhabited:

> We went to the Converzazione of the Fabian Society in Bloomsbury Town Hall. A collection of cranks, native and foreign: young women in extraordinary costumes, one a perfect Burne-Jones, played the violin; young men with long hair and velvet coats. Most people were in evening dress so that a conspicuous

figure was George Bernard Shaw in grey Jaeger get-up, flirting
outrageously with all the girls in the room.[10]

Levy repeatedly records in her calendar that she "Kept the office" or
"Helped in the office" (once "Clemmy read a paper to M. Smart and myself in the office"). That office belonged to the Woman's Protective and
Provident League (WPPL), located near the Levys' home in Bloomsbury. Was Levy giving her time to the WPPL only because of her friendship with Black, its secretary? Olive Schreiner, who was intensely involved
with left-wing politics, told the poet Arthur Symons that Amy Levy was
"the most interesting girl she had met in England!"[11] This, together with
Levy's relationships with people like Clementina, the Radfords, Eleanor
Marx, and Stepniak, suggests that Levy was able to offer a critique of her
society that met the standards of people who dedicated their lives to social change. We know that Levy did not make a similar commitment, but
it is possible that she helped out in the WPPL office in 1889 because Black
had helped her to become more sensitive to the troubles of working-class
women than she had been when she expressed lack of sympathy for the
hardships of "girls fr. the streets" (letter 31).[12] It should be remembered
that Levy at first disapproved of the Black sisters' servantless flat only to
make just such a living arrangement look like a delightful adventure in
Romance of a Shop less than two years later.

What the calendar does *not* tell us is what Levy was thinking and
feeling. When she wrote *"Reuben comes,"* did she have trepidations
about how the Jewish press and the Jewish community would respond to
her novel? How did she feel about the fuss over the book? The *Jewish
Chronicle* did not review it although it gave enthusiastic notice to every
other book Levy produced before and after. The editors may have
wanted to avoid public criticism of Levy, who, after all, had been a contributor to its pages. Toward the end of January the *Chronicle* published
an editorial titled "Critical Jews" that, without mentioning Levy or her
book, was obviously a response to *Reuben Sachs* as well as to *Dr. Phillips:
A Maida Vale Idyll,* Julia Frankau's novel about Jewish life (published

under the name Frank Danby).[13] The editorial in the *Jewish Chronicle* is reasonable, citing both the Bible and the old joke "Wherever there are two Jews, there are two critics." The piece concludes with the observation that "ill-natured sketches" by a Jew can have a deleterious effect on "the outside world," so that "those who are prone to it should check them in themselves."[14]

The *Jewish World* showed no such restraint when it responded to Levy's Jewish novel in late February, lumping it together with Frankau's book. Levy was attacked more ferociously than Frankau (reviled for not even having the decency to hide her name behind a pseudonym) even though *Dr. Phillips,* influenced by Naturalism, is unmodulated in its sordid portrayal of Anglo-Jewry. Its Jews are materialistic, coarse, and heartless, and the protagonist, a Jewish physician (whose diabolic qualities of character are linked to his "Hebraism"), kills his wife. At the novel's end Dr. Phillips is performing experiments on his patients—"maiming men and unsexing women." The review of the two novels in the *Jewish World* accuses Levy of "delighting in the task of persuading the general public that her own kith and kin are the most hideous types of vulgarity; she revels in misrepresentations of their customs and modes of thought, and she is proud of being able to offer her testimony in support of the anti-Semitic theories of the clannishness of her people and the tribalism of their religion."[15]

Nor was the *Jewish Standard* gentle with Levy's Jewish novel. *Reuben Sachs* was literally conflated with *Dr. Phillips,* when, in March, the *Standard* published a parodic piece of doggerel titled "Dr. Reuben Green: A Study of the Maida Vale Jewish colony."[16] Signed by "Amy Danby," this heavy-handed satire written by Israel Zangwill (using his pen name "Marshallik") caricatures the vulgarity and avarice that Zangwill saw in the Jewish characters from Frankau's and Levy's books. This parody was followed by an editorial in the *Standard* (possibly also written by Zangwill) in which Frankau's and Levy's depictions of Jewish life are described as so "venomous" that they are like "the bipedal cuttle-fish squirting its nauseous black fluid on to clean paper and calling the result a picture."[17]

Not surprisingly, the writers for the *Jewish Standard* did not appear to notice that by referring to the Gwendolen Harleth plot (i.e., the "Christian" part) of *Daniel Deronda*, Levy signals to the reader that in its materialism and its willingness to commodify women the Jewish community is a microcosm of the larger society. Nor did they remember that in *Romance of a Shop* middle-class (gentile) society, in addition to being snobbish and shallow, is predatory toward women and contemptuous of them (Gertrude Lorimer's friend Conny complains that the men who come courting are "sneaks who want one's money" and "bad imitations of fashionable young men, who snub, and patronize, and sneer at us all" [New's ed. 136]).

Did it never occur to Levy that a novel by a Jew critiquing Anglo-Jewish life would inevitably generate concern among Jews (a despised minority) about the book's impact on the way the larger culture perceived them? Meri-Jane Rochelson, who records the responses to Levy's novel in both the gentile and the Jewish press on both sides of the Atlantic, points out that the Jewish reviewers were all preoccupied with the same question: "How will it look to the outside community?"[18] Rochelson observes that "writers in the secular press of the day often treated *Reuben Sachs* as documentary evidence," and she cites some of the reviews to show that the book was indeed read by many critics as a confirmation of their racist preconceptions (e.g., "The reviewer for *Blackwood's* . . . referred to Reuben's choice of 'ambition, advancement, [and] wealth' over love as 'the instinct of his race').[19]

Levy's calendar betrays no sign that she noticed anything pertaining to herself in the Jewish newspapers or that her novel was being used in mainstream periodicals to support negative stereotypes about the Jews. Given the effort she had made to forge a personal reconciliation with Anglo-Jewry, however, she cannot have felt comfortable when she read remarks like the following: "In *Reuben Sachs* . . . she writes for the most part with vitriol instead of ink, and throws passion and a scorn in her work. . . . The central element in the book . . . is a deep and bitter hostility to modern Judaism, and, we might almost add, to modern Jews."[20]

What we lack is a letter to Katie, fervid and frank, expressing Levy's concern, disappointment, embarrassment, anger, or whatever it was that she felt about the controversy ignited by her novel.

Richard Garnett addresses the question of how Levy handled the cause célèbre created by *Reuben Sachs* when he writes that "the criticism . . . was far from affecting her spirits to the extent alleged."[21] The implication is that Levy was saddened, not devastated, by the furor. This assessment would seem to be accurate although her mood appears to have darkened as the months went by. The letters to Katie from previous years show that Levy could keep to a surprisingly busy schedule, even making friends and maintaining relationships, when she was unhappy. While the months after the publication of *Reuben Sachs* cannot have been easy for her, instead of becoming depressed she seems to have thrown herself into what appears in the calendar to be a vigorous "Miss Creak" existence. The activities recorded in the diary—until August 5—are not compatible with the impaired concentration and general dysfunction that are symptomatic of a major episode of clinical depression.

The comparison between what the calendar offers and what we might learn if we had any substantive letters written by Levy in 1889 reminds us of the advantages and the limitations of different kinds of sources to the biographer. For other perspectives we turn at this point to the way Levy was described during May and June by those who did not know her well. In July Elizabeth Pennell recorded in her journal that she saw Amy Levy at the party given by William and Elizabeth Sharp ("Amy Levy asked to be introduced to me, and I thought her very attractive").[22] Katharine Tynan, who remembered Levy's "charming little Eastern face," wrote, "I have a letter somewhere from Amy Levy, asking me to tea one day that summer. I could not go, and afterwards I had poignant regrets, as though I might have done something if I had come to know her better. But I dare say she was doomed, poor, gifted little soul."[23] Like Pennell, Tynan saw Levy at the Sharps' in July: "I talked that day with Amy Levy again. I find a memo in my diary, 'Sunday 21st. A. Levy. 4:30. At home Wednesdays.' Perhaps that indicated a meeting which did not come off."[24]

Louise Chandler Moulton, writing in 1892, remembers Levy at what was probably the party she gave in May:

> She invited me to the University Club for a tea, at which the other guests were all members of the club, and in some wise connected with literature. . . . I can see her now, as she poured tea, that July afternoon, at the little round table, in one of the home-like sitting-rooms of the University Club.[25] She wore a white gown, as, indeed, she almost always did. Her face . . . matched the cream-white of her dress. It was a face illumined by great dark eyes, from which looked the sweetest, saddest soul that ever fell out of love with life.[26]

W. B. Yeats, who met Levy at the end of July, wrote, "I saw [Amy Lévy] no long while before her death. She was talkative, good-looking in a way and full of the restlessness of the unhappy."[27]

That these recollections include comments on the attractiveness of Levy's appearance is poignant since she was convinced that she lacked physical charm, and it is important, of course, that Yeats and Moulton could see that she was unhappy. Yeats's observation that Levy was "restless" confirms the impression of frenetic activity that one gets from the calendar. Was she keeping busy so as not to have time to muse over what she had referred to as her "sunken ships" in her letter to Katie from Florence (letter 35)? It is interesting that Levy asked to be introduced to Pennell and that she invited both Tynan and Moulton to tea (a letter Levy wrote to the latter, postmarked April 1, shows that before Levy and Moulton even met, Levy proposed that they get together).[28] That she would make overtures to these women and invite eighty people to a reception at her club suggests that Levy was forwarding her career.

Levy's motives for wanting to befriend Tynan (a poet of some reputation, with important literary connections) and Moulton (a journalist in a position to help Levy win public attention) were almost certainly professional. Other letters that Levy wrote to Moulton in the spring and summer of 1889 support this interpretation, and one letter reveals an additional reason why Levy would have pursued Moulton: the latter had written an article on Jewish novels.[29] As for what Louise Moulton says about Levy always dressing in white, we should remember that in letters to Vernon Lee written in 1887 Levy describes wearing a dress that was "maize, brown and orange" and another dress that was black. Why would she have started clothing herself only in white?

My guess is that Levy might have been trying to create an image—a "look"—that would make her a memorable literary personality, an authoress who had a mystique about her. Perhaps it is relevant that Mme. De Staël's Corinne always wore white when she recited improvised poetry in front of awed multitudes. After the demise of her hopes for a romance with Dorothy Blomfield in 1888, Levy may have decided that she would learn a lesson from the myth of Corinne/Sappho and, stifling the yearnings of the Hungry Poet, concentrate on the construction of an impressive career. Levy's determination to make the professional side of her self the mainstay of her identity may have helped her to maintain composure in the face of the criticism she received as the author of *Reuben Sachs.*

The literature Levy produced in the last year of her life constitutes almost the only remaining evidence from this period. *Miss Meredith,* written hastily in the winter, was serialized in the *British Weekly* in April and June. Despite well-written descriptions of the Duomo, the Campo Santo, the Baptistery, and the tower at Pisa, the novel is slight. Elsie Meredith, an English girl, goes to Pisa to be a governess for an aristocratic Italian family. The Brogis live in a palace that is cold even in good weather, their manners are stiff and formal, and their conversation is trivial. There are overt and covert allusions to *Jane Eyre* and references to Shelley, Mary Shelley, Byron, and the others in the so-called Pisan circle who lived in Pisa from 1820 to 1821, but these are only literary window dressing. Actually *Miss Meredith* has nothing much to say. When the Brogis' handsome son Andrea returns from America, he and Elsie fall in love at first sight; the opposition of Andrea's parents serves to complicate the plot.

As an article in the *Academy* points out, by the end of the nineteenth century the governess was such a tired figure in fiction that when she appeared at all she was "mainly the invaluable puppet of the penny or threepenny novelette."[30] Levy's last work of extended fiction transcends those subliterary genres, but her decision to write a courtship novel about a governess indicates that she relished the challenge of working with materials that might seem to be used up. Writing in 1892, Harry Quilter greatly overvalues *Miss Meredith* (calling it "very high art"), but he is right that "from a technical point of view" it shows "a complete mastery over its material and method."[31] As with *Romance of a Shop*, Levy purposely held in her hand. But her final novel, unlike her first, is not much more than a well-written fairy tale.

Her heroine is interesting only in that Elsie is *not* a New Woman, and Levy calls attention to qualities in her personality that are stereotypically feminine. Elsie says about herself, "I am neither literary nor artistic . . . but I have a little talent for being fond of people" (New's ed. 295). And she is so upset by the hostility Andrea's admiration for her has engendered in his family that she cries out, "They do not like me, and I cannot bear it any more. . . . No one has thought me very wonderful, very clever, very beautiful, very brilliant; but people have always liked me, and if I am not liked I shall die" (340). This recalls Lallie, the eponymous protagonist of Levy's early, unpublished story, another girl whose aspirations are bounded by the sphere of the affections. Levy may have felt a sneaking affiliation with such women, for in her Confessions Book entry she responded to the questions about "favourite qualities in men and women" with a list that culminated with the candid "A tendency to like me."

In March Levy published "Addenbrooke" in *Belgravia*, another story with a courtship plot. "Readers at the British Museum" came out in *Temple Bar* in April and "Cohen of Trinity" in May. In July she sold "A Slip of the Pen" and "Eldorado at Islington." What was the quality of this work? "Addenbrooke" is superior to the potboilers Levy had tossed off in earlier years only because the heroine in the end chooses the lesser man over the better—thus the story shows the irrationality of passion. Levy's article about the British Museum is informative and has moments of charm, and the two stories published in July are contrived, clever, and slight, with "Eldorado at Islington" showing the sympathy for the "small bourgeoisie" that Levy had expressed in her letter to Vernon Lee back in 1887 (letter 32).

But "Cohen of Trinity" is a masterpiece. In this story, as in *Reuben Sachs,* Levy embodies the epistemological issues involved in trying to understand a people about which British culture harbored so many deeply held, unexamined notions that a writer could not ignore them and the imagery they generated. But the story goes further than the novel: it opens questions about Jews without even hinting at any answers. Levy's narrator here is definitely a gentile. Describing Cohen, a student at Trinity College, as "slight, ungainly . . . an awkward rapid gait, half slouch, half hobble," with "full prominent lips" and a nose which is a "curved beak" (478), this man provides an anti-Semite's view of what a Jew looks like. What he tells us of Cohen's loud behavior with companions— "yelling and shrieking with laughter" (479)—conforms to received assumptions about how Jews behave. Levy's tactic is to present Cohen only through this unsympathetic lens, and the story emphasizes the impossibility of seeing and representing Jews with any clarity.

Before writing "Cohen of Trinity" Levy would have had time to read numerous reviews in mainstream literary journals. Most of these were certain that her novel told the ugly truth about the Jews, and some, like the one in the *Cambridge Review,* assumed she had written it out of hostility toward her people. Such notices from gentile reviewers, appearing in January and February, are likely to have had a greater effect on the story than the criticism in the Jewish press because they came out earlier and because Cohen commits suicide after publishing a book that is hailed by the non-Jewish intellectual elite. His despair is the result of his conviction that he will never be understood by the larger society.

Levy's calendar shows that she corrected the proofs for "Cohen of Trinity" on March 9, which allows us to think about whether the story might be a response to the way *Reuben Sachs* was received by the Jewish press. The *Jewish Standard* had published its outraged parody of the novel only eight days earlier, and the *Standard's* angry editorial came out on

March 8. Clearly Levy composed "Cohen" before reading those pieces although they might have influenced her last-minute revisions. Similarly, the *Jewish World's* angry review in late February could have caused her to make changes while correcting the proofs, and it might even have appeared early enough to have influenced its composition.

It is also possible that as soon as the novel appeared in January individual Jewish readers told Levy that they were upset by *Reuben Sachs*. The inclusion of Leopold Leuniger in "Cohen of Trinity"—a minor character who "turns the cold shoulder" to Cohen—brings out an important theme: that a highly anglicized Jewish person may find it no easier than a gentile to understand a less assimilated Jew and feel affinity with him. The reaction to Levy's "Jewish novel" would have given her a heightened appreciation of this. Having failed to anticipate the anxiety *Reuben Sachs* would generate in many Jews, she must have feared that the "Leopold Leuniger" voice within her psyche, unvanquished after all, had coauthored the novel without her realizing it. In all of Leuniger's appearances he is a person who is hostile to Jewish life and Judaism, but only in "Cohen of Trinity" is his characterization entirely unsympathetic. Dubbed "Little Leuniger" (with no first name), he is not even allowed to be a speaking subject, and he has lost the status as an artist that he had in "Leopold Leuniger" and *Reuben Sachs*. All we hear of his music is that he "played the fiddle." Still driven by his desire to gain acceptance by "the aristocrats and scholars, the flower of the University," Leuniger is probably Levy's caricature of herself as a Cambridge student eager for acceptance by her gentile classmates. If so, the portrait indicates that she was now ashamed of herself.

The gentile narrator thus sifts through his consciousness two Jews, Leuniger, the "gatecrasher," and Cohen, a Jew of the kind that Sander Gilman says is "the quintessential Jewish literary persona" and calls the schlemiel.[32] Cohen functions as Leuniger's *Döppelganger*, just as, according to Gilman, the Eastern Jew became the "reification of the anti-Semitic caricature of the Jew in the West."[33] Like the *Ostjuden* in the imagination of West European Jews, Cohen is the externalization of all that is different, irrational, and repugnant, the reification of everything "bad" associated with the Jewish stereotype that an enlightened Jew like Leopold Leuniger would try to expel from his own being. The gentile speaker manages by the briefest of sketches to make it clear that for him, no matter how different from Cohen young Leuniger manages to be, he will always be only another unattractive type of what remains an alien species.

Levy reveals almost nothing about her narrator except that he is a Cambridge man (presumably a don), that his relationship with the man he describes "could not bear the name of friendship," and that he has "scraped acquaintance" with Cohen in order to study him in a manner that is peculiarly clinical. That this speaker makes the same kind of generalization about Jews that the seemingly omniscient narrator in *Reuben Sachs* makes repeatedly should not go unnoticed, for it reinforces the argument that the narrator of *Reuben Sachs* is neither reliable nor Levy's mouthpiece when he makes such statements. The gentile narrator of "Cohen of Trinity" pronounces, "A desire to stand well in one another's eyes, to make a brave show before one another, is, I have observed, a marked characteristic of the Jewish people."

Even though Cohen's acquaintance admits that he possesses "little information," he does not hesitate to give a detailed description of Cohen's background:

> *I seemed to see it all before me:* the little new house in Maida Vale; a crowd of children, clamorous, unkempt; a sallow shrew in a torn dressing-gown, who alternately scolded, bewailed herself, and sank into moody silence; a fitful paternal figure coming and going, depressed, exhilarated according to the fluctuations of his mysterious financial affairs; and over everything the fumes of smoke, the glare of gas, the smell of food in preparation. [emphasis added] (481)

Levy uses the opening words of this passage to subvert the reader's trust in what the narrator will say since he acknowledges openly that he has constructed his picture of Cohen's family entirely out of an imagination that draws its images from the cultural storehouse of notions about Jews. Thus Cohen's father is assumed to be obsessed with "mysterious" financial dealings, his mother a shrew and a slattern, his siblings noisy and disorderly, and the entire household emotionally volatile, vulgar, and incomprehensible.

Cohen is expelled from Cambridge but achieves success with a book that is described as "Half poem, half essay . . . with a force, a fire, a vision" but "appalling lapses of taste" (483). The narrator again meets the now famous author. Cohen's words at this encounter reveal that his literary success has failed to satisfy him: "'They *shall* know, they *shall* understand, they shall feel what I am.' That is what I used to say to myself in the old days. I suppose, now, 'they' do know, more or less, and what of that?" (485). Despite the literal meaning of his last sentence, which seems to say that his book succeeds in explaining its author to the larger society, the phrases "I suppose" and "what of that?" indicate that the Jew has come to realize he can never make himself known.

That Cohen is denied any direct voice until the story is more than half over, speaking, when he is allowed utterance at all, only to quote W. S. Gilbert and Robert Browning, increases our sense of his unknowability. When he is finally given some dialogue, the disparity between the crude intensity of Cohen's speech and the restrained rhetoric of the narrator—except when he paints what he imagines to be Cohen's home life—sharpens our sense of the chasm that divides them. At the end we are told of Cohen's suicide, and the narrator admits that he "was wholly unprepared by my knowledge of Cohen for the catastrophe" (485). Given their final conversation, one sees that no attempt at objective scrutiny, no degree of frankness on Cohen's part, could give this representative of the dominant social order the key to the enigma of the Jew.

If we turn to *A London Plane-Tree* for signs of Levy's mood in the spring and summer of 1889, we can be certain only that three of the poems were written in those last months of her life.[34] Levy's calendar shows that "The Old House" and "London Poets" were written in April and "The Old Poet" in early May 1889. As a pair of poems, the first two are revealing since the former expresses an unambivalent wish for death while the latter offers the comforting thought that maturity (as opposed to youth) enables a person to derive joy from nature even when life has been disappointing. "The Old Poet" has an inspiring "message"; that is, it seems to say what Levy thought she ought to feel or what she thought might help—if she could only manage to believe it. And so it is not surprising that most of the imagery in "The Old Poet" is stale (e.g.,"I will be glad because it is the Spring; / I will forget the winter in my heart"). The discrepancy between these poems—in theme and artistry—reveals the weakness of the forces within her that battled to overcome hopelessness.

The deep pessimism of "London Poets" is quietly shocking, no doubt because Levy honestly gives voice to the logic of a person in despair. As we know, her earlier poems frequently express a desire to stop living, but the death wish always stems from the sense of having been deprived of joys that others experience. In contrast,"London Poets" takes it for granted that the longing for oblivion unites past, present, and future poets. The speaker, taking comfort from the realization that the sorrows of dead poets who used to pace the city's streets are "now only the shadow of a dream," muses that another poet will find solace in the thought that the speaker's life too is over. The proofs for *Plane-Tree* show that Levy made one alteration in the text: in the last line—"No more he comes, who this way came and went"—she changed the pronoun from "she" to "he," apparently an effort to make the autobiographical nature of the lyric less obvious.

Levy sold and published four lyrics in this period, the first half of 1889. In addition to "The Old House," two of these were probably new: "The Village Garden" and "A Wall Flower."[35] I will treat four more as belonging to the last year of Levy's life: "A March Day in London," "On the Wye in May," "The End of the Day," and "In the Nower."[36] Since these can be classed thematically (with some overlap), I will examine a few others—poems for which there is no evidence of earlier composition—that fall into these same categories. My analysis of this work (like my discussion of "The Old Poet") will enable us to imagine Levy's state of mind in the period leading up to and including her final depression. I will also provide some understanding and measure of what she accomplished poetically in the last part of her life and note the traditions she was drawing on. There is a need for serious discussion of Levy's final volume of poems, and the remarks made here should prompt other critics to enter the conversation (so far, most of the attention her poetry has received in our time has emphasized the dramatic monologues from *A Minor Poet*).[37]

Levy's "Oh, Is It Love?" would seem to be a late poem because it expresses the epistemological anxiety that informs "Cohen of Trinity."[38] Levy's speaker asks, "O is it Love or is it Fame, / This thing for which I sigh?" The sheer audacity of such an explicit reference to the tired theme of conflict between love and fame cancels the cliché and captures the reader's attention; it seems that the speaker is going to explore and reveal primal feeling. Instead of leading to self-knowledge, however, the question at the start of this short lyric produces only another question. She asks about her emotional tumult, "Has it then no earthly name / For men to call it by?" By once again polarizing love and fame, Levy uses this highly conventional linguistic paradigm to expose the inadequacy of language to make sense of and articulate a woman's inner life.

In the second stanza of "Oh, Is It Love?" Levy's speaker elaborates on her indecision and confusion, establishing that she suffers from a diagnostic problem for which she knows no anodyne: "I know not what can ease my pains / Nor what it is I wish." Understanding that unfulfilled sexual desire is part of her trouble, she gives figurative expression to the difficulty she has in reining in her passion. But her passionate yearnings are not only erotic. Because she longs for both personal fulfillment and recognition for her poetic gift, her problem is larger in scope: the framing of her problem as if *either* private *or* public fulfillment should represent her feelings thus becomes a barrier to their disclosure. The simile in the last two lines—"The passion at my heart strings strains / Like a tiger on a leash"—conveys more than the pull of sexual desire. It is also a bold image of the tug-of-war between the speaker's drive for self-expression and comprehension of her dilemma and the constraints on both.

The dominant emotion in "A March Day in London" is once again anxiety about the difficulty of making sense of things. In the second stanza Levy finds an objective correlative for her obsessional ruminations: "The little wheel that turns in my brain; / The little wheel that turns all day, / That turns all night with might and main." The next stanza begins with a direct question—"What is the thing I fear and why?"—and goes on to show that "the world is all awry" by saying that "The wind's in the east, the sun's in the sky / The gas lamps gleam in a golden line." The *OED* notes that in England the east wind is proverbial for "bleak, unpleasant, and injurious to health," and the sun should not shining when darkness calls for gaslights. The speaker's contemplation of this confusing external world somehow leads her at the end of the poem to the achievement of a "weary peace" that feels unearned.

The language of "A March Day in London," though it seems to express clearly the speaker's restless search to know why she is afraid and why the "world is all awry," partly drowns out the feelings it represents. The poem is heavily indebted to Swinburne: "'Tis the wind of ice, the wind of fire / Of cold despair and of hot desire, / Which chills the flesh to aches and pains, / And sends a fever through all the veins." The heavy use of alliteration in this poem, its driving rhythm, the many repetitions and antitheses allow Levy to create a beautiful poem by singing mellifluously about feelings that are far from pleasing aesthetically. Like Swinburne, she uses musicality to muffle personal suffering at the same time that she voices it.

"On the Wye in May" and "A Wall Flower" should be coupled because they are about what Isobel Armstrong calls the "flight across the boundary." She explains that Victorian women poets imagine an escape from the restrictions of bourgeois society into the "other" through fantasy. In "On the Wye in May" Levy evokes perfection experienced in a natural setting just at the start of spring, when the air "is neither fierce nor keen," the sun is "temperate," and the speaker is with her "beloved" (and all is as it was at the beginning of their love). Levy knows that such a moment in the real (the fallen) world can only be "brief." The final two lines express Levy's vision of a flight across a boundary into a timeless place where fulfillment is possible: "I see that clime, unknown, without a name / Where first and best and last shall be the same." In "A Wall

Flower," where the speaker's spirit is torn between the liberation promised by waltz music and "a leaden fiend" (the devil of depression again) that keeps her stationary, she remembers a perfect place—"Somewhere . . . not here, / In other ages, on another sphere"—where she danced "in perfect motion" and "To perfect music" with the beloved to whom she speaks.[39]

In "The Village Garden" the speaker, instead of seeing solace in a realm that has no actual existence on earth, voices the untraditional idea that the city is the best place for a troubled person. Away from "The roar and hurry of the town" the speaker finds that "the burden of individual life . . . weighs me down." Levy derives the idea that the submergence of self is desirable from Schopenhauer and from Heine and Lenau. "The Village Garden" is full of feeling, but the speaker does not demand the joys and satisfactions of life as do so many of the speakers in *A Minor Poet and Other Verse,* whether they are fictionalized narrators of dramatic monologues or voices seemingly close to Levy's own, as in the lyrics. Instead, the tone of "The Village Garden" is calm and, at the end, hopeful, but its measured cadences suggest a struggle to maintain a facade of serenity that the speaker admits is at present unattainable because her mind is too turbulent.

In a number of the poems probably or definitely written in her last year the voice is far from calm although the speaker often expresses an intense yearning not just for calm but for diminished feeling. "The Old House" is one of Levy's most powerful lyrics of this kind: an example of what Angela Leighton calls poetry about "self-encounter" in which "there is a deep-rooted split in the nature of the female self."[40] Leighton refers specifically to "The Old House," calling it a "mirror poem," and compares it to two of Augusta Webster's dramatic monologues ("Faded" and "By the Looking Glass"), Alice Meynell's "A Letter from a Girl to Her Own Old Age," and a few lyrics by other poets.[41] How the self changes over time is a theme in most of these poems in which a grown woman encounters herself as a girl. Levy's lyric is strikingly different from the poems of Webster in that its speaker does not welcome the opportunity to reestablish a connection with her youthful self. And even though the speaker in Meynell's poem ends by telling her aged self to forget the youthful writer of the letter, the relationship between the two is tender, not abrasive. For one thing, the girl has initiated the encounter by taking up her pen. In Levy's late poetry the facets of the self are often hopelessly at odds, whether she is looking at them chronologically or at a particular moment.

In "The Old House" the speaker returns to a house she knew in the past. The journey up the "silent stair" where the "dead come to meet me" takes place in the house of memory. It is clear that those were happier days, a time when "the dream was dreamed." When a "shade" turns her face, the speaker feels a rush of agonized emotion, exclaiming, "O God, it wore / The face I used to wear when I was young!" She is flooded by grief, but most of all she is "shamed / Before that little ghost with eager eyes" so that she cries out, "O turn away, let her not see, not know! / . . . How should she understand?" And so the poem ends with the speaker trying not to be noticed by the person she had been as an expectant girl. It is impossible to read this poem and not think of Levy's expostulation in an 1888 letter to Clementina Black—letter 36 (already quoted in chapter 3)—"O Clemmy, Clemmy, is everybody's life like this? I ought to have made something out of mine, but it's too late."

Leighton uses the phrase "the art of minimal feeling" to describe many of Christina Rossetti's melancholy poems and says that they are often "strikingly free of any sentiment at all."[42] Levy's "Old House" is by no means a poem of minimal feeling, but it is about emotion that pushes against the defenses that the speaker employs to keep it in check. Released from repression, the speaker experiences not relief but pain that is almost unendurable. Armstrong says that when emotion is repressed in the poems of Victorian women, the emotion is "consciously known,"[43] and this is the case in Levy's poem. Her speaker acknowledges that she has held her consciousness of shame and disappointment in check by means of self-discipline: "I thought my spirit and my heart were tamed / To deadness; dead the pangs that agonise."

Although this is Levy's only poem about a meeting with an earlier self, it is one of a number in *Plane-Tree* in which identity is probed through a confrontation (unwanted or fiercely desired) or an intense exchange with another person who is an aspect of the self. Usually this person is a beloved woman, and on the surface these seem to be love lyrics. In "London in July," published and probably written back in 1887, the speaker begins by asking why "all the people in the street / Should wear one woman's face?" First, the speaker identifies her beloved as a confirmed urbanite ("My love, she dwells in London town, / Nor leaves it in July"); at the end of the last stanza the speaker reveals that she is an urbanite too and proclaims, "The summer in the city's heat—/ That is enough for me." The two are counterparts—in this lyric the distinction between subject and object collapses quite openly—and yet they cannot meet, no matter how indefatigably the speaker seeks her double through the "various and intricate maze, / Wide waste of square and street." On the literal level, the poem is about obsessional love, but on another level it is about the frustrated desire to bring together parts of the psyche that are at odds.

The other poems in *Plane-Tree* that use a similar trope to represent the fragmentation of consciousness are much darker than "London in July," closer to the mood of "The Old House," published in April of 1889. The others are about a beloved person who has died, who is dying, whose death the speaker has dreamed, or who is suffering terribly. None of these lyrics appeared in print before the publication of Levy's posthumous volume of poetry, and I would be surprised if they were not all written in the last summer of her life. "The Lost Friend" belongs in the group although it is far more anguished than most, and it is different in another way that proves helpful. The difference is that this moving sonnet is *explicitly* figurative. There can be no doubt that the lover whose loss the speaker laments is the vehicle and the joyful component of her personality the tenor of this metaphor. Levy personifies both sorrow and joy, with the speaker insisting that "Joy is my friend, not sorrow" and that "in some far land we wandered long ago." Then her feelings well up, and she invokes "Joy" in a passionate outburst: "O vanished treasure of her hands and face!— / Beloved—to whose memory I cling." "The Lost Friend" substantiates my claim that Levy wrote poems in which her speaker, appearing to express her feelings about a lover, is giving voice to a state of inner alienation.

A quick glance at "In the Mile End Road" will suggest how an apparently simple (and yet cryptic) poem opens up when approached from this perspective. What Melvyn New calls its "tight little drama"[44] is actually about the dramatic confrontation with a self that has experienced death in life. My interpretation rests in part on the abstract way in which the encountered woman is represented. Mention is made of her "motion and mien" and her "airy tread," but the reader is given no more detail (just as the woman sought in "London in July" is never described physically). As a result, "my only love" seems to be a reification of a side of the self, not an actual woman. The lyric ends with the kind of startling reversal that Levy learned from Heine: "For one strange moment I forgot / My only love was dead." In this lyric Levy uses the experience of an illusionary encounter with a dead beloved to represent what was probably her own sense toward the end of her life of being among the walking dead.

"Impotens," another very short lyric, does not describe an actual or imagined meeting, but it too involves a splitting of the self. The speaker addresses another person who is "dear," saying how hard it is to endure the suffering the other experiences as a result of "The pitiless order of things / Whose laws we may change not break." The evolutionary diction seems to refer to the biological bad luck of being born flawed, and the invention of a double allows Levy to say that what has happened to her is horrifying and unfair, without specifying the form of suffering and without falling into self-pity or risking the charge of self-dramatization. "Impotens" is moving because the emotional burden falls on the speaker's compassion for an other, mentioning her own victimization only incidentally. These late lyrics may be the ones Nord has in mind when she says (in a note) that Levy's love poems "seem rather like exercises, often spirited ones, in which she carries convention to the point of taking a male poet's voice. Rather than revealing intimate feeling, they seem instead to be burying it completely."[45] The reason that most of these poems lack intimate feeling and none is erotic is that they are actually about the self, not romantic love.[46]

In Levy's poems about fragmentation of the self, feeling is usually held in check, minimized, but present. "The End of the Day" and "In the Nower," almost certainly written very near the end of her life, are lyrics in which exhaustion has won out. In the former (dedicated to "B. T." or Bertha Thomas, with whom, the calendar reveals, Levy went rowing in late July), rhythm, rhyme, imagery, and theme converge. The speaker tells about the conversation she and her friend have had while rowing until they are "Dead-tired, dog-tired." They have had their say "On life and death, on love and art, / On good or ill at Nature's heart. / Now, grown so tired, we scarce can lift / The lazy oars, but onward drift." While their topics are philosophical, the iambic tetrameter of these lines is monotonously regular and the rhymes inevitable. Instead of stimulating the speaker, the talk has dulled her mind, and what she has undergone mentally is echoed by nature, for the "vivid day" has become "shrouded" by clouds until "blurred and grey the landscape lies." In the last stanza the speaker acknowledges openly that far from regretting such mental fatigue, she welcomes it as a kind of anesthesia: "far better than thought I find / The drowsy blankness of the mind. / More than all joys of soul or sense / Is this divine indifference."

"In the Nower" (which the *OED* says is an archaic word for "nowhere") there is even less energy. The final words articulate what is surely Levy's own desire for the obliteration of sensation and consciousness: "I close my tired eyes—it were / So simple not to wake." In these two poems Levy has finally achieved minimal feeling, but, unlike Christina Rossetti, Levy could not dampen her desires to such an extent that she could live on and write important poetry that was "free of any sentiment at all." It is painful to compare "The End of the Day" and "In the Nower" with the clamor of grievances in Levy's youthful, unpublished *"Poeta Esuriens"* or with the angry demands and refusal to live of the despondent speaker in "A Minor Poet" (he retains enough feeling to be outraged at cosmic injustice).

As Levy struggled to channel into art the magnitude of her growing distaste for life, she developed methods to represent what was happening to her. The lyrics just examined convey Levy's inability to make sense of life; display her determination to lighten the "burden of individual life" that weighed her down; reveal her desire for escape into a realm of the imagination where she could be free and happy; and evoke her sense of inner discord and estrangement. "In the Nower," one of Levy's final poetic utterances, shows a numbing of the emotions that goes beyond Rossetti's art of minimal feeling to the extinction of all affect; after such a poem one does not expect anything other than silence.

The calendar shows that Levy kept up her busy pace through July and early August though her activities were almost entirely social. On August 6, 1889, Levy took her nephews on a picnic and visited Jenny. At that point the calendar becomes a graphic representation of Levy's plunge into what was certainly a major episode of depression. From August 7 through August 30 the words "Ill At Endsleigh Gardens" are slashed across the page; after August 16 she added, "Corrected proofs of *A London Plane-Tree*, et.c." During this time she wrote two notes to Louise Moulton. In one Levy invites Moulton to tea at Endsleigh Gardens, the only evidence that Levy did not completely cut herself off from the outside world after she retreated to her parents' house. The other, written at the very end of the month, indicates that she still hoped to recover from her bout with depression: "I am still very unwell, and am going off tomorrow to the country, to see if that will do me any good . . . . I hope we shall meet next year."[47]

During that August, while in seclusion, Levy probably wrote, in addition to the poems about dissociation from the self, two others—"In the Nower" and "The Promise of Sleep"—and the story "Wise in Her Generation."[48] Three of these poems and the story appeared in *Woman's World* in 1890 after her death.[49] Her final story may have been written earlier in 1889 because its power as a work of fiction makes it unlikely to be the product of a mind in the grip of a major depression although the bitterness of its vision is reason to believe that it dates from her final summer.

"Wise in Her Generation" is additional evidence that Levy's discomfort with an ethos that celebrated the cynical pursuit of self-interest was by no means confined to a critique of Anglo-Jewry. The first-person narrator, a young woman, tells how, in her first social season, the preceding year, she fell in love with Philip, but the handsome and flirtatious young lawyer dropped her to marry a wealthy woman who could further his career (this, of course, is what Reuben Sachs does to Judith Quixano). Philip and Virginia, the narrator, meet again a year later at a ball. At the same social event she also meets Sir Guy, an aristocrat and "socialist of an advanced type." Not able to fall in love with Sir Guy and still responsive to the personal magnetism of Philip, Virginia is determined to be tough and cynical, ready to treat men as she has been treated; in this way she resembles Levy's speaker in "Félise to Her Lover." Understanding the courtship ritual for what it is, she has "no intention of playing a losing game."

The phrase "last year" recurs as it does in Levy's early poem, and Levy returns to the question of constancy in love that had been such a preoccupation in her writing, but Virginia, while admitting that "life can hold no such moment in store" for her than the way she felt during her courtship by Phillip, tells him flatly (in a conversation that occurs only in her mind) that she no longer loves him. Remarks such as "It is the third day and I have risen again" and "You were right, Philip; and I who once believed myself your victim, crushed beneath the juggernaught-car of your ambition—I was wrong" (the latter uttered in another imaginary conversation) reveal Virginia's determination to abjure self-pity and reproach (New's ed. 487). The double bind that women find themselves in is exposed in an actual ballroom exchange between Virginia and her former suitor. When she says, "For thorough-going untiring support of one's own interests, there is, after all, no one like yourself," Philip is shocked: "Don't! . . . don't! It doesn't do for a woman to talk like that!" (492).

After Sir Guy proposes marriage in a letter, she sits in front of her mirror: "The reflection of my face caught my vision; its expression was scarcely one of triumph. And surely there must be some mistake in the calendar, some trick in the sand and quicksilver; I was not twenty, with smooth cheeks—I was a hundred years old and wrinkled!" The image of her double—herself grown old and corrupt—makes Virginia realize she must turn her suitor down despite his "thirty-thousand a year." She says, "I will take no undue credit to myself; had no choice in the matter; I simply could not do it" (495). And yet she wonders whether, by the time of the next social season, she will be "capable not only of stalking, but also of killing my game" (several meanings of the word *game* are played with throughout). While I am not offering Levy's story as a challenge to the scholars who have named various narratives as sources for *The Picture of Dorian Gray*, it is possible that "Wise in Her Generation" played some part in Oscar Wilde's creative process.[50]

In Levy's final story her attack on the unrestrained individualism and savage competitiveness of her era could not be more explicit. As in her novel about Jewish life, she uses the language of Social Darwinism to challenge the Victorian doctrine that there was a boundary that protected the private sphere of life from the brutality of market relations. "Wise in Her Generation" ends with the protagonist looking out the window at London: "Black, black in its heart is the City; the blackness of man's heart is in its huge, hideous struggle for existence. . . . Better be unfit and perish than survive at such a cost" (497).

Emerging from seclusion on the last day of August, a Saturday, Levy went on an overnight trip with Olive Schreiner to the seaside and returned to spend Monday, September 3, at home. On Tuesday she went away again with Schreiner to St. Alban's, another resort, returning to Endsleigh Gardens on September 6. Bella Duffy, in a letter to Vernon Lee written after she heard of Levy's death, says that Levy had "looked ill all the summer" and gives us a glimpse of Levy's state just before she took her life:

> I had miserable scraps of notes from her all the time I was at Brighton, telling me she was ill, but just at the last, speaking of herself as *very* ill. Her last note . . . told me she had been for three days at the seaside with Olive Schreiner, but feeling no better, she had returned London and "crept back into her hole."[51]

On the day after returning from the seashore, a Saturday, Levy recorded that she "Dined at Katie's" (Lewis, Isabel, and the younger children were away). On Sunday she made her last entry: "Alone at home all day." Levy died early Tuesday morning, the 10th of September. Her death certificate states that the cause of death was "asphyxia from the inhalation of Carbonic Oxide Gas from the burning of charcoal. Suicide when of Unsound Mind."

Grace Black wrote to Ernest Radford:

Clemie wrote to me on Friday this:—"When I arrived here on Tuesday morning I found the woman who was in charge of the house at Endsleigh Gardens had been to say that Amy was ill and would I come round. I went as soon as I had had some breakfast expecting to find her slightly unwell and found Mrs. Levy and Katie in the most terrible grief. She had got charcoal, shut herself into a little room and so painlessly killed herself during the night."[52]

Olive Schreiner wrote two letters about Levy. In the first, to Edward Carpenter, she said:

I should have written yesterday but I had a blow that somewhat unfitted me. My dear friend Amy Levy had died the night before. She killed herself by shutting herself up in a room with charcoal. We had been away together for three days last week. But it did not seem to help her; her agony had gone past human help. The last thing I sent was the "Have Faith" page of *Towards Democracy*. She wrote me back a little note, "Thank you, it is very beautiful, but philosophy can't help me. I am too much shut in with the personal."[53]

Schreiner's second letter about Levy was written to Havelock Ellis in 1892. She wrote:

I was only trying to cheer Amy Levy . . . and professing that I found life delightful and worth living. I've often thought since that if I'd been more sympathetic to her melancholy mood, I might have done more for her. In her last note to me she said, "you care for science and art and helping your fellow-men, therefore life is worth living to you; to me it is worth nothing."[54]

What triggered Levy's last struggle with and defeat by "the great devil who lyeth ever in wait in the recesses of my soul"? There is no definitive answer, and this is not only because the record is forever incomplete (documents, such as letters that Levy may have written or received that addressed her final depression, have been destroyed or lost).[55] Most important, as this entire account of her life shows, the fatal act was overdetermined, resulting from the interplay between historical and cultural forces as well as from biology and happenstance.

Levy came of age at a time when her society promised her, as a woman and as a Jew, unprecedented mobility, and entering Cambridge she must have felt as though it were possible to be and do anything. Discrepancies between the ways the dominant culture and Anglo-Jewry defined womanliness must have facilitated her deconstruction of gender, making it easier for her to accept the new ideas she encountered at Brighton and Newnham. While *"Poeta Esuriens,"* "Lallie: A Cambridge Sketch," "Euphemia," and even "Between Two Stools" betray anxiety and ambivalence about the freedom to choose a "Miss Creak" existence, there is no sign that Levy ever tried to take up the activities of a conventional Jewish young woman of the period. Despite ambivalence, New Womanhood and life outside of what the narrator in *Reuben Sachs* refers to as "the tribal duckpond" must have looked enormously inviting. Yet, as we have observed, late Victorian England was at odds with itself about the Jews—highly tolerant and increasingly racist. While at Cambridge and in the years before 1886 Levy was forced to realize that although she might modify her subject positions (become an emancipated woman and an assimilated Jew), she had to accept many limits.

Levy found it much easier to achieve literary success than to establish an enduring attachment that might have stabilized her emotional life. Her shyness and hearing loss are probably factors, but these did not keep her from establishing deep and durable friendships. What (if any) relationship exists between Levy's sexual orientation and what she tells us about relations between women and men in the Anglo-Jewish community invites speculation (e.g., in "Middle-Class Jewish Women of To-Day," Levy says, "frank and healthy intercourse between both sexes is almost impossible"[56]). Whether "race" was a factor in Levy's inability to forge the lasting relationship with a woman that she seems to have needed is again open to conjecture. Was her Semitic background a liability with gentile women? Was a liaison with a Jewish woman less likely because the Jewish community (single-mindedly focused on marriage and children, as Levy says) had no place for the kind of romantic friendship between women that Martha Vicinus and others tell us was accepted in certain sectors of gentile society in this period?

From 1879 to 1886 Levy must have found that—romance apart— while she was welcome in gentile circles, acceptance was not unqualified. Many of those in the artistic and left-wing circles in which she moved, open to all sorts of new ideas, still perceived Jews as a racial other. As noted in the Prologue, this could take a relatively benign form—alterity could be imaged as exotic and mysterious—but more unpleasant stereotypes were common even among those who prided themselves on being advanced thinkers. Vernon Lee gives us a sample of the unreflecting anti-Semitism that was probably common even among Levy's friends and acquaintances. Writing to Bella Duffy from Tangiers about the Jews she saw there, Lee comments, "They are all Spanish, mostly handsome & intelligent & amiable, without any of the caricature and vulgarity of our Jews."[57] That she would express herself so openly in this way suggests either that she knew Duffy shared her prejudices or that she assumed everyone did.

Beatrice Webb's notions about the Jewish character were expressed less casually than those of Vernon Lee. In 1889 she published an essay called "The Jewish Community" in which she says that "the Jewish drive and ability to compete are . . . the most dangerous enemy of a harmonious society" and asks the Jews rhetorically, "Why bluster and fight when you may manipulate and control in secret?"[58] People in Levy's social circle may not have included her when they generalized about Jews, but many were probably incapable of forgetting that in their terms she was racially different. In the first half of the 1880s she seems to have been thin-skinned about anti-Semitic stereotypes—and prone to internalize them.

But 1886 was the first of nearly three stable and highly productive years for Levy. No longer aspiring to become as anglicized as possible, she constructed a usable self, one that was positioned to move comfortably within the Anglo-Jewish community as an unusually independent-minded Jewish woman and in the larger society as a Jew who was highly assimilated. Animated by the power of Lee's charismatic personality, Levy seems to have been content to admire her idol mainly from afar while becoming her pen pal and gaining acceptance by her London circle of friends and acquaintances. The friendship with Vernon Lee would have seemed particularly tonic when it appeared to lead to a romantic relationship with Dorothy Blomfield.

By 1888, when Levy wrote *Reuben Sachs,* she must have thought of herself as unusually fit for the literary representation of Anglo-Jewry to both Jewish and gentile readers since, after recovering a positive sense of Jewish identity, she was able to take advantage of what had once been felt as discord but now felt like healthy cultural hybridity. In May 1889, however, when "Cohen of Trinity" appeared, Levy was in a far different frame of mind. On a personal level, her hopes for a relationship with Blomfield were over and her friendship with Vernon Lee attenuated.[59] Moreover, Levy's Jewish novel had been treated as an act of treason by the Jewish press (except for the *Chronicle,* which did not specifically acknowledge its existence) and as an exposé of Jewish life by most of the gentile reviewers. "Cohen of Trinity" reveals what the calendar does not: the controversy generated by *Reuben Sachs* caused Levy to shift from the belief that she could be at home in both the gentile and the Jewish worlds to the conviction that she did not belong in the former and could not be content with the latter.

When her protagonist Cohen cites a portion of "Caliban upon Setebos"[60] he delivers more of Browning's lines than does Melissa in "Out of the World" quoting from the same passage. Melissa cites only the part about a fish from an icy stream that attempts to exist in the warmer ocean but sickens there and so returns to the stream where it originated. In "Out of the World" Levy uses Browning to make a statement about how acceptance of one's limits is a necessary step toward defining one's identity. But when Cohen quotes the passage more fully, the meaning that emerges, especially in the context of the story, is bitter: the fish "'flounced back from bliss she was not born to breathe / And in her own bonds buried her despair, / Hating and loving warmth alike'" (New's ed. 480). Cohen's implication is that Jews who would assimilate are like the unfortunate stream-bred fish. Forced to return to the Jewish community because they cannot thrive in gentile society, they live lives of constraint and despondency. The three identity narratives Levy wrote during her Cambridge years show how preoccupied she had been by the possibility of conversions of identity. Then she modified her objectives so that what she wanted was not self-transformation but mobility between the two worlds she knew. Now in 1889, when Levy has Caliban express the impossibility of swimming in two different kinds of water, he is speaking not only for Cohen but for herself.

But Levy misquotes Browning, substituting "bonds" for "bounds," a substitution, whether deliberate or inadvertent, that carries two meanings: bonds of affection and bondage. Perhaps her affection for her fellow Jews was heightened by the furor over the novel (at the same time that she continued to feel the narrowness of Jewish life). The *Jewish Chronicle*, after all, had not criticized her overtly, and (despite what Garnett says about how the novel "brought upon the author much unpleasant criticism")[61] most of Levy's Jewish friends and acquaintances may have taken a reasonable attitude toward *Reuben Sachs*. Max Beer reports that Eleanor Marx told him: "The Jewish community did not relish the book, but did not show the animosity of which the many-tongued *fama* gossiped. Amy told me that she was treated to the last with great kindness by the best families of the community."[62] And the smugness with which the gentile press (for the most part) assumed Levy was pillorying her people may have engendered the "hate" part of the love/hate relationship with the larger society to which Caliban refers. Her calendar shows that Levy by no means swam exclusively in the stream of Jewish life in 1889, but she saw Jewish friends with a frequency that may have been unprecedented in her adult life and may have been a response, albeit a paradoxical one, to the brouhaha over *Reuben Sachs.*

Catherine Belsey posits that while subjectivity is inevitably "displaced across a range of discourses in which the concrete individual participates," contradictions among subject positions can produce "intolerable pressure" and that "one way of responding to this situation is to become sick."[63] Even without knowing about Levy's life, the reader of her fiction and poetry feels the clash of what the narrator of "Cohen of Trinity" calls "the warring elements within that discordant nature." Levy's susceptibility to major depression made it easy for her to develop a genuine sickness. But one is forced to speculate about why she was unable to recuperate from her final breakdown as she had from previous ones; her depressive illness made the tragedy possible but was not in itself a sufficient cause.

The net that Levy was unable to extricate herself from appears to have been woven from many strands. In addition to the collapse of her conviction that she could bridge the gentile and Jewish worlds, she felt anxiety and guilt—expressed in "Cohen of Trinity"—over whether in writing *Reuben Sachs* she had misrepresented her people by unwittingly looking at them through the lens of an outsider. The notion that, as the *Cambridge Review* put it, she had written the novel out of hostility to modern Judaism and to modern Jews must have been felt with particular keenness because she had worked so hard to defeat the "Leopold Leuniger" voice within.

An unrelated but perhaps equally important factor may have been the fear, expressed in her 1888 letter to Clementina (letter 36), that she did not "have many more sane years." Then there was her poor physical health, particularly her deafness. And the failure of Levy's last romantic attachment cannot be underestimated. In *"Neue Leibe, Neues Leben"* Levy (with Vernon Lee in mind) had written, "this time is the last," but she had tried yet one more time to satisfy the Hungry Poet. What had begun in Levy's adolescence as an insatiable desire for emotional experience became, as she neared her thirties, a longing for the annihilation of feeling.

I have noted what looks like Levy's resilience in the face of harsh criticism from the Jewish press in the preceding January, February, and April.[64] In a note to Louise Moulton dated August 1, Levy wrote, "I cd. come to you any time to-morrow. . . . I am greatly interested in yr. article on Jewish novels, & shd. like to talk it over with you."[65] The calendar shows that she did see Moulton at her home late on August 2. That Levy remained eager to discuss the Jewish novel indicates a spirited determination not to let the negative response to *Reuben Sachs* keep her from writing more fiction about the Jews (which she had already done in "Cohen of Trinity").

But on August 2 the *Jewish Chronicle*, which up to that point had never mentioned Levy or her book by name, reviewed yet another novel offering a critical representation of Jewish life—Mrs. Andrew Dean's *Isaac Eller's Money*—an indictment of Anglo-Jewry for, among other things, its supposed lack of genuine religious feeling. It took the position that the Jews can become good British citizens only by converting to Christianity. The *Chronicle* reviewer wrote, "'Isaac Eller's Money' . . . is a clever performance in the style of 'Reuben Sachs,' but less intentionally offensive. . . . The clever ill-natured fiction of Jewish life has now reached a high level of development."[66] Since the *Chronicle* would already have come out by the time of day that Moulton and Levy met, their talk, on Levy's side, must have been laden with emotion.

How could Levy not have felt misunderstood? Her own novel interrogates Jewish life and raises the question of what it means to be a Jew. Granted, it offers a variety of negative stereotypes about Jewish people, but it also casts them in doubt, and it gives expression to the idea that Jews have a particular tenderness for one another (Judith Quixano, removed from her people, yearns to be back with them). But now even the *Jewish Chronicle* (the Jewish newspaper with which she had a particular relationship) found her novel more offensive than one that called for the conversion of the Jews and their disappearance as a people!

Levy's calendar shows that she left town on Saturday as planned, kept busy for the three days following, and, starting on Wednesday, the 7th of August, was "Ill at Endsleigh Gardens" for the rest of the month.

The proximity between the day the *Chronicle* published its review and the day Levy withdrew to her parents' house supports the inference that the article deflated her determination to be impervious to criticism of *Reuben Sachs*. Although the calendar shows what looks like normal activity during the five-day interval before her collapse, she must have been sliding into an episode of clinical depression.

A postcard from Vernon Lee to her mother written in early September raises the possibility that near the end Levy felt hurt and humiliated by the recognition that she was valued only opportunistically by Lee. Again on the lookout for someone to serve as secretary to her invalid half-brother, Lee wrote, "In despair at not bringing Eugene anybody I have asked Miss Levy. I don't love her, but she's a poor little person & clever & can talk poetry. . . . No answer yet."[67] Although Levy never saw this card, Lee may have been unable to disguise her condescension and exploitative attitude, and her attempt to recruit Levy could not have come at a worse time. Vernon Lee's invitation would have arrived at Endsleigh Gardens just before or after Lee's postcard to her mother, dated September 5, was written; Levy must have read Lee's letter on September 2 or on September 6—upon returning from one of the two trips to resorts that she took with Oliver Schreiner in a last attempt to regain the will to go on with life.

In a letter to Duffy written in October after the suicide, Lee seems gleeful about being the bearer of a delicious nugget of gossip. She says: "Poor Miss Levy! The truth has little by little dribbled out. She killed herself with charcoal. . . . But she had every right: she learned in the last 6 weeks that she was on the verge of a horrible & loathsome form of madness apparently running in the family, & of which she had seen a brother of hers die."[68] The brother, of course, would have been Alfred, whose death may have been from syphilis, which medical science now understands he would have had to contract on his own. The Victorians believed that syphilis could be transmitted congenitally and reveal itself in an adult who had appeared normal (Ibsen's *Ghosts* is a record of that misconception).[69] That Levy worried about madness is documented by her own letter to Clementina (letter 36) and Garnett's statement about her "fear of insanity."[70] Suffering from a variety of physical problems,[71] Levy may have experienced symptoms in the summer of 1889 that made her think she detected in herself the disease that had killed Alfred.

Is it possible that Levy, depressed and wondering if she was doomed, began to play with the idea of herself as another Sappho, the protagonist in one last narrative fashioned to give form and meaning to her end?[72] This notion does not require the assumption that Levy had made a firm decision to kill herself before she actually did so. We know from poems like "To Myself," written at Newnham, and morbid jokes in letters to Katie that thoughts of suicide always hovered in her consciousness. The idea that Levy had Sappho in mind toward the end of her life—that she constructed yet another one of her personae—comes from the fact that three of the poems in Levy's posthumous *London Plane-Tree* appear under the heading "Songs from THE NEW PHAON" (unpublished).[73] Details about the suicide handed down in Levy's family—for example, that the bed was surrounded by vases of flowers[74]—support the idea that it was enacted as a scene from a narrative, but as for the nature of that narrative, it is easy to pose questions, hard to provide answers. Why "The NEW PHAON" rather than "The NEW SAPPHO"? The significance of Levy's projected book title (certainly provocative) can never be understood.

Amy Levy's death elicited a variety of responses. Beatrice Webb, acquainted with Levy as one of the crowd of women who regularly worked at the British Museum, assumed that Levy was defeated by the difficulties of being an emancipated woman trying to bring about social justice. Deborah Nord quotes from Webb's diary about "the brilliant young authoress . . . who has chosen to die rather than stand up longer to live. We talk of courage to meet death; alas, in these terrible days of mental pressure it is courage to live we most lack, not courage to die."[75] Failing to take into account the particularities of the human lot and the unevenness of the way life's burdens are distributed, Webb assumed Levy's troubles were much like her own. (She would have done well to contemplate the words of Levy's minor poet: "I am myself, as each man is himself—/ Feels his own pain, joys his own joy.")

Bella Duffy, who knew Levy well, captured some of her friend's specific qualities and gauged her valor: "I was quite fond of her, with a fondness born of admiration for her clear-cut, luminous mind. . . . What made her so interesting to me was a forlorn sort of courage that she had, and the manner in wh. at the *very* worst an intellectual stimulus could rouse her."[76] Ellen Darwin, who hinted in her review of *A London Plane-Tree* that she too was a friend, also recognized Levy's bravery, understanding it not as forlorn but as heroic: "To live as she did, with an eager vital temperament, continually under the shadow of a great mental depression which fettered and chilled all her energies . . . is tragic. For it is not only events that make tragedies, and heroism is sometimes merely the lonely struggle with temperament."[77]

Underlying one of Levy's lyrics is the stoic philosophy of Epictetes, who saw courage in choosing death over living a highly compromised life. Vernon Lee, in her reminiscence of the conversations she and Levy had about happiness when they first met, implies (without stating definitively) that Epictetes' ideas were part of that discussion.[78] The tragic heroism that Darwin saw in Levy's life is expressed in "To Death":

> *If within my heart there's mould,*
> *If the flames of Poesy*
> *And the flames of Love grow cold,*
> *Slay my body utterly.*
>
> *Swiftly, pause not nor delay;*
> *Let not my life's field be spread*
> *With the ash of feelings dead,*
> *Let thy singer soar away.*

This lyric probably offers a better explanation of Levy's final act than anything else that has been said.

Epilogue

In the immediate aftermath of Amy Levy's death, various literary figures appraised her work. In the obituary that Oscar Wilde published in *Woman's World* he asserted that a handful of her poems "would be enough to mark their writer as a poet of no mean excellence" and that "no intelligent critic could fail to see the promise of greater things" in her poetry. About *Reuben Sachs* Wilde wrote: "Its directness, its uncompromising truth, its depth of feeling, and, above all, its absence of any single superfluous word, make it, in some sort, a classic. . . . The strong undertone of moral earnestness never preached, gives a stability and force to the vivid portraiture, and prevents the satiric touches from degenerating into mere malice. Truly the book is an achievement."[1]

Richard Garnett found Levy's "Xantippe" her most powerful poem, mentioning its "passionate rhetoric" and "keen, piercing dialectic." As for Levy's fiction, he called *Reuben Sachs* "remarkable," praising the "condensed tragedy of the main action" and "the striking portraiture of the principal characters." Like Wilde, he foresaw greater achievement ahead if Levy had lived: "Her writings offer few traces of the usual immaturity of precocious talent; they are carefully constructed and highly finished, and the sudden advance made in 'Reuben Sachs' indicates a great reserve in undeveloped power."[2] We see that while Garnett and Wilde admired Levy's poetry, her potential as a novelist elicited their eloquence.

My own assessment is that *Reuben Sachs* and "Cohen of Trinity" are remarkably experimental in their use of narrative strategy, representation of subjective states of mind, and exploration of the multiplicity and indeterminacy of truth. And despite Levy's departure from classic realism in these narratives, her "Jewish" novel stands out from all but a few works of Victorian realism in the extraordinary verisimilitude of its characters. Levy paints even the important characters—Reuben, Judith, Leo, and Esther—with relatively few brush strokes (the novel is subtitled "a sketch"), yet these people are so deeply imagined and complex, their identity so fluid, that one feels that behind what they say and do lie past lives containing far more than what we have been told. Indeed, the reader has the illusion that these characters have futures that will unfold with the same mysterious mix of the predictable and the unforeseeable that is found in life.

The sketchiness of Levy's prose, both in her novels and in her short stories (her brevity and short paragraphs), starting with "Sokratics in the Strand" in 1884, shows a desire to move away from the Victorian novel—its length, detail, and sometimes ponderous prose—to a seemingly easier, more "journalistic" style that she must have thought was in keeping with a modern sensibility. At the same time, when Levy is writing well, her language, apparently simple, is rich in irony, parody, and allusion, its layers allowing her to probe the emotional dilemma of her characters with a lighter touch than would otherwise be the case given the heaviness of their predicaments and the moral inadequacy of her society without being (as Wilde observes) the slightest bit preachy.

A good many of Levy's short stories were written for the market and should be disregarded when the quality of her work is weighed. Wilde wrote in the obituary that "she herself was the first to speak slightingly" of some of her stories although in his view only "two or three are slight and careless."[3] In my opinion, only seven or eight should be taken seriously. Among the good ones—"The Doctor" and "Leopold Leuniger: A Study" (even though they show the marks of their author's immaturity), "Between Two Stools," "Sokratics in the Strand," "Cohen of Trinity," and "Wise in Her Generation"—are in a class with the finest short fiction of their time.[4] Levy's prose style in her serious fiction is always witty, and as she developed it grew increasingly graceful and elegant without ceasing to be wry and colloquial.

W. B. Yeats encouraged readers to take Levy's poetry seriously too. Having read only the poems, he wrote, "Had she cared to live, a future of some note awaited her."[5] Ellen Darwin was right in saying that the range of the poetry is narrow, with much of its power coming from Levy's "struggle for life and joy continually beaten back."[6] The narrow range of the poems in *A Minor Poet* comes in part from their being written in a minor key; my reference, of course, is not simply to the melancholy tone of this work but to its evocation of agonized states of mind that are different from those most people ever experience. The poems in *A Minor Poet and Other Verse* are boldly transgressive in their refusal to see any inherent harmony and meaning in the order of things.

In *A London Plane-Tree and Other Verse* the lyrics are so various that it is difficult to summarize Levy's achievement briefly, but they differ from her earlier work. Her language is more colloquial, and she abandons classical subjects, using allusions to Greek and Latin literature and mythology sparingly and almost always for witty effect.[7] Abandoning the dramatic monologue, she uses the lyric to express moods and states of mind that, paradoxically, often seem less personal, not because they do not express her own feelings but because she develops techniques that create distance. In these later poems her pitch remains for the most part in the melancholy register most natural to her temperament, but the reader is often struck by the irony of her lyric voice, rare in a Victorian woman poet.

Levy had a wonderful sense of humor (as her letters show), and so it should not be surprising that her comic poetry (especially "Reading," her unpublished satiric verse drama) is genuinely amusing. And we should not forget the subtle wit Levy's "serious" poems can have—for example, "Ballade of an Omnibus" and "A Ballad of Religion and Marriage." These and some of her other best poems are not melancholy (among them "Sinfonia Eroica," "Borderland," "Lohengrin," "Philosophy," and "The Birch-Tree at Loschwitz"). From the start Levy's poems are notable for their extraordinary emotional integrity, and a good many of the lyrics she wrote after *A Minor Poet and Other Verse* stand out, whether they are joyful or sad, because of their condensed power.

Levy's death at such a young age was a loss for letters, and yet the work that she did in her twenties would deserve to be read and remembered even if she had lived out the time on earth allotted to the most fortunate. Until recently she has been a figure obscured by misconceptions and myths when she was not entirely neglected; before Melvyn New's edition, her work had been accessible only to the most determined readers. This book too should play a part in allowing Amy Levy to take her rightful place in literature.

Appendix

Letters from Amy Levy, ca. 1870
to August 1889

■ These letters that Amy Levy wrote to her parents when she was a child already show her sense of humor and her interest in verse. The first is undated and contains two notes, one to Mama and one to Papa.

1

My Dear Mama,

I was of course not at all surprised when I [word omitted] that the house was dull without us; for am I not the glorious star, in fact the angelic treasure of our small community? We went today to St. Peters and were very much interested in the ancient church (which is 800 years old) and graveyard. One curious inscription on a head stone attracted our attention particularly; Miss Pateman[1] wrote it down and I will now give you a copy of it:

RICHARD JOY (CALLED THE
KENTISH SAMSON) DIED IN 1702
Herculean hero formed for strength
At last here lies his length and breadth
See! How mighty man is fall'n

> To death the strong and weak are all one
> And the same judgment doth befall
> Goliath great and David small!

Is it not comical? There was another one equally amusing but it was so digust-
ing [sic][2] Miss Pateman would not let me send it to you. We have caught such
a lot of fish and shrimp, prawns and crabs. Tell Tub that . . . I have collected
many shells. With love to all. I remain et.c.

Your affectionate Amy

Dear Papa,

I have time before tea to write to you, a few lines so that you may not think I
have forgotten you. I wish you would come down with Mama to see us; it is so
very nice here. You would like to see St. Peter's old church it is so curious and
antique.

Adieu. with love I remain

Yours affectionately—

[on back of page] P.S. I am very very very sorry about the bathing. I have
grown as fat as this.

[drawing of a very round person]

1. Emily Pateman (b. 1848) was the family governess. After the four older children
no longer needed her, she taught their cousins for a while, then started a small school.
Her birth date shows she was only thirteen years older than Amy Levy and therefore
no more than twenty-four when this first letter was written, for Amy was surely no
more than ten or eleven. Pateman filled out a page in Levy's Confessions Book (probably in the late 1870s, when Levy was in high school); given her pupil's precocious commitment to feminism, it is interesting that she wrote "The Women's Rights" in answer
to a question about her "pet aversion."

2. I will note misspellings and errors in syntax (probably accidents) with sic, but
will either ignore or correct errors in punctuation in Levy's letters.

2   October 30th, 1872

My Dear Papa,

It was very kind of you to answer my letter so soon, for I did not expect
that you would do so at all. I am very sorry on account of my bad characters,[1]
but I will try in the future to have better ones. . . . I have composed a piece of
poetry, on Mr. Balda's Spoils of War. It runs thus:

"As from that burning city
The hapless maid doth rush,
There is a voice within her,
A voice she cannot hush."

Pateman purposed taking us to St. Paul's Cathedral, but the weather being so unfavorable we shall spend our half holiday at home.[2] Having no more news I must conclude, with love to yourself & Mama, with thousands of kisses for Puffball, I remain,

Your fond child.

Amy J. Levy.

1. Eleven-year-old Amy makes both "characters" and "ones" plural, so she must be referring to her handwriting and not to her character.

2. The reference to St. Paul's Cathedral and to "our half holiday at home" indicates that this letter was written at a time when the children remained in London with their governess while their parents were away.

■ In 1876, when she was almost fifteen, Amy Levy began attending Brighton High School for Girls (in the seaside resort town of Brighton). The school had just opened. Run by the Girls Public Day School Company, it was one of the reformed secondary schools for girls that opened in the last three decades of the nineteenth century. Unlike the old-fashioned "ladies seminaries," which flourished until the end of the century, these schools were "committed to higher, or at least a more regularized, academic standard, classes streamed according to age, examinations, a flat, limited fee, and trained teachers."[1] The Girls Public Day School Company was founded in 1871 by sisters and feminist reformers Maria Grey and Emily Shirreff. The schools that were under its aegis "stressed the value of academic attainment over and above domestic skills," had entrance requirements for prospective pupils, and "espoused a . . . philosophy of women's rights."[2]

Most of the children who attended the school lived in boardinghouses while some lived at home. Although it was primarily a secondary school for girls, Brighton High took young boys, so Alfred, Willy, and Ned (Edmund), three of Levy's brothers, received instruction there too. Levy's parents apparently were in Brighton during part of the time she attended the school, but she and her six siblings were all born in London. The family residence from 1872 to 1884 was 11 Sussex Place, Regents Park. Perhaps the Levys did not live in Brighton but visited extended family there, sometimes for substantial periods of time.

The letters that Levy wrote from high school to her sister Katie[3] are notably high-spirited, even exuberant; they resound with ironic amusement, both about others and herself. The voice could be that of an irreverent, self-dramatizing, precocious adolescent of our own era although her openness in regard to her obsession with her adored headmistress, Edith Creak, belongs to her own period.

1. See Martha Vicinus, *Independent Women: Work and Community for Single Women, 1850–1920* (Chicago: University of Chicago Press, 1985), 166.

2. See Philippa Levine, *Feminist Lives in Victorian England: Private Roles and Public Commitment* (Oxford: Basil Blackwell, 1990), 136.

3. Katie, born on March 3, 1860, was sixteen in the autumn of 1876.

■ All of the letters from Brighton are undated, but internal evidence establishes that this one and the one that follows were written in 1876.

3

The Wick[1]

My dear Mama,

Thank you very much for the money, buttons, and the letter you sent me. I have quite recovered from the "blues" which it was horrid of me to mention.[2] Alfred says he told you today of Willy[3] having sprained his foot; it is so trifling that Mrs. Creak[4] did not think it necessary to mention it to you; his foot being rather swollen, he is to remain in bed for a few days; I have visited him several times today; he seems very lively and feels well; don't bother in the least about him; Mrs. Creak says that you are now to decide if I am to stay next term at school, and, if so, if the music is to be continued, it being just a month to the holidays. I am reading now a very nice book, "Hitherto"; it is American. As I am rather busy tonight please excuse this short letter. My conscience pricks me that I bother you a great deal. . . .

With love to you all.

I am—

Yr. fond child

Amy Levy

1. The Brighton High School building was often referred to as the "Wick," as it is here, or the "Temple," as in other letters; many of the letters from Levy's school years

have street addresses, presumably that of the boardinghouse where she resided. Perhaps she gave the "Wick" as a return address on letters she wrote while in the school building.

2. Levy refers to having had "the blues," the first mention of what was very likely an early episode of the depressive illness she grappled with all her life; apparently she felt she ought not to have burdened her parents by telling them of it.

3. Alfred would have been thirteen and Willy eleven years old in autumn of 1876.

4. Levy refers to "Mrs." instead of "Miss" Creak, possibly designating Edith Creak's mother, who may have owned the boardinghouse and served as a housemother. Edith Creak was from a family in the Brighton-Hove area. See Richard Garnett III's biography of his grandmother, *Constance Garnett, a Heroic Life* (London: Sinclair-Stevenson, 1991).

4

The Wick

My dear Mama,

I have just written to Mrs. Rosie to thank her for, & decline her invitation. I suppose you like your dinners with Aunt Matilda; who treats? This afternoon Alfred & I went to Preston Street before school, & therefore refreshed to the amount of 5 [pence] & also bought something for the prostrate William, who rather enjoys his captivity. His foot is getting on all right.[1] I must congratulate you on your new nephew; poor Aunt Bessie with 10 children![2] . . . The tea-bell will soon ring so I must leave off. Do you visit Grandmama? With love to all & hope you are quite well. I am your fond child. Amy Levy

1. Willy's foot is still healing so this letter is obviously written soon after the previous one.

2. The "new nephew" is Reginald Saul Solomon, the son of Amy's father's sister Elizabeth and her husband, Saul. This cousin was born in 1876, thereby dating these two letters from Levy's first year at Brighton High School.

5

49 Brunswick Place
Brighton

My Dear Katie,

Mama is rather surprised that she has not heard from you. Are you gay, lazy, or sick? Belle has already given you a graphic account of our [turtling?], it was rather rich. This morning Connie[1] came, and we fetched Grace,[2] & all four went for a walk. We went over to the Pavilion[3] (it being the 1st Monday in the month) & enjoyed ourselves, sentimentalizing, lounging in the drawing rooms, and inspecting the pictures. Belle & Grace explored the kitchens et.c.—After we went to Cowleys where I stood (the proud spirited Sloman paid for itself). After lunch I obtained the maternal consent to visit my heart's love,[4] and accordingly at about 3:45 with a clean face, a beating heart and Ella[5] for a protector, set out (in my green!) for the Temple (i.e. the Wick). But the [illegible] informed me that Miss Creak had "gone out for a *holiday*"! (I suppose she meant a *jaunt*.) Tomorrow I intend to repeat the experiment, with more success I hope.—Have I not grown bold since yr. absence? I am reading "Shirley;"[6] it is clever but heavy; I am resolved to eschew *very* light literature. I had my Latin lesson to-day. Mr. Lomus complimented me on my Latin generally, and on my translation of Ovid, particularly—said worms[7] often go up for exams with less knowledge than I have. Also he wondered if She were a good Classical scholar, and said that what she had passed in, in mathematics, would not be recommendation enough for a private mathematical master! Alas! Conny, the Old Birds, and George dine here Saturday—aren't you sorry that you won't be here?[8] I saw the Orleans Plum, by the bye, riding with Butter to-day, rather to my surprise; to-morrow I mount my steed once more. Conny related to me to-day an incident of some Brightonian—now that long years ago, the. . . . [The letter ends here; the last page or pages are missing.]

    1. There are references to both a "Connie" and a "Conny" in these letters. Two girls named Constance attended Brighton High with Levy, and she makes no consistent distinction in the spelling of their names. Constance Black, who later married Edward Garnett, the well-known editor, was to become the famous translator of Russian literature. She attended Newnham College with Levy and is mentioned frequently in the letters from Cambridge. The other "Conny" or "Connie" was Constance Leon, a Jewish girl whose family seems to have been friendly with the Levys.

    2. Grace is likely to be Grace Black, Connie Black's sister, who may not have been a student at the school. The Black family lived in Brighton, and Levy became acquainted with them all; Clementina, the eldest, ultimately became her closest friend.

    3. The Royal Pavilion is the palace erected in Brighton by the prince regent in 1818. Built in an ornate, monumental Indian style, it is furnished lavishly, with paintings and other works of art, many of them Eastern.

    4. This is the only letter in which the woman on whom the adolescent Amy Levy had a crush is explicitly identified: Miss Creak is Levy's "heart's love." In other letters the object of her affections is designated only as "the O. A.," initials that must had stood for some administrative title. Despite what Levy says here about Edith Creak's

education, Creak had distinguished herself in both mathematics and classics while at Cambridge (see Garnett's biography).

5. Ella was the youngest daughter in the Levy family, and she would have been four at this time since she was born in 1872; Amy's parents apparently were staying in Brighton at this point because she obtains "the maternal consent" to go visit Miss Creak at the school building.

6. "Shirley" must be Charlotte Brontë's second novel, published in 1851.

7. The term *worms* appears to be schoolgirl slang for abject, contemptible creatures, a meaning found in the *OED*, which labels it Old English.

8. Because Levy assumes that her sister is familiar with the people she mentions, it seems likely that Katie had previously been a student at Brighton.

■ The next three letters are from the same address (the same boardinghouse), so they probably are from the same year.

6

27 St. Michael's Place

My Dear Katie,

I utterly despise you![1] I never did think your passion" (?)[2] worth much & now my suspicions of its spuriousness are confirmed. Fancy even comparing the leering O.B. to the sweet, sweet O.A.! Thursday at algebra she came up to me spontaneously & asked if I had learnt with Miss Orme, if you liked her, (I said "awfully!") & what she was like, tall or short, etc.? Was it not rich? I think she wanted to identify her from among the worms she'd seen at Burlington House. She was actually imprudent enough to discuss this year's matric with Nelly Huggett, & lent her the papers. I saw from some sweet little dashes around them that she did all the geometry and heaps of natural philosophy. I carefully sounded Nelly, but I don't think she knows. Please find out as soon as possible if she has passed. It is fearfully rich here; Maggie & I don't know how to sit sometimes, for there is a kind of guerilla warfare between "Grandma,"[3] & one of the small boys [illegible]. The wretched old woman, too, loves to make filthy remarks about the O.A.; as, the other day at dinner we were discussing whether Bessy or Edith suited her best, when she put in viciously "I shd. say "Crummy!" Of course, wrathful as we felt, we burst; and the crone, encouraged, went on about her being "rather stout,"[4] and wanting more exercise than boating in the holidays. Wasn't it horrid? I met and skated with the Hopkins party yesterday at the rink; Bella told me that the O.A. had been reproaching her for overwork, and that she was only to prepare half her

"Delectus." Nelly, and *not* Miss Creak, takes our French; Ugh! Yesterday the Eversheds, Johnsons, Cutler, Collin, Bookbird, and Conny went to Arundel. [The final page or pages of the letter are missing.]

1. Under the address on the manuscript is a picture of a heart with an arrow piercing it (Levy drew that same picture under the return address in the following two letters). On this one, next to the heart is a girl's profile, with the word "fiend" written below it; it is likely that the face is meant to be Katie's.

2. The question mark is in the original letter. It would seem from Levy's mockingly scornful mention of Katie's passion that she too has or has had a crush that is either waning (and therefore contemptible) or that Amy cannot respect, perhaps because she does not respect its object.

3. Probably someone who helped supervise the children.

4. The dinner-table conversation about whether the name "Bessy" or "Edith" was more suitable for the "O.A." is more evidence that Levy's beloved O.A. was Edith Creak. She is described in Garnett, *Constance Garnett,* as "large and fat and plain" (27), and her photo shows that she was very heavy (see Figure 6). Levy is probably pretending to be outraged that Miss Creak has been described as stout.

7

27 St. Michael's Place
Brighton

My dear Katie,

It's awfully good of me, wasn't it? to write—tho' I daresay you won't appreciate my goodness being too wholly absorbed in your best-best.[1] This week we have a screaming joke at school—an examiner of sober mien & middle age; he & the O.A. patrol the place; morning and afternoon, pestering the ignorant girls with viva voce exams. Our turn comes tomorrow. This morning we had a written grammar exam in wh. I played the fool; but She says if I don't do well it's not to be in the report, as I've been away half the term.[2] I send you the papers (beastly hard, even She [illegible] they are) but please return them directly you've finished with them. Yesterday afternoon, & evening, & early this morning I have been grinding[3] Morris, and then of course scarcely anything was asked out of it. This afternoon exhausted nature refreshed itself! cold-creamed, on the bed (you've no idea how sweet an anointed Pegtop can look) while Conny looked on admiringly. Then the fair trio set off for Milton[4] and had an exquisite talk with their respective divinities.[5] Mine looked lovely. She grows more passion-inspiring daily; how after having known and liked her you can think of sacrificing an hour of her company for that little——[6] passes my comprehension. After the interview we cooled our hot souls at Gatti's. Tomorrow's Geography, ugh—I must grind, and am just thinking of wet towels & Page. Today a table was laid in the Sanctum[7] for Creak, Sully, and the examiner.

What wd. you have given to have been present at the repast? Peg sends her love. Sentiment & fatigue stay my pen. Do explain the "Sedens pro gaudio" & family feed. How do you feel? What do you think about when you're alone? I can't imagine. How weak the "Harum" is this month.[8] Conny Leon doesn't shine, but I don't think the Mosely's bad, though she personally is odious. I've sent sketches & poem.

Yours scornfully,
Amy Levy

1. The term "best-best" would seem to refer either to Katie's best friend or, perhaps, to a person she has a crush on.

2. Levy's remark that she has "been away half the term" is important—was she ill? Could she have been in a depression? She is certainly exuberant in this letter.

3. The word *grind* in this and other letters means "study hard," slang that is still used today, but here Levy uses it as a transitive verb, and in other letters she uses "ground" as the past tense of the verb: these usages have died out.

4. This must be Milton Hall on Montpelier Street, where the school was located during its first four years.

5. The implication is that the "divinities" whom Levy and her two schoolmates visit at the school are female teachers whom they have crushes on.

6. The line is in the original.

7. The ironic reference to "the sanctum" links an early, unpublished story, "Miss C's Secretary" (written while Levy was at boarding school) to Brighton High School; in the story the headmistress's office is called "the sanctum."

8. "Harum Scarum" is the name of the manuscript literary journal that Amy and Katie put out during the years Amy was at Brighton. The sketches and poem that she is sending with her letter must be for its next issue.

8

27 St. Michael's Place
Brighton

My dear Katie,

Thanks for yr. letter. Perhaps it sounds bad but I'm awfully sorry the family's coming down—it's so luxurious living away from everyone & not being rubbed all the wrong way. Yesterday morning the Geo[1] came off—I did filthily; in the afternoon we had viva voce (French and History). It was a perfect farce. All of us were scared, excepting Conny who poured volumes at his head (wrong facts & all), wh. he accepted with a sort of reverential bewilderment. We had to translate a piece of "Le Menteur" (Mary Haycroft distinguished herself awfully in this) and had a question each. Peg and I didn't answer some compound tense—mad? He then distributed idiotic questions at the rate of one each, on early English Hist., nearly all of which were answered. This rot occupied about an hour and a half; the Divinities sat in the room all the time and the O.A. declared afterwards that she nearly exploded. The examiner appeared an awful fool & ignoramus & the Sweet One was awfully scornful; but he was a real man so *you* wd. have honored him. Conny was jubilant because Sully offered to give her a swimming lesson that afternoon where Both were going—but my poor Trojan couldn't accept.

After a converse with the worshipped Ones, we [illegible] at Clifford till tea after wh. muggy repast we simply ground German; indeed I worked so hard that I was too tired to bother with the paper this morning. First I had striven to cool my head with a "dip" before breakfast in company with Alice & Dottie. Today that blessed woman mounted guard for 4 hours—so you may imagine my eyes were not bent solely on my paper—She did look sweet—just working mathematics contentedly to Herself. She has flung out minute crumbs of sweetness lately to her wormy adorer, who bagged a divine passion-inspiring—whenever-I think-of-it—embrace today at the sanctum door. Frankly I'm more in love with her than ever—isn't it grim? I don't believe it will go for ages;[2] and I can never care for anyone or anything else while it lasts. Don't you like these egotistic outpourings? Of course this is quite confident-like. I make such different future pictures to what I used to—you married maternal, prudent & [illegible] with a tendency to laugh at the plain High School Mistress sister who grinds, and lodges with chums and adores "without return."[3] [No signature so the letter may have continued.]

1. This would seem to be a reference to a geography or geology exam.
2. This statement could be interpreted to mean that Levy doubts that her feelings for Miss Creak will endure, but in context it means just the opposite: she is saying that she believes her passion will be long-lasting.
3. What is perhaps most striking about Levy's expression of feelings for her head-

mistress is her exaggerated drama and self-mockery. Amy teases Katie by saying that though the examiner was "an utter fool" her sister would have "honored him" because "he was a real man." This, together with her prediction that Katie will marry, suggests that a significant distinction between them had already emerged: Katie was interested in men.

9

[no return address]

My dear Katie,

Even my fertile brain has not yet had success in inventing "news" and I merely write to send you Mrs. Mason's lean invitation wh. Mama is going to answer, as it was accompanied by a tender note, asking you to stay there for the ballette. Being Friday you can't go—sorry?[1] Yesterday Conny called for me as I had expected; she happened to mention that my spouse[2] was pining for me, when I said I wondered she had not called as such was the case & learned that the pious Mary & family "did not like to visit Jews, no orthodox persons did." Rich? Of course I do not mind the verdant notions of the Haycrofts, but what if she shared them? The thought has quite haunted me. Do you remember a quarrel I had with Nelly about Mary, when she said, alluding to the [illegible] tragedy, "you of all persons ought not to speak." Conny told me that she was alluding to my "race & religion"; filthy?[3] We lounged on the beach, & then went to the High for some books, but of course She wasn't there. Awful news! The Norris has these holidays, translated the whole of the Ovid, unaided & now "assists" at the Wednesday class! she told me yesterday afternoon that she did it from the time she got up, till the time she retired. Really she must be very clever, don't you think so?

Today I gave Ned[4] his lessons; his conduct is decidedly ahead of his mathematical & mnemonic powers. Give the girls my "love" & congratulate Ann for me; is she coming down before Monday? I have not yet copied any "Edgar"[5] but intend doing so today; if my suspicions of her anti Hebrew notions were confirmed, I should feel inclined to leave in all the objectionable parts, shouldn't you? Yesterday the Rouses & Nevilles called, & Mama was out![6] Tragical? I am fearfully bored, &. . . . [The remaining page or pages of the letter are missing.]

1. Levy probably assumes Katie cannot attend the "ballette" because it will take place on a Friday, the Jewish sabbath.

2. The reference to Amy's "spouse," who seems to be Mary Haycroft, is not surprising in its context. When Victorian girls or women were close friends, they often called each other "spouse" (in letters written in her late twenties, George Eliot [Mary Anne Evans] addressed her intimate friend Sarah Hennell as "spouse"). Levy's letter indicates that Conny Black was a far more important friend than Mary Haycroft, which suggests that, at least for adolescents, the spousal relationship might be quite shallow and short-lived.

3. The theme of anti-Semitism is introduced as a factor in Levy's life in this letter. "Conny" is almost certainly Constance Black, not Constance Leon, because it does not appear that the girl who tells Levy about Mary Haycroft's anti-Semitic sentiments is also Jewish.

4. Ned would have been six at this time.

5. The "Edgar" Levy says she is "copying" is probably the story mentioned in note 7 to letter 7. Finally named "Miss C.'s Secretary," its protagonist, Edgar, is secretary for the headmistress of a school. In the original version there may have been a character who corresponded to Mary Haycroft.

6. Levy seems to be staying with her parents.

■ Amy Levy entered Newnham (the second college for women at Cambridge) at the start of the Michaelmas term, in October 1879. Newnham College had begun taking women students in 1871, and when Levy arrived, there were approximately 230 students while the first Cambridge college for women, Girton, had 100.[1] Levy's friend Connie Black and another girl from Brighton, Ellen Huggett (Nelly), mentioned in letters 6 and 9, entered at the same time, so Levy had friends and acquaintances from the moment she arrived. Edith Creak, as Levy's letters show, was still very much involved in the life of the college and visited frequently. The Newnham records show that Creak was one of three "Old Students" in residence at the college during the "Long Vacation" of 1880; Amy Levy was also in residence.

During Levy's first year at Cambridge she lived in Norwich House, which opened in 1877 to house students for whom there was no room in Newnham Hall, the first building. Newnham Hall was constructed for the college in 1875 on a site of two and a half acres in the parish of Newnham, just outside the town of Cambridge. When North Hall was opened in 1880, Newnham Hall, which had been full to overflowing, was designated South Hall.

Levy left Newnham in 1881 without having taken her Tripos (exams taken at the end of the designated three years of study); women students won the right to take the Tripos in 1881, Levy's final year. While she was at Cambridge women were denied permission to attend university lectures and refused the Cambridge degree—which was not granted to women until 1948.[2]

1. Rita McWilliams-Tullberg, "Women and Degrees at Cambridge University, 1862–1897," in *A Widening Sphere: Changing Roles of Victorian Women*, ed. Martha Vicinus (Bloomington: Indiana University Press, 1980), 130.

2. Ibid., 120.

10

■ This is only a fragment of a letter, having no first page and leaving off in the middle of a sentence; it appears to date from just after Levy's arrival at Newnham. The diction and tone indicate that it is addressed to Katie.

& echo splendidly down the huge building, with its great stained glass windows, & high roof. It's simply a delicious place, with old deep carved stalls such as one reads about, and the candles in the middle only make the unlit part look more mysterious. Yesterday we went down to Latin lecture; Mr. Hicks is a nervous, [illegible] little man, who snorts abominably; we have to put our cards & address on his desk, & he questions us singulatum on what we have done et.c. Fortunately I brought some of your cards, as we have often to use them. After Latin Conny & I called on Madge, & we all four (Nelly was there too) went to look at Jesus College which we had not seen before. We then deposited Nelly & Conny at the Hall for Analytical [illegible], & Peg accompanied me home. On the way we took the Local Museum, a really fine place, with a rather good collection of pictures—there is one specially famous one where John the Baptist is represented in specs! We roared at the rich sight. After lunch (a sort of cold meat, cheesy, informal affair) I ground a little, till it was time to go down to French lecture. M. Bocquet is a sort of male Madame Abrassart; he lectures in French, to the dismay of some fair pupils; he gave us a dictee to test our grammar. One rich person there nearly killed me; she was old, fat, giggling, & highly excited, & kept up a sort of chorus of "Wee Monsieur," to his general remarks, whenever she understood them, which was rather infrequent. I looked round in vain for a twinkling orb, but only encountered feeble smiles at M. B's copious wit (?). Afterwards Madge, Nelly, Alice & I went to King's; Conny & Miss Bond were there also; the latter had been to see me, and asked me to call on her; I think it was very kind, as I know her very little. Nelly & I have called on Miss Kennedy but she was not at home. This morning I am going down to Greek for the first time. The girls here are a rum lot; one rich person (by name of Miss Green) is the very image of Cotkin; I have never seen such a likeness, another is exactly like a tall Mary Haycroft, & prowls about in the same way; she is always coming in & out of my room with messages, etc. She has a room which is the pride of her heart, quite gorgeous with china, pictures, etc.;[1] last night she gave a whist-ball, to which I was bidden, but I wanted to grind so did not go, it being invitation no. 2 which I had rejected.[2] There is another girl from Oxford High disposed. . . . [The rest of the letter is missing.]

1. The description of Miss Green's room is an example of how a student might by her own efforts do much to counter the spartan atmosphere inside the women's colleges at Cambridge. Such efforts correspond to accounts of life at the new women's colleges at Cambridge, including Levy's account in the *Alexandra*, March 4, 1881 (a published copy on newsprint is in the Amy Levy collection in London). In *Independent Women* Martha Vicinus mentions "the round of formal cocoa parties" which began at 9:30 P.M., after an hour or two of intensive study, which in turn followed such evening activities as dancing, literary clubs, and debate (131).

2. Levy acknowledges no trepidations about being accepted socially; nevertheless, it is possible that her decision to turn down invitations in order "to grind" came as much from social awkwardness as from dedication to her studies.

11

■ This fragment begins in the middle of a sentence (which I have omitted), but the word "soror" in the closing indicates the letter was to Katie, as does the prose style.

(I had an awful lot of sweetness from the O.A.). Sunday afternoon Nelly & I gave a D.V. ball, about which you will hear from "Creakine lips."[1] (They were both grimly polite, & appeared not to see the joke of it.) This week I have been working with tolerable steadiness. I do an average 6 hours a day—sometimes 7, sometimes only 5. I get so grimly fagged that I can't do more; the teaching here (excepting the French) is really crack—I feel myself getting on with my classes, though the modern languages aren't so satisfactory. Tonight we have a debate—subject Browning & Tennyson; I was to have led the opposition (in favour of R. B.) but backed out of it, yet think of speaking. Madge is coming, but Conny can't as the Newnham Shakespeare reading takes place, with Miss Gladstone as Portia[2]; I wish I were there if only to hear her—she is a most subtle person, for whom younger Newnhamites have violent G.Ps. [Grand Passions]. She is about 30, with a grand, rather large face, with the sweetest smile & manner you can image. I had the bliss of being helped by her the other day in the gym. when I was practising—she has a sort of queenly graciousness for all young or new girls, & is a sort of "cock" at Newnham. She spoke the other night at the Debate, and her speech was made even more effective than it otherwise wd. have been by the expression of her face, wh. is habitually calm & serious, but lights up occasionally with big smiles. There is a dear little creature here by name Miss Lloyd, who strikes me as particularly pretty. She is slight & dark, with a half solemn, half humorous face, & a lot of rough black hair always falling over her face. There is one Norwich House girl whom I like particularly; she is rather pretty, & "intensely" dressed, & we have had several long talks. I see a good deal of Madge & Conny. The other day Conny & I went for a long country walk, and came back laden with lovely, tinted berries. I have invested in gorgeous coffee-cups, real Chinese, greenish grey outside, with blue sprays inside.[3] Madge has pathetically worked me a kettle-holder, wh. was presented with howls. Indeed, I have howled a good deal since I have been here. I must look up some Greek for the benefit of the worthy Mr. Jenkinson, at whose class we invariably roar, so adieu.[4] Write soon to your fair soror

      Amy Levy

    1. Since Amy tells her sister that she will get an account of a Newnham event from "Creakine lips," Katie must have been in Brighton frequently and thus in regular contact with Edith Creak.

    2. While Levy is still reporting on the "sweetness" she has received from "the O.A.," there are now other stars in her galaxy. Helen Gladstone, who made such an impression on Levy, was the daughter of the prime minister William Gladstone and was vice principal of Newnham College for over a decade, leaving in 1896. In 1901 she became head of the Women's University Settlement, an organization that brought college women to work with women in the slums. At the bottom of the page Levy drew a picture of a woman's face in profile, labeling it "H. Gladstone." This sketch, together with the admiring description of Helen Gladstone's looks, manner, and charisma, brings to mind Levy's obsession with Miss Creak although there is no reason to think that Levy's feelings for Gladstone ever became a full-blown crush. There is a picture of Gladstone in Levy's photograph album (now in the possession of Katie's granddaughter).

The reference to "G.Ps" and the remark about Miss Gladstone as "a sort of 'cock' at Newnham" reminds us that in the women's colleges, as in the reformed secondary schools, intense feeling for other women, often with a significant erotic component, was common; it is impossible to estimate the extent to which these homoerotic feelings were sublimated or expressed physically.

3. Levy's purchase of pretty coffee cups—she clearly plans to entertain in her room—tells us that she participated in the social life of the college.

4. This fragment would seem to have been written fairly early in Levy's first year because she reports on how she spends her time, evaluates the quality of her teachers, and tells of new acquaintances.

12

■ Levy is still in her first year at Newnham even though the year is 1880 because she mentions going to visit Girton for the first time, and she is still living at Norwich House.

Norwich House

1880

My Dear Mama,

I am very sorry that you were vexed at not receiving another letter from me; I am really so much occupied that it is difficult for me to write more than once a week. When I am not actually grinding there is always plenty of walking to do; going to lecture seems to waste a lot of time. Today for instance I ground for about 1/2 hour after a hurried breakfast, then went to lecture; after that I came back, ground again, lunched, & went to another lecture. Then I went with Conny to Newnham [this must mean Newnham Hall], where I had tea, & we afterwards went for a walk with Maggie (on the way I bought some tennis shoes, (3/3 [shillings and pence]). We rested a little at Norwich House, then went to King's Chapel to hear the organ, & I did not get home till time to dress for dinner. This evening I have been grinding for a few hours, but not as hard as usual, as tomorrow is an easy day. We have a great deal of work, but of course it varies every day; I rather wish I had not so many subjects. My coffee pot is a useful object—Saturday afternoon all the Brighton-High Sch. people, including Miss Bond, came to my room, & we had great fun. At Newnham [the Hall] the girls give tea-parties at night, but here they only ask one or 2 to spend a little time in their rooms. There is one charming student here, with whom Nelly & I [read?] the other night—rather suggestive of Miss Pateman &

Miss Sullivan. Tomorrow I am going to the gymnasium as a performer for the first time [illegible]. My dress looks very nice, & I hope to use the tennis skirt this week. Yesterday, after dinner, Nelly & I went for a long walk as far as Girton. It looks a delightful place; red-brick, forming 2 sides of a quadrangle, with tennis courts in front. I have heard that it's not so nice as Newnham, as it is so troublesome driving in & out of Cambridge to Lecture. Miss Creak & Miss Sullivan come down on Friday; they have taken lodgings near here, & of course we are looking forward to their arrival with great pleasure.[1] I have heard again from Katie, & once from Willy. I'm afraid you must be rather lonely without Katie;[2] I shall by no means be sorry to come home, though it is very nice being here. You'll be glad to know Joseph Jacobs has been down to try for his fellowship. If he gets it he'll stay down here & lecture; I only hope he won't lecture me, as Ephraim would urge him to pluck me![3] Your fond child, AL

I am going to a little dance Thursday, if you do not object, to my getting some shoes; I can get mittens for 1/4 [shillings and pence] unless you could find time to send some. Please write soon, or ask Alfred to, & say if you mind. I'm only going for a joke.[4] Please thank Papa for the caricature. Julian is splendid. AL

1. Miss Creak continues to be part of Levy's social world although her feelings have apparently cooled considerably. Of course, she may mention her former headmistress so matter-of-factly because this letter is to her mother, not to Katie, her confidante.

2. The census of 1881 reveals that at this point Katie was a student at the London Academy and residing there (I have not been able to find out anything about this school).

3. Joseph Jacobs and Ephraim—both Jewish names—must be friends of the family; when Levy jokes that Ephraim would "pluck" her, she is using university slang meaning he would get her expelled.

4. The last paragraph was scribbled at the top of the letter, sideways, as if a last-minute addition. Although it would seem from the syntax that Levy is asking whether her mother objects to her getting shoes, the sense of this postscript is that she thinks her mother would not approve of her going to a dance, and she will go only with permission. Socializing with the other sex seems to have been parentally monitored, even for a young woman of eighteen (while homosocial relations—however intense—were free from scrutiny). Or perhaps Levy thinks her mother might mind her socializing

with gentile young men. In any case, she seems to believe that her mother will be reassured if she gives the impression that the dance is unimportant to her.

■ There are no letters from Levy's second and final year, though the records show that in November 1880 she was a resident of the newly renamed North Hall. There is a fragment, probably from a letter to her mother, written from Italy. She says, "I expect to be quite well long before 3 months & to be in full work for the summer term." She is traveling with Clementina Black, Constance's sister, with whom she had a friendship that lasted for the rest of her life. Levy writes that "Clemmie is now writing a novel by the fire" and asks about a manuscript that has been returned, so she is sending out her writing. She closes: "I have often thought of Papa in my walks—& of how he would enjoy the narrow picturesque street & clean air. Yesterday we walked through the Jewish quarter on our way to S. Lorenzo, but the old ghetto is deserted."

■ The next four letters were written in 1881 from a pension at 15 Luttichau Strasse, Dresden. Whether or not Levy returned to Newnham for the summer term of 1880 or 1881, in the autumn she was in Germany, traveling with her friend Madge (probably the same Madge mentioned in letters 10 and 11 from Newnham). Levy's first letter from Europe is dated November 10, her twentieth birthday. Her book *Xantippe and Other Verse* was receiving attention from the reviewers, and at Newnham it was winning her recognition in absentia. Levy writes with zest about work and social activities, but her tone can, in a flash, become melancholy or even despairing.

13   15 Luttichau Strasse
                                                                            Dresden
                                                                    November 10th

Dear Mama,

Thank you very much for your letter & present—I liked the photographs *awfully*. We have roared over Ned; I rather think he admires himself in his new clothes. I will write to the children to-morrow, meanwhile thank them, Alfred & Papa very much for their letters & cards. I had a very funny letter fr. Willie;[1] he seems to take gt. interest in his work, & moreover his handwriting is excellent—don't you think so? I'm glad the Heymann row has not terminated fatally. I haven't seen the Whitehall, the reviewer sent me the draft of what he'd written, but I should like to have the printed notice if you don't mind sending it. This morning I attended a meeting in connection with some tableau vivants in wh. I am to take part. It was held at the house of a Dresden poet—a very rich & very vain old woman, whose house is got up in imitation of a Venetian palace & adorned with her own portraits, wreaths, & works (richly bound). She is very funny—her vanity is quite a disease, I think. There is to be a dance after the tableau vivants wh. are given by a literary club where I have been several times and where yesterday I met a gorgeous woman fr. San Francisco who knew the Castles. Mrs. Fred K. Castle was in Dresden last week; she has been putting her children to school in Hanover. Maggie[2] gave me a gorgeous photograph to-day. I am going out now to see about getting a frame for it. My pupil has lately been taken up with her love troubles & joys—her fiancé (an awful creature) has been staying here; it is a secret engagement etc. I don't like being twenty at all; I think my arrival in the world was rather an unfortunate occurrence for everyone concerned.[3] A new poetry club at Newnham was inaugurated the other day with the reading of "Xantippe." Thanks again for thinking of me.

> Your fond child,
> Amy Levy

1. At this time Ned would have been eleven, Alfred eighteen, and Willie sixteen.

2. Maggie could be another name for Madge.

3. This remark could be a variant of the thinking that the *DSM IV* says is characteristic of some people with recurrent major depressive disorder: "a belief that others would be better off if the person were dead" (322).

14

> 15 Luttichau Strasse
> Dresden
> Nov. 27th

Dear Mama,

You are mistaken—I have no particular desire to return home, & should be very sorry to cause such an unnecessary expense as Alfred's journey. Some friends of mine are coming out from Cambridge, very probably at Easter, & I might perhaps return with them. Meantime, please don't imagine I am miserable here. I have some new pupils—two boys (15 & 16) for English, but don't begin with them till after next week. They will bring in 3/ a week, so I shall be earning 5/ a week [the unit of currency would be shillings]. I am also reading Greek with a Cambridge man here, to whom Mr. Gilderdale (the English clergyman) recommended me. I don't know how much it will be—he wanted to do it for nothing, but of course I didn't want that, & he said we wd. settle it afterwards. I will ask him about it next time, & only hope it isn't much: if it is, I won't go on long. I'm going to-morrow to a Shakespeare reading at his house. The dance (most completely decent, I can assure you—rather too much so!) I found very amusing as a spectator, but knowing no one I didn't take much share in it. We had 3 old ladies with us (including the Baron) so were well chaperoned. I'm sorry to hear Willy is unhappy, but he's at the age for his troubles to come on, poor boy. It seems to me it wd. be a gt. pity to break off his education just as he is getting some real good & enjoyment out of his work, after the drudgery.[1] I hope Papa doesn't think of sending him to a foreign school. Please thank Papa for his letter wh. I will answer soon; I am glad to see fr. the magnificent way in wh. he talks that he has at last struck oil! But, you know that I can't feel very happy about myself & the money I spend, in spite of all his kindness.

Here is a notice of my book in last week's *Academy*, not so stupidly gushing as the other ones, but favourable on the whole; & the Academy is a good paper. The book still continues to sell, moderately. It has been reduced to 9 [shillings] that is to say the other booksellers sell it with discount—& Mr. Johnson is consequently obliged to do the same. Love to all.

Fr. Yr. Affec. Dtr. Amy Levy

1. It is noteworthy that Lewis Levy was unsure about further schooling for sixteen-year-old Willie since the Levys provided a daughter with a university education. Perhaps if we knew what "the Heymann row," referred to in letter 13, was about, we would understand, but it may be that the Levys saw higher education as impractical for a son, who would, presumably, have to support a family. None of Levy's brothers attended a university.

15	15 Luttichau Str.—Dec. 2nd.

My dear Mama: Thanks for the letter and papers. You will see fr. my letter to Papa that I have given up the idea of teaching those boys, though I can't see the matter from your point of view. As to my coach—he has a wife and baby, both of them very nice of their kind; the former called on me yesterday, and I go to a Shakespeare club at their house. But seriously, you needn't have any fears on my account. I regret to say that I am as safe as Grandmama could be; there wouldn't be any impropriety (excepting from an outside point of

view) in my teaching any number of young men. I have never excited in anyone a desire to "forget themselves" in any way, which has its advantages, especially in my present circumstances. I went to see Mabel Kent the other day, as
Katie told me to, but she was out. I have not answered Katie's last letter partly
because of my uncertainty of her address—partly because I have had neuralgia all the week[1] and haven't written letters or done anything else, so perhaps
she will excuse me. The *Academy* where my book is noticed is for Nov. 19th.

I wore my madras muslin dress at the dance—it was not in its first fresh-
ness but did very well. I have heard again from my Whitehall critic; he is indignant with the editor for having altered his original notice of my poems, wh.
was even more complimentary than the one you saw. But I'm sorry to-day,
judging fr. his own poems, that I think he is mad—a sort of kind, of wh. there
are a good many on the borders of Literature. I really can't think of anything
else to say. Thanks for yr. offer of sending me something—I bought a book of
children's music (Schumann's) the other day for strumming purposes & will
consider it a present from you. Love to the children fr.

Yr. affectionate child Amy Levy.

1. The reference to her neuralgia is the first of many remarks about poor health
that runs through these letters, written when she was in her twenties.

16   15 Luttichau Strasse
                                             Dec. 4th
Dear Katie,

Thanks for your letter which I think there is time to answer before the arrival of my 1st (& at present, only) pupil. Things are going on with the same
amount of humour as before & we continue to marvel at everything we see &
hear; as Maggie says, it will be nice to go to England again to see a little normal life for a change. The scenes at dinner are richer than ever & suggest our
old game of "and-then-the company-roared!" For nothing seems too pointless
to evoke gales of laughter from all assembled. Sunday evening there was
"[German word—illegible]" with a [illegible] English girl (fr. Birmingham), 2
German frauleins of doll-like mien & a sort of German King shared the
evening meal. In the evening we played games, tableaux, charades, etc. of a
rich variety. This week there have been two fresh arrivals—a Scotch person,
Mrs. Stewart, & her daughter. The girl, a sort of Grace-Neo,[1] only younger,
curtseyed low on being introduced to us. They are the rummest people I have

seen; they live it seems at some German village & the mater has brought the girl here for a week or two for her holidays; they are bent upon seeing everything they can; rise at cock-crow for the galleries & go to some place of amusement in the evenings. The mater (a broad Scotch accent distinguishes her) is really a "character." She is always talking of her travels (a la [illegible]) in China & elsewhere & her daughter for whom she seems to have a G.P. [Grand Passion]). She informed me that last year the girl had gone to a "bal maskay" as "Red-Riding-hood" ("& very pretty she looked") but had been permitted by her father to dance with no one but himself! However, in spite of that, she allowed her to dance a reel & a polka with von [Gondon?] the other night—the sight of which was too much for Madge & myself. The mater appears to regard me as a chummy maiden-lady for she confides to me all her educational plans for her children & is always desiring my company on her expeditions; hitherto I have got off, tho' I believe that Madge & I are in for going to a Beethoven concert with her tonight.

I am going in for a course of German reading at present; I have finished "[German title—illegible]" & begin "[German title—illegible]" to-day. Yesterday I read for two hours at the public Library of the [illegible]—a huge building on the other side of the Elbe. I read [German title—illegible] wh. doubtless you know.

I have just been interrupted by the arrival of Mr. Minden who came to bid us for a walk. I cdn't go—of course, but poor little Madge has been borne off. I hope her German will not fail her. Please tell Mama that I went to Synagogue yesterday—& a beastly place it was. Zion unventilated & unrefreshed sent forth an odour wh. made me feel [illegible] for the rest of the day. The place was crammed with evil-looking Hebrews. Lots of the shops were shut yesterday. When you write do you mind sending me some English stamps—I want them for literary purposes. This afternoon we call on the Sulzburgers— some wealthy Hebrews of our "acquaintance" who, for Js [Jews], don't seem half bad. I say, "for Js" because the German Hebrew makes me feel, as a rule, that the Anti-Semitic movement is a most just & virtuous one. It is rumoured that three English girls are coming to our pension—I pray that such is not the case. We have just begun fires & have got reconciled to our great white china stove on discovering its capabilities for boiling a kettle, warming the hands, & above all for sending forth "the firelight's flickering glow" wh. we thought we were doomed to forego all the winter. How did everybody fast? . . . & did you

not miss your stalwart escort of last year?[2] Really, this letter deserves a prompt
& long answer. By the bye, I shd advise you to take B. with the other groups;
the more you take the greater is yr. chance of a scholarship; other people who
miss a group scholarship get them for general excellence in some mysterious
way.[3] Love to all including the sisters Izzard and the sisters Isaac.[4]

            Yrs. Amy Levy

    1. "Grace-Neo" is probably Levy's jocular way of saying that the Stewart girl looks
like someone named Grace whom she and Katie know—possibly Grace Black,
Clementina's sister, who was considered a beauty.

    2. Levy's questions—about whether Katie misses her "escort of last year" and
about fasting—almost certainly refers to Yom Kippur (the Day of Atonement), on
which Jews are not supposed to eat or drink to atone for the sins of the past year. This
letter, written in early December, is a response to Katie's last letter, so the mails must
have been very slow—Yom Kippur occurs in either September or October (the Jewish
year is on a different calendar, and its days shift from year to year in relation to the
Roman calendar).

    3. Katie seems to be preparing herself for entering the university.

    4. The sisters Isaac are Emma and Isabel Isaac, whose names appear on the
printed playbill for a production of *The Merchant of Venice* performed at the Levy home
at Sussex Place, Regents Park (its date was February 5, but no year is given). In 1880
Emma Isaac played the governess in a home performance of Levy's own "The Unhappy Princess." As teenagers, she and her sister filled out pages in Levy's Confessions
Book, and in 1889 Levy spent Easter Sunday with them.

17

                                        15 Luttichau Strasse
                                                 Dec. 8th

Dear Katie,

    I presume you are at home by now & I venture to send this to Sussex
Place. I write to you out of the very depths of affliction brought on by a diseased body. God must love me awfully for he chasteneth me without cease;
now alas! to my many woes of the spirit & flesh he has added a ceaseless
neuralgia, not to speak of a stye-eye & an abscess beneath the arm, wh. had to
be cut (ugh!) Altogether I've been having a fine time of it, & have spent a small
fortune in doctor & plasters. I have resided in my apartment, cross & doing
nothing but reading novels for a week, but as the pain shows no sign of abat-
ing I may as well return to normal life again. With a maternal shawl bound

round my classic head. I feel so bad, that I think if all my Pecks wrote &
"popped" that it would afford but small consolation.

Mrs. Kent & a daughter & cousin floated in on Tuesday afternoon; she
nearly filled our salon, colossal as it is. We haven't called on her yet, tho' of
course bidden. I have had to miss my Greek wh. pains me, for the lessons are
nice, & so is my coach, as far as I can tell. The Shakespeare reading is rich—I
cdn't go last weak because of my confounded body;[1] at it appeared a perfect
group of people to whom Madge & I have given names—I was specially re-
joiced at seeing two men known to us as the Honorable Fringe Cravatte & Mr.
Le Chaste respectively. There is an Anglo-Dresden edition of Sal. here whom
we have christened the Avah because we heard her loudly asking a friend to
"ave a cup o' tea." Her look, accent, dress, in short her gauges [illegible] are
identical with those of the immortal lady of number 3, Sussex Pl.[2] I did secure
those boys as pupils but was not allowed to teach them. Don't you call that
simply absurd? So I go on fr. day to day consuming the paternal substance. I
don't see why you shld. fling yr. little pennies away at Polish Bank or any other
game because you have not succeeded in finding a husband. I really am sorry
for you, for I don't see who there is to rescue you from old-maidism unless it's
Brouette.[3] But never mind, my child: "thank with brief thanksgiving whatever
gods there be, that no life lives for ever et.c." & go yr. little journey gravewards
as cheerfully as you can. As for me—my youth is dead, my ♥ is Broken—sour
& Sara-like old age has come upon me ere my time. Madge & I sit like two
aged crones & talk about the past—by mutual consent avoiding any reference
to the future. Really if this confounded neuralgia don't stop I shall have to hie
to a chemist—no, not a chemist—the river; for the German chemist is alas!
not permitted to retail the death-fraught drug to the chance customer.[4] Write
soon to the profoundly miserable. AL

1. Despite the jokes, Levy's health problems are a big problem: she is uncomfortable and unable to engage in activities she would enjoy.
2. Evidently a neighbor, for the Levys lived at 11 Sussex Place.
3. The reference to Katie's "old-maidism" suggests that it may not have been easy
for Levy to view her own single state with equanimity, no matter how she felt about
men—and women.
4. Levy's jokes about buying a lethal drug, presumably because of her broken
heart and her health problems, show her preoccupation with death.

■ The next two letters were written from Lucerne in Switzerland in 1882. We know this because in the following letter Levy says that she has finished "Medea." Levy's own copy of *A Minor Poet and Other Verse*[1]—in which she inked in dates and places of composition—reveals that "Medea" was written in Dresden and Lucerne in 1882. It is surprising that she is already asking Clementina Black to help her find a publisher, for *A Minor Poet* was not to appear until 1884; indeed, some of the poems that appear in the volume had not yet been composed at the time this letter was penned.

1. Now in the possession of Levy's grandniece.

18   Hotel & Pension
                                          Sonnenberg-Selisberg
                                                      Lucerne

Dear Clemmy,

I got yr. letter to-day for wh. many thanks; I knew Cassell was no good— if you don't mind really, & if Mary Campbell is willing wd. you try Warne, Routledge, Dean & Shaw (48 Paternoster Row). I know it's a case of fighting with the Fates, but fighting passes the time & after all is better than sitting still. Still, when it's a case of deputing the fighting to another person it's a little hard on that person; I hope I'm not asking too much. Is Nelly Huggett a March Hare or a Hatter?[1] One or other she certainly is. What cd. possibly have been pressing enough to keep her fr. accepting the Lily's kindly invitation? If I'd had such a chance (O woful mockery) I'd have gone if I'd had to die for it the next day; in any case the morbid result wd. have been welcomed—for the rest of my life I shd. have had wine instead of blood in me. Fancy Fidelio under such circumstances! Of course Clemmy any feeble twaddle I write is only meant for your benevolent eye.

Well, as to work, for work I suppose is what one's life will be until the undertaker or crematorium official is called in—I have finished *Medea* after a fashion & suppose I shall begin on *Eustace*[2] to-morrow, but I feel very down. I have amused myself to-day lying about in the sun & reading *Les Misérables* & writing nonsense verse wh. I enclose; very good employments in their way but hardly satisfactory. We both feel very wholesome & if one weren't a [illegible] leech's daughter always crying out "More, More" I shd. be happy.[3] Miss Crofts is simply delightful; she makes one feel utterly mean & dirty, she is so simple

& clean & strong & very charming withal. Did you get my other letter? If E. Radford's⁴ book is not of great price I wish you wd. send me a copy—I will remit the funds per Katie. I don't feel much like letter writing to-night because I've rather got "heartache" (to quote Conny) & it's the same old story, so you can imagine what I wd. say. So here are the verses to make up. Write soon to

Yrs. Amy Levy

> *Is it worth, in life, to join the strife?*
> *Ay, for striving brings many fair things:*
> *Wealth & health & name,*
> > *Riches & fame;*
> *More than I can write*
> > *Men win in fight.*
> *But the things, the best, think not to wrest*
> *Fr. the Fates. Strife, pain;*
> > *All were in vain—*
> *For the Fates give these*
> > *To whom they please.*

> *Ere I go down into the grave*
> > *Four things I crave:*
> *Much love, much sunshine & much health,*
> > *A little wealth.*
> *When these be gone, Good Death, I pray*
> > *bear me away.⁵*

1. Nelly Huggett attended Brighton High School and Newnham College with Levy and is mentioned in those letters. Her name (Ellen Huggett) appears in the attendance book of the club to which Levy belonged in the first half of the 1880s. In this letter Levy finds it remarkable that Nelly turned down a chance to see the opera *Fidelio*—hence Levy's hyperbolic, humorously self-dramatizing response. Levy's love of music and opera is apparent in many of her poems, for example, "Lohengrin," "Sinfonia Eroica," "In a Minor Key," and "A June-Tide Echo" (subtitled "After a Richter Concert").

2. Levy is probably referring here to Trollope's *The Eustace Diamonds* (1873), one of his Palliser novels, the one that is unpleasant in its treatment of its Jewish characters.

3. When Levy refers to herself as a "leech's daughter," she means a person who

always wants more from life than she can get. In the biography I call this persona the Hungry Poet ("*Poeta Esuriens*" in Latin, the title of one of her early poems).

4. Ernest Radford and Dollie Maitland, who married in 1883, were friends of Levy's. He was a poet, journalist, barrister, and socialist, who, by 1884, became active in William Morris's Socialist League. In 1882 he published *Translations from Heine and Other Verses* (in which about half of the poems are his own). He and Levy admired and translated Heine's poems, had their first books published by E. Johnson of Cambridge, and had T. Fisher Unwin bring out their second books in 1884. In the 1890s Ernest was a member of the Rhymers' Club, along with Ernest Dowson, Arthur Symons, and W. B. Yeats.

5. This verse (which Levy refers to as "nonsense," meaning that she did not take it seriously as a poem) asserts that death would be preferable to a life without love and health; it is an eerie foreshadowing of Levy's end. The suicidal poets in Levy's "A Minor Poet" and "Sokratics in the Strand" take the position that random luck determines whether one gets the important things in life

19

Hotel Sonnenberg

July 18th

Dear Katie,

Thanks for yr letter wh. I got yesterday. I am rather sad because my inspiration ceaseth to flow, otherwise I am joyful for the weather is glorious. Alack! My Pegasus was ever a sorry jade. It's no good trying to put her in harness.

The mass of the Ford party has departed in full Alpine rig to ascend a mountain, but Mrs. Ford is still here; she seems very nice. She edits a M.S. magazine to wh. I am going to contribute; we are going for a walk this morning. Sunday evening we had rather a joke; we went down in the dark to the little lake near here & hired the solitary tub & drifted about for an hour—One of the party (a Dublin undergrad.) produced a flute & made night hideous with Irish melodies. Monday morning I walked down to Lake Lucerne with three of the party & we took a most remarkable boat with very quaint oars; we had to stand up to row, but it was rather fun. The hotel gets fuller & fuller. My dear, the sight of yr. co-religionists wd. delight you utterly; I simply sit & watch, sad but infinitely amused. Charles Moke is here in the flesh wedded to Mrs. Magnus & it seems a very happy marriage[1]; I wish you cd. see the pair; there are also present—myself in youth with a pigtail, Amy Mo., Mrs. Annette Cohen, et.c. et.c.

Among the English people are Miss & Mr. Cross (George Eliot's husband); Miss Crofts & the Fords knew them a little to start with & the friend-ship is on the ripen. Miss Crofts is next to Mr. Cross at dinner & says it seems like a daily dinner party. I am writing on the verandah & opposite to me is E.C. being sketched by Miss Cross[2] to whom I am also going to sit; at least Miss Cross offered me a model, but I hope it won't come off, for I hate sitting.

Poor Jane & the British!

I am simply sticking in Les Miserables. I have read about half & it has lately become so inutterably dry that I don't know what to do. Victor Hugo is at times a little elaborate as when he describes Waterloo & says, "Les Ecossars tomberant en pesant de Ben Lomand!" Are we going to be in a very bad way financially all this winter? I mean to get regular work of some sort if I possibly can. O why doesn't Mary Robinson or Algernon Charles want a secretary?[3] I have sent my tale "Periwinkles" to the aged Clementina[4] & asked her if she thinks it is any good from a magazine point of view. I believe being educated has taken away all chance of my producing "potboilers"—wh. is a grim reflec-tion. Let's grind [illegible] to-gether in the Winter & cultivate lots of friends. I'm happier in one way because I'm beginning to get on so much better with people in spite of my accursed shyness. How rich about the Michael Green ro-mance. Write soon. Yrs. AL.

1. Mrs. Magnus is Lady Katie Magnus, a woman from a prominent Jewish family and a writer on Jewish subjects. Lady Katie was also the founder of the first club for immigrant Jewish girls in the East End. Even into the twentieth century, clubs for im-migrant Jewish girls, teaching "religion, refinement, and recreation," were called Lady Magnus clubs. Levy's sister Katie is likely to be the Katie Solomon mentioned as one of the women active in the "Butler Street Jewish club, modelled on Lady Magnus's pio-neering enterprise" (see Eugene Black, *The Social Politics of Anglo-Jewry, 1880–1920* [Ox-ford: Basil Blackwood, 1988], 129). Levy's remark about Magnus and Charles Moke is, from the tone, almost certainly a joke.

2. Miss Cross, the sister of George Eliot's widowed husband, could be either John Cross's sister Eleonora or his sister Edythe. Edythe Cross, who contributed poetry to Oscar Wilde's *Woman's World* in 1888 and 1889, may have been a painter as well as a poet.

3. Algernon Charles is, of course, Swinburne, whose work Levy admired and whose poetry influenced her own. In *Romance of a Shop* Levy quotes from his tragedy *Chasteland,* and the epigraph to chapter 11 of *Reuben Sachs* is from *Chasteland.* In chapter 15 of *Reuben Sachs,* Judith's epiphany comes after reading from Swinburne's "Triumph

of Time," and chapter 16 begins with an epigraph from "A Leave-Taking." It is unlikely that Levy knew Swinburne personally because by the early 1880s he was quite reclusive. For information about Mary Robinson, see note 3 to letter 26.

4. Levy does not appear to have published anything called "Periwinkles," nor has the manuscript been found among her surviving papers. She refers to Clementina Black as "aged" because Black was six years older. Levy looks to her for advice on how to get a story published because Clementina, in addition to her political work, was a rather prolific fiction writer. In 1881 Clementina had helped Levy find a publisher for her first book, *Xantippe and Other Verse.*

Black's first novel was the autobiographical *A Sussex Idyll* (1877), and her fictional work includes *Mericas* (a collection of stories) that came out in 1880, *Orlando* (1880), *The Agitator* (1894), and the *Linleys of Bath* (1911). She also published extensively on women's trade unionism and on other social and political issues such as women's suffrage. In "On Marriage: A Criticism," in the *Fortnightly Review* 47 (1890): 586–94, she asks for relationships between husband and wife that would be "mutual" and thus constitute a new form of marriage. In August 1893 she reviewed Gissing's *Odd Women* in the *Illustrated London News,* expressing disappointment that the love affair between the feminist heroine Rhoda and Everard Barfoot, a man with progressive ideas, ends unhappily: "We feel, as we read, that between two persons so clear-sighted, so outspoken and so fully aware of the pitfalls of married life, the natural end would be a real marriage—that is to say, an equal union, in which each would respect the freedom and individuality of the other, and in which each would find the completest development" (cited by Elaine Showalter in her introduction to *The Odd Women* [New York: Penguin, 1983], xix).

■ The following letter is from London and to Dollie Maitland Radford (Levy spells her friend's name "Dolly" but Radford herself spelled it "Dollie"). Dated 1884, it apparently was written during the first part of the year since the Radfords became parents on July 23, 1884, and there is no mention of their baby.

20

11 Sussex Pl. NW / 84

Dear Dolly,[1]

Many thanks for yr. note. Alas, I fear you must not come & see me, for an ulcerated sore throat is among my maladies. (Extreme distaste for this particular planet is another of them.) I hope you will soon come to dine. Thanks for the offers of light literature; if by any chance you shd. venture to call (I'm nearly well to-day) you might bring with you anything particularly sparkling, airy, piquant—in right character to be lying around. [The last six words are not clear.]

The intrepid Clemmy sought me in my sick chamber yesterday. To-day I have moved down a flight, but the world is very dark.

I'm glad the Residential Flat is so robust. (This sounds a little personal but I don't mean anything.[2]) I'm so sorry about the hero; at any rate, it's better he shd. be silent than carry on an elaborate [pointed stutter?] through 3 vols. like the man in Mrs. [illegible] new book. Heroes don't want many "lines"; give them, and insist upon, some pleasing point, a rare grave smile, a white hand, & "celebrated sneer." I am at present taking a young man through scene after scene of most thrilling interest solely by means of a loud, genial laugh & an electric eye. The cultured but passionate heroine makes a speech, then "their eyes met" or she hears that laugh neighing out sympathetically from some hidden & remote corner. It is very subtle.[3] I've just had a ticket for the Tennyson Tableaux at Prince's Hall. Isn't it riling I can't go?

I wonder if you will ever come here or if the Fates seriously object. Pray for me in yr. little prayers.

AL.

[Scrawled in the left margin of the first page] Has Mr. Radford anything "out," in any of the magazines?]

1. Dollie Maitland Radford, like her husband, was a poet. In the 1880s she published in magazines and later produced books, *A Lighter Load* (1896), *Songs and Other Verses* (1895–96), and *Collected Poems* (1910). Dollie was a close friend of Eleanor Marx's and appears as a character in Judith Chernaik's *The Daughter*, a novel about Eleanor (New York: Harper & Row, 1979).

2. Levy's apology suggests that she has said something that could have sexual connotations, but it is unclear what she is embarrassed about.

3. These jokes about how a writer manipulates various of conventional characters are important because they show that Levy was conscious of the formulaic nature of popular fiction.

■ The next three letters were written in 1884, the first two from the Gasthaus Zum Titisee in Baden, Germany, in the Black Forest. In the third letter, Levy tells Katie that she is no longer staying at that guest house but is now in a nearby village, at a pension belonging to a family named Ochs. The first and third letters in this group mention Blanche Smith, evidently Levy's traveling companion, who (as she later tells Vernon Lee in letter 29) attended Newnham and, probably after this trip to Germany, studied to be an actress and went on the stage. These letters, all obviously written around the same time, are probably from the summer and fall of 1884, for in October 1884 Levy published in *London Society* a piece called "In the Black Forest," and in letter 23 she mentions receiving payment from *London Society*. Her poem "In the Black Forest" (titled "After Heine") appeared in the *Cambridge Review* in October 1884.

21

Gasthaus Zum Titisee
Altenweg: Baden
Friday

Dear Katie,

Thanks for yr. letter, with the enclosure of the mad Magn. This is a most satisfactory place. I wish we had come here fr. the first. But I daresay the first raptures will wear off & that I shall have had enough of it before we leave. Blanche Smith is regularly seedy[1]—she talks of sending for her sister & staying here all the summer, in wh. case I shd. have to return on my own fair hook, wh. I fear, as it's a long journey.

Harry Bond is sort of headnurse at this place; goes round with a gang of little German girls, whom he teaches rowing, as far as one can teach with these old tubs. We find him very slow: he affords us little satisfaction, the only point in his favour being his sex.

Carl Pearson[2] came over yesterday afternoon to fetch us for a walk. We went to his village, had coffee & were introduced to his villagers, with whom he chums & who regard him as a sort of King. We went into one little house where a horrible old woman exclaimed: "Ach Herr Professor! [German—illegible] . . . No wonder you are fond of Titisee when there are such beautiful ladies there! et.c. et.c." (at great length.) I suppose one oughtn't to feel uncomfortable on such occasions but I think I did. He hawked us all round the place, introducing us as the first English ladies who had ever been to Saig. We are going to give a return coffee party to wh. Messrs. Pearson and Bond are to be coyly bidden.

Today we make an excursion to a little town, going there by post-wagen & returning on our [illegible]. I wish I had a more lively companion, but I suppose it's seediness makes Blanche so dismal. However, I console myself with the abnormal wholesomeness of my body, & live the soulless life of a cow, trying to ignore the great devil who lyeth ever in wait in the recesses of my heart.

There is a rumour of the invasion of a gang of Newnhamites, Ada Radfords[3] & things—I pray to the gods they won't come.

This letter sounds very cheerful, doesn't it, but the devils are awful bad in the intervals of basking.[4] I wish I could think of some plan for the winter wh. would include going to a warm place—my deafness is in a bad way.

I'm afraid there's no chance of a watery grave in the Titisee, the boats are so safe, & David Jones has no liking for Continental steam-packets. [illegible.]

There are some Jews here, of course—Belle Slo. all a-blooming & a-growing, & a little boy with an exaggerated Alfredian head. They regard me with a knowing eye, but I think I puzzle them. Everyone speaks English here—I don't know where my German has gone.

I'm not interested in the Slo. [illegible]. I suppose it's "a good match" even for a Slo. to go off with an unknown being called Marcus. However, he is a very [illegible] cad, that's one thing in his favour—"gentlemanly but not polished"—as Rachel puts it, "but that can soon be altered!" So I suppose the youth is ultimately to be anointed with the oil of the Vale—a Slo.'s notion of polish.[5]

It's now about 8:30, & I have breakfasted, [illegible], & written my letter home already. One gets long basking days here wh. are delightful. When I've finished this, I shall take a turn on the lake, & then set off for Lenzkirch.

How is Jenny?[6] . . .

Are yr. Essengers et.c in Folkestone, or has that rising young barrister J. M. S. taken himself & his household gods to Southsea—there to enact in person one of those French novels with wh. he is wont to beguile his leisure hours?[7] Do reward my virtue with a long letter—give my love to Jenny & Dorothy & Harry & Charles.

Do you do much Fannying, in consideration of Ned's bed & board?[8]

Adieu. Pray for the soul of

Amy Levy

1. *OED*: slang, meaning "Unwell, poorly, 'not up to the mark.'"

2. Karl (originally Carl) Pearson became a professor of applied mathematics at University College, London, in 1885. An evolutionary biologist, socialist, and future eugenicist, he wrote several books, among them *Socialism in Theory and Practice* (1885). The Men and Women's Club, which he founded, discussed new ways for men and women to relate to one another socially and sexually. Pearson is portrayed by Levy as a self-important egotist in letters 21 and 22. Judith Walkowitz discusses him in *City of Dreadful Delight: Narratives of Sexual Danger in Late-Victorian London* (Chicago: Univer-

sity of Chicago Press, 1992), saying that he and the other men in the group "dominated and intimidated" the female members.

3. Ada Radford, mentioned in letter 21, was Ernest Radford's sister and attended Newnham College from 1881 to 1883. She married Graham Wallas, political scientist and founding member of the Fabian Society, who was George Bernard Shaw's best man at his wedding in 1897. In June 1883 Ada had spent a weekend at Cambridge with Amy Levy, Dollie Maitland, and Constance Black. Later, as Ada Wallas, she published "The Poetry of Amy Levy" in *Academy* 57 (1899): 162–63.

Levy's negativity about the arrival of the Newnhamites, people who must in some sense have been friends, may reflect the "accursed shyness" mentioned in letter 19, but it also foreshadows an increasingly critical attitude toward the "culture" of Cambridge that emerges in letters to Vernon Lee written in 1886 and afterward.

4. Levy's remarks about "the great-devil who lyeth ever in wait" and "the devils [that] are awful bad in the intervals of basking"—allusions to her bouts of depression—provide a sense of how she must have lived always in fear of the next episode.

5. Levy is gossiping in a snobbish way about "Belle Slo.," whom she and Katie evidently knew. A component in Levy's's disdain is that Belle is from "the Vale" (Maida Vale), a section of London inhabited at the time by Jews who were new to the middle class and perceived by more established Jewish families as vulgar. Characters in both *Reuben Sachs* and "Cohen of Trinity" speak of Maida Vale disparagingly.

6. "Jenny" is Jennette de Pass, a Jewish woman (b. 1859), who, at least by 1889, had become a close friend of Levy's. "In the Nower" is dedicated to "J. de P."

7. The Essengers were related to Katie's future husband, Joseph Maurice Solomon (referred to archly here as "J. M. S"). Levy is being satiric in fancying Joe Solomon as a character in a French novel when, in fact, he was a sober widower with three young sons. Folkestone, in Kent, was a genteel seaside resort and is now a large seaport.

8. I cannot guess what Levy meant by "Fannying"; she seems to be asking her sister if, at a school Katie and Ned attend, she performs some services to help cover the cost of Ned's expenses.

22

■ In this letter to Dollie Maitland Radford, Levy repeats some of what she told Katie in the previous letter.

Gasthaus Zum Titisee

Altenweg: Baden Aug. 10th

Dear Dolly,

I am so glad to hear you are flourishing: please thank Mr. Radford for his nice letter. Is it not exciting to have a baby of one's own? I am sure it is a nice one if there is anything in heredity. (Is not that neatly put?) I am most anxious to behold "Maitland" & to sport with him. I suppose he will be made an honorary member of the Club. I sympathize with Mr. Radford on the subject of reviews. It's a good thing we are not of Keats-like sensibility, otherwise we shd. have long ago been "snuffed out" by the various "articles" of kind critics. I suppose you've seen the *Literary World?* I don't know which makes one more scornful of one's reviewers—their praise or their blame.[1]

Harry Bond is here—very much in his element, the centre of a crowd of admiring little German girls. We have dubbed him 'The Head Nurse" but do not betray us. Carl Pearson has been staying at a village a little way off; we went to coffee at his inn the other day and were introduced to his peasants. He is a sort of little god among them—wh. he rather enjoys I fancy in spite of much philosophy and mathematics. He has gone to Freybourg today to meet Mr. Parker[2] whose marriage has been put off till next month.

I saw Mr. Shaw's article in *To-day.* Perhaps he thinks it is criticism—I don't. I'm sure Mr. Radford feels with me the indignity of figuring in a "comic" article. However, I'm getting accustomed to the high spirits invariably produced by my work in my critics.

This is a lovely place, much better than the [illegible], where, by the bye, there are no springs where Truth or cholera may lurk. My novel progresses slowly. Perhaps it's the critics' fault, but I'm losing all faith in myself as a literary person, and thinking [of] sheep-farming in the Far West.

'O that I were a man—'[3]

I hope you will have a good time in the country; I am going on to the romantic town of Worthing after this: I suppose we shall meet in the autumn.

Have any more sub-editors lost their hearts to the fair Unknown, & how about the late?

Good-bye, my dear little Dolly. Please "remember" me to Maitland[4] & to his father and ask Mr. Radford if he thinks it worse to be accused of "drivelling idiocy" or "wild & insensate folly."[5]

Miss Smith sends her love.

> Believe me
>
> Yrs. affectly,
>
> Amy Levy

1. Levy's remarks suggest that Radford's *Measured Steps* took a beating from reviewers, but perhaps both he and Levy were as sensitive to negative notices as legend

has it that Keats was (her specific allusion is to what Byron says about Keats in *Don Juan*). George Bernard Shaw did mock both volumes of poetry in the unsigned review in *To-Day* that Levy mentions further on in this letter (see "Recent Poetry," *To-Day* 2 [August 1884]: 156–58). The reviews of *A Minor Poet* were mixed but on the whole good.

2. Probably Robert Parker, a member of the club, who is discussed in note 36 to chapter 6.

3. I have not been able to find the source of Levy's quotation, but she may have in mind Christina Rossetti's "From the Antique," where the speaker says, "I wish, and I wish I were a man."

4. Levy's interest in baby Maitland is undoubtedly genuine: her letters consistently show involvement with her own younger siblings and Katie's children, and her 1889 calendar shows that she took her friend Effie Stevens's son and her nephews on outings.

5. Levy is probably quoting from what reviewers said about her volume of poems and Radford's.

23

■ The following fragment lacks a first or last page: the diction, tone, and level of intimacy tell us it is to Katie.

Zum Ochsen: Saig
Beu Lenzkuech

[sketch of the pension]

Behold me in my village retreat! I am in a state of naked impropriety—absolutely unchaperoned. My first night of exile was a failure. I cdn't get room at the Ochs, so had one found at the Pfarrer-house, with the arrangement that I was to board at the inn. The word Pfarrer suggested a lovely domestic spot to myself and Miss Corfe who led me up. Not until I was fairly established did I identify it with the grim individual in a cassock who is to be seen curtsying about the churchyard at all hours of the day. When I came back fr. supper at the Ochs a sort of funk seized me, I bolted my room & put chairs against an inner door. The nasty old woman who brought my bath saw the chairs & scoffed at my fears, & I tried to settle down with my books. Presently a knock came. I opened the door & beheld a tall figure in a cassock, candle in hand, grinning & chuckling in a way wh., when taken with his normal solemnity, was grim in the extreme. He came to soothe my fears (a irony) assured me that I was "bei ihm" ["at his place"] & that the hostess at the inn had been wrong, & that my room was not besitzt ["occupied, taken"] for the next night. He kept on repeating "Ich behalte Sie so lange als Sie wolle" ["I will look at you as long as you want me to"] so often & with so much fervour & coming so close, that had it not been for his profession I might have considered myself entitled to hang up my 'at in the 'all. I kept the door very narrowly open, tho' he was evidently anxious to pay me a pastor-ly visit, & waxed pale & funky, wh. was silly, for of course he meant well—but he was a hale man in the 30's & I was quite at his mercy. I had a grim night; kept on remembering that all the villains in German tales are priests.

I am now at the Ochs & like my new quarters immensely. It is a most rustic building but everything is awfully good. I have to go in to *table d'hôte*[1] alone & created much surprise at first. All the people are Germans, so it doesn't matter. I am now on the track of the German owl (cocks only examined). There is a little group of simple-hearted Studenten with whom I rather chum. One, strange to say, is a friend of Walter Gottieil; he is a Wagner-schwaermer,[2] & is going to play me bits of the *Walkure* to-night. Yr. hair wd. have stood on end to have seen me last night, after dinner, sitting at the table with no less than three German mashers[3] engaged in animated converse. I think the matrons believe me to be no better than I shd. be, but my men are awfully nice & polite. I have had 2.10 fr. L.S. *[London Society]* & the proofs of one of my potboilers, so shall probably stay till Wednesday week & return home with Miss Corge, as Blanche stays on. The latter joins me at Saig on Friday. I have been working, but O the novel is so bad—it's no go. I have been wasting my substance in riotous living—had a coffee-party, & breakfast-party, the same day: guests, Radfords et.c. As a matter of fact I am writing this at Titisee; I came over for letters & stayed for dinner because of the rain. I must go soon & summon Miss Gardner who is going to walk up with me. She has asked me to call on her in London.

I am sorry you are so sad. Fr. my point of view you are such a lucky beggar! Fixed income, good ears,[4] loving friends, & a credit-account with the Heavenly Powers! My own melancholy is too large for words—O if I needn't go home & begin the old struggle for existence.[5]

Yr. gaiety does not entice me, not even the mention of Henry's roses: a sort of north villa, by the sea.

Is Arthur Lawrence mad to go near that silly fool when Edith Elkin is to be had? Give the latter my "love", also Jenny (without the inverted commas).

I have just read *Rudder Grange*[6] & am wrestling with a dull selection of Heyse's[7] novellen. Poor Clemmy writes me a letter with her left hand to say she has been down with rheumatism. Her holidays always go wrong. I shall probably go home via Gregburg [spelling unclear] & Basel. A clever German lady here, has asked me to go to dinner & have some music with her at Treybourg on my way through. She is very witty, a sort of good-looking Magna; she &. . . . [The rest of the letter is lost.]

1. In 1891 the Radfords told Katherine Bradley and Edith Cooper (who published poetry together as "Michael Field") that Levy had said that the oil mills near their home in Hammersmith "smelt like a German *table d'hôte.*" See "Works and Days," the diary of Michael Field, April 14, 1891, British Library Add. MS 46779, f. 33.

2. Since in German "schwaermerei" means "enthusiasm, ecstatic fondness or love, fanaticism," Levy must mean that this person is ardent in his enthusiasm for Wagner's music.

3. Flirts or people who make sexual advances (slang).

4. The remark about envying Katie's ears indicates that Levy's increasing deafness—at age twenty-three—weighs heavily.

5. It is interesting that Levy expresses her dread of going back to England in evolutionary language.

6. The novel *Rudder Grange* by Frank Stockton was published in 1879.

7. The novelist referred to here is a German, Paul Heyse, whose mother was Jewish.

■ The next two letters to Katie were written from 7 Endsleigh Gardens in Bloomsbury, London, the summer of 1885, just after Katie's wedding. We know that the Levys moved from Sussex Place, Regents Park to Ulster Place, Regents Park sometime in 1884, and then to Endsleigh Gardens in the second half of 1885 because Ella Levy's application for admission to North London Collegiate, dated January 3, 1885, gives the Ulster Place address. Amy lived with her family when she was not traveling.

24

7 Endsleigh Gardens
August 19th / 85

Dear Katie,

The enclosed came after you left, also a hideous gift fr. the bereaved Julyanne. We all think the War-horse must be mad. After you left there was a great rush of departure. I don't wish to run down yr. new family, but each lady seemed to have brought her double with her (in lieu of a spouse); I stood at the bottom of the stairs shaking-hands, & really & truly I saw Miss Sylvester come down *three* times. I think of communicating with the Psychical Society. Stray beings of Papa's floated in, in time for dinner, among them "Dora", who has purchased you a gift (so he says.) There was a big spread at 8—each lady succeeded in collaring a man; Jenny had Phillip, Emmy, a being called Mac-Carthy, Annie, Hubert, Lizzie, Willy, Charlotte, Uncle Fred, myself, Wesche, et.c. et.c. Afterwards we had a song or so, & Jenny & I concluded with a wild caper with "Lieutenant Rouse" & Willy, to the sound of Wesche's strumming.

Wedding cake is now on the cut—a warm gentleman from Buzzard's officiating—he is very free with the use of his hands. By the bye, your list is not to be seen (yr. cake list.) Where is it? Mind you let us know.

You were supposed to look *something*—yesterday, really you weren't half bad. Are you having a good time? Do you feel solemn? Has J-sh M-r-e S-L-n[1] revealed any strange traits, hitherto unknown to you; a club foot or a bad temper? Phillip thinks the bridegroom a very lucky man—such indeed was the prevailing sentiment amid the gay throng yesterday afternoon—perhaps it resulted fr. the glamour cast by the bridal veil et.c. Jenny & I have been slaying the time preparing a pot-pourri for you, made from yr. wedding bucket,[2] also a small bunch of flowers drawn from the same source. Touching? Lots of people had flowers fr. the bucket after you left. Jenny missed her train this morning & has only just left. Both she & Paul. urged me to stay with them, but it's not fair to go a-visiting a la Z. [illegible] Leoni—all take & no give (to quote Mrs. Barber.) Did you survive my two kisses? I felt rather bad afterwards. The feature, by the bye, of yesterday's festivity was a desperate flirtation between Yiah & Doctor Oppenheim; they simply stuck in a corner for an hour or more & Leoni Jane reported that he proposed & was refused. By the bye, Leoni made cat-like remarks, worthy of record. Sorry. Joseph Solomon of Linden Gardens (79)[3] seemed quite out of it—I asked why Belle didn't come, & he said he didn't know; he had come fr. the City. Evidently she was at home! Excuse this scrawl—am I not good to write?

Mama is alright [*sic*]: I am very happy & my head is very clean.

Give my kinds regards to Mr. Joseph Maurice Solomon.

> Yrs. Affectly
>
> Amy Levy

Did Broo. turn up? Jenny said he wd. wear a bucket; I thought even he wd. draw the line at so insane a deed.[4]

1. Levy teasingly refers to Katie's bridegroom, Joseph Maurice Solomon, by his Hebrew name, "J-sh" (for Joshua).

2. This is probably a joking reference to the wedding bouquet, but given that the word appears again in the postscript, perhaps it is an alternative Victorian spelling for "bouquet."

3. This Joseph Solomon (not to be confused with Katie's husband or anyone in his family) was a young man at the time of Katie's wedding: the number "79" does not refer to his age. He was the son of Elizabeth and Saul Solomon, Amy Levy's aunt and uncle; Elizabeth was Lewis Levy's sister, and she is the woman about whom young Amy says in letter 4, "Poor Aunt Bessie with 10 children!"

4. Katie's wedding seems to have been very lively; it is unlikely that the wedding of upper-middle-class gentiles would have been as boisterous. Levy refers to people without giving last names here, so it is impossible to trace most of them, but the guests—relatives and family friends—are unlikely to have been eminent enough to be traceable. Jenny (de Pass) is mentioned again; Charlotte, "Paul" (Pauline), and Dora, guests at the wedding, are women whose names appear frequently in Levy's 1889 daily calendar. "Emma" is probably Emma Isaac. That Levy does not mention the surnames of her Jewish friends in her letters or her calendar is a sign that she knows them well; she never mentions Clementina's last name either.

25

■ The next letter is written shortly after the previous one, and Katie and Joe, evidently, are still on their honeymoon.

7 Endsleigh Gardens

Aug. 22nd

Dear Katie,

I was glad to get your letter though it did rather make me swear. However, I'm glad you're having such a good time.

There is positively nothing to tell you. Willy is at Folkestone, Papa is at Ben Rhydding & reports that the heir apparent is considerably better.[1]

The latest thing is your own great beauty started by "the aunts" to while away the August hours in London, I suppose. Such terms as "very beautiful (!)" "sweetly pretty"' "her great, big eyes" float about freely & goad me to paroxysms of envious sadness. Monty[2] came last night. Don't be jealous, but Lyons has given his young woman diamond bracelets, a diamond star, et.c. It quite annoys Monty to see him spend his money! By the bye, the latter offered to take me to the Antwerp exhibition (seriously quite a bona fide offer) but I refused on grounds of inability to knock about a-pleasuring. The children are not going away, wh. really is a shame. It does Donald moral as well as physical harm, for the poor kid is so "fretful" that he has to be "humoured" & moreover feels aggrieved at the breaking of the parental promise. *Do* write to Papa about it, & point out how necessary it is.[3]

Mama seems alright [sic] & I am simply bubbling over with vitality & Lebenlust.

There is an impression in this family that Joe has been rather remiss in not writing to Mama or Papa, but certainly he was not well-treated.[4]

Donald refused to receive Joe's portrait—he says he can't help it, but he doesn't want it! The wedding-baked meats[5] continue to coldly furnish forth the family table—we are a little tired of cream puddings & chicken.

"Dora's" gift has arrived—of all things, a French book on Japanese art, worth (according to Monty) 8 guineas. The other Dora's Ruskin has turned up—a beautiful edition, barring the binding.

Write again & next time remember to stamp yr. letter.

AL

1. When Levy refers to "the heir apparent" she means Alfred, the oldest son in the family, who, in 1885, would have been around twenty-two. His health problems in 1885 may have been serious because he died in 1887.

2. "Monty" is likely to be Montague Solomon, Levy's first cousin (one of Lewis Levy's sister's ten children); he is listed as the violinist on the playbill for the Levys' performance of *The Merchant of Venice*.

3. Levy's criticism of her parents for not taking " the children . . . away" (apparently breaking a promise) and her concern about Donald (around eleven at the time) are part of a pattern of criticism about the way her younger siblings are treated.

4. The Levy parents seem quick to take offense, for Katie and Joe have been married for only four days and already there is tension and reproach.

5. The "wedding-baked meats" is an allusion to "the funeral baked meats / did furnish forth the marriage tables" (Act I, scene II of *Hamlet*).

■ The following seven letters, written from 7 Endsleigh Gardens, London, between fall of 1886 and August 1889, are to Violet Paget (1856–1935), who began using the pseudonym "Vernon Lee" in her teens. (An eighth letter to Lee, No. 37, follows three more to Katie and one to "Clemmie.") A scholar, a fiction writer, and an aesthetician, Vernon Lee lived in her mother's villa in Florence when she was not in London or traveling, and Levy met her there in 1886. She seems to have been in love with Lee, at least at first. At the time Levy met her, Lee was in a romantic partnership with Mary Robinson (a poet); in August 1887 she began a liaison with Clementina (Kit) Anstruther-Thomson.

These letters, in the Vernon Lee Collection at Colby College, are all that survives of Levy's correspondence from 1886 and 1887; in addition to shedding light on the Levy-Lee relationship, they provide a picture of Levy's life while in London during the two years that preceded the final year of her life.

26

■ This letter was written in November 1886.

7, Endsleigh Gardens, N.W.

Nov. 26th

Dear Miss Paget,

It is beginning to be very foggy in London and my thoughts turn often to Florence. I don't think, however, that I shall come out before February if I am able to come at all. Miss Blomfield[1] seems doubtful about her plans, so I wrote to Miss Wimbush,[2] who as you know, has a flat in the Via Romana, but she doesn't expect to have room for me in the spring. I am expecting to see Miss Blomfield appear, & then we can discuss plans. Miss Robinson[3] actually did come to see me the other day. She was so nice & pretty, and looked, for her, quite robust. I had had several distant prospects of Mr. Cross[4] in the Reading room lately, his beauty quite marred by spectacles. Miss Black & her sister are living on the top floor of a house in Fitzroy St; they do their own housework, & are quite & completely domestic, unless when they are attending Socialist or Anarchist meetings. I confess, that my own Philistine, middle class notions of comfort wd. not be met by their *ménage*. As for me, I am rather good; wrestling with a story & reading solid literature at the Museum! And a great crisis has occurred in my career; I have been asked to dance by Fisher Unwin! I met him the other day at a very remarkable party, & instead of thrusting me a sheaf of advertisements & saying that he cdn't take my MS's. on any consideration (his usual course of conduct) he blushingly murmured that he thought we cd. manage a quadrille. Considering that I have owed him 3.10 [pounds and shillings] for the last 5 years, it was rather magnanimous [*sic*] of him; but I did not think myself worthy of such an honour and declined it.

I was in Cambridge last week for some days, & found people rather depressing and depressed as usual. Stimulating themselves with tea & steadying themselves with bromide of potassium, & taking no pleasure in anything apparently. A big price for intellectual exclusiveness.[5] I am looking forward to see yr. story in the Fisher Unwin annual.

Have you been doing anything since I saw you? But of course you have. My sister sent the Phantom Lover to my brother in America,[6] but there has not been time yet to hear his opinion on it. Do you know I am almost afraid to go to Florence; it was so nice last year; & nice things never come over again. Whether I can go again or not, it will always have been a good thing to have gone at all. I can't tell you what a difference it has made to me to have known you. I thought I was beyond the reach of human aid as it were (this sounds rather melodramatic, but you know what I mean) & if you have not converted me to optimism, you will say, I know, that you are not an optimist yrself, you have made things look & feel a great deal better.

How is Mr. Hamilton?[7] I was sorry to hear fr. Miss Robinson that he had been ill. And has he been making any verse? I send you some little verses of my own.[8] I am, dear Miss Paget, yrs. very sincerely, Amy Levy.

1. A good friend of Vernon Lee's, Dorothy Blomfield became important to Levy. She was a poet and fiction writer. The only published work that I have found are two poems in *Woman's World* ("A Roman Love-Song" and "Disillusioned") and a story, "The Reputation of Mademoiselle Claude," which appeared in *Temple Bar* in 1885. She is likely to have published other works, but I have not been able to track them down. Blomfield, whose name suggests that she might have been Jewish, had emigrated to Canada by 1894 (letter from Dorothy Blomfield to Vernon Lee, August 7, 1894, Vernon Lee Collection). See note 36 to chapter 7 for full citations of her published work.

2. Evelyn Wimbush was a friend of Lee's; Levy makes an openly nasty remark about her in letter 28. This may mean that she had reason to think that Vernon Lee did not care for her much; alternatively, Levy may have known Wimbush too was in love with Lee (as is clear from Wimbush's letters at Colby College) and was nasty because she was jealous. The 1889 daily calendar shows that Levy saw Evelyn Wimbush socially upon occasion.

3. Mary Robinson (Agnes Mary Frances Robinson) was a celebrated writer of the period and came to be part of Levy's social network once she met Vernon Lee. Robinson was Lee's lover (or, at least, romantic friend); they had been involved with each other since 1880. Robinson was to marry James Darmesteter, an Oriental scholar (and a Jew) in 1887; after his death she married Emile Duclaux, director of the Pasteur Insti-

tute in Paris. Robinson's work includes books of poetry and novels, among them *The New Arcadia and Other Poems* (1884), *An Italian Garden, a Book of Songs* (1886), *Arden: A Novel* (1883), and three biographies—*Emily Brontë*, (part of the Eminent Women series), *Margaret of Navarre*, and *Marie de Seveigne*. Her parental home was frequently the scene of literary gatherings that attracted writers of varying degrees of fame, including Robert Browning, Oscar Wilde, and Henry James. Elizabeth Pennell, an American who kept a journal about the artistic set that she met in London, says in her January 20, 1889, entry that Henry James had wanted to marry Mary Robinson.

4. John Cross, the late George Eliot's husband, mentioned in letter 19.

5. The disillusionment with Cambridge expressed here animates Levy's 1888 story "The Recent Telepathic Occurrence at the British Museum," exists in embryo in "Between Two Stools" (1883), and underlies "At Prato" (1888).

6. *The Phantom Lover*, one of Lee's supernatural tales, was first published as a story "Oke of Okehurst." The brother in America was probably Willie, who was twenty-one at this time.

7. Eugene Lee-Hamilton was Vernon Lee's invalid half-brother, who was a poet and playwright. His several books include *The Fountain of Youth: A Fantastic Tragedy in Five Acts* (London: E. Stock, 1891). Veneta Colby says in *The Singular Anomaly* (New York: New York University Press, 1970) that he was a helpless cripple for twenty years—a "victim of neurasthenic paralysis"—but that after his mother's death he made a complete recovery (278). After Levy's suicide he wrote a poem about her, "Fumes of Charcoal," that New includes in his edition.

8. The manuscript of this letter has Levy's "The Birch-Tree at Loeschwitz" (spelled "Loschwitz" when she published it in *Plane-Tree*) following her signature, with "To Vernon Lee" on the other side of the page. The Vernon Lee Collection also has three other lyrics that Levy sent to Lee with this first letter: "Lohengrin," the sonnet that was published in *Plane-Tree* as "The Two Terrors," and *"Neue Liebe, Neues Leben"* (translated as "New Love, New Life" when it was revised and included in *Plane-Tree*)." Important for biographical reasons, *"Neue Liebe, Neues Leben"* has two stanzas that come between the second and what is the third stanza in "New Love, New Life." Since these are not available in print or on the Internet, I will include them here as they appear in the manuscript:

II

Why did you come to my dreams last night,
And wring my heart with the old, old pain?
Did you come in love, did you come in despite,
> *Yr. coming was in vain.*
For the old, old pain is dead;
And there is a new pain in its stead.

III.

Nay, my friend,
I wd. not deny
What none can know
So well as I.

27

■ This letter ends with "good wishes for 1887," so there is no question about its date.

Did Medea da Carpe[1] ever really exist?
[scrawled in the upper right-hand corner]
7, Endsleigh Gardens, N.W.

My dear Miss Paget,

It is very ungrateful of me not to have written to you before, but I have been waiting to see Miss Blomfield again before writing. The Raphael angel is quite beautiful, & I need not say how much I value it.

Miss Blomfield came yesterday afternoon & we have agreed to read some Italian together, beginning on a modern novel. Miss Blomfield attracts me immensely; there is something so generous about her; generous in an extended sense; & her sort of mind is so refreshing, after the academic mind wh., till within a comparatively short time, represented culture to me as distinguished fr. Philistinism.

I went some time ago to see Miss Robinson; she is very charming, but hasn't the same personal attraction for me that Miss Blomfield has. I think her *Vincent Hadding* very clever, but striking a false note at the close.[2]

I have finished Villari,[3] and contemplate attacking Macchiavelli's History of Florence; & my story is finished & in the act (or rather state) of being copied out. But please don't have an idea that I am very industrious! It makes me blush to think of people like you or the Robinsons. Have you been doing anything pleasant for Christmas? My people are in Brighton & I have been staying with a married schoolfellow, but am now at home alone with a chum, wh. is my favorite form of existence.[4] As for Florence, I cannot be quite sure, but I expect I really shall go out, in the 2nd week of February. Perhaps I shall take advantage of yr. kind offer, & ask you to negotiate a room for me, either at Miss Godkin's or at an Italian pension of wh. Mabel Robinson[5] told me. The idea of the Italian pension rather takes hold of me, as diligent perusal of Miss Blomfield's [illegible] has given me quite an enthusiasm for Italian! The weather here has taken a turn for the better; it is cold & clear, reminding me of the Florence climate for wh. I never cd. get any one to share my affection.

I have to thank you for two delightful letters; it really must have been a case of telepathy—I mean the crossing of the first of them, with mine.

Sixty Years After (Tennyson's new book) is, of course, the nearest approach at present to a "literary sensation." It looks to me quite hopelessly bad, but the press is kinder to it than it generally is to Tennyson's later poems. I am reading *Jane Eyre* (it is 10 years since I read it first.) What an astonishing book!

I have seen nothing of the Crosses since I have been home, but contemplate calling on Miss Cross one day—I think Miss Blomfield & I are going together. Lucy Matthews was here the other day on her way to the [illegible], & remembers Florence as a dull hole where there were no parties! Isn't that simply terrible?

Miss Black has been sleeping here for a night or two, but is now in Brighton. She had an article on Ugly Men the other day in the St. James Gazette. I talked about you the other night to a Mr. Julian Marshall[6] who sat next to me at dinner; a moody, humorous, discontented sort of person. Do you remember him? With every good wish for 1887, I am, yrs, always sincerely

Amy Levy.

1. Medea da Carpe is a character in Lee's story "Amour Dure," one of her supernatural tales. See Irene Cooper Willis's edition of Vernon Lee's *Supernatural Tales* (1955).

2. While it is possible to interpret Levy's negative remarks about Robinson here and elsewhere as jealousy, I think it much more likely that she is speaking her mind freely because it has not occurred to her that Lee and Robinson are lovers.

3. Luigi Villari was an Italian historian who wrote a biography of Macchiavelli. In an 1888 letter Levy mentions seeing him and his wife socially while in Florence; Villari's wife was Linda White Villari, an English novelist.

4. The married schoolfellow is probably Euphemia Malder Stevens ("Effie"), the wife of Thomas Stevens, a solicitor. Levy met her (when she was Effie Scott) at Brighton High School, and they remained very good friends, but she was not part of Levy's intellectual and artistic set. The poem "The Village Garden" (in this volume) is dedicated to "E. M. S." The "chum" is Clementina, as Levy makes clear further on in the letter.

5. Mabel Robinson, whose full first names were Frances Mary, was the sister of Mary Robinson. Like her sister, she graduated from University College, London, and she became a secretary of Bedford College (London University's principal college for women). Translating many works from French, she also wrote six novels, mostly with feminist themes, including *Mrs. Butler's Ward* (1885), *Disenchantment: An Everyday Story* (1886), which is dedicated to her sister, and *A Woman of the World* (1890).

6. Julian Marshall had belonged to Levy's discussion club.

28

■ This letter can be dated precisely because Levy mentions that Clementina Black has been elected secretary of the "Woman's Protective League" (actually the Woman's Provident and Protective League, or WPPL), which occurred in February 1887.[1]

University Club for Ladies
31, New Bond Street, W.

My dear Miss Paget,

I have been meaning to answer yr. nice letter before, but have been in the depths rather, not so much fr. abstract pessimism, as fr. various tangible causes.[2] It wd. be so nice to have been with you for a few days; the sort of thing that the Fates evidently think too good for me.

Mr. Thicknesse's[3] address is, I believe, 1 Stone Buildings, Lincoln's Inn. Poor Man, I hear he does not get on at the Bar & wants badly to be married to a person he has been engaged to for years. Miss Black has just been made secretary of the Women's Protective League, & editor of the Woman's Union Journal. She was elected out of 72 candidates.

No, I like the *Phantom Lover* better than Medea da Carpe; perhaps because I read it first. It took hold of me entirely at the time. And I think Medea loses by being split up into parts.

I am now expecting Miss Robinson to tea here; knowing her habits & customs I shall not be surprised if she fails to turn up. Miss Blomfield is coming too perhaps; she has been away the last week or two at Godalming. Miss Bessy Ford was in here with a friend a moment ago—odd little person.

Miss Cross came to see me the other day & we had a long talk; she really is a very interesting person below her crust of respectable spinsterhood. I liked her better than I have ever done before. Whether it is that yr. Apollo inspires me, or fr. other causes—I have been abnormally productive, both of prose & verse of late. Quantity, however, seems to transcend quality, & I have no vision

of myself among the immortals. I have met a striking person or twice lately—
Laurence Tadema[4]; there is so much "possibility" about her, to use an affected
expression. She gives one such an impression of youth & innocence, & simplicity & strength. I think more of her book now that I have seen her. And
what sweet eyes! Miss Blomfield & I took to talking about the infinities the
other day; we do not agree on that rather wearisome subject, as no doubt you
know. The vaguely pious person, disbelieving & believing in Christ, is an
anomaly beyond my comprehension. If you go in for vague belief, fling away
the bible you ought to [illegible].[5]

I met a man who knew you, at dinner, last week. He said: "Is not Miss
Paget a very delicate person?" I said, No; I didn't think you were. You're not,
are you?

I have been turning over Dowden's Shelley;[6] it's rather heavy & sentimental, but some of the journals & letters that I've not seen before, interest me
immensely. I am finishing this at home; Miss Robinson & Miss Blomfield met
on the steps, & appearing to-gether, put an end to my letter-writing. Miss
Robinson came fr. Mr. Gosse's[7] lecture, & wore a little green Philistine hat wh.
I didn't like, & wh. D. F. B. [Dorothy Blomfield] pointed out exactly matched
her eyes. She told me, to my astonishment, that Eleanor of Toledo is the first
idea of Medea. She is a being for whom Miss Black & I share an odd sort of
personal antipathy; derived fr. the account of her in Benvenuto Cellini & fr.
the numerous Bronzinos in Florence. Indeed, I once had a scheme of getting
the photographs of her & all her ghastly family & framing them to-gether;
there's that same look of badness about them all, even in that small boy with
the bird—Don Garcia, I think. A sort of family rejoicing in a traceable hereditary curse, like that in Stevenson's *Odala*. Apropos, I have been re-reading
Markheim, & am much struck with it; people tell me it's nabbed fr. somebody's
Le Châtement et le Crime (at least I suppose 'Le Crime' comes first, in the natural order of things).[8] I am so tremendously glad that there is to be some sort
of chance of seeing you.

You are something of an electric battery to me (this doesn't sound polite)
& I am getting faint fr. want of contact!

This is nonsense, & I will leave off, as it appears to be time to do so. By
the bye, Miss Robinson looked immensely well; but Miss Blomfield, is, I fear, a
dreadfully seedy person; & what a sweet, delicate nature she has.

Please remember me to Mr. Hamilton & believe me, with love,

Yrs. sincerely Amy Levy.

The idea of *you* taking lessons from Miss Wimbush amuses me. I didn't know there were any brains stowed away in that flaxen, bird-like head; a sort of vaguely cultured stupidity I have always regarded as her characteristic. I hear Mr. James[9] has the Crosses' old rooms. I remember seeing you there, so well, one evening last year; with Mr. Cross, & Mr. Benson & some American cigarettes.

1. For more about Black's work with the WPPL, see Liselotte Glage, *Clementina Black: A Study in Social History and Literature* (Heidelberg: Carl Winter Universitatsverlag, 1981), 26.

2. Levy is possibly alluding here to her brother Alfred's death in May 1887.

3. Judith Walkowitz mentions Ralph Thickness as a member of Karl Pearson's Men and Women Club in *City of Dreadful Delight*.

4. Laurence Alma-Tadema was the daughter of the distinguished Victorian artist Sir Lawrence Alma-Tadema. She published two novels, *Love's Martyr* (1886) and *Wings of Icarus* (1894). *The Crucifix*, consisting of three long stories, came out in 1895. In the 1880s and 1890s she contributed prose and verse to magazines, notably the *Yellow Book*, the chief organ of the aesthetic movement from 1894 to 1897. According to Sally Mitchell's reference book, *Victorian Britain*, Alma-Tadema played a significant part in the success of that journal.

5. The conversation with Dorothy Blomfield that Levy speaks of here is the only reference to God and religious belief in her letters. Her attitude toward the uncertainty, so pervasive in her time, about the existence of God and, especially, an afterlife would have been different from that of most Victorians because she was not a Christian, and Judaism does not emphasize what happens after death. Several of Levy's poems insist that there is no afterlife and imply that there is no God; however, "Lohengrin" is an impassioned expression of the loss of God and the implications of that loss for society.

6. Edward Dowden, whose life of Shelley came out in 1887, was an important Shakespearean scholar. He also wrote biographies of Southey, Browning, and Montaigne. Levy's timely reading of his Shelley shows that she kept up with scholarly work on English literature.

7. Sir Edmund Gosse, best known today for his autobiographical *Fathers and Sons* (1907), was a poet who was close to the Pre-Raphaelites when he first came to London in 1875. He became Clark lecturer at Cambridge in 1883.

8. Apparently Robert Louis Stevenson was suspected of plagiarizing his story "Markheim" from *Crime and Punishment;* Levy has obviously never heard of Dostoyevski. Her observation about the sequential illogicality of the way the title *Crime and Punishment* was translated into French is amusing.

9. Probably Henry James

29

■ Levy mentions reading Thomas Hardy's *The Woodlanders*, which came out in 1887, so we know this letter is from that year.

7 Endsleigh Gardens

My dear Miss Paget,

I have to thank you for a long & delightful letter; how nice it will be when you come to London; I do so want to see you.

I am so good that you wd. hardly know me, am in the 19th chapter of my novel, & am thinking seriously of a new volume of verse.

I saw a notice about *Zuvenilia*[1]—that it is coming out—in the Athenaeum; is it political-economical?

A friend of mine, Blanche Smith,[2] is going to Florence, & I have ventured to introduce her to you. I think, if you are able to see anything of her, that you will find her a very interesting woman. She read natural science at Newnham, then studied for the state, & went on a dramatic tour with Frank Benson. Miss Blomfield has gone for some months to Godalming to stay with the Leonard Huxleys. I saw a good deal of her when she was in town, as I have already told you, & found her a delightful person.

I was staying down near Godalming, the other day, with Miss Bertha Thomas,[3] but D. B. [Dorothy Blomfield] was in Canterbury, so we did not see her as we had hoped.

I saw something there of the Allinghams (William & Helen)[4] nice, simple, people; are not Mrs. Allingham's pictures delightful?

I met your Count (I will not venture on his name) at the Blacks the other day; Miss Black, by the bye, is flourishing; has the first part of a story in this month's *Eng. Illus.*, and works a great deal for the *St. James.* Last Friday, I went to see the Robinsons, and found them both rather knocked up with hard work, particularly Mary; who looked pale & weak, but was very charming.

There are two novels this season worth reading; I wonder if you have read them? The Woodlanders; a finished, unpleasant, clever book; & *The Silence of Dean Maitland*;[5] a crude, unsympathetic extravagant production, yet powerful in its way, & carrying very many absurdities by the force of the author's belief in them. It is by an invalid woman of 40, who has lived in the country all her days; it has had a great success (it is pious); I think you might hate it.

I am much occupied, at present, in procuring for myself a new evening dress; it is to be of yellow silk; don't you think that will look nice? but I vibrate between maize & gold & orange; wh. last is the fashionable colour, but not so pretty as the others, I think. I have not seen anything of Miss Laurence Tadema lately; I hear she is too busy to work; as she is practicing for a minuet to be danced before the Prince of Wales at a Costume Ball at the Institute of Water Colours!

I hear you have Helen Zimmern[6] in Florence; have you seen anything of her, & is she at all better; it is dreadful, the way in wh. she is broken up. When are you coming here? Is it true that you are going to live en garcon instead of staying with the Robinsons?[7] I wonder if I shall see anything of you? It seems simply ages ago that I said good-bye to you in the Underground Railway (of all places); do you remember?

I hope yr. mother is better; & will you please remember me to Mr. Hamilton? This is such a stupid letter, but you don't know how difficult it is to write to a person like yr. self; talking is so much easier & so very much pleasanter. Perhaps soon I shall be talking to you.

Yrs. always sincerely Amy Levy.

1. Vernon Lee's *Zuvenilia* is a collection of essays on aesthetic questions.

2. Smith is mentioned as Levy's traveling companion in letters 21 and 23.

3. Bertha Thomas, although sixteen years older than Levy (b. 1845), became a good friend; the 1889 daily calendar shows them spending a good deal of time together. Levy's poem "The End of the Day" is dedicated "to B. T." Thomas was the daughter of the Reverend John Thomas Canon of Canterbury from 1862, and the granddaughter of John Bird Sumner, archbishop of Canterbury from 1848. A contributor to many prominent magazines, she had published an article in *Frazier's* in 1874 called "Latest Intelligence from Venus," which is a satire on male attitudes to women's suffrage. Her dozen novels include *Elizabeth's Fortune* (1887) and *Son of the House* (1900). Her study of *George Sand* (1883) is part of the Eminent Women series. Thomas and Levy seem to have become friends through Vernon Lee although they would have known each other since Thomas had been a member of the discussion club.

4. William Allingham (1824–189), a poet born in Ireland, was friends with Carlyle, D. G. Rossetti, and Tennyson. His first volume, *Poems* (1850), includes "The Fairies," his best-known work, but he continued to publish throughout his life. Allingham's *Diary*, published in 1904, contains four decades of vivid portraits of his contemporaries. His wife, Helen Paterson Allingham, was a watercolorist.

5. *The Silence of Dean Maitland* was written by Maxwell Gray.

6. Helen Zimmern (b. 1846 in Hamburg) contributed to the *London Athenaeum*, the *Spectator*, and other British and German periodicals. Much of her scholarly life was devoted to German philosophy: she published *Arthur Schopenhauer, His Life and His Philosophy* (1876), and translated the work of G. E. Lessing, Schopenhauer, and Nietzsche. Her biography *Maria Edgeworth* came out in 1883 as part of the Eminent Women series. Zimmern and Bertha Thomas were very close to each other, possibly romantic friends. Thomas's letters to Richard Garnett mention Helen Zimmern repeatedly and imply that they shared a house in Canterbury; the two frequently traveled together.

7. Levy asks Lee about not staying with the Robinsons so casually—which suggests to me that she still does not know about Lee's romantic relationship with Mary.

30

■ This undated letter was also written in 1887 because Levy refers to H. Rider Haggard's *She,* which came out that year, as a book that "Everyone is talking about."

7 Endsleigh Gardens, N.W.

My dear Miss Paget

Here is bad news; fr. my own point of view, at least, very bad news indeed. I am not coming to Florence after all. I can't exactly give the reasons as they concern other people besides myself.[1] But I am horribly disappointed. I had been so looking forward to seeing you again; I can hardly say how much.

I try not to curse the Fates too audibly, as that wd. be taking the world too much in one's confidence, wh. weak-minded people like myself are always in danger of doing. But I felt all along, that Florence was too good to come over again. Miss Blomfield has been at Canterbury & I have therefore not seen her for a week or two, but I look forward to her return. I find her curiously stimulating; she is the only person I have ever met with whom it gives me any real satisfaction to talk about verse & verse-making—a very isolating sort of industry, by the way. Apropos, I hear that Mr. Hamilton has a new book coming out; I look forward greatly to seeing it. And how about yr. own work? "Are you writing anything:" as the casual person is so fond of saying to one at afternoon tea or over the dinner-table (I always say 'no' at once, wh. is the best way of stopping the horrid subject.) Do the Social Science & Political Economy (I am always hearing people say that it is an exploded science!) proceed, & are they going to have interesting results? (This question has a horrid ring—sounds in fact like something far more personal; I hope you don't think me coarse.[2]) I have not seen Miss Robinson lately, but have met Mabel Robinson once or twice at the Museum, in the Luncheon Room. I believe she is a person of unknown depths! I called this week on Miss Cross, but she was out, so my hopes of a Florentine gossip were baffled.

Everyone is talking about Mr. Haggard's *She;* I don't think much of it, personally; the writer has such a vulgar mind, & such a John Bull sort of imagination. How are you my dear Miss Paget? I hope you sometimes think of me. I think so often of Florence, & of the little rooms with the big fires in the Via Garibaldi. By the bye, I really do mean to write a novel, & you are to be not the heroine, but the hero![3] At least he is to have elements of you in his composition; & to suffer fr. psychological spasms, wh. the poor heroine is to find rather misleading. Are you not interested in the coming work? Will you write to me one day, when the spirit moves you and tell me about yourself! I am beginning to wonder if I shall ever see you again. When people are a long way off it is inconceivable to me that they shd. remember my existence, & sometimes indeed they don't. Yrs. very sincerely Amy Levy.

1. This could again be a reference to Alfred's illness or death or, perhaps, to the family's economic situation.

2. As in her letter to Dollie, Levy worries that she has said something improper: perhaps she thought her phasing could suggest the outcome of a pregnancy.

3. Levy's remark about writing a novel in which Vernon Lee is the *hero* is worth noting. Its gender-bending brings to mind the fact that Vita Sackville-West was the inspiration for Woolf's eponymous Orlando—who starts out as a man but becomes a woman.

31

■ This undated letter was written in June 1887. There is no internal hint of when it was written, but Vernon Lee is in London, and Lee's letters to her mother show that she visited London in June of that year.

University Club for Ladies,
31 New Bond Street. W

Dear Miss Paget,

You are simply too good to me. The flowers were like a breath of Florence wafted into the room; I had a distinct vision, when they came, of Parma

violets heaped against the Strozzi stones, & those fields on Bellosguardo with
the anemones. Miss Blomfield & I owned to being quite overwhelmed by the
appearance of our respective boxes.

I dined with Miss Blomfield on Tuesday & went down with her to a
working girls Club at Westminster. Somehow those girls fr. the streets, with
short & merry lives, don't excite my compassion half as much as small bourgeoisie shut up in stucco villas at Brosdesbury or Islington. Their enforced "respectability" seems to me really tragic.[1] I saw the Robinsons on Sunday at Miss
Thomas's; Mary Robinson was in a good vein & I enjoyed talking to her immensely. Mabel always repels me a little; she is cold, rather "standoffish."

I went Tuesday to see the Dramatic Students in Heywood's Woman
Killed With Kindness. What a fine play!

How are you? & Mr. Hamilton? I see no advertisements of his book.

I am seedy, but apart fr. that, find life opening up, somehow. But the seediness is a drawback. I wore some of yr. flowers last night at a dinner-party—
they are still fresh & sweet; I wore a black dress, open in front, & sticking out
behind as much as even you cd. desire; & went in with a person of the master
species![2] Yrs, with love Amy Levy

1. Levy's sympathy for "the small bourgeoisie"is expressed in her 1889 story "Eldorado at Islington."

2. Vernon Lee seems to have been trying to get Levy to wear a bustle and probably a corset instead of the so-called artistic dress, loose and flowing, that women students at Cambridge wore, which she apparently had not given up. The reference to "a
person of the master species" is another of Levy's gibes about male supremacy and
male arrogance.

32

■ This letter dates from at least the middle of 1888. Levy mentions correcting
the proofs of one novel, Romance of a Shop, and writing another, Reuben Sachs.
The former came out in October 1888 and the latter, though it has an 1888
date of publication, did not appear until January 1889. Levy says she hopes to
go to Switzerland with a "pal" (instead she went alone to Florence in the autumn).

7 Endsleigh Gardens

My dear Miss Paget,

This is indeed bad news—that you are here, & too smashed to see people.

Do you think there is no chance of yr. being visible in London either on yr. way to or fr. Scotland. You really mustn't be one of the people to get heavy & smashed—it takes away the ground fr. one's feet; you are such a rock— morally & mentally speaking—that one cannot reconcile oneself to the idea of yr. being physically out of sorts.[1] This is a very selfish view to take of it, is it not?

I have been spending a few days with Dorothy Blomfield at Geddington; we talked all the time, & drove about in the rain, in a high dog-cart with a frisky horse. She is such a delightful creature.

I have been seeing a little of Miss Anstruther-Thomson, who excites my admiration in many ways[2] tho' I feel that I cd. never become intimate with her, as with Dorothy.

But she is very unique & full of all sorts of beauties.

I am working hard, correcting proofs & writing. I think there is some stuff in the novel on wh. I am at work, but I don't much care for the other one—wh. is slight & aims at the *young person*. You mustn't pitch into me about it—it fills its own aims, more or less, & I have purposely held in my hand.

But, one way & another, I am knocking up & looking for a pal to go to Switzerland with.

My dear Vernon Lee, when am I going to see you again? Dorothy & I agreed that you made life interesting & vivid in quite a wonderful way; although I hardly ever see you, that time in Florence has made all the difference to me, & has made it more possible to carry on the—to me—burdensome business of living.

This is not a letter but an expression of feeling. Yrs. sincerely Amy Levy.

1. Lee's letters to her mother and others show that she was grappling with depression and ill health during this period. Her romantic partnership with Anstruther- Thomson began just as Lee and Robinson were breaking up; Vernon and Kit's romance continued until 1898, and the two remained friends throughout their lives. In 1912 and 1913 they published their work on psychological aesthetics in art—*Beauty and Ugliness* and *The Beautiful*. Bernard Berenson falsely accused them of plagiarizing (see Phyllis Mannochi's article about their relationship, "Vernon Lee and Kit Anstruther-Thomson: A Study of Love and Collaboration Between Romantic Friends," *Women's Studies* 12 [1986]: 129–48).

2. As with Mary Robinson, the way Levy mentions Kit Anstruther-Thomson suggests that she is unaware of the romantic nature of Kit's relationship with Lee.

■ The following three letters to Katie are written from Florence in the autumn of 1888, the first two in November, the third either in November or December. Levy wrote to Macmillan (which was about to bring out *Reuben Sachs*) on October 27 and said that she was about to leave for Italy.[1]

1. Levy's letter to Macmillan is in the Macmillan Collection at the British Library (MS. 201/269).

33

Casa Guidi

Thursday

My dear Katie,

I have just heard yr. sad news. Poor little Humphrey. I was surprised to find how sorry I was. Don't be down about it—after all, as life goes, it is a great piece of luck for him.[1]

How is my dear Bing?[2] Please congratulate him on his birthday for me. His portrait adorns my mantelpiece, & even the hard heart of Helen melted at the sight. I wd. give anything to have him here, prancing around. I have now been here a week & am, so far, not particularly spry. It's a bit lonely. If it weren't for kind little Bertha[3] & *La Guerre et La Paix* I don't know where I shd. be. I think the latter the most enthralling book I have ever read. It has carried me through several wet solitary days, attends me at meals, & is, in short, my guide, philosopher & friend for the time being. I glide lightly over the military part, but even that strikes me as eminently readable. Helen is established here, as she remarks, till she shall be carried up the hill to the crematorium. She seems alight with some secret joy, wh. I have at last traced to the fact that she boards & lodges cheaper at the price than anyone in Florence. I attended her at home on Monday. She adheres strictly to the Italian custom of no tea or food. Lee-Hamilton has sent me his poems with a well-turned compliment scrawled on the fly-leaf. I called the other day, but thank God, he was out. However I have had a special request to go again. The poems are dreadful; I must look through them, I suppose, before I go. I had my first Italian lesson, yesterday, with a lady of Helen's recommending, & rather enjoyed it. Mme. Villari fell upon me at Viesorieux's (the library, & general meeting place) & congratulated me on the success of my book & on *Griselda*.[4] She is going to write & fix a day for me to go up there. Hope to goodness she won't forget—it *is* rather dull. More people will be turning up—Vernon & Miss Wimbush have promised various introductions wh. have not had time to come yet, & I expect Mrs. Townsend & Miss Gibson will be out soon.

The weather is awful. One can't go for long walks, but simply flutters about at the library & streets & churches. I am going through all the sights again, as a matter of fact & began yesterday with San Lorenzo.

The reviews continue mildly good,[5] but as they are evidently written by fools I don't much care, except for sale purposes; & it's as well to have the way paved for Reuben.[6]

Tell Bing, the Strapper, that Auntie Amy will bring him home lots of Italian things; & give him six kisses, if you don't mind—three on either cheek. *Make* Joe read *La Guerre et La Paix*. In the words of Shoulders of the Vale, he will never regret it.

I read *Peres et Enfants*[7] on the way out & liked it immensely. Do read it.

I hope you're not very down. Can't you manage to go away for a few days?

Love to yr. Charlies. Write, won't you?

Yrs. ever.

A.L.

1. Katie and Joseph Solomon's little son, Humphrey Joseph, died in infancy. It is impossible not to wonder how Levy's sister and brother-in-law took her typical, even reflexive, remark about the luck of those who die young.

2. Levy's nephew Billy, Katie's oldest surviving child, was apparently called Bing as a young child.

3. Helen Zimmern and Bertha Thomas were in Florence too.

4. Levy's story "Griselda" came out in *Temple Bar* in 1888.

5. *Romance of a Shop* was published by Fisher Unwin in early October 1888.

6. Again we see that the novel Levy took seriously was *Reuben Sachs*.

7. Levy is reading Tolstoy and Turgenev in French; these and other Russian writers were not available in English until her friend Constance Black Garnett translated their work in the years between 1894 and 1928.

34

■ Internal evidence in the first paragraph establishes that this letter was written on the fifteenth, and since it is evident that little time has passed since Levy's last letter to Katie, the month was still November.

Casa Guidi

Thursday

Dear Saint—

I will write at once, as letters take an awful time coming. Yours dated Sunday only reached me this morning (15th).

I'm afraid you must have been having a bad time. Poor Bing. Kiss his shrunken cheeks for me, and keep my memory green.[1] I look critically in all the toy & sweet shops with a view to him. I often hear him to-whooming, as I sit over my blazing logs with *La Guerre et La Paix*. Yes—the latter is too long & unworthy, but has such splendid bits, that it is more than worth while being a little bored between. I am now about half through the third volume. Things are looking up, as regards people, but I'm not well & horribly sad. I don't think so much time for thinking over one's sunken ships[2] is exactly good for one. Vernon has been most kind in sending people to see me, & I have 5 tea-parties booked for this week. Her great friend, Miss Bella Duffy,[3] is the most hopeful. She has simply urged me to go there at all hours & days. She is a very handsome woman, but terribly lame; and awfully witty & charming. She is considered rather terrible & cynical, I find, but she fell upon me with apparent mash at once,[4] and we rather hit it off, I think. There is a tea-ball at her haunt to-day, where Helen & Bertha are also bidden.

Helen, by the bye, is so benevolent, that I can't help thinking my star must be in the ascendant. (This is a mean thing to say, & it is only for yr. private orb.) I went to tea at the Villaris on Tuesday: various literary females & a broken down man, also literary, with a shrill voice & a partially dislocated jaw. Yesterday as I was in the Reading Room who shd. come in but Maude Weeks & her mother—looking much the same as ever, if perhaps a little sapless. Also, the great name of Mrs. Barton Kent is in the library list, but I haven't seen her or Mabel.

My revised proofs are now dispatched to Macmillan. The title page has 1888 on it, so any day you may wake to find yrself once more an aunt. (& Joe an uncle) Reviews of *The Shop* continue good, in a damn-with-faint-praise fashion, with the exception of one in the *Bradford Observer*, wh. Ned tells me the governor[5] attributes to the machinations of [illegible]!!! Ned has come out as a wit. I had a letter fr. him to-day wh. simply caused me to shriek aloud in the solitude.

The Italian proceeds slowly. Its dull just having lessons with a visiting hack when one wanted to read Dante with a great soul. Such is life.

I hope to hear that you & Bing are well & that I've played my last card & lost. (Don't mention these lugubriosities at home, or to anyone else, will you?) I have such a ghastly headache that I must leave off. Do write. Everyone seems to have forgotten one's existence—not a line fr. Clemmy.

Much love to Bing.

Fr. yrs. ever,

A.L.

Remember me to Emma[6] & the Charlies.

1. "Keep my memory green" is a quotation from Charles Dickens's "The Haunted Man," which is in *The Haunted Man and the Ghost's Bargain* (1848).

2. Levy had a habit of repeating a well-turned phrase or a powerful image: the narrator of "Wise in Her Generation" also speaks of her "sunken ships."

3. Bella Duffy was a close friend of Vernon Lee's; many of her letters to Vernon Lee—written over a span of many years—are at Colby College. As the next letter indicates, she painted, but she also wrote books: a novel, *Winifred Power* (1883), a biography, *Madame de Staël* (1887 [part of the Eminent Women series]), and two histories, *The Tuscan Republics* (1893) and *The Story of the Jews Under Roman Rule* (1895).

4. The 1889 calendar referred to so often in the biography and in the notes to these letters is inscribed "Amy Levy—In Memory of Nov. From Bella Duffy." Levy's remark about how Duffy fell upon her "with apparent mash" shows that she could still joke with Katie about romantic relationships between women.

5. Presumably their father, Lewis Levy.

6. Emma may be Emma Isaac again, or else Emma Hicks, nursemaid to Katie's son Billy (Bing).

35

Casa Guidi

Wed.

Dear Saint—

Our accounts (as regards letters) have got rather mixed, but as I am rather bored I will be generous. I am glad to hear such good accounts of your strapper, whom I shd. greatly like to behold.

There isn't much to tell, but I will take up what I can. Friday I made myself look very nice and sped to the Villaris, only to find that spiteful cat, Miss Pargiter, for fellow-guest. However, we had a fine meal, cigarettes & much gossip.

Saturday I was asked to drive out to a Mrs. Smilie's—an old Scotch lady who has a charming villa just beyond the gates. But I was engaged to go to the opera. Monday I made a walking expedition with some rather nice Philistines I know here. We were escorted, mirabile dictum [illegible] by a man—a gt. booby of the Captain Tribe,[1] who related one plot of a Bootle's Baby story while we were standing in an old, old church, of great solemn beauty! Afterwards I went back with them to tea, where I met Miss Horner of "Walks in Florence" fame, who asked me to go & see her. As my hostess remarked afterwards, it's dull but very respectable.

Yesterday the Duffys took me to an afternoon at home in a wonderful old palace. The hosts combined business with pleasure, for their works of art (the whole family painted) were [illegible], priced, about one of the loveliest suite of rooms I have ever seen. There were gangs and gangs and gangs of women—with an occasional Kahlkoff or infant to represent the male sex. The people—they are half English, half-Italian, are giving a musical party on Friday evening, to wh. they have invited me & I wonder if it will be conducted on the same business principles as yesterday's *fête*. I am—as you see, now fairly launched on a stream of quaint pals. Miss Duffy is the chief social feature of Florence for me, & I see her nearly every day. We have begun to read Dante together & have set apart two evenings a week for the purpose. She is one of the cleverest people I have ever met & I greatly enjoy my intercourse with her. She is Vernon's great friend out here. I heard fr. Tom Stevens to-day. They move into their flat quite soon. I am so glad to think Effie will be in London. Tom said a friend of theirs, Miss Williams, wrote to Effie that everyone was reading *The Romance*. As she belongs to a quite different set to any I know, that is good news. Saturday, if it is fine, Bertha & I go to Lucca for the day, starting off at 7 a.m. & returning about the tens. I see a good deal of Bertha, who I like, as you know. It is in the cards that I may go to Rome after Christmas, at least if the periodical financial smash hasn't come off.[2] Kiss Bing for me many times. I shd. like to have a sport with him. I am rather better and the likeness to June Levin has slightly diminished. But I continue to think the world a heartache.

Write me every fact you can gather on any subject.

Adieu.

A.L.

1. The remark about the man ("of the Captain Tribe") who chatters in a beautiful church is yet another gibe at masculine insensitivity and self-importance.

2. Levy's reference to "the periodical financial smash" is another indication of her family's economic instability.

36

■ The following is a fragment, undated, and, as is apparent from Levy's direct appeal to "Clemmy," addressed to Clementina Black. I place it here with the letters Levy wrote from Florence because Levy is clearly writing from abroad, and her mood, though far more anguished, is in keeping with remarks in the three previous letters about how "horribly sad" she is. The words that begin the first sentence of this letter express Levy's fear of insanity.

have many more sane years, am standing as it were with my hand on the Colney Hatch door-knob [a London insane asylum]. I wish I cd. say something interesting. How has yr. "Auf der Hoke" thing prospered? When I come back I mean to act our "Mingled", if it's practicable—I wish I never were coming back but I am in for another 60 years. O Clemmy, Clemmy, is everybody's life like this? I ought to have made something out of mine, but it's too late. Forgive me if I trespass too much on yr. friendship—& tell me; but it's a relief instead of dragging round all day, crying half the night. What a charming sentimental [illegible] I am. Burn this & don't think too badly of

A.L.

[Levy ends this letter with the following poem, which she never published.]

IMITATION OF HEINE
Last night there was piping and fiddling,
A blowing, a scraping of strings;
The men & the maidens were dancing,
The hours flew by as on wings.
The ladies were twirling & twisting,
The gentlemen bowed, ev'ry one;
I kicked up my heels with the others
And found 'twas rather good fun.

We laughed & we leaped & we chattered,
We said silly things not a few;
Then someone went by in the brightness—
A woman with eyes like you.

> *The laughter, the leaping, the chatter,*
> *Went on as before without rest;—*
> *I wished that the walls wd. close round me*
> *And crush the life from my breast.*[1]

1. This location of this poem suggests that Levy's despondency, while bound up with fear of insanity, is at least in part related to losing a woman she loved. If she was clinically depressed when she wrote this letter, she pulled herself out of it, for her calendar for 1889 tells of a whirlwind of professional and social activities, which end suddenly in early August 1889.

37

■ This short letter to Vernon Lee, dated only "Saturday," was written either on August 31 or on September 7, 1889, both Saturdays.[1] Levy mentions John Sargent's oil painting of Kit Anstruther-Thomson, which, in a letter dated August 28, Vernon Lee told her mother that Sargent had just decided to paint.

7 Endsleigh Gardens

Saturday

My dear Miss Paget—

I have put off answering yr. most kind note, as I wished to tell you how good I think it of you to have asked me to stay with you, &, had circumstances been otherwise, I shd. have been delighted to come. But I'm not well—either in soul or body—& I have refused all invitations to stay with my friends. And I must refuse yrs. too, one of the most attractive. I hope "the back of your head" will get right. Please remember me to Miss Wimbush & Miss Anstruther-Thomson—I'm so glad Mr. Sargent has painted her. Will it be exhibited?

Yrs. with many thanks & good wishes. Amy Levy.

1. Sargent, a friend of Vernon Lee's since childhood, painted a famous portrait of Lee, now owned by the Tate Gallery in London.

2. Levy's daily calendar records that on August 31 she emerged from seclusion and left for a resort with Olive Schreiner; September 7 was the day after she returned from their second trip to a resort. She committed suicide early Tuesday morning, September 10, 1889.

Bibliography

A Publishing History of Amy Levy's Writings

(where they first appeared and important reprintings)

1875

"Ida Grey: A Story of Woman's Sacrifice," Part 1. *Pelican* 2 (April): 20.

1879

"Run to Death." *Victoria Magazine* 33 (July): 248–50; rpt. *Xantippe and Other Verse* (1881). Rpt. Melvyn New's *The Complete Novels and Selected Writings of Amy Levy, 1861–1889.* Gainesville: University Press of Florida, 1993.

1880

"Xantippe," *Dublin University Magazine* (May). Rpt. *Xantippe and Other Verse*; rpt. *A Minor Poet and Other Verse* (1884); rpt. New's edition.

"The Shepherd" (From Goethe). *Cambridge Review,* June 9, 158.

"Euphemia: A Sketch" [Parts 1 and 2]. *Victoria Magazine* 36 (August–September): 129–41, 199–203.

"Mrs. Pierrepoint: A Sketch in Two Parts." *Temple Bar* 59: 226–36.

1881

"Imitation of Heine." *Cambridge Review,* December 7, 127; rpt. as "A Farewell." *A Minor Poet*; rpt. New's ed.

"Newnham College." *Alexandra*, March 4, pages unknown.

Xantippe and Other Verse. Cambridge: E. Johnson.

1882

"From Grillparzer's Sappho." *Cambridge Review*, February 1, 141.

"From Heine." Trans. of Heine's "Mein Herz, mein Herz ist traurig." *Cambridge Review*, April 26, 270.

"To Death" (from Lenau). *Cambridge Review*, February 8, 157; rpt. New's ed.

"The Sick Man and the Nightingale" (from Lenau). *Cambridge Review*, February 8, 157; rpt. New's ed.

"To Sylvia." *Cambridge Review*, March 15, 239; rpt. *A Minor Poet*.

1883

"Between Two Stools." *Temple Bar* 69:337–50; rpt. New's ed.

"Diary of a Plain Girl." *London Society* 44:295–304.

"James Thomson: A Minor Poet." *Cambridge Review*, February 21 and 28, 240–41, 257–58; rpt. New's ed.

The Unhappy Princess: An Extravaganza. London: Samuel French; rpt. *Fairy Plays for Home Performance*. Samuel French, 1898.

"A Ballad of Last Seeing." *Cambridge Review*, May 1, 337.

"A Cross-Road Epitaph." *Cambridge Review*, May 9, 353; rpt. *A Minor Poet*; rpt. *Victorian Women Poets: An Anthology*, edited by Margaret Reynolds and Angela Leighton. Oxford, 1995.

"Epitaph." *Cambridge Review*, May 9, 353; *A Minor Poet*; rpt. New's ed.; rpt. *Victorian Women Poets: An Anthology*.

1884

"After Heine." *Cambridge Review*, December 3, 123 ; rpt. *A London Plane-Tree and Other Verse* (1889) as "In the Black Forest"; rpt. New's ed.

"Mariana in the Ballroom." *London Society* 45 [Special Supplement]: 76.

"The Dream." *The Cambridge Review*, Oct. 22, 29; rpt. *Plane-Tree*.

A Minor Poet and Other Verse. London: T. Fisher Unwin; 2d ed. 1891 (The Cameo Series).

"The New School of American Fiction." *Temple Bar* 70:383–89; rpt. New's ed.

"Sokratics in the Strand." *Cambridge Review*, February 6, 163–64; rpt. New's ed.

"Olga's Valentina." *London Society* 45 (February): 152–57.

"In Holiday Humour." *London Society* 46 (August): 177–84.

"In Retreat." *London Society* 46 (August): 332–35.

1885

"Easter-Tide at Tunbridge Wells." *London Society* 47:481–83.

"Revenge." *London Society* 47 (April): 389–99.

Translation of J. B. Pérès, *Historic and Other Doubts; or The Non-Existence of Napoleon Proved.* London: E. W. Allen.

"Last Words." *Cambridge Review*, February 11 [Supplement]: lxxi.

"Philosophy in the Ballroom." *London Society* 48:175; rpt. as "Philosophy" in *Plane-Tree*; rpt. New's ed.

"Captivity." *Cambridge Review*, December 9, 142–43; rpt. *Plane-Tree*.

1886

"Out of the World." *London Society* 49 (January): 53–56.

"Lohengrin." *Academy*, March 20, 201; rpt. *Plane-Tree*; rpt. New's ed.

"To E." *London Society* 49 (May); rpt. *Plane-Tree*; rpt. New's ed.

"The Ghetto at Florence." *Jewish Chronicle*, March 26, 9.; rpt. New's ed.

"The Jew in Fiction." *Jewish Chronicle*, June 4, 13.

"Jewish Children." *Jewish Chroncle*, November 5, 8; rpt. New's ed.

"Jewish Humour." *Jewish Chronicle*, August 20, 9–10; rpt. New's ed.

"Middle-Class Jewish Women of To-Day." *Jewish Chronicle*, September 17, 7; rpt. New's ed.

"Lost and Won." *Lawn-Tennis*, August 4, 152–53.

"A Game of Lawn-Tennis." *Lawn-Tennis*, June 16, 66.

"A Meadowshire Romance" [4 parts]. August 18, 176–77; August 25, 186–88; September 1, 202–3; September 8, 214–15.

1887

"Alma Mater." *Cambridge Review*, June 1, 362; rpt. *Plane-Tree*.

Two poems called "Sonnet." *Women's Voices: An Anthology of the Most Characteristic Poems by English, Scotch, and Irish Women*, edited by Mrs. William (Elizabeth) Sharp. London: Walter Scott; one of these rpt. as "The Two Terrors" in *Plane-Tree*, the other (beginning "Most wonderful and strange") first pub. *Xantippe* and rpt. *Minor Poet*.

"London in July." *Academy*, July 30, 70; rpt. *Plane-Tree*.

1888

"Rondel (dedicated to Mrs. Fenwick-Miller)." *Pall Mall Gazette*, February 24, 13.

"Roundel." *Star*, February 29; rpt. as "Between the Showers" in *Plane-Tree*.

"Straw in the Streets." *Star*, February 29; rpt. in *Plane-Tree*; rpt. in *Victorian Women Poets:An Anthology*, edited by Angela Leighton and Margaret Reynolds (Oxford: Blackwell, 1995).

"Ballade of an Omnibus." *Star*, February 18; rpt. *Plane-Tree*; rpt. New's ed.

"A London Plane-Tree." *Star*, February 3; rpt. *Plane-Tree*; rpt. New's ed.

"Ballade of a Special Edition." *Star*, May 5; rpt. *Plane-Tree*; rpt. New's ed.

"The First Extra." *Court Society Review* (Autumn) [month and pages not available]; rpt. *Plane-Tree;* rpt. New's ed.

"Griselda." *Temple Bar* 84: 65–96; rpt. New's ed.

"The Poetry of Christina Rossetti." *Woman's World* 1:178–80.

"The Recent Telepathic Occurrence in the British Museum." *Woman's World* 1:31–32; rpt. New's ed.

Translations of poems by Jehudah Halevi and Heinrich Heine. In *Jewish Portraits,* edited by Lady Katie Magnus (London: Routledge, 1988); two by Halevi rpt. New's ed.

"Women and Club Life." *Woman's World* 1:364–67; rpt. New's ed.

"At Prato." *Time* 19 (July): 168–74.

The Romance of a Shop. London: T. Fisher Unwin; Boston: Cupples and Hurd ("The Algonquin Press"), 1889; rpt. New's ed.

Reuben Sachs: A Sketch. London: Macmillan; 2d ed. Macmillan, 1889; rpt. New York: AMS Press, 1971; rpt. New's ed.

1889

"The Village Garden." *Spectator,* February 9, 199.

"The Old House." *Spectator,* April 20; rpt. New's ed.; rpt. *Victorian Women Poets: An Anthology.*

"The Birch-Tree at Loeschwitz." *Woman's World* 2:429; rpt. *Plane-Tree;* rpt. New's ed.

"A Wall Flower." *Woman's World* 2:320; rpt. New's ed.

"Cohen of Trinity." *Gentleman's Magazine* 266 (May): 417–34; rpt. New's ed.

"Eldorado at Islington." *Woman's World* 2:488–89.

"A Slip of the Pen." *Temple Bar* 86:371–77.

"Addenbrooke." *Belgravia* (March), 24–50.

A London Plane-Tree and Other Verse. London: T. Fisher Unwin ("The Cameo Series").

Miss Meredith. Serialized in *British Weekly,* April–June; London: Hodder and Stoughton; Montreal: John Lovell and Son (n.d.); rpt. New's ed.

"Readers at the British Museum." *Atalanta* (April), 449–54.

1890

"Wise in Her Generation." *Woman's World* 3:320–23; rpt. New's ed.

"The Promise of Sleep." *Woman's World* 3:52; rpt. *Plane-Tree.*

"Peace." *Woman's World* 3:65; pub. as "In the Nower" in *Plane-Tree;* rpt. New's ed.

"At Dawn." *Woman's World* 3:65; rpt. *Plane-Tree.*

UNDATED

A Ballad of Religion and Marriage (twelve copies printed privately by Clement Shorter), 1915; rpt. New's ed; rpt. *Victorian Women Poets: An Anthology.*

Poems rpt. in *Victorian Women Poets: An Anthology* (and not in New's edition):
"A March Day in London" [from *Plane-Tree*]
"Twilight" [from *Plane-Tree*]

Amy Levy's poems in *A Minor Poet and Other Verse* and *A London Plane-Tree And Other Verse*
   are on the Internet and can be accessed at http://www.indiana.edu/~letrs/vwwp
   or by conducting a search using the titles of these books + Amy Levy.

$\mathcal{N}otes$

PREFACE AND ACKNOWLEDGMENTS

1. *Woman's World 3* (1890): 52.

2. Levy's work became accessible because of the publication of Melvyn New's *The Complete Novels and Selected Writings of Amy Levy, 1861–1889* (Gainesville: University Press of Florida, 1993); several recent anthologies of poems by Victorian women also include a sampling of her work. The manuscripts of all but seven of the letters by Amy Levy included in this book and the manuscripts of the unpublished stories, poems, sketches, and other items referred to in this biography (if not otherwise stated in these notes) are in the Camellia Collection: Amy Levy Archive in London. Some of Levy's writings—at least two important stories, some interesting essays, and a few examples of her light verse—exist only in the nineteenth-century newspapers and magazines where they were first published. See the complete bibliography in this volume of Levy's published work for where her writings first appeared. All references to works by Levy that refer to New's edition will be cited parenthetically in the text; the words "New's ed." precede the page number for the first reference to that particular text.

CHAPTER 1. PROLOGUE

1. That late Victorian women writers were forgotten until recently is widely accepted; for an excellent discussion of why women novelists had limited opportunities to

be taken seriously, see Gaye Tuckman and Nina E. Fortin, *Edging Women Out: Victorian Novelists, Publishers, and Social Change* (New Haven: Yale University Press, 1989).

2. Deborah Nord's article "'Neither Pairs Nor Odd': Female Community in Late Nineteenth-Century London" discusses Levy as part of a network of independent late Victorian women. See *Signs* 15 (1990): 733–54; rpt., with revisions, in Nord's *Walking the Victorian Streets* (Ithaca: Cornell University Press, 1995).

3. The Victorian Women Writers Project at Indiana University has put the poems from Levy's last two published volumes of poetry on the Internet at <http://www.indiana.edu/~letrs/vwwp>.

4. James Warwick Price, "Three Forgotten Poetesses," *Forum* 47 (1912): 367. The others are Emily Dickinson and Emma Lazarus.

5. Katharine Tynan, *Twenty-Five Years: Reminiscences* (New York: Devin Adair, 1913), 330.

6. Harry Quilter, "Amy Levy: A Reminiscence and a Criticism," in *Preferences in Art, Life and Literature* (London: Swann Sonnenschein, 1892), 138.

7. Grant Allen, "The Girl of the Future," *Universal Review* 7 (1890): 56.

8. *Athenaeum*, October 5, 1889, 457.

9. Gail Kraidman, *Encyclopedia of British Women Writers*, ed. Paul Schlueter and June Schlueter (New York: Garland, 1988), 294–95.

10. Nord, *Walking the Victorian Streets*, 183–84.

11. Angela Leighton and Margaret Reynolds, eds., *Victorian Women Poets: An Anthology* (Oxford: Blackwell, 1995), 589. This story apparently has its origin in Edward Wagenknecht's 1983 *Daughters of the Covenant*, where he explains that the Beaumont Trust raised money for the "People's Palace," established in the 1880s to offer technical courses as well as cultural and recreational facilities for the poor of the East End. Although Levy had nothing to do with the People's Palace, her friend Constance Black (later Garnett) was its librarian in 1888–89.

12. Recent examples of the tenacity of these myths include the entries in *The Oxford Guide to British Women Writers* and the *Dictionary of Literary Biography*; both mention a factory, a garret, and teaching. The notion that Levy lived in a garret is likely to have originated in or at least has been bolstered by a biographical reading of her poem "A London Plane-Tree," where the speaker says, " Here from my garret-pane, I mark / The plane-tree bud and blow."

13. The term "New Woman" was coined in 1894 by Sarah Grand. See Sally Mitchell, ed., *Victorian Britain* (New York: Garland, 1988), 539. I use the term in discussing Levy and attitudes toward women's nature and role in the late 1870s and 1880s because the ideological and behavioral changes that led to its coinage are already apparent in those periods.

14. Eileen Sypher, *Wisps of Violence: Producing Public and Private Politics in the Turn of the Century British Novel* (London: Verso, 1993), 1; James's remark, cited by Sypher, is from Leon Edel, *Henry James: 1882–1885, the Middle Years* (Philadelphia: Lippincott, 1962), 84.

15. These papers make up the Camellia Collection: Amy Levy Archive. Liselotte Glage says in her biography of Clementina Black that after Levy's death her family destroyed some of her papers. See *Clementina Black: A Study in Social History and Literature* (Heidelberg: Carl Winter, 1981), 22.

16. The records of the Beaumont Trust reveal that the Lewis Levy who was involved with this organization had a different address than that of Amy Levy's family and that the "A. Levy" was actually an "Alexander Levy." These records are held by the Greater London Record Office at 40 Northhampton Rd, London (Ref. no. A/BPP/2). As for the Men and Women's Club, London University Library has confused the record by organizing its Karl Pearson Collection so that a club to which both Levy and Pearson belonged is conflated with the later and more radical Men and Women's Club.

17. Bryan Cheyette, "Introduction: Unanswered Questions," in *Between "Race"and Culture: Representations of "the Jew" in English and American Literature,* ed. Bryan Cheyette (Stanford: Stanford University Press, 1996), 13. The idea that "the Jew"as a sign is the embodiment of indeterminacy runs through Cheyette's *Constructions of "the Jew" in English Literature and Society: Racial Representations, 1875–1945* (Cambridge: Cambridge University Press, 1993).

18. The *Diagnostic and Statistical Manual of Mental Disorders (DSM IV)*, 4th ed. (Washington, D.C.: American Psychiatric Association, 1994), discusses what it calls "Major Depressive Disorder (Recurrent)" in considerable detail and says that "the pathophysiology of a Major Depressive Episode include norpinephrine, serotonin, acetylcholine, dopamine, and gamma-aminobutryric acid" (324). Today this disorder can usually be treated effectively with antidepressants that block the reuptake of these neurotransmitters. The *DSM IV* adds criteria for specific features not characteristic of all manifestations of the disorder. Some of these—e.g., "the belief that others would be better off if the person were dead" (322)—call to mind remarks that Levy makes from time to time in her letters (see, e.g., the end of letter 13). Richard Garnett in his *Dictionary of National Biography* entry for Levy said that she "responded more readily to painful than to pleasurable emotions, and this incapacity for pleasure was a more serious trouble than her sensitiveness to pain" (1041); in light of his remark, the criteria for "Melancholic Feature Specifier" in the *DSM IV* seem particularly applicable to Levy's case: "The essential feature . . . is loss of interest or pleasure in all, or almost all, activities, or a lack of reactivity to pleasurable stimuli" (383). As the name "Major Depressive Disorder (Recurrent)" suggests, the disorder is characterized by episodes that come and go. Levy's letters and the reminiscences of friends and family indicate that when she was not going through an episode she was capable of experiencing pleasure.

19. See letter 22 in this volume. All further references to letters included in this book will be cited parenthetically in the text. Virginia Woolf referred to her episodes of depression as her "blue devils."

20. Margaret Reynolds, "The Woman Poet Sings Sappho's Last Song," in *Victorian Women Poets: A Critical Reader*, ed. Angela Leighton (Oxford: Blackwell 1996), 306 n. 12. Reynolds believes this moment "runs from about the end of the 1840s to the beginning of the 1890s."

21. In her essay "Middle-Class Jewish Women of To-Day" Levy says that the Jewish community was even more insistent about marriage and family for women than was the larger society; Levy's essay on Jewish women is discussed in chapter 7.

22. Judith Walkowitz, *City of Dreadful Delight: Narratives of Sexual Danger in Late-Victorian London* (Chicago: University of Chicago Press, 1992), 68.

23. For more about these reformed secondary schools, see Philippa Levine, *Feminist Lives in Victorian England: Private Roles and Public Commitment* (Oxford: Basil Blackwell, 1990), 135–36.

24. Elaine Showalter, *Sexual Anarchy: Gender and Culture at the Fin de Siècle* (New York: Viking Penguin, 1990), 40.

25. Todd Endelman, *Radical Assimilation in English Jewish History, 1656–1945* (Bloomington: Indiana University Press, 1990), 209.

26. Ibid., 92.

27. Todd Endelman, "Native Jews and Foreign Jews in London, 1870–1914," in *The Legacy of Jewish Migration: 1881 and Its Impact*, ed. David Berger (New York: Brooklyn College Press, 1983), 109.

28. Endelman, *Radical Assimilation*, 209.

29. Endelman, "Native Jews and Foreign Jews in London," 110.

30. "Middle-Class Jewish Women of To-Day" reveals Levy's determination to establish that England's Jews were English. Arguing that the Anglo-Jewish community has narrow attitudes toward women, she says that such notions "flourish with more vigour, more pertinacity, over a more wide-spread area, with a deeper root than in any other English Society." She takes a similar stance in "The Jew in Fiction," and in *Reuben Sachs* Leo and his cousins seem to be making the same point when they jokingly ask each other whether a would-be convert to Judaism who came to dinner expected "to see our boxes in the hall, ready packed and labelled *Palestine?*"

31. Ned married a Spanish-speaking Catholic woman, and his descendants do not consider themselves to be Jewish. (Willy remained a bachelor.) Ned's descendants moved to California in the 1980s, and a child born to his granddaughter is named Amy Levy.

32. See Michael Ragussis, *Figures of Conversion: The Jewish Question and English National Identity* (Durham: Duke University Press, 1995), 217, 227–28, and Cheyette, *Con-*

structions of "the Jew," 19–22. In the discourse of Victorian ethnology, Semites were not classified as Indo-European.

33. Cited in Andrea Freud Loewenstein, *Loathsome Jews and Engulfing Women* (New York: New York University Press, 1993), 20.

34. Ibid.

35. Ragussis, *Figures of Conversion,* chap. 6.

36. See Ragussis, *Figures of Conversion;* Cheyette, *Constructions of "the Jew";* Eric Hobsbawm, *The Age of Empire, 1875–1914* (New York: Pantheon, 1987).

37. Michael Galchinsky, "The New Anglo-Jewish Literary Criticism," *Prooftexts: A Journal of Jewish Literary History* 15 (September 1995): 274.

38. Todd Endelman, "The Frankaus of London: A Study in Radical Assimilation, 1837–1967," *Jewish History* 8 (1994): 132. In *Radical Assimilation,* Endelman provides numbers: "In 1870, before the first wave of emigration broke, there were only 60,000 Jews in Great Britain; at the outbreak of World War I, there were over a quarter of a million, most of whom were immigrants or the children of immigrants" (173).

39. Stephen Greenblatt, "Culture," in *Critical Terms for Literary Study,* ed. Frank Lentricchia and Thomas McLaughlin (Chicago: University of Chicago Press, 1990), 229–30.

CHAPTER 2. CHILDHOOD AND FAMILY

1. Marks's handwritten memoir, penned in the 1950s. Dr. Anthony Joseph, the head of the Jewish Genealogical Society of England and a distant relative of both Lucy Marks and Amy Levy, has the manuscript and made a copy for me.

2. Todd Endelman, *Radical Assimilation in English Jewish History, 1656–1945* (Bloomington: Indiana University Press, 1990), 73.

3. Ibid., 94–95.

4. In a letter to Linda Hunt Beckman dated September 19, 1993, Katharine Solomon, Katie's granddaughter, wrote that her "grandmother brought up her children to celebrate Christmas, telling them that it was an old English festival far older than Christianity (i.e., the northern European festival of Yule)." Katie's children married gentiles, and their children were brought up in the Church of England.

5. Michael Ragussis, *Figures of Conversion: The Jewish Question and English National Identity* (Durham: Duke University Press, 1995), 11.

6. Published by Samuel French in 1883; rpt. in French's *Fairy Plays for Home Production* in 1898. Its plot is based on a short story by George Macdonald called "Double-Story." Only the playbill for the 1880 performance survives, but Katie Levy, in her own copy of the published play, noted that it was staged again in January 1883 at the family home at Sussex Place.

7. The Mocattas were a prominent family in London's native Jewish community. The Mocatta Library for Jewish Studies at the University of London is a beneficiary of the philanthropy of one branch of this family.

8. A clipping of this essay about the biblical David is in one of Levy's childhood scrapbooks in the Amy Levy Collection.

9. *Jewish Chronicle*, February 17, 1879, 5.

10. Marks's memoir. One sign of the intimacy of the two families is that Miss Pateman, the governess, was passed on to Lucy's household when Katie, Amy, and the two older boys were too old for her instruction.

11. This letter is dated December 4. The holy day occurs no later than October, so the mails were slow.

12. In 1926 Beth Zion Lask (later Abrahams) read a paper about Levy before the Jewish Historical Society of England: "Amy Levy," *Transactions of the Jewish Historical Society of England* 11 (1926): 168–89.

13. *Pelican* 2 (1875). This issue contained part 1 of the poem; part 2 never appeared because the journal ceased publication. Clippings of Levy's essay and poem are in the Amy Levy collection.

14. Lask mentions the friendship in "Amy Levy and 'The JC,'" *Jewish Chronicle*, November 17, 1961, 13; the description of Asher Myers is from Tony Kushner, "Heritage and Ethnicity: An Introduction," in *The Jewish Heritage in British History: Englishness and Jewishness*, ed. Kushner (London: Gainsborough House, 1992), 31.

15. Census of 1881.

16. Meri-Jane Rochelson, "Jews, Gender, and Genre in Late-Victorian England: Amy Levy's *Reuben Sachs*," *Women's Studies: An Interdisciplinary Journal* 25 (1996): 311.

17. Endelman, *Radical Assimilation*, 92–93. Also see Endelman, "The Frankaus of London," 130. Endelman says that even at the end of the century most Jews took "no interest in art, literature, or science."

18. Katie Levy eventually became a writer too. After her duties as a mother abated, she published stories in popular magazines under the pen name of Katherine Sylvester.

19. Levy's story "A Meadowshire Romance," which appeared in *Lawn-Tennis* in August and September 1886, quotes the saying from which she derived this pen name: "Give a dog a bad name and then hang him for it."

20. Its pages were filled out by Levy herself, her family and friends, her governess, and her beloved high school headmistress, and, though most are undated, the earliest date (on Lewis Levy's entry) is 1874 (when Levy was twelve or thirteen) and the one by Edith Creak is dated 1878. Most of these entries were probably done in the 1870s, when Levy was in her teens, although the one by Levy herself (in this book) seems to have been done when she was slightly older, probably when she was at Newnham. The Confessions Book is in the possession of Katharine Solomon.

21. Ned Levy's handwriting tells us that his page in the Confessions Book was filled out when he was quite young (certainly preadolescent), and all of his responses are jokes: in answer to the question, "What characters in history do you most dislike?" he answered, "Queen Victoria."

22. British slang for feet.

23. According to Katharine Solomon, Katie's granddaughter.

24. It would seem from the notes in the Amy Levy Archive in Abrahams's handwriting that she planned to use the documents in her possession to write other scholarly papers after delivering the paper cited in note 12; she may even have planned a book although she never published further work on Levy. These papers were not available to the public before Abrahams's death in 1990. She acquired the papers of another Jewish woman writer, Grace Aguilar, which she donated to the Jewish Museum of London in the early part of this century. As Rachel Beth Zion Lask, she read a paper on Aguilar before the Jewish Historical Society of England: "Grace Aguilar: A Centenary Tribute," *Transactions of the Jewish Historical Society of England* 16 (1952): 137–48; see Michael Galchinsky, *The Origin of the Modern Jewish Woman Writer* (Detroit: Wayne State University Press, 1996), 9. As Beth-Zion Abrahams, she also translated, edited, and wrote an introduction for *Memoirs* [Gluckel of Hameln: Life 1646–1724] (New York: Thomas Yoseloff, 1963).

25. Macmillan did not publish these stories.

CHAPTER 3. BRIGHTON HIGH SCHOOL FOR GIRLS

1. Philippa Levine, *Feminist Lives in Victorian England: Private Roles and Public Commitment* (Oxford: Basil Blackwell, 1990), 28, 135.

2. Alfred's birthday was April 30, 1863, so in fall of 1876, when the Levy children began studying at Brighton High School, Levy was going on fifteen, Alfred (b. April 30, 1863) was thirteen, Willie (b. June 13, 1865) was eleven, and Ned (b. October 6, 1872) was about to turn six.

3. Constance and Clementina Black were the daughters of David Black, a solicitor and for many years town clerk of Brighton; his wife died when Clementina, the eldest, was still an adolescent, and she took over the maternal role. There were eight children in the Black family, five girls and three boys.

4. Junior Prize Review of "Aurora Leigh," *Kind Words*, n.d. [probably 1874].

5. Designed by John Nash, it is still open to the public.

6. Richard Garnett, *Constance Garnett: A Heroic Life* (London: Sinclair-Stevenson, 1991), 28.

7. Martha Vicinus, *Independent Women: Work and Community for Single Women, 1850–1920* (Chicago: University of Chicago Press, 1985), 187–210. Levy's feelings for Miss Creak were evidently commonplace, as was her openness about them, for Vicinus says

that these crushes were "highly public" (187) and that "differences in age and authority created a distance that intensified desire" (188).

8. Ibid., 188, 197.

9. The *Newnham College Register* says that Edith Creak (1856–1919) became the first headmistress of King Edward's High School for Girls in Birmingham, serving in that position from 1883 until 1910. "A pioneer in modern methods of girls' education," she became quite famous. Creak introduced into her school ideas of self-government and followed the educational ideas of Matthew Arnold.

10. A comment in letter 9 about not yet having "copied any Edgar" suppports my assumption that Levy wrote the story while she was at Brighton High School for Girls.

11. In the letters that Levy wrote and in poems and stories for which she did not make a "fair copy," she regularly uses certain abbreviations for commonly used words. I have kept them since they are easy to decipher, but the following is a complete list: affec. = affection; affectly. = affectionately; cd. = could; cdn't = couldn't; dtr = daughter; fr. = from; gt. = great; shd = should; shdn't. = shouldn't; wh. = which; wd = would; wdn't. = wouldn't; yr. = your; yrs. = yours.

12. Israel Zangwill has an amusing, tongue-in-cheek, hyperbolic paean to fried fish in *Children of the Ghetto: A Study of a Peculiar People*, ed. Meri-Jane Rochelson (Detroit: Wayne State University Press, 1998), 115. In *Reuben Sachs* Levy has the dinner eaten to break the fast on the Day of Atonement include "cold fried fish."

13. The Amy Levy collection has a copy of the poem from *Victoria Magazine* with "1876" written in pen on the first page.

14. Levy's notes in her own copy of *A Minor Poet and Other Verse*, now in the possession of her grandniece, say that "Xantippe" was composed in 1879 in London and Brighton.

15. Letter from Clementina Black to Richard Garnett, October 9, 1879, Richard Garnett Collection, Harry Ransom Research Center, University of Texas, Austin. Garnett was a distinguished scholar and had an important post at the British Museum.

CHAPTER 4. NEWNHAM COLLEGE

1. Ann Phillips, ed., *A Newnham Anthology* (1979; rpt. Cambridge: Newnham College, 1988).

2. Philippa Levine, *Feminist Lives in Victorian England: Private Roles and Public Commitment* (Bloomington: Indiana University Press, 1990), 145. See also Carol Dyhouse, *No Distinction of Sex: Women in British Universities, 1870–1939* (London: UCL Press, 1996), and Martha Vicinus, *Independent Women: Work and Community for Single Women, 1850–1920* (Chicago: University of Chicago Press, 1985).

3. Levine, *Feminist Lives*, 144.

4. The book by Mill that Levy would have had these young women's rights advo-

cates read would probably be John Stuart Mill's *On the Subjection of Women* (1869); it is not as easy to guess which work by Thomas Henry Huxley Levy had in mind. The author of numerous scientific papers and volumes of essays, he propounded a theory of scientific naturalism that made physical causation, as determined by scientific method, the criterion of knowledge. He coined the term *agnosticism*, using it in *Man's Place in Nature* (1863).

5. Vicinus, *Independent Women*, 129.

6. In the manuscript this word appears as "Psha! (w)."

7. Levy is in love again (or, perhaps, still in love).

8. Vicinus, *Independent Women*, 121–62.

9. There is a picture of Helen Gladstone in Levy's photograph album, now in the possession of Katharine Solomon.

10. Published as "Imitation of Heine" in the *Cambridge Review* in 1881 (after Levy had left) and again, as "A Farewell," in *A Minor Poet and Other Verse*. The other Cambridge poems are "Cambridge in the Long" and "Alma Mater."

11. See E. Cobham Brewer, ed., *The Reader's Handbook of Famous Names in Fiction, Allusions, References, Proverbs, Plots, Stories and Poems* (Philadelphia: Lippincott, 1899), 2771. Undine is the title and heroine of an 1814 romance by De La Motte Foqué. Christina Rossetti, whose poems Levy was reading in the years she was at Newnham, has a poem called "Undine."

12. Cited in Elaine Showalter, *Sexual Anarchy: Gender and Culture at the Fin de Siècle* (New York: Viking Penguin, 1990), 25.

13. Levine, *Feminist Lives*, 156.

14. For a scholarly discussion of the malleability of women's sexual orientation, see Carol-Smith Rosenberg, "The Female World of Love and Ritual: Relations Between Women in Nineteenth-Century America," *Signs* 1 (1975): 1–30. This article appeared early in the history of women's studies as a discipline and has become a classic.

15. "A Prayer" is in New's edition, and the manuscripts of all these poems are in the Amy Levy Archive.

16. The first series of Swinburne's *Poems and Ballads* came out in 1866. Levy again quotes from Swinburne's "Félise" in the story "Between Two Stools" (1883); see my discussion of its significance in the story in chapter 6, and see note 3 to letter 9.

17. Edward Wagenknecht, *Daughters of the Covenant: Portraits of Six Jewish Women* (Amherst: University of Massachusetts Press, 1983), 84. Of course, Wagenknecht had access only to Levy's published poetry, but even so, many poems, e.g., "Sinfonia Eroica" and "Borderland," express passion.

18. Angela Leighton, *Victorian Women Poets: Writing Against the Heart* (Charlottesville: University Press of Virginia, 1992), 63.

19. Ibid., 61.

20. Ibid.

21. The Levy family had a copy of Christina Rossetti's *Sing-Song: A Nursery Rhyme Book* (London: Routledge and Sons, 1872), now in the possession of Katharine Solomon. When the Levys moved to Endsleigh Gardens in 1885, their next-door neighbor was William Rossetti and his family, so Amy is likely to have had a nodding acquaintance with Christina, who lived elsewhere but surely visited her brother. In 1888 Levy published "The Poetry of Christina Rossetti," in which she mentions "Mrs. Hemans."

22. Isobel Armstrong, "'A Music of Thine Own': Women's Poetry—An Expressive Tradition, " in *Victorian Women Poets: A Critical Reader*, ed. Angela Leighton (Oxford: Blackwell, 1996), 251. A longer version and slightly different version of this essay is in Armstrong's *Victorian Poetry: Poetry, Poetics and Politics* (London: Routledge, 1993).

23. "A Music of Thine Own," 247.

24. Ibid., 251.

25. That Levy used male personae at times will be discussed more fully in chapter 5.

26. Martineau, review of *Villette* (in the *Daily News*, February 3, 1853), cited in Winifred Gérin, *Charlotte Brontë: Evolution of a Genius* (Oxford: Clarendon Press, 1967), 598.

27. And not just the female *poetic* tradition; cf. Brontë's *Jane Eyre* and *Villette*. Matthew Arnold was repelled by *Villette* because "the writer's mind contains nothing but *hunger,* rebellion and rage" (emphasis added). Quoted in Barbara and Gareth Lloyd Evans, *The Scribner Companion to the Brontës* (New York: Charles Scribner's Sons, 1982), 375.

28. Published in Levy's first and second volumes of poetry (1881 and 1884) and in *Women's Voices*, ed. Elizabeth Sharp (London: Walter Scott, 1887), included in New's edition.

29. Marks's memoir.

30. Elaine Showalter, "Toward a Feminist Poetics," in *The New Feminist Criticism*, ed. Showalter (New York: Pantheon Books, 1985), 248.

31. See essays by these critics in *Victorian Women Poets*, ed. Leighton.

32. Until H. T. Wharton translated Sappho's fragments in 1885, reproducing her feminine pronouns in English for the first time, her homoeroticism was largely unknown in England. See Margaret Reynolds, "The Woman Poet Sings Sappho's Last Song," in *Victorian Women Poets*, ed. Leighton, 294.

33. It would seem that Levy found this sentiment striking, for in 1883, a year later, she quotes the same line from Grillparzer's *Sappho* in German in her essay "James Thomson: A Minor Poet" (see New's ed. 507).

34. Richard Garnett, "Amy Levy," *Dictionary of National Biography* (Oxford: Oxford University Press, 1892), 1041.

35. Its title means self-murder, i.e., suicide. Levy had it reprinted in *A London Plane-Tree and Other Verse* (1889), her last volume of poems.

36. Alfred W. Dole, "A Newnham Student's Poems," *Literary World*, August 5, 1881, 90–91.

37. This article, on newsprint in a periodical called the *Alexandra*, is in the Amy Levy Archive; the page numbers are missing. I have been unable to locate other copies or find out anything about this newspaper.

38. Dyhouse, *No Distinction of Sex*, 91.

39. See "'Life at Girton' (by a Girtonian)," in *A Newnham Anthology*, ed. Phillips; Vicinus, *Independent Women*; Levine, *Feminist Lives*; and Dyhouse, *No Distinction of Sex*.

CHAPTER 5. LEVY'S FICTIVE SELVES: THE HUNGRY POET, "MISS CREAK,"
AND "LEOPOLD LEUNIGER"

1. When I did research in the Amy Levy collection I was allowed to photocopy these never-published stories; at the time I planned to include them in an appendix to this biography, but this became impossible. Readers who want further information on "Leopold Leuniger: A Study" and "The Doctor" should contact me at Ohio University's English Department.

2. The first address on the back of the last page is "South Hall, Newnham College."

3. Clifford Geertz, review of Jerome Bruner's *The Culture of Education*, *New York Review of Books* 44 (April 10, 1997): 24.

4. Walter Pater, *Norton Anthology of English Literature*, 6th ed., 2 vols. (New York: Norton, 1993), 2:1534. Levy was highly aware of the aesthetic movement and would certainly have read this piece.

5. "Works and Days," the diary of Michael Field, entry for April 14, 1891, British Library Add. MS 46779, f. 33v.

6. Vernon Lee, *Laurus Nobilus: Chapters on Art and Life* (London: John Lane, the Bodley, 1889), 155–57.

7. Richard Garnett, "Amy Levy," *Dictionary of National Biography* (Oxford: Oxford University Press, 1882), 1041.

8. Catherine Stimpson, "Gertrice / Altrude: Stein, Toklas, and the Paradox of the Happy Marriage," in *Mothering the Mind: Twelve Studies of Writers and Their Silent Partners*, ed. Ruth Perry and Martine Watson Brownley (New York: Holmes and Meier, 1984), 36.

9. In *Walking the Victorian Streets* (Ithaca: Cornell University Press, 1995), Deborah Nord says that in Levy's love lyrics she takes on the voice of a male persona (199), and in the introduction to *The Complete Novels and Selected Writings of Amy Levy, 1861–1889* (Gainesville: University Press of Florida, 1993), Melvyn New for the most part agrees (38).

10. "The Last Judgment" is the only lyric in which the speaker is specifically a man.

11. Elizabeth Spelman, *Inessential Woman: Problems of Exclusion in Feminist Thought* (Boston: Beacon Press, 1988), 123.

12. The entry probably dates from Levy's Newnham years. Although those that are

dated are from the 1870s and most of the contributors are people Levy knew at Brighton High, some are friends from Newnham, and Levy's handwriting in the entry under discussion is mature—the handwriting she started using while at Cambridge.

13. Browning's poem raises questions about the existence of God and about whether there is meaning and order in the universe (and in the end answers those questions affirmatively).

14. "'Life at Girton' (by a Girtonian)," in *A Newnham Anthology,* ed. Ann Phillips (1979; rpt. Cambridge: Newnham College, 1988). 606.

15. M. M. Bakhtin, *The Dialogic Imagination* (Austin: University of Texas Press, 1981), 293.

16. Todd Endelman, *Radical Assimilation in English Jewish History, 1656–1945* (Bloomington: Indiana University Press, 1990), 101.

17. Reuben's surname name is spelled "Saxe" instead of "Sachs" in this story, the earliest of the works of fiction in which he appears. The spelling suggests that Levy sees her character as English (i.e., Anglo-Saxon) as well as Jewish. Even when his surname is spelled "Sachs," as in the novel, she is probably making the same point. One of the twelve tribes of Israel was named after Jacob's son Reuben; the first name of her protagonist refers to the Jewish component in his character.

Levy uses the name Reuben Saxe/Sachs in three fictional narratives. The character who bears that name in "Leopold Leuniger: A Study" plays no role in the story; in another early, unpublished story (discussed in chapter 6) a Reuben Sachs makes a brief appearance, but he has no resemblance to the eponymous hero of Levy's Jewish novel; in contrast, Leopold Leuniger's character is for the most part consistent in the three stories in which he appears. It is, of course, fascinating that Levy recycles names and characters from fiction to fiction, but the inconsistency of the Reuben character indicates that Levy was not creating a coherent series of narratives. Nevertheless, the names Leopold Leuniger and Reuben Saxe/Sachs certainly had a place in an internal drama that was part of her struggle to come to terms with her Jewishness. See chapter 8, note 24, for more about the different characters named Reuben Sachs.

18. The *OED* tells us that "Jew" as an attributive is "now mainly offensive" and by its examples shows that this was so throughout the nineteenth century. Ragussis gives many instances of Trollope's use of "Jew" as an anti-Semitic modifier, e.g., "Mr. Emilius, the Jew-preacher" in *The Eustace Diamonds* (1873).

19. Cited in Michael Ragussis, *Figures of Conversion: The Jewish Question and English National Identity* (Durham: Duke University Press, 1995), 224.

20. George Eliot and Matthew Arnold wrote appreciative essays about Heine. Eliot's is "German Wit," first published in the *Westminster Review* in 1856, and Arnold's are "Heinrich Heine" and "Pagan and Religious Sentiment," published in *Cornhill Magazine* in the 1860s.

21. See Trollope's Palliser novels, e.g., *The Eustace Diamonds* (1873) and *The Way We Live Now* (1875). Levy did not read the former novel until 1882 (see letter 18).

22. Dickens is also absent. In "The Jew in Fiction" Levy says, "Dickens, as might be expected, places himself on the crudely popular side, but tries to compensate for this having affixed the label 'Jew' to one of his bad fairies by creating the good fairy Riah."

23. In her Confessions Book Levy lists Mrs. Gaskell, C. Brontë, Goethe, George Eliot, Thackeray, Heyse, and Henry James as her favorite novelists. By 1886 Levy knew Thackeray's *Codlingsby*, unpleasant in its attitude toward the Jews, because she mentions it in "The Jew in Fiction," but she had singled Thackeray out for high praise in her 1884 essay "The New School in American Fiction." Her admiration for his fiction may have dwarfed any discomfort about his representation of Jews.

24. Endelman, *Radical Assimilation*, 109.

25. Martha Vicinus, *Independent Women: Work and Community for Single Women, 1850–1920* (Chicago: University of Chicago Press, 1985), 140.

CHAPTER 6. EUROPE AND LONDON: 1881–1885

1. This is almost certainly the same "Madge" mentioned in letters 10 and 11. Madge's full name was Margaret Johnson.

2. After Levy began to earn money from her writing, she painstakingly recorded in her notebooks how much she made from each transaction.

3. See Judith Walkowitz, *City of Dreadful Delight: Narratives of Sexual Danger in Late-Victorian London* (Chicago: University of Chicago, 1992), 137. Levy spells Pearson's first name "Carl" in the letters because that was his spelling until he teutonized it to "Karl." For more on Pearson, see note 2 to letter 21.

4. George Eliot had died two years earlier, in 1880.

5. *About the Jews Since Bible Times* (1881). In 1885 Katie Magnus published *Outlines of Jewish History from B.C. 586 to C.E. 1885*. She was the wife of Sir Philip Magnus and the mother of Phillip Magnus. Her son became a member of Parliament, a director at Routledge, and, in 1919, editor of the *Jewish Guardian*, a newspaper that took an anti-Zionist stand. For more about Lady Magnus, see note 1 to letter 19.

6. Katie Magnus, *Jewish Portraits* (London: T. F. Unwin, 1888). Jehudah Halevi (born around 1080) was a Jewish poet and philosopher who wrote in Hebrew, but Levy's translations are from Abraham Geiger's 1851 German version. Katie Magnus, in chapter 4 of *Jewish Portraits* (titled "*Daniel Deronda* and His Jewish Critics"), criticizes George Eliot for having Daniel and Mirah, her important Jewish characters, set sail for Palestine at the end of the novel. Magnus argues that England's Jews are thoroughly English and therefore should stay in England. Levy probably agreed. As mentioned in the prologue, in *Reuben Sachs* the cousins joke about the notion that English Jews would be likely to set sail for Palestine. Leo says, "I have always been touched . . . at the immense good faith with

which George Eliot carried out that elaborate misconception of hers" (New's ed. 238).

7. The book is now in the possession of Katharine Solomon.

8. Levy's "In Retreat," published in *London Society* in 1884, is about a visit to a convent in Alsace.

9. John Sunnerson, *Georgian London* (London: Pelican Books, 1962), 182.

10. Levy was first admitted to the British Library on November 15, 1882 (Register of Readers' Signatures, Central Archives of the British Museum, London).

11. Walkowitz, *City of Dreadful Delight*, 69.

12. Beatrice Potter married Sydney Webb in 1892.

13. Dollie Maitland and Ernest Radford, both poets, were good friends of Levy's before and after their marriage. See note 4 to letter 18 for more about them.

14. Black published a total of six works of fiction. See note 4 to letter 19 for more about her varied publications.

15. Garnett resigned from this position to compile the General Catalogue of Books.

16. G. B. Burgin, "Some British Museum Stories: A Chat with Dr. Garnett," *Idler* 5 (1894): 371–74.

17. G. F. Barwick, *The Reading Room of the British Museum* (London: Ernest Benn, 1929), 136, cited by Sharona Levy in "Amy Levy: The Woman and Her Writings" (Ph.D. dissertation, Oxford University, 1989), 20, n. 39. Sharona Levy's study also brought to my attention Burgin's article in the *Idler* (cited in note 16). For more about male objections to the presence of women, see Walkowitz, *City of Dreadful Delight*, 69.

18. Yvonne Kapp, *Eleanor Marx*, 2 vols. (New York: Pantheon, 1976), 2:32–33.

19. Deborah Nord, *Walking the Victorian Streets* (Ithaca: Cornell University Press, 1995), 182.

20. Ibid., 181.

21. Max Beer, *Fifty Years of International Socialism* (London: Allen & Unwin, 1935), 72.

22. Kapp, *Eleanor Marx*, 2:260.

23. Ibid., 1:224–26.

24. Chushichi Tuzuki, *The Life of Eleanor Marx, 1855–1898* (London: Clarendon Press, 1967), 265.

25. Jerrold Seigel, *Marx's Fate: The Shape of a Life* (University Park: Pennsylvania State University Press, 1978), 285.

26. Tuzuki, *Life of Eleanor Marx*, 253–54.

27. Dollie Radford, Diary, May 24, 1883, November 30, 1884, Radford Papers, William Andrews Clark Library, University of California, Los Angeles.

28. I have found record of only two socialist functions that Levy attended—a meeting of the Socialist League that she attended with the Radfords (Dollie's diary, June 3, 1888) and an "At Home" sponsored by the Fabian Society in 1889, described in chapter 7.

29. Kapp, *Eleanor Marx*, 2:526.

30. Discussed in chapter 3.

31. Entry for November 9, 1889, in *The Diary of Beatrice Webb*, 2 vols. (Cambridge, Mass.: Belknap Press of Harvard University Press, 1982), 2:303.

32. Letter from Ann MacEwen, Dollie's granddaughter, to Linda Hunt Beckman, January 21, 1993. Dollie's diary shows that Dollie and Amy (sometimes with Clara or Ernest) played tennis "at the Levys." Their game was lawn tennis, played in Regents Park, close by Sussex Place.

33. Letter from Ann MacEwen to Linda Hunt Beckman, February 19, 1993.

34. Radford, Diary, February 21, 1884.

35. Ibid., December 29, 1884.

36. The Attendance Book of the club to which Levy belonged, in the Karl Pearson Collection at University College, London, shows that its first meeting was November 4, 1879. This is the club that is sometimes confused with the Men and Women's Club. The latter was more radical, its purpose to bring the two sexes together in an effort to define new ways for men and women to relate to each other sexually and socially. Karl Pearson, a member of the first, organized the second in 1885 when the first club disbanded. The only people transferring from the first club (which seems to have had no name) to the Men and Women's Club were men: Pearson, Ralph Thickness (a friend of Pearson's who, like Pearson, was an evolutionary thinker), Robert Parker (another evolutionary theorist and friend of Pearson's), and Hume C. Pinsent.

37. The club's members were figures from London's political and artistic circles, many of them distinguished. Members and guests whose names show up in the club's Attendance Book include Ernest and Dollie Radford, Clementina Black, Constance Black, Grace Black, Louie Jeeves (who had gone to Newnham and was a friend of Dollie's and the Radford clan), William Thompson, Frederick Wedmore (author and art critic for the *Standard*), Martha Wedmore, Ellen Huggett, Grace Gilchrist (the wife of Herbert Gilchrist, a painter), the poet Mary Robinson (see note 3 to letter 26), Julian Marshall (an art collector who published *The Annals of Tennis* and *Handel*, a biography of the composer), Helen Zimmern, Bertha Thomas, Caroline Radford, Charles Radford, Arthur Popham, Annie Eastly, Edith Eastly, Minnie Eastly, George Bernard Shaw, Eleanor Marx, Winifred Patterson, Augustine Birrell (author of many books, including *A Life of Charlotte Brontë*, who became a member of Parliament, and, in the 1890s, was on the staff of the *Speaker*), Sidney Lee (assistant editor in 1883 and editor in 1891 of the *Dictionary of National Biography*), Frances Rowe, Louis Rowe, Meta Shaw, Dora Shaw, Frances Hoyle, and Robert and Olive Garnett (two of Richard's children).

38. Deborah Nord, *Walking the Victorian Streets* (Ithaca: Cornell University Press, 1995), 205.

39. Judith Walkowitz, *City of Dreadful Delight: Narratives of Sexual Danger in Late-Victorian London* (Chicago: University of Chicago Press, 1992), 69.

40. Walkowitz has several references to Robert J. Parker in *City of Dreadful Delight*. He was a close friend of Karl Pearson's, and, like Pearson, his intellectual life was shaped by evolutionary theory.

41. Attendance Book of the Men and Women's Club [*sic*], June 28, 1884.

42. Attendance Book.

43. Entry for November 9, 1889, *Diary of Beatrice Webb*, 2:303.

44. This poem appeared in the *Cambridge Review* in May 1883. No previous critic writing about Amy Levy's oeuvre seems to have been aware of it. Because "Ballad of Last Seeing" is not included in *A Minor Poet*, where Levy recorded dates of composition in her own copy, there is no way of knowing for certain when it was written. I am considering it a later poem because it was not published until 1883.

45. Some of the poems ostensibly addressed to a beloved woman written in the last phase of her life are not erotically charged, but this is not because she was taking on a male persona; see chapter 9.

46. "The Last Judgment" is the only love poem in which the speaker is specifically a man; in "Sequel to a Reminiscence" the missing lover to whom the speaker refers is a man.

47. "To Sylvia" was published in the *Cambridge Review* in March 1882. It is written in Sapphics, four-line stanzas, three in tetrameter, followed by a short line in dimeter. Levy may have used this form as a way of saying that her art was inspired by a woman, but it is unlikely that she knew that Sappho's lyrics were homoerotic because this became known in England only after Henry Wharton's edition came out in 1885. As an admirer of Swinburne, she would have known Swinburne's early poem "Sapphics" (in *Poems and Ballads* [1866]), which is written in Sapphic stanzas.

48. I quote "A Ballad of Last Seeing" in full because it is not otherwise available except in the *Cambridge Review*, May 2, 1883, 337.

49. Isobel Armstrong, "Women's Poetry—An Expressive Tradition?" in *Victorian Women Poets: A Critical Reader*, ed. Angela Leighton (Oxford: Blackwell, 1996), 254.

50. Hearing loss must have run in the family because Katharine Solomon, Levy's grandniece, told Linda Hunt Beckman, in a letter dated June 18, 1993, that Levy's younger sister Ella also became prematurely deaf.

51. "Works and Days," the diary of Michael Field, April 14, 1891, British Library Add. MS 46779, f. 33v.

52. One of these is the essay on James Thomson, and the other is "The New School of American Fiction"; published in *Temple Bar*, it is about the work of William Dean Howells and Henry James.

53. Judith Butler, *Gender Trouble* (New York: Routledge, Chapman and Hall, 1990), 136.

54. See, for example, New, Introduction, 38.

55. I am taking the liberty of assuming that this poem is in large part biographical because of its title: a dedication to a specific person. Like "To Sylvia," "To E." is written in Sapphic stanzas. It is possible that Levy used Sapphic form in "To E." as an acknowledgment that "E." was a woman—the poem was published in 1886, a year after Wharton's book came out.

56. *The World as Will and Idea* (1833) by Schopenhauer, an articulation of his philosophy of pessimism.

57. There were two Greeks named Aristarchus. The one that Levy must have had in mind here was head of the Alexandrian library (ca. 216–144 B.C.) He is known for initiating "scientific scholarship" and "his work covered the whole range of grammatical, etymological, orthographical, literary, and textual criticism" (Simon Hornblower and Anthony Spowforth, eds., *Oxford Classical Dictionary* [Oxford: Oxford University Press, 1996], 159). Aristarchus could be considered a pedant, and Levy may be suggesting in this poem that the soul-voice, which urges intellectual effort, has nothing to offer but arid erudition.

58. "Another Morning in Florence" (1886) is about Melissa and one of her frequent traveling companions, but it is not epistolary.

59. Angela Leighton, *Victorian Women Poets: Writing Against the Heart* (Charlottesville: University Press of Virginia, 1992), 175.

60. Levy almost never signed the pieces she published in *London Society*, an indication that she did not want writing that she considered hackwork to be considered part of her oeuvre. Only one of these *London Society* stories, "Revenge" (1885), has Levy's name on it. The other short stories are "Diary of a Plain Girl" (1883) and "Olga's Valentine" (1884).

61. Another sign that Levy was determined to earn money as a writer is that in 1885 she undertook the assignment of translating from the French J. B. Pérès's *Historic and Other Doubts; or, The Non-Existence of Napoleon Proved* (London: E. W. Allen). Pérès's piece is a parody of the "higher criticism" (scholarship on the Bible as a text written at a particular time in history); Richard Garnett arranged for her to take on this work.

62. In my view, most of the short stories that Levy published are potboilers—and she knew it. The fiction in *London Society* is obviously hackwork (as are both of her stories in *Lawn-Tennis*), but other short fiction she wrote before and after the 1881–85 period, including "Mrs. Pierrepoint" and "Griselda" in *Temple Bar* and "Addenbrooke," published in *Belgravia* in 1888, also seem to have been written solely for the market. In contrast, "Euphemia," in many ways an immature and amateurish story, comes from a deeper place in Levy's imagination.

63. Lenau's real name was Nikolaus Franz Niembsch von Strenlenau (1802–50). After Goethe, Heine (1797–1856) is regarded as Germany's best lyric poet. Born a Jew, he converted in 1835 to attend the university and advance in German society. Levy's "To Death" and "The Sick Man and the Nightingale" have "From Lenau" in parenthesis under their

titles. When Levy uses "From" before the name of a Heine or Lenau in a title or subtitle, she is saying that the poem is a fairly direct translation. When she uses "After" or "In Imitation of" before the name of a poet in a title or subtitle, she means that her poem is written in the spirit of that writer. Levy was not alone in writing poems inspired by Heine: throughout the 1880s the *Cambridge Review* published poems imitating his style and sensibility.

64. Review of *A Minor Poet and Other Verse*, *Oxford Magazine* 17 (October 15, 1884): 334.

65. "Some Recent Poetry," *Literary World*, 1884. A copy of this review was found among Levy's papers in the Amy Levy Collection, but the date and page number are missing.

66. Review of *A Minor Poet and Other Verse*, *Court Circular*, June 24, 1884, 509.

67. Angela Leighton, in *Victorian Women Poets: An Anthology*, ed. Leighton and Margaret Reynolds (Oxford: Blackwell, 1995), 591. For a full discussion of sexually transgressive women in Victorian women's poetry, see Leighton's "'Because men made the laws': The Fallen Woman and the Woman Poet," in *Victorian Women Poets: A Critical Reader*, ed. Angela Leighton (Oxford: Blackwell, 1996).

68. Isobel Armstrong, *Victorian Poetry, Poetics, Politics* (London: Routledge, 1993), 374. For a different, provocative analysis of "Magdalen" that "challenges the conventions of Christian poetry," see Cynthia Scheinberg, "Canonizing the Jew: Amy Levy's Challenge to Victorian Poetic Identity," *Victorian Studies* 39 (Winter 1996): 173–200.

69. Cited in a letter from Clementina Black to Richard Garnett, October 9, 1879, Richard Garnett Collection, Harry Ransom Research Center, University of Texas, Austin. Whatever Garnett may have said about "Xantippe" in 1879 to prompt Levy's response, his estimate of the poem was high in 1892, when he published his *DNB* entry.

70. Dorothy Mermin, "The Problem of the Damsel and the Knight," in *Victorian Women Poets*, ed. Leighton, 207–8.

71. See ibid., 211. Mermin seems unaware that Levy and Webster wrote poems that boldly revised—from a woman's point of view—stories traditionally told from the male perspective, and, though she says that Barrett Browning and Christina Rossetti do this "timidly and unobtrusively," she seems to think that such revisions barely existed until poets of today took on such work. For another discussion of how Victorian dramatic monologues by women differ from those by men—and the effects of excluding those by women from critical discourse—see Cynthia Scheinberg's "Recasting 'sympathy and judgment': Amy Levy, Women Poets, and the Dramatic Monologue," *Victorian Poetry* 35 (1997): 173–92.

72. Leighton, in *Victorian Women Poets*, ed. Leighton and Reynolds, 591.

73. Graham Tomson's "The Smile of All Wisdom" is an exception; Louise Sarah Bevington and Mathilde Blind also wrote poems that could be considered philosophical.

74. Cynthia Scheinberg, "Canonizing the Jew: Amy Levy's Challenge to Victorian Poetic Identity," *Victorian Studies* 39 (1996): 180.

75. For some of my thinking about the inaccessibility of the suffering expressed in "A Minor Poet" and in many of Levy's other poems, I am indebted to Suzi Morrison's unpublished essay, "'Pain Is King': The Unapproachability of Amy Levy's Poetry," presented at the Conference of the Midwest Modern Languages Association, November 1996.

76. *Jewish World*, August 8, 1884: 14. The *American Israelite* reprinted part of this review on August 29, 4.

77. "Recent Poetry," *To-Day* 2 (August 1884): 157.

78. Melvyn New, Introduction to *The Complete Novels and Selected Writings of Amy Levy, 1861–1889* (Gainesville: University Press of Florida, 1993), 12.

79. "Recent Poetry," 157. Shaw did not sign this review but, as letter 22 reveals, Levy and Ernest Radford knew who it was that had made fun of their new books.

80. Leighton in *Victorian Women Poets*, ed. Leighton and Reynolds, 591.

81. *The Shorter Oxford English Dictionary*, 3d ed., 1256.

82. Review of *A Minor Poet and Other Verse*, *Jewish Chronicle*, September 5, 1884, 12.

83. This review of the second edition of Sharp's anthology, titled "Women Poets," appeared on September 21, 1891. A copy of it is in the Amy Levy collection, but the pages do not give the name of the journal, and I have not been able to locate it. Sharp's anthology includes two of Levy's sonnets.

84. Frank Harris, *My Life and Loves*, 2 vols. (New York: Grove Press, 1925), 2:304. Since "To Clementina Black" was published as part of *Plane-Tree* in late 1889, Harris may not have intended to imply that Levy's poem was part of his conversation with Marston although it is possible that he read it in manuscript.

85. *Speaker*, October 3, 1891, 413.

86. E. K. Chambers, "Poetry and Pessimism," *Westminster Review* 138 (1892): 366.

87. May 1, 1883, cited in a letter from Ann MacEwen to Linda Hunt Beckman, January 21, 1993.

88. This is the story, mentioned in note 16 to chapter 5, in which a character named Reuben Sachs has a bit part; he is not at all like the Reuben in Levy's novel.

89. The addresses and the fact that the manuscript is a fair copy indicate that Levy attempted to publish "St. Anthony's Vicarage." The manuscript is in the Amy Levy Collection.

90. Sander Gilman, *Jewish Self-Hatred: Anti-Semitism and the Hidden Language of the Jews* (Baltimore: Johns Hopkins University Press, 1986), 3.

91. Todd Endelman, *Radical Assimilation in English Jewish History, 1656–1945* (Bloomington: Indiana University Press, 1990), 167.

92. Gilman, *Jewish Self-Hatred*, 5.

93. Subtitled *A Physical Enquiry into the Influence of Race over the Destinies of Nations*, it first came out in 1850 and was reprinted in 1862. Ragussis includes illustrations from it in *Figures of Conversion*; see 213, figure 16. For a look at Levy's sketch that I have dubbed "Jewesses" and two of the sketches discussed in chapter 3, see figures 23–25 in my article

"Leaving 'The Tribal Duck Pond': Amy Levy, Jewish Self-Hatred, and Jewish Identity," *Victorian Literature and Culture* 27 (1999): 185–201.

94. Levy herself and everyone else in her world thought of the Jews as a "race"; if one believes that race is culturally constructed, then the Jews of England in the 1880s *were* a race.

95. In Valerie Steele, *Fashion and Eroticism: Ideals of Feminine Beauty from the Victorian Era to the Jazz Age* (New York: Oxford University Press, 1985), 102.

96. Nord, *Walking the Victorian Streets*, 200.

97. Armstrong, *Victorian Poetry*, 375.

98. Attendance Book for the Men and Women's Club [*sic*].

99. Katie Levy noted in her published copy of *The Unhappy Princess* that in the 1883 performance of the play "Emmy" Isaac was cast as Girtonia, the governess, evidence that even after Amy Levy left Newnham she continued to be in contact with Jewish friends from her girlhood.

100. In "Amy Levy: A Reminiscence and a Criticism," *Preferences in Art and Life* (London: Swann Sonnenschein, 1892), Harry Quilter says that he found Levy's photograph in an inn in Cornwall and that the owner told him she came there several times to recover her health.

CHAPTER 7. FLORENCE, LONDON, and FLORENCE: 1886–1888

1. Liselotte Glage, *Clementina Black: A Study in Social History and Literature* (Heidelberg: Carl Winter, 1981), 21.

2. Even when the Brownings lived at the Casa Guidi, it was divided into apartments that were rented.

3. Letter from Clementina Black to Richard Garnett, March 23, 1886, Richard Garnett Correspondence, Harry Ransom Research Center, University of Texas, Austin.

4. "Clementina Black: A Character Sketch," *Young Woman* (1892): 315–16. Clementina's character seems exemplary in many respects. In addition to mothering her younger siblings when their mother died and shouldering important political and social work on behalf of working women, she adopted her brother Arthur's infant daughter Speedwell in 1892 after he committed suicide.

5. The protagonist of "Euphemia" is half-Jewish; though nothing is made of that in the story, it must have had significance for Levy.

6. "Amy Levy & 'The J.C.,'" *Jewish Chronicle*, November 17, 1961, 13.

7. Melvyn New, Introduction to *The Complete Novels and Selected Writings of Amy Levy, 1861–1889* (Gainesville: University Press of Florida, 1993), 29.

8. "Vernon Lee," in *Feminist Companion to Literature by Women*, ed. Virginia Blain, Isobel Grundy, and Patricia Clements (New Haven: Yale University Press, 1990), 644.

9. Later, in collaboration with Kit Anstruther-Thomson, Lee theorized about the relationship between psychology and aesthetics in several essays and books such as *The*

Beautiful (1913) and *The Handling of Words* (1923); in 1920 she wrote *Satan the Waster*, a pacifist drama.

10. Veneta Colby, *The Singular Anomaly: Women Novelists of the Nineteenth Century* (New York: New York University Press, 1970), 249. Colby says that James too stopped speaking to Lee in 1892 when he became the object of her satire in her short story "Lady Tal."

11. Preface to *Vernon Lee's Letters*, ed. Irene Cooper Willis (Privately published, 1937), xiii.

12. Willis, draft of the preface to Lee's letters, Vernon Lee Collection, Department of Special Collections, Colby College Library, Colby College, Waterville, Maine.

13. Peter Gunn, *Vernon Lee: Violet Paget, 1856–1935* (Oxford: Oxford University Press, 1964), 76. Robinson was a poet, biographer, and literary critic who, in the 1880s, had a considerably larger reputation as a poet than Levy did.

14. See various letters from Vernon Lee, *Vernon Lee's Letters*. For information about Mary Robinson, see note 3 to letter 26.

15. Levy probably met Dorothy Blomfield through Vernon Lee.

16. See the June 19, 1886, letter from Vernon Lee to her mother, Matilda Paget. The manuscripts of Vernon Lee's letters to various people cited in this biography and the manuscripts of the poems and letters Levy sent to Lee that are included in this book are all in the Vernon Lee Collection, Colby College. Many, but not all, of Vernon Lee's letters are also in the book cited above that was edited by Irene Cooper Willis.

17. The three other lyrics that Levy enclosed were the sonnet eventually published in *Plane-Tree* as "The Two Terrors," "Lohengrin," and "The Birch-Tree at Loschwitz." The latter appeared below Levy's signature as it does in letter 26 in this book (Levy changed the spelling to "Loschwitz" when it was published). "Lohengrin" was published in the *Academy* in May 1886 before Levy sent it to Lee in manuscript the following autumn.

18. "Out of the World," *London Society* 49 (1886): 55. Further references to this essay will be cited parenthetically in the text.

19. Stuart Hall, "Ethnicity: Identity and Difference," *Radical America* 23 (October–December 1989): 18.

20. Levy was to cite more of this passage in her story "Cohen of Trinity" (1889); see my discussion in chapter 9.

21. Stuart Hall, quoted in Henry Louis Gates, "Black London," *New Yorker*, September 18, 1998, 203.

22. "The Jew in Fiction," the only article in the series that New does not include in his edition, came out in June 1886. It will be discussed in chapter 8.

23. Cynthia Scheinberg, in her review of Melvyn New's edition in *Victorian Poetry* 33 (1995): 169–73, also notes the connection between Levy's urban poetry and the historically urban character of Anglo-Jewish life.

24. *Spectator*, February 9, 1889, 197. It is possible that Levy is the author of this unsigned article.

25. *Plane-Tree* has a quotation from Austin Dobson opposite the frontispiece which reads, "Mine is an urban muse / And bound / By some strange law to paven ground." Levy and the few other English poets in this period who wrote about the city would have known Baudelaire's *Fleurs de Mal* (1857), but its influence has to have been convoluted since Baudelaire represents the urban scene as hell.

26. Cynthia Scheinberg, "Canonizing the Jew: Amy Levy's Challenge to Victorian Poetic Identity," *Victorian Studies* 39 (1996): 188. Scheinberg emphasizes Levy's rejection of the idea that the poet has access to universal truth, which she says is "the very crux of the British literary tradition." She attributes Levy's rejection of universals to her Jewish background and her Judaism. I agree that there is a connection, but my research into Levy's life leads me to downplay any direct religious influence.

27. In "Middle-Class Women of To-Day" Levy is more than likely reporting accurately in her generalizations about Anglo-Jewish attitudes toward women's roles; however, when she says that "the Jew is . . . more Oriental at heart than a casual observer might infer" and that "the shadow of the harem has rested out womankind" (New's ed. 525), she may be using a strategy that Joyce Zonona discusses in her article "The Sultan and the Slave: Feminist Orientalism and the Structure of *Jane Eyre*," *Signs* 18 (Spring 1993): 592–617. Zonona's argument is that Victorian feminists attempted to reform Western patriarchal attitudes by developing a discourse that targeted the East for particularly atrocious treatment of women while making comparisons between British and "Oriental" men so as to shame the former into being more enlightened. In *Reuben Sachs* Levy again attributes Anglo-Jewry's treatment of women to its "Orientalism."

28. Levy's article drew a hostile response titled "Middle-Class Jewish Women of To-Day—Another View of Them" by "Another Jewess." See *Jewish Chronicle*, September 24, 1886, 7.

29. The person Levy refers to as "Miss Marks (now the wife of Professor Ayrton)" was Hertha Ayrton (born Sarah Marks), the first Jewish woman at Cambridge. While a student at Girton College she became a kind of foster daughter to Barbara Bodichon and Emily Davies, the chief founders of Girton. Sarah changed her name to Hertha (after the earth-goddess in a poem by Swinburne) and married Will Ayrton, a gentile scientist. George Eliot met Sarah/Hertha through Bodichon, and the characters of Romola (in the novel with that title) and Mirah the Jewish heroine of *Daniel Deronda*) are said to be partially based on Hertha.

30. Candidates Book of the University Women's Club, 1886–87.

31. Despite the emotional growth and upheavals that Levy underwent in 1886, it was a productive year. See the publishing history of Levy's work in this volume for the writings that appeared in 1886. In addition, of course, she wrote the five poems that she sent to Vernon Lee, four of which were not published until 1889.

32. Beth Zion Lask, "Amy Levy," *Transactions of the Jewish Historical Society of England* 11 (1926): 179.

33. Elizabeth Sharp, *Women's Voices* (London: Walter Scott, 1887), 348–49; Sharp reprinted "Most Wonderful and Strange" and published the sonnet that Levy was to call "The Two Terrors" when it appeared in *Plane-Tree*.

34. New, Introduction, 19.

35. For information about Bertha Thomas and Helen Zimmern, see notes 3 and 6 to letter 29.

36. Blomfield had published "The Reputation of Mademoiselle. Claude" in *Temple Bar* 74 (July 1885): 358–70 before she and Levy became acquainted, and she subsequently published two poems in *Woman's World*: "A Roman Love Song" 1 (1888): 363 and "Disillusioned" 2 (1889): 352. Another poem, "The Ballad of Rydal Vale," appeared in an American magazine, *Living Age*, December 24, 1892. See note 1 to letter 26 for more about Dorothy Blomfield.

37. Judith Walkowitz, *City of Dreadful Delight: Narratives of Sexual Danger in Late-Victorian London* (Chicago: University of Chicago Press, 1992), 164.

38. In letter 29 Levy calls it the "Women's Protective League," but the name was changed to the Women's Provident and Protective League (WPPL) in 1887.

39. We know from Dollie Radford's diary that she and Levy saw each other three times in 1888 (March 24, June 3, and June 14), and, judging by the names in Levy's 1889 daily calendar, she remained very close to Clementina Black and continued to see Effie Stevens. Levy saw Ernest Radford a few times in 1889, but she did not see Dollie Radford or Eleanor Marx that year.

40. Grace Black shared Clementina's interest in working women and had helped to establish the first trade union for laundresses in Brighton. She became a pacifist and eventually married an engineer who had worked in the armaments industry but made a career change at Grace's request. After her marriage she did social work on behalf of prostitutes. See Glage, *Clementina Black*, 19.

41. Glage says that Clementina, Emma, and Grace Black moved to Fitzroy Street in 1879, but Levy, in letter 26, is referring to a new living arrangement; perhaps Emma moved out, and Clementina and Grace relocated to a different flat on the same street in 1886, at that point dispensing with the services of a maid.

42. Letter from Vernon Lee to Matilda Paget, June 13, 1887.

43. Stepniak's real name was Sergius M. Krachvinsky. He was a Russian revolutionary whose ideas were influenced by nihilism and anarchism. A friend of Eleanor Marx's, he settled in London in 1885.

44. Vernon Lee became politically active as a pacifist during and after World War I; Zimmern wrote on Schopenhauer and also translated the work of G. E. Lessing and Nietzsche.

45. In 1883 Robinson published a biography of Emily Brontë, Zimmern a life of Maria Edgeworth, and Bertha Thomas a biography of George Sand, all brought out as

part of John Lane's Eminent Women series. Bertha Thomas wrote novels about women taking on new roles, and her novel *Son of the House* (1900) has a socialist hero.

46. Clementina Black never married, and nothing is known about her romantic life; however, her writings about marriage suggest that she was heterosexual. Her determination to believe that marriage could become an egalitarian institution and the tone in which she writes about it seem likely to have resulted from a personal investment in the ideal. See note 4 to letter 19 about Black's writings on the subject of relationships between women and men.

47. See letters from Bertha Thomas in the Richard Garnett Collection, Harry Ransom Research Center, University of Texas, Austin.

48. "The Reputation of Mademoiselle Claude," 360.

49. Although much work has been done on male homosexuality in the literature of this period, I have been unable to find similar scholarship on the homoerotic fiction written by British women. One important book on homoerotic literature by and about men is Joseph Bristow's *Effeminate England: Homoerotic Writing in England After 1885* (Buckingham, U.K.: Open University Press, 1995).

50. Introduction II to *Victorian Women Poets: An Anthology*, ed. Angela Leighton and Margaret Reynolds (Oxford: Blackwell, 1991), xxxvii–xxxviii.

51. Letter from Dorothy Blomfield to Vernon Lee, December 9, 1885.

52. See letters from Evelyn Wimbush to Vernon Lee, 1887–89.

53. The style called "artistic dress" was a descendant of the Pre-Raphaelite clothing that Elizabeth Siddal, Jane Morris, and other Pre-Raphaelite women adopted in the 1860s.

54. Letter from Vernon Lee to Matilda Paget, June 11, 1887.

55. *OED*: "unwell, poorly, not up to the mark" (used by Dickens in 1858).

56. Marks's unpublished reminiscences, handwritten in the 1950s.

57. Lewis Levy's death certificate shows that he died in Johannesburg, where he was employed as a stockbroker. Isabelle died in London in 1928.

58. Alfred's death no doubt explains the will that Levy wrote in December 1887, appointing her longtime friend Euphemia Malder Stevens the executrix and asking her to "have my body cremated." Levy left "all I possess to be divided equally among my brothers & sisters except that I bequeath to Clementina Black . . . all books papers letters & documents of every kind & copy rights if any."

59. Candidates Book of the University Women's Club, undated, but it would have to have been between late autumn 1887 and early January 1888 because of the preceding and succeeding entries.

60. Richard Garnett, "Amy Levy," *Dictionary of National Biography* (Oxford: Oxford University Press, 1892), 1041.

61. Florence Fenwick-Miller, a journalist, ran for the London School Board three times in the 1880s, attracting much attention for her skills as a public speaker. Her name

appears to have been spelled with and without the hyphen. She authored an article that appeared in *Woman's World* in 1888, and her name is hyphenated in the table of contents.

62. In *City of Dreadful Delight*, Judith Walkowitz says that Fenwick Miller (Walkowitz's spelling) and other "platform women" were "part of the spectacle of London life in the eighties, provocative signs of modernity" (66–67) and that in October 1888 Fenwick Miller wrote a letter to the *Daily News* saying the Whitechapel murders "were not just homicides but 'womenkilling,'" making an association between public and domestic violence against women (225).

63. "Canonizing the Jew," 195. Scheinberg was unaware of "Rondel" (Dedicated to Mrs. Fenwick-Miller) until I sent it to her after "Canonizing the Jew" appeared in *Victorian Studies*.

64. *Observer*, July 7, 1929, 10.

65. The proofs of *Plane-Tree* in the Amy Levy collection show that in August 1889 when Levy made corrections she deleted a statement that had appeared with "Ballade of a Special Edition" when it first came out in the *Star* (March 5, 1888): "This was written and published before the recent Whitehall murders."

66. Twelve copies were printed by Clement Shorter, an editor and literary man. The British Library gives the date as 1915, but the pamphlet itself has no date.

67. Terry Castle, *The Apparitional Lesbian: Female Homosexuality and Modern Culture* (New York: Columbia University Press, 1993), 9. In a note to pages 9–10 Castle says, "A subterranean 'lesbian' meaning may be present in odd and its derivatives . . . as early as 1755," and adds, "Later in the nineteenth century, and on into the twentieth, the word inevitably crops up whenever female-female desire is hinted at—especially in fiction." She gives Henry James's *The Bostonians* as an example of a nineteenth-century text that uses *odd* as a code word for homoerotic desire, but does not mention Gissing's *The Odd Women;* I do not think that Gissing's use of *odd* has homoerotic connotations.

68. Isobel Armstrong reads "The Ballad of Religion and Marriage" as a lesbian poem, but she does not explain the basis for her interpretation. See *Victorian Poetry: Poetry, Politics, Poetics* (London: Routledge, 1993), 319.

69. Elaine Showalter, *Sexual Anarchy* (New York: Viking Penguin, 1990), 64. Showalter cites Penny Boumelha's *Thomas Hardy and Women*, 63–64, as her source for the quotation from Hepworth-Dixon.

70. Male critics in our century, with the exception of Richard Ellmann, write about it disparagingly. See, for example, Richard Aldington's introduction to *The Portable Oscar Wilde* (New York: Penguin Books, 1946). In "The Invention of Oscar Wilde," Adam Gopnik says that in *Woman's World* Wilde "helped invent the still current women's magazine formula of campy frivolity and feminist earnestness" (*New Yorker*, May 18, 1998, 81). My own view is that while its material is uneven, *Woman's World* was a publication that Wilde took seriously and had reason to be proud of.

71. Levy's "Dirge" is closer to Heine's lyric than to Rossetti's.

72. Sharp, Introduction to *Woman's Voices*, v, viii.

73. Frederick Rowton, *Female Poets of Great Britain* (Philadelphia: H. C. Baird, 1850), xxxix. I am indebted to Veronica Schuder for calling my attention to Rowton's anthology and to his heavy-handed editing of the poems he includes.

74. William Rossetti, *Christina Rossetti: A Literary Biography* (London: Jonathan Cape, 1994), 338.

75. Amy Levy, "The Poetry of Christina Rossetti," *Woman's World* 1 (1888): 180 (further references to Levy's essay will be given in parentheses in the text). It is interesting that, with the possible exception of "Maude Clare," these are not the Rossetti poems to which today's critics pay attention.

76. Angela Leighton in *Victorian Women Poets*, ed. Leighton and Reynolds, 353.

77. Showalter, *Sexual Anarchy*, 64.

78. Letter from Oscar Wilde to Helena Sickert, in *The Letters of Oscar Wilde*, ed. Rupert Hart-Davis (London: Rupert Hart-Davis, 1962), 208.

79. Amy Levy, "At Prato," *Time* 19 (July 1888): 68 (further references to this story will be cited parenthetically in the text). Meri-Jane Rochelson "discovered" this story and brought it to my attention.

80. In the Victorian period the British regularly referred to the Italians as a race.

81. See chapter 4 ("Queen George") of Showalter, *Sexual Anarchy*.

82. "The words "your Bradshaw" refer to *Bradshaw's Monthly Railway Guide*, published 1841–1961.

83. See the letter from Vernon Lee to Matilda Paget, June 28, 1888, about Lee's emotional and physical distress at this time.

84. New, Introduction, 22–23.

85. See Meri Jane Rochelson, "Jews, Gender, and Genre in Late-Victorian England," *Women's Studies* 25 (1996): 311–28, for a full discussion of *Reuben Sachs* as "a late nineteenth-century feminist novel." Also see my article "Amy Levy and the 'Jewish Novel': Representing Jewish Life in the Victorian Period," *Studies in the Novel* 26 (1994): 235–53, for a discussion of how Levy widens the implications of her feminist critique in *Reuben Sachs* so that it extends beyond the Jewish community.

86. Letter from Vernon Lee to Matilda Paget, August 30, 1887.

87. Phyllis Mannochi, "Vernon Lee and Kit Anstruther-Thomson: A Study of Love and Collaboration Between Romantic Friends," *Women's Studies* 12 (1986): 132; Vernon and Kit's romance continued until 1898, and the two remained friends throughout their lives.

88. Veneta Colby, *The Singular Anomaly: Women Novelists of the Nineteenth Century* (New York: New York University Press, 1970), 290.

89. Mannochi, "Vernon Lee and Kit Anstruther-Thomson," 132.

90. Willis, Preface to *Vernon Lee's Letters*, x.

91. Letters from Evelyn Wimbush to Vernon Lee, e.g., May 28, 1888, July 17, 1888, Vernon Lee Collection. Letters Lee wrote in November and December 1888 show that her exploitation took the form of allowing Wimbush to serve as a combination of nurse and travel companion when, hoping that travel would improve her health and spirits, she went to Tangiers, Gibraltar, and Spain.

92. Supplement to *Spectator* 61 (November 3, 1888): 1536.

93. Letter from Amy Levy, October 29, 1888, Macmillan Collection, MS 201/269, British Library.

94. Garnett, "Amy Levy."

95. Levy's *Minor Poet*, now in the possession of Katharine Solomon, has "Casa Guidi, Firenze, 1888" written just above Morley's words. The choice of this inscription at this point in Levy's life indicates that while Vernon Lee and the Radfords remembered rightly that she insisted on happiness, they did not know that she came to believe that this insistence was part of her problem.

96. Letter from Vernon Lee to Matilda Paget, October 2, 1888. Lee-Hamilton was a poet and playwright; see note 3 to letter 26 for more information about him.

97. In 1888 when Levy met Duffy, she was the author of *Winifred Power* (1883), a novel, and *Madame de Staël* (1887), a biography written for the Eminent Women series. See the note to letter 34 for more about Duffy.

98. Although it is impossible to be certain, the evidence points so strongly in Blomfield's direction that I will let her serve in the role of Levy's last love for the purposes of this narrative.

CHAPTER 8. TWO NOVELS: *ROMANCE OF A SHOP* AND *REUBEN SACHS*

1. Ann Ardis, *New Women, New Novels: Feminism and Early Modernism* (New Brunswick: Rutgers University Press, 1990), 3.

2. Quoted in Deborah Nord, *Walking the Victorian Streets* (Ithaca: Cornell University Press, 1995), 201. The cited passage is from *Romance of a Shop* (the reader might note the similarity between the imagery in this passage and in Levy's "A March Day in London"). All page references to *Romance of a Shop* and *Reuben Sachs* will be cited parenthetically in the text and refer to New's edition.

3. Nord, *Walking the Victorian Streets*, 200-201.

4. See Ann Ardis, "Retreat with Honor: Mary Cholmondeley's *Red Pottage*," in *Writing the Woman Artist*, ed. Suzanne Jones (Philadelphia: University of Pennsylvania Press, 1991).

5. *British Weekly* 4 (October 26, 1888): 420.

6. *Academy*, November 10, 1888, 302. Thus Gissing may have owed nothing to *Romance of a Shop*. Nord says in her article that in his diary Gissing mentions taking *Reuben*

Sachs out of the library in April 1892, a few months before he started to write *The Odd Women*. If that fact has any importance, it may be because of the feminism in Levy's Jewish novel, not because of any significant connection between *Romance of a Shop* and *The Odd Women*. See Nord's "'Neither Pairs Nor Odd': Female Community in Late Nineteenth-Century London," *Signs* 15 (1990): 749.

7. Supplement to *Spectator* 61 (November 3, 1888): 1536.

8. Ibid.

9. Ardis, *New Women, New Novels*, 113.

10. See *Romance of a Shop* in New's edition 185. The language of this passage ostentatiously echoes that of the proposal scene in *Jane Eyre*.

11. See Catherine Belsey, *Critical Practice* (London: Methuen,1980), 67–84, 112–17.

12. On the subject of multiplicity of truth in the Victorian novel, see, for example, Rosemary Clark Beattie, "*Middlemarch*'s Dialogic Style," *Journal of Narrative Technique* 15 (1985): 199–218.

13. Penny Boumelha, "On Realism and Feminism," in *Realism,* ed. Lilian R. Furst (London: Longman, 1992), 320. This essay provides a good discussion of what is meant by the term *classic realism*. To problematize the notion of the so-called omniscient narrator as a truth voice, consider the narrator of Thackeray's *Vanity Fair,* who often cites Tom Eaves, a voyeur and a gossip, as the source of his "omniscience."

14. Examples would include Dickens's *Bleak House* and Charlotte Brontë's *Jane Eyre;* of course these novels owe much to the romance, but my point is that in addition to transcending what are considered its conventions, the great Victorian novels are often generic hybrids.

15. Regina Gagnier, *Idylls of the Marketplace: Oscar Wilde and the Victorian Public* (Stanford: Stanford University Press, 1986), 5.

16. Meri-Jane Rochelson, "Jews, Gender, and Genre in Late Victorian England: Amy Levy's *Reuben Sachs,*" *Women's Studies* 25 (1996): 318.

17. Levy may have had in mind Vernon Lee's brother Eugene Lee-Hamilton, whom she disliked, when she named this character (see letter 33).

18. Levy is alluding to and parodying Trollope's Ethelbert Stanhope in *Barchester Towers* (1857), which parodies Disraeli's *Coningsby* (1844). Trollope says that Bertie Stanhope went "to Judea, but being unable to convert the Jews, was converted by them" (cited in Michael Ragussis, *Figures of Conversion: The Jewish Question and English National Identity* [Durham: Duke University Press, 1995], 239); Stanhope was a convert to Roman Catholicism before his conversion to Judaism.

19. It is useful to compare Judith's treatment in the home of her relatives with that of Fanny Price in Jane Austen's *Mansfield Park:* Fanny, like Judith, is reared in the home of her aunt and uncle and has cousins near her own age, but, though she is treated kindly, she is never allowed to forget that she is a poor relation that the Bertrams have taken in.

20. Ragussis, *Figures of Conversion*, 247.

21. Levy misremembers Clough's *Amour de Voyage* (Canto III, Section VII). She alludes to this part of Clough's poem again in *Romance of a Shop* when the narrator says that "life was opening up for Gertrude and her sisters because they were coming into contact with people in many ways more congenial to them than the mass of their former acquaintance; intercourse with the latter having come about in most cases through 'juxtaposition' rather than 'affinity'" (New's ed. 139).

22. In *Reuben Sachs*, Levy repeatedly alludes to George Eliot's *Daniel Deronda*, a novel that, as Ragussis establishes, also has Jewish self-hatred as a theme. See Ragussis, *Figures of Conversion*, 283–87.

23. That Levy created this relationship between the two texts when she knew readers of *Reuben Sachs* would not have read the early story is a sign of the degree to which these characters had a vivid existence in her imagination.

24. While the Reuben Sachs who makes a brief appearance in "St. Anthony's Vicarage" is in no way like the Reuben Sachs in Levy's novel because of the harshness of his sentiments and the way he expresses himself, it is interesting that in this story he is a man who, despite regarding the Jews as "the finest race in the world," is eager for them to assimilate so thoroughly through intermarriage that they will be absorbed into the general population. In *Reuben Sachs*, published at least four years later, Reuben says, in response to Leo's expressed desire for the absorption of the Jews, that "should I live to see it borne out, I should be very sorry " (New's ed. 239).

25. "Letter to the Editor of the *'Jewish Chronicle,'*" October 12, 1883, 4.

26. *Academy*, February 16, 1889, 109.

27. Macmillan reader's report, October 4, 1888, British Library, BM Add. MS 55941, ff. 146–47.

28. See Linda Hunt, "Amy Levy and the Jewish Novel: Representing Jewish Life in the Victorian Period," *Studies in the Novel* 16 (1994): 235–53, esp. 241–45.

29. Oxford: Oxford University Press, 1983, vol. 2, 329.

30. Lucy Lane Clifford, *Mrs. Keith's Crime* (London: Richard Bentley and Son, 1885).

31. Cited in Ragussis, *Figures of Conversion*, 244–45.

32. Cited in Bryan Cheyette's *Constructions of "the Jew" in English Literature and Society: Racial Representations, 1875–1945* (Cambridge: Cambridge University Press, 1993), 31.

33. Julia Frankau, *Dr. Phillips: A Maida Vale Idyll* (1887, rpt. New York: Garland, 1984), 5.

34. Jonathan Culler, *On Deconstruction* (Ithaca: Cornell University Press, 1982), 95.

35. Boumelha, "On Realism and Feminism." Critics writing in the 1990s have tended to be no more able than commentators in the 1880s to recognize that in *Reuben Sachs* Levy uses methods that depart significantly from conventional realism in order to create a mélange of varied and opposing voices on Anglo-Jewry; Geoffrey Alderman, for example, asserts that *Reuben Sachs* is unusually "realistic" because, unlike philo-semitic

Victorian novelists who provide "blatantly false portraiture" of English Jews, Levy "set out to expose" Jewish life "in all its ultra-opulent and self-satisfied glory." See Geoffrey Alderman's *Modern British Jewry* (Oxford: Claredon, 1992).

36. Reuben's phrase from the title of Walter Besant's novel *All Sorts and Conditions of Men* (1882), which inspired the founding of the People's Palace.

37. Yvonne Kapp explains Marx's interest in Levy's book by emphasizing the debate between Leo and Reuben; she says, in regard to Reuben's defense of the Jews, that he offers "a viewpoint that Eleanor was coming more and more to share." See *Eleanor Marx*, 2 vols. (New York: Pantheon, 1976), 2:260.

38. Maeera Y. Shreiber, "The End of Exile: Jewish Identity and Its Diaspora Poetics," *PMLA* 113 (1998): 274. Meri-Jane Rochelson describes a pattern in English novels about Jews (whether by Jews or gentiles) "in which Jewish survival hinges on a woman's fate"; she goes on to suggest that in Zangwill's *Children of the Ghetto* the destiny of the Jews seems to be predicated on who Esther Ansell will marry, which remains undecided when the novel ends. See Rochelson's introduction to her edition of *Children of the Ghetto* (Detroit: Wayne State University Press, 1998), 33–34.

CHAPTER 9. LONDON: 1889

1. While in Paris she was taken by Kit Anstruther-Thomson to meet Charles Emile Auguste Carolus Duran, the famous French painter noted for his realistic portraits with whom Kit had studied.

2. Margaret Bateson published an article called "Dress in Character" (about how clothing expresses identity) in *Woman's World* 2 (1889): 482. Her book *Professional Women upon Their Professions* (1895) is made up of interviews with women physicians, actresses, journalists, and the like.

3. Judith Walkowitz, *City of Dreadful Delight: Narratives of Sexual Danger in Late-Victorian London* (Chicago: University of Chicago Press, 1992).

4. Bessy May was a Newnham classmate whose membership in the University Women's Club Levy sponsored in 1888; she and Levy saw each other occasionally throughout the year.

5. Stepniak was the Russian nihilist mentioned in chapter 7. In 1889, when Stepniak and Levy saw each other socially a few times, he was thirty-seven years old. The freedom with which they exchanged calls shows how unchaperoned Levy's life was.

6. The parenthetical "80" may refer to the number of guests although the rooms at the University Women's Club were small for such a large party.

7. George Fleming was Julia Constance Fletcher, an American writer of New Woman fiction, who lived in England. Her books include *For Plain Women Only* (1885) and *The Truth About Clement Ker* (1889). Oscar Wilde expressed admiration for her writing, and she sometimes published in *Woman's World*.

8. "Ouida" was the pen name of Louise de la Ramée, a popular fiction writer whose first novel appeared in 1863 and whose last novels were published in the 1880s. She generally wrote melodramatic tales of love and intrigue, but her fiction sometimes addressed social issues.

9. Caird was a feminist polemicist and novelist. She published a series of essays about marriage as a patriarchal institution that were collected as *The Morality of Marriage* (1897). Two of her novels are *The Wings of Azrael* (1889) and *Daughters of Danaeus* (1894).

10. Elizabeth Pennell was the wife of the artist Joseph Pennell. Living in London in the late 1880s, she kept a journal about the artistic and political scene there; Pennell's unpublished journal is at the Harry Ransom Humanities Research Center, University of Texas, Austin, and the quoted passage is from her April 12, 1889, entry. The Jaeger suit was invented by a Dr. Jaeger; this was an all-wool garment said to be more beneficial to the health than the common garb of the day. Pennell reports that Shaw said about it, "I want my body to breathe."

11. Quoted in Karl Beckson, *Arthur Symons, a Life* (Oxford: Clarendon Press, 1987), 50.

12. The possibility that Levy came to have an emotional investment in the welfare of the working women who belonged to the WPPL is supported by what Liselotte Glage says in *Clementina Black: A Study in Social History and Literature* (Heidelberg: Carl Winter, 1981), 24, that after Levy's death "some of the books that had been in her possession were presented to the Woman's Protective and Provident League by Amy's sister, Mrs. Solomon. Amy had been a supporter of the League and is mentioned in its donations list."

13. Julia Frankau, *Dr. Phillips: A Maida Vale Idyll* (1887, rpt. Garland, 1984).

14. *Jewish Chronicle*, January 25, 1889, 11. This was followed in early May by a review of a novel called *Angela's Tempters*—also critical of Jewish life—that probably refers critically to Levy but again refrains from mentioning her by name. See *Jewish Chronicle*, May 3, 1889, 12.

15. "The Deterioration of the Jewess," *Jewish World*, February 22, 1889, 5.

16. "Morour and Charoseth," *Jewish Standard*, March 1, 1889, 9–10. Meri-Jane Rochelson says Levy's experience with *Reuben Sachs* is "believed to be the source of a major plot thread" in *Children of the Ghetto* ("Jews, Gender, and Genre in Late-Victorian England: Amy Levy's *Reuben Sachs*," *Women's Studies: An Interdisciplinary Journal* 25 [1996]: 311). Zangwill cooled off, for the character based on Levy is treated sympathetically; moreover, he defended Levy in a 1901 *Jewish Chronicle* article (cited in Bryan Cheyette, "From Apology to Revolt: Benjamin Farjeon, Amy Levy and the Post-Emancipation Anglo-Jewish Novel, 1880–1900," *Jewish Historical Society of England Transactions* 24 [1982–86]: 260).

17. "A Misunderstood Marshallik," *Jewish Standard*, March 8, 1889, 6.

18. Rochelson, "Jews, Gender, and Genre," 316.

19. Ibid.

20. *Cambridge Review,* January 31, 1889, 182.

21. Richard Garnett, "Amy Levy," *Dictionary of National Biography* (Oxford: Oxford University Press, 1892), 1041. Garnett may be referring only to the criticism in the Jewish press, not to how Levy was treated personally.

22. Journal of Elizabeth Pennell, July 19, 1889.

23. Katharine Tynan, *Twenty-Five Years: Reminiscences* (New York: Devin Adair, 1913), 290.

24. Ibid., 301.

25. Moulton was an American journalist who lived in England in 1889 and wrote about London writers and artists for the *Boston Herald* and other periodicals. She says that the gathering she attended took place in July. There is nothing in Levy's calendar for July that corresponds to Moulton's description, but Levy did attend two of Mrs. Moulton's "At Homes" during July. Writing three years later, Moulton must have remembered inaccurately the month of Levy's University Club party.

26. *British Weekly,* September 8, 1892, 317. (The article says that Mrs. Moulton's account is reprinted from another journal, the *Arena.*)

27. W. B. Yeats, *Letters to the New Island,* ed. Horace Reynolds (Cambridge, Mass.: Harvard University Press, 1934), 87. The book is a collection of the columns Yeats wrote between August 1889 and November 1892 for two American newspapers.

28. Letter from Amy Levy to Louise Moulton, April 1, 1889, Louise Chandler Moulton Collection, Library of Congress.

29. Letter to Amy Levy from Louise Chandler Moulton, August 1, 1889, ibid.

30. "The Governess in Fiction," *Academy,* August 12, 1899, 163.

31. Harry Quilter, "Amy Levy: A Reminiscence and a Criticism," in *Preferences in Art, Life and Literature* (London: Swann Sonnenschein, 1892), 135.

32. Sander Gilman, *Inscribing the Other* (Lincoln: University of Nebraska Press, 1991), 53. Gilman makes this remark while discussing eighteenth-century drama by German Jews.

33. Ibid., 124.

34. Since many of the poems in *Plane-Tree* first appeared in various journals, it is possible to establish when quite a few were published (and we know that she composed the five she sent to Vernon Lee in the first half of 1886). The earliest are "The Dream," "In the Black Forest" (originally called "After Heine"), and "Last Words," all published in the *Cambridge Review;* the first two appeared in autumn 1884 and the latter in February 1885.

35. The fourth, "The Birch-Tree of Loschwitz," sold to the *Woman's World* in June 1889, is one of the lyrics sent to Lee back in 1886, and its energy and vigorous eroticism place it in that year of rejuvenation.

36. "A March Day" and "On the Wye" are likely to have been written in spring of 1889 because of their themes, mood, and tone. The proofs for *Plane-Tree* show that Levy

added "The End of the Day" to her volume while correcting the proofs, which, together with the poem's mood, suggests that she wrote it in August, just before her death. "In the Nower" was published posthumously in *Woman's World* as "Peace" (1890).

37. Isobel Armstrong is certainly aware that Levy wrote in other modes: e.g., both her essay in the *Critical Reader* and the chapter on the female poetic tradition in her book on Victorian poetry begin with "A Ballad of Religion and Marriage"; however, she groups Amy Levy with Augusta Webster, saying that "these last two wrote consciously as dramatic monologuists." See "Women's Poetry—an Expressive Tradition?" in *Victorian Women Poets: A Critical Reader*, ed. Angela Leighton (Oxford: Blackwell, 1996), 253. For an important discussion of the lyrics in Levy's last book, see Joseph Bristow's "'All out of tune in this world's instrument': The 'Minor' Poetry of Amy Levy," *Journal of Victorian Poetry* 5 (1999): 76–103.

38. The way Levy uses this anxiety links some of her late poems to the female tradition defined by Isobel Armstrong. Although she says that Levy is one of the later Victorian women poets who "were able to depart from the expressive model," "Oh, Is It Love" and some of Levy's other late lyrics have the qualities that Armstrong refers to in defining the aesthetics of expressive poetry. In her words, there is a "disjunction between the secret feelings of the mind and the form of representation," "expression and repression, although in conflict with one another, become interdependent," and "the verbal forms of language are inadequate, ineffable." See "Women's Poetry," 270.

39. Levy's "Captivity," first published in 1885 in the *Cambridge Review*, also belongs in this category even though the speaker, likening herself to a caged lion or a bird straining for freedom, wonders if these creatures, released from their bonds, might not return voluntarily to their fetters. Armstrong observes that the impulse to be released from the constraints of bourgeois society is frequently allied "with a metaphor of prison, or of slavery" ("Women's Poetry," 252), and Kathleen Hickok discusses the prevalence of captivity and imprisonment imagery in women's poetry in *Representations of Woman: Nineteenth-Century British Women's Poetry* (Westport, Conn.: Greenwood Press, 1984), 29–30.

40. Margaret Reynolds's "The Woman Poet Sings Sappho's Last Song" and Dorothy Mermin's "The Damsel, the Knight, and the Victorian Woman Poet" also address the question of how nineteenth-century women poets use themselves as subjects *and* objects to raise questions about the self. Both essays are in *Victorian Women Poets*, ed. Leighton.

41. Introduction (II) to *Victorian Women Poets: An Anthology*, ed. Angela Leighton and Margaret Reynolds (Oxford: Blackwell, 1995), xxxvii. Leighton also discusses the mirror poem (without mentioning Levy) in *Victorian Women Poets: Writing Against the Heart* (Charlottesville: University Press of Virginia, 1992), 186–90.

42. Leighton, *Victorian Women Poets*, 145.

43. Armstrong, "Women's Poetry," 270.

44. Melvyn New, Introduction to *The Complete Novels and Selected Writings of Amy Levy, 1861–1889* (Gainesville: University Press of Florida, 1993), 37.

45. Deborah Nord, *Walking the Victorian Streets* (Ithaca: Cornell University Press, 1995), 199.

46. "Contradictions," "On the Threshold," "At Dawn," and "In the Night" are also poems about dissociation from and confrontation with dimensions of the psyche. These contrast with Levy's other love poems, which are sexually-charged—e.g., "A Ballad of Last Seeing," "Sinfonia Eroica," "To Vernon Lee," and "Borderland."

47. In her other note to Moulton (postmarked August 17) Levy says she is not well enough to make calls but invites her correspondent to tea.

48. "Wise in her generation" (or, at least, variations on the phrase) is proverbial. Roget's *Thesaurus* (1911) gives the meaning of "wise in one's generation" as "adj., prudent." The source is Luke 16:8: "for the children of this world are in their generation wiser than the children of light" (King James Version).

49. These writings are not on the list of items that Levy sold and published in periodicals in 1889 (on the back of her calendar the list ends with pieces sold in July).

50. Richard Ellmann says that Wilde told the story of "a man and a picture" to various young men for several years before he actually wrote it down. After meeting J. M. Stoddart, the editor of *Lippincott's*, Wilde agreed to send him the story by October 1889 but "does not seem to have delivered it until the next spring." Wilde's tale did not appear in *Lippincott's Monthly Magazine* until June 20, 1890 (the July issue), and Levy's story was published in Wilde's *Woman's World* earlier in 1890. If she submitted it herself, Wilde would have had it before September 10, 1889 (the day of her death)—before the composition of *Dorian Gray*. Even if Levy's story was submitted later by a family member or by Black, Wilde would have read it before he completed the composition of *Dorian Gray*. See Ellmann's *Oscar Wilde* (New York: Knopf, 1988), 314. Levy's "Wise in Her Generation" contains a passing reference to a woman poet named Medora Gray.

51. Letter from Bella Duffy to Vernon Lee, September 23, 1889, Vernon Lee Collection, Colby College, Waterville, Maine.

52. Letter from Grace Black to Ernest Radford, September 16, 1889, in Ann MacEwen's private collection.

53. Letter from Olive Schreiner to Edward Carpenter, September 1889, *Olive Schreiner's Letters*, vol. 1, *1871–1899*, ed. Richard Rive (Oxford: Oxford University Press, 1988), 157.

54. Letter from Olive Schreiner to Havelock Ellis, April 23, 1892, in *My Other Self: Letters from Olive Schreiner to Havelock Ellis, 1884–1920*, ed. Yaffa Claire Draznin (New York: Lang, 1992), 474.

55. In *Clementina Black: A Study in Social History and Literature* (Heidelberg: Carl Win-

ter, 1981), 22, Liselotte Glage says, "Most of Amy's books, papers and manuscripts were left in possession of her family who destroyed some of them."

56. See "Middle-Class Jewish Women of To-Day," New's ed. 526.

57. Vernon Lee to Bella Duffy, December 7, 1888, also in *Vernon Lee's Letters* (Privately published, 1937), 299.

58. Quoted in Yosef Gorni, "Beatrice Webb's Views on Judaism and Zionism," *Jewish Social Studies* 40 (1978): 102–6.

59. When Lee was in England in the summer of 1888 she and Levy did not even see each other. The Vernon Lee Collection has only one letter from Levy to Lee written in 1888 (letter 33 in Appendix A). It is possible, of course, that letters were lost.

60. That Levy made a connection between the Jew and Caliban is interesting. She may have been inspired by George Eliot; in *Daniel Deronda* Eliot has Daniel explicitly identify with Caliban, who is said to have caused the anticolonial uprising in Jamaica. Today, of course, Stephen Greenblatt and other postcolonial theorists use Caliban as a figure for the racialized other: see, for example, Greenblatt, "Learning to Curse: Aspects of Linguistic Colonialism in the Sixteenth Century," in *First Images of America: The Impact of the New World on the Old*, 2 vols., ed. Fredi Chiapelli (Berkeley: University of California Press, 1976).

61. Garnett, "Amy Levy."

62. Max Beer, *Fifty Years of International Socialism* (London: G. Allen & Unwin, 1935), 73.

63. Catherine Belsey, "Constructing the Subject: Deconstructing the Text," in *Feminisms: An Anthology of Literary Theory and Criticism,* ed. Robyn Warhol and Diane Price Herndl (New Brunswick: Rutgers University Press, 1991), 598.

64. The *American Hebrew* took Levy to task in its review of *Reuben Sachs,* April 5, 1889, 142.

65. Letter from Amy Levy to Louise Moulton, August 1, 1889, Moulton Collection, Library of Congress.

66. "New Books," *Jewish Chronicle,* August 2, 1889, 12. Mrs. Andrew Dean also used the name Cicely Ullman Sidgwick.

67. Letter from Vernon Lee to Matilda Paget, September 5, 1889, Vernon Lee Collection. Lee had valued Levy more highly earlier in their relationship: in a letter to her mother dated June 11, 1887, she lists Levy as one of the five people she "was most pleased to see" in London.

68. Letter from Vernon Lee to Bella Duffy, October 14, 1889, Vernon Lee Collection.

69. In a letter to Kit Anstruther-Thomson dated January 7, 1904, Vernon Lee criticizes a young blind man for marrying "when his own blindness is due to double syphillis, inherited and personally acquired."

70. Garnett, "Amy Levy."

71. One of Levy's chronic health problems, deafness, can actually be the result of a untreated infection resulting from syphilis, as she may have known. While Vernon Lee's letter to Duffy, cited above, makes it unlikely that Duffy and Lee knew of Levy's fear that she had syphilis, Duffy's September 23 letter says, "I only trust that she did not put an end to herself. She had looked ill all the summer, perhaps she died of natural causes." To make this statement, Duffy must have believed that Levy, at twenty-seven, suffered from physical disabilities that could lead to death.

72. My speculations should be distinguished from Germaine Greer's snide and simplistic linking of Levy's suicide to Sappho's legendary leap. I am not suggesting that imagining herself as Sappho was in any way a cause of Levy's death. Greer's explanation of Levy's suicide is as off-base as her observation that "Levy's suicide at twenty-eight added glamour and gravitas to her reputation." See *Slipshod Sybils: Recognition, Rejection and the Woman Poet* (London: Viking, 1995), 423–24.

73. Phaon was Sappho's legendary male lover. Scheinberg also notices the title of Levy's projected book as it appears in the table of contents of *Plane-Tree*. She criticizes Melvyn New for not commenting on this, saying that New "may have inadvertently obscured Levy's explicit interest in Sapphic conventions and likewise some important clues to her own poetic experimentations with lesbian poetic address." See Scheinberg's review of New's edition, *Victorian Poetry* 33 (Spring 1995): 169–73. I discuss the question of whether Levy's poems are homoerotic most fully in chapter 6. Unlike eleven of Levy's love poems, the three in the NEW PHAON section of *Plane-Tree*—"The First Extra," "Wall Flower," and "At a Dinner Party"—are not specifically addressed to or about women, and they provide no hints of what Levy had in mind in choosing her title. Levy uses Sapphic meter in "To Sylvia" and "To E.," and New also comments on Sapphic form in the latter poem.

74. Letter to Linda Hunt Beckman from Katharine Solomon, Katie's granddaughter, March 5, 1996.

75. Quoted in Deborah Epstein Nord, *The Apprenticeship of Beatrice Webb* (Amherst: University of Massachusetts Press, 1985), 134.

76. Letter from Bella Duffy to Vernon Lee, October 14, 1889, Vernon Lee Collection.

77. Ellen Darwin, "The Poems of Amy Levy," *Cambridge Review,* January 23, 1890, 158.

78. Vernon Lee, *Laurus Nobilis: Chapters on Art and Life* (London: John Lane, the Bodley Head, 1889), 155.

CHAPTER 10. EPILOGUE

1. Oscar Wilde, "Amy Levy," in *Woman's World* 3 (1890): 52.

2. Richard Garnett, "Amy Levy," *Dictionary of National Biography* (Oxford: Oxford University Press, 1892), 1041.

3. Wilde, 52.

4. In my view, two additional short stories should be included in Levy's canon—"At Prato" and "The Late Telepathic Occurrence in the British Museum," although the latter is slight compared to the others. As mentioned in note one to chapter five, I have photocopies of Levy's unpublished stories; therefore, readers who want further information about the two unpublished stories that I consider among Levy's best—"Leopold Leuniger: A Study" and "The Doctor"—should contact me at Ohio University's English Department. We must hope that the owners of these manuscripts will soon permit publication of unpublished material.

5. W. B. Yeats, *Letters to the New Island*, ed. Horace Reynolds (Cambridge, Mass.: Harvard University Press, 1934), 87.

6. Ellen Darwin, "The Poems of Amy Levy," *Cambridge Review*, January 23, 1890, 158.

7. In a sense, Levy makes Frank Jermin in *Romance of a Shop* speak for her when he says that artists have "to get off [their] high horse," giving as an example of his new attitude toward art that he took his *Death of Oedipus* and put "its face to the wall" (New's ed. 126). The difference between Levy and Frank Jermin is that while she too was unashamed about produced popular art, she did not give herself over to it: her artistic aims were as high as or higher for most of the work she did in her later, more contemporary mode.

Index

Note: Page numbers in **boldface** refer to illustrations. Amy Levy is abbreviated "AL" in sub-headings. References to letters in the appendix appear in *italics*.

"In the Nower" (Levy), 190, 197, 198
"Independent Jewess" persona, 138
indirect discourse, 166
Isaac, Annie, 15
Isaac, Emma (Emmie), 15, 177, 237n. 4
Isaac, Isabel, 177, 237n. 4
Isaac Eller's Money (Dean), 207
Isaac family, 15

James, Henry, 5, 120, 262n. 9, 295n. 23, 298n. 52, 303n. 10
"James Thomson: A Minor Poet" (Levy), 61, 103, 105, 292n. 33, 298n. 52
Jane Eyre (C. Brontë), 157, 184, 292n. 27, 310n. 14
Jeeves, Louie, 85, 297n. 37
"Jew in Fiction, The" (Levy), 124, 159, 160, 167, 171, 286n. 30, 295n. 22
"Jewish Children" (Levy), 24, 124, 127–28, 167
Jewish Chronicle (newspaper), 17, 107, 118, 125, 138, 165, 179–80, 204, 205, 207, 208
"Jewish Community, The" (Webb), 203–4
"Jewish Humour" (Levy), 124–26
Jewish Portraits (Magnus), 77, 144
Jewish religion. *See* Judaism
Jewish Standard, 180–81, 186
Jewish stereotypes: in AL's drawings, 111–12; and prevailing anti-Semitism, 9; "scientific" basis of, 10. *See also* anti-Semitism
Jewish women, traditional expectations for, 8, 286n. 21
"Jewish Women and Women's Rights" (Levy), 17
Jewish World, 103, 180, 187
Jews: assimilation of, 6, 9, 13, 29, 37, 69, 71–72, 73–74, 203–7; British cultural construction of, 71–72, 302n. 94; conversion of, 10; education of, 8–9; English political rights of, 8; numbers in Great Britain, 287n. 38; refugees from Eastern Europe, 10, 11, 84, 110–11; self-hatred of, 110, 126, 162, 163; social cohesion among, 13; social position of, 83–84; suspicion of, 10; university education for, 8–9
Johnson, Margaret (Madge), 75, 87
Joseph, Dr. Anthony, 287n. 1
Judaism: and dietary laws, 13, 14; and religious education, 13; and religious observance, 13, 14
"June-Tide Echo, A" (Levy), 105, 106–7, 240n. 1

Kapp, Yvonne, 83, 312n. 37
"Katie's Courtship" (Levy), 36–37
"Kettledrum" (Levy), 21–23
Kind Words (magazine), 17, 18
King Lear (Shakespeare), 178
Knox, Robert, 112, 113
Kraidman, Gail, 3

Ladies Literary Dinner, 178
"Lady of Shallot" (Tennyson), 33
"Lallie: A Cambridge Sketch" (Levy), 22, 42–44, 54, 58, 185, 202
Landon, Letitia (L.E.L.), 33, 46, 47, 54–55, 61
"Last Judgment, The" (Levy), 293n. 10, 298n. 46
"Last Words" (Levy), 314n. 34
Lawn-Tennis (magazine), 288n. 19, 299n. 62
Lazarus, Emma, 284n. 4
Lee, Sidney, 86, 297n. 37
Lee, Vernon (Violet Paget), 61, 119–22, **121**, 128–32, 148–49, 150, 177, 200, 203, 204, 206–7, 208, 210, 268n. 1; correspondence with AL, 120, 128–30, 131–32, 134–35, 147, 152, 176, 184, 208, *255–68*, *275*
Lee-Hamilton, Eugene, 150, 208, 257n. 7, 310n. 17
Leighton, Angela, 4, 46, 51, 98, 101, 102, 104, 133, 144, 193, 194
L.E.L. (Letitia Landon), 33, 46, 47, 54–55, 61
Lenau, Nikolaus, 82, 99, 193
Leon, Constance (Conny), 15, 36, 220n. 1
Leon family, 15
"Leopold Leuniger: A Study" (Levy), 59, 62, 69–74, 119, 161, 162, 163, 213
"Leopold Leuniger" persona, 62–64, 74, 112, 119, 187, 206
lesbianism, 7. *See also* homoeroticism
"Letter from a Girl to Her Own Old Age, A" (Meynell), 193, 194
Levine, Philippa, 38
Levy, Alfred (brother): birth, 13, 289n. 2; death, 136, 208–9, 262n. 2; education, 29; health, 254n. 1
Levy, Amy: abbreviations used by, 34, 290n. 11; bibliography of her published works, 277–81; birth, 1, 13; calendar for 1889, 151, 152, 175, 176, 186, 197, 198, 208, 272n. 4; education, 1, 19, 29–57 passim, 75, 226–32; family, 12–28 passim; family relationships, 24–28, 177; feminism, 5, 6, 8, 18, 138; financial self-sufficiency, 76, 99, 178;

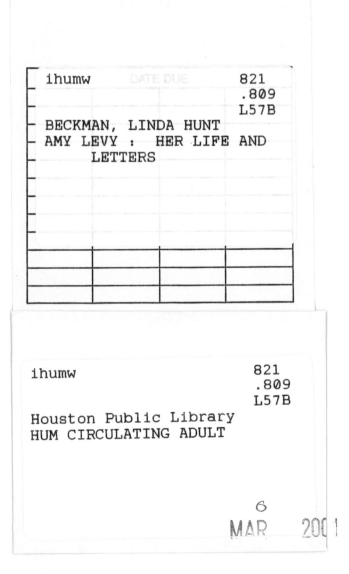